THE BEST DVDS YOU'VE NEVER SEEN, JUST MISSED OR ALMOST FORGOTTEN

31
36
47
48
61
71
79
81
95
97
98

Ararat
Brideshead Revisited
Dancer Upstairs
Wilde
George Washington
In the Mood for Love
I am Love
A Christmas Tale
Billy Elliot
Little Women   the Vanish
House of Mirth   the Circle
Salvador   Tango
Sarajevo
the Prisoner

Recommended by
the Leading Film Critics of

The New York Times

THE BEST DVDS

You've Never Seen, Just Missed or Almost Forgotten

A GUIDE FOR THE CURIOUS FILM LOVER

Edited by PETER M. NICHOLS

With an Introduction by A. O. SCOTT

St. Martin's Griffin ⚜ New York

Book design by Gretchen Achilles

Library of Congress Cataloging-in-Publication Data

The best DVDs you've never seen, just missed or almost forgotten : a guide for the curious film lover : recommended by the leading film critics of the New York Times / edited by Peter Nichols ; with an introduction by A. O. Scott.—1st ed.

  p. cm.

   ISBN 0-312-34362-0
   EAN 978-0-312-34362-0
   1. Motion pictures—Catalogs. 2. Motion pictures—Plots, themes, etc. 3. DVD-Video discs—Catalogs. I. Nichols, Peter M.

PN1998.B458 2005
791.43'75—dc22

                                        2005047053

10   9   8   7   6   5   4   3

CONTENTS

ABOUT THE CONTRIBUTORS

A. O. Scott is the chief film critic of *The New York Times*. **Stephen Holden** is a film and cabaret critic for the paper, and **Caryn James** is the critic at large. **Peter M. Nichols** formerly wrote the DVD column for *The Times*; **Dave Kehr** currently writes the column.

INTRODUCTION

by A. O. SCOTT

In Michael Almereyda's luminous modern-dress screen adaptation of Shakespeare's *Hamlet* (page 165), the hero, reimagined as an aspiring New York filmmaker played by Ethan Hawke, utters his most famous soliloquy—the one that begins "to be or not to be"—in a video store. At first, this may seem like an odd place to give voice to a grave existential dilemma, but when you stop to think about it, the choice seems oddly appropriate. The local Blockbuster (or its online counterpart, the Netflix queue) is, as often as not, a place of doubt and indecision, where modern Hamlets spend hours in endless dithering and fruitless contemplation, scrutinizing empty boxes. Should we face the slings and arrows of another mindless action blockbuster, or is it nobler to suffer through an Oscar-winning tearjerker? And as for outrageous fortune, that was the one with Bette Midler and Shelley Long, right? Didn't we see that the other night on basic cable?

Every year something like 500 new movies make their way to American theaters—sometimes only in a few cities, sometimes only for a short time—and sort themselves into familiar categories. Not just according to the usual video-store genres—action, drama, comedy, foreign—but also with respect to more subjective criteria. There are the movies you wanted to see but never got around to, the movies all your friends kept telling you not to miss, the movies all your friends hated, the movies you would probably have loved but never heard about, the movies you probably would have hated but were curious about anyway, and so on. Included are also movies and mini-series that were made for television, which you didn't think were worth your time until someone said you shouldn't have missed them. This book, though it follows the more conventional classifications (and adds some new ones of its own), is for the most part a guide to those movies—the ones you may not have even known you were missing. Its intentions are advisory and, in a sense, therapeutic. In corralling the unruly enthusiasms of a motley crew of *New York Times* film critics into one portable package, the editors hope to ease the anxious quandary you may face wandering up and down the video-store aisles in search of something to watch.

Of course, there is always the chance that a book like this one will only make matters worse by reminding you of just how many interesting movies are available for home viewing on DVD, and just how little time you have to watch them. The number is daunting indeed, and the 500 or so selections offered here represent only a small sampling of what is out there. This guide does not pretend to comprehensiveness or to the kind of false objectivity represented by star- and letter-grade based rating systems. This is not the place to look for appraisals of recent blockbusters and acknowledged classics—we assume you know about *Lord of the Rings* and *Citizen Kane* already—but rather a source of information about films that might have been neglected or overlooked or, conversely, well known at one time and now worth a reminder. Many could be defined as "art films": small-scale independent features, foreign-language films, and other movies that are marketed to rarefied tastes. Others, though, belong to genres—coming-of-age comedies, for example, or thrillers—that flourish on the far side of respectability, and are therefore often unfairly ignored by serious movie lovers.

Not every one of them is a masterpiece—though more than a few might qualify. Nor is every selection likely to satisfy every taste—movies that try to do that never stay interesting for very long. What the movies discussed here have in common, quite simply, is that one or more of *The Times*'s critics thought enough of them at the time of their release to try to convince our readers that they were worth seeking out. Some readers agreed, some did not (we tend to hear from both groups), and a great many others never had a chance to see for themselves. Perhaps they couldn't book a babysitter, or persuade their friends to go along, or find the movie at the local multiplex. Perhaps there were other things to do.

But the DVD is the medium of second looks and second chances—for actors who pad out the commentary tracks demystifying their work to filmmakers who put together "director's cuts" full of scenes the studios or the ratings board made them cut. And, above all, for movie fans, who can fill in the gaps and make up for lost time. We hope this book helps.

THE BEST DVDS
YOU'VE NEVER SEEN,
JUST MISSED OR ALMOST
FORGOTTEN

ABOUT A BOY

*Hugh Grant, Nicholas Hoult, Toni Collette,
Rachel Weisz*

Directed by Paul and Chris Weitz
2002. 101 minutes. PG-13.

Nothing about the premise here is too unexpected; what's surprising are the chemistry among the characters and the high level of execution.

Essentially this is the story of two boys who help each other grow up, only in this case one is 38. Living slothfully on the royalties from a Christmas song written by his father, Will Freeman (Grant) loads his apartment with electronic toys and ventures forth for food and to connect with women, whom he attracts by the droves before they ascertain his total shallowness.

Will figures single mothers are good targets, since they are lonely to begin with and responsible enough to dump him fast when they see how irresponsible he is, which saves him the trouble of dumping them. To help seal the deal, he invents a 2-year-old of his own, always conveniently absent, to establish early camaraderie.

Pursuing one of these prospects, Will meets Fiona (Collette), the suicidally depressed mother of Marcus, a bright, suffering 12-year-old who, in addition to dealing with a mother who lies on the couch weeping all day, is regularly persecuted at school. Marcus needs rescuing by an adult, preferably male.

Despite himself, Will finds himself drawn in to being the boy's mentor, especially in all things modern, masculine and cool. When it comes to deeper matters, he at first shies from involvement, but then a latent sense of caring starts to emerge. It's Marcus who makes Will finally realize that others are necessary.

Grant is fine as a cad with a heart, and the Weitz brothers' film, adapted from Nick Hornby's novel, handles the sentimentality with a sweet, light touch.

ADAPTATION

Nicolas Cage, Meryl Streep, Chris Cooper, Tilda Swinton, Brian Cox, Cara Seymour, Judy Greer, Maggie Gyllenhaal, Ron Livingston, Jay Tavare

Directed by Spike Jonze
2002. 114 minutes. R.

In Jonze's brilliantly scrambled film, the screenwriter Charlie Kaufman stands back to take a look at his inability to produce a script.

Years earlier Kaufman was assigned to write a film based on *The Orchid Thief,* Susan Orlean's dense and elusive book about a poacher and man of the swamps named John Laroche. When he found no good way to do that, he decided to write a film about himself trying to write the film.

In *Adaptation,* the tortured Kaufman (Cage) gives himself an easygoing twin brother named Donald (also Cage), who is a screenwriter himself and a fount of crass banalities that make him and his derivative serial-killer script a success in Hollywood.

Meanwhile, poor Charlie labors on in pursuit of truth and art, avoiding all cliché and convention—and coming up empty as the deadline approaches. In desperation he seeks help from Robert McKee (Cox), a voluble script doctor and screenwriter guru who rumbles on about structure and other tactics of little use to Charlie.

Occasionally the shuffled narrative goes off into the jungle with Orlean (Streep) and Laroche (Cooper) to look at the source material for an exhilarating film whose ideas pop up like blossoming flowers.

THE ADVENTURES OF SEBASTIAN COLE

Adrian Grenier, Clark Gregg, Aleksa Palladino, Margaret Colin, Marni Lustig, John Shea

Directed by Tod Williams
1998. 99 minutes. R.

A man in a dress is an unlikely candidate for Father of the Year, but as a man named Hank, who is about to become Henrietta, Gregg brings unexpected depth, wit and poignancy to this affecting coming-of-age film. Nominally, the central character is Sebastian (Grenier, now better known as the star of the HBO series *Entourage*), a high school student living with his mother, sister and stepfather in upstate New York in 1983. When the stepfather, Hank, announces that he has decided to undergo sexual reassignment and become a woman, Sebastian's mother flees to England with her son, but Sebastian soon returns to New York to live with Henrietta, who is now wearing a long shag wig and dresses.

When Sebastian goofs off in school and nearly does himself in during a one-night drinking binge, Henrietta is a stern disciplinarian. But she also fiercely defends Sebastian and, in one of the best scenes, takes a swing at someone who insults him. (The lady in the dress is surprisingly tough.)

The film is framed by weak opening and closing scenes in which Sebastian tells the story of his relationship with Hank/Henrietta, but the true end of the story is as touching and surprising as the eloquence of the love between Sebastian and the man who becomes his stepmother.

This semiautobiographical film is the first by Tod Williams, who lived through much of what Sebastian did and went on to make the even stronger *Door in the Floor*.

THE AGE OF INNOCENCE

Daniel Day-Lewis, Michelle Pfeiffer, Winona Ryder, Miriam Margolyes, Robert Sean Leonard, Richard E. Grant, Alec McCowen, Geraldine Chaplin, Mary Beth Hurt

Directed by Martin Scorsese
1993. 133 minutes. PG.

Based on Edith Wharton's elegant, wry novel about Old New York society in the late 19th century, this may be one of the most underrated films of the 1990's because it seems like such an unlikely movie from Scorsese, the director of tough-guy classics like *Mean Streets, Raging Bull* and *Goodfellas*. But he is simply focusing on a more subtle kind of savagery in a hierarchical world where a cutting glance can be lethal.

Ellen Olenska (Pfeiffer) is the black sheep of the aristocratic Mingott family because she has left her dissolute husband. Her grandmother (Margolyes as the matriarch) puts the family behind Ellen but wants to discourage divorce and further scandal, and so she asks Newland Archer (Day-Lewis) to try to dissuade her. Although the proper Newland is engaged to Ellen's cousin, the shy, innocent May (Ryder), he falls irresistibly in love with the worldly Ellen.

Whether Ellen and Newland will defy society and run off together seems to be the underlying question, but the real strength of the film is in the passion raging under the surface. Scorsese creates a film of such eloquence that the sight of Ellen's gloved hand can drive Newland mad. If Pfeiffer seems a trifle too modern to be wholly convincing, Day-Lewis makes up for it with a sympathetic performance that captures Newland's impossible dilemma.

The voice of the narrator is Joanne Woodward's, bringing just the right tone of grace to the world she describes, which is gorgeously filmed as it goes from the opera to elegant drawing rooms, and is so precise that it gets the forks right in a grand dinner scene. The film ends with a coda that leaps ahead by decades, in which Archer's son (Leonard) leads him to a heartbreaking moment of recognition about his life.

ALL ABOUT MY MOTHER

Cecilia Roth, Eloy Azorín, Marisa Paredes, Candela Peña, Penélope Cruz, Toni Cantó, Antonia San Juan

Directed by Pedro Almodóvar
1999. 101 minutes. Spanish with English subtitles. No rating.

A story that gets around, to state it mildly, begins with a mother, Manuela (Roth), who sees her son, Esteban (Azorín), run down by a car on his 17th birthday. As an organ transplant specialist, she must decide who will receive the boy's heart.

Esteban was a devotee of *A Streetcar Named Desire*, and Tennessee Williams's play figures prominently. Traveling to Barcelona, Manuela finds Esteban's father, with whom she once starred in a production of *Streetcar* and who is now a femme fatale named Lola (Cantó). A drag supernova named Agrado (San Juan) turns out to be an old friend of Manuela and comes to her aid and comfort. At a prostitute's shelter we meet the beautiful Sister Rosa (Cruz), also from Manuela's past.

Joined by the *Streetcar* actresses Huma (Paredes) and Nina (Peña), the women sustain each other. Almodóvar sets up the world of acting as a source of inspiration as they improvise their way through their own lives in a film about how tragedies of the flesh can still lead to hope and renewal. Almodóvar has called the style "screwball drama." But with this film about compassion among strangers, his work moves on to a new level of sophistication and depth of feeling.

ALL OR NOTHING

Timothy Spall, Lesley Manville, Alison Garland, James Corden, Ruth Sheen

Directed by Mike Leigh
2002. 128 minutes. R.

Leigh's look at the hard luck and domestic distress of the contemporary English working class could have brought obsessive dreariness, but somehow it blossoms into a tableau of extraordinary vividness and variety.

Phil (Spall) and Penny (Manville) are shoehorned into a South London housing project with their glum daughter, a cleaner at a nursing home, and angry son, an overweight layabout addicted to the tube. Phil, a livery car driver, and Penny, a supermarket checkout clerk, may be married, but Penny says he never proposed and there wasn't a wedding.

Pain and resilience in the projects isn't a new subject for Leigh, and here we have a ragged family unit that, for all its inertia and difficulty, carries on with dignity and in the faint hope that things will be better.

In theater and television as well as film, Leigh involves actors in a long collaborative process, which produces extraordinarily deep performances, especially from Spall, a mainstay in Leigh's films.

Leigh is tough-minded and democratic, and it would be a mistake to look down on these characters. They are neither puffed up by sentimentality nor diminished by mockery. Leigh probes unsparingly into their awfulness, hoping they will surprise him with their decency, and they do.

ALMOST FAMOUS

Patrick Fugit, Kate Hudson, Billy Crudup, Frances McDormand, Jason Lee, Zooey Deschanel, Fairuza Balk, Anna Paquin

Directed by Cameron Crowe
2000. 122 minutes. R.

Immersing itself in the joyful, reckless energy of rock in the 1970's, Crowe's warm, affectionate film recalls the days when he had the same ambitions as the budding young journalist William Miller (Fugit). "You're not out there to join the party," a *Rolling Stone* editor tells William. "We already have one Hunter Thompson."

Never having met William face-to-face, the editor is as yet unaware that, on the strength of a few good clips, the magazine has assigned a 15-year-old to report on a fast-rising rock group called Stillwater.

The year is 1973 when William joins the band's tour bus in Tempe, Arizona, and starts getting acquainted with Russell Hammond (Crudup), the group's guitarist and rising star. He also encounters Stillwater's lead groupie, a warm and wise teenager who calls herself Penny Lane (Hudson).

"The enemy: a rock writer," somebody warns. But William is all honest boyish charm, which earns him a certain amount of affection from Hammond and the others and a deflowering at the hands of Penny Lane and her fellow groupies, themselves part of a groupie group that calls itself the Band-Aids.

Don't tell Mom, however. On the road there are messages from William's anxious mother (McDormand), a good-hearted and wonderfully expressive worrywart back in San Diego. Her William survives larger and wiser for the experience in an upbeat film that recognizes the demonic power and decadent excesses of the life but declines to wallow in them.

AMERICAN BEAUTY

Kevin Spacey, Annette Bening, Thora Birch, Wes Bentley,
Mena Suvari, Chris Cooper, Peter Gallagher, Allison Janney

Directed by Sam Mendes
1999. 122 minutes. R.

Spacey's performance as the hapless suburbanite Lester Burnham may be his best, and Mendes's scathing satire, which won five Oscars, makes an interesting accommodation with the deceptively complex world it excoriates.

The droll Burnham, who has been shot dead, talks from the beyond about his whole miserable existence before he liberated himself and adopted a new take on life.

A victim of downsizing at work, Lester takes a job with a fast-food chain. That leaves the money-making to his wife, Carolyn (Bening), a frantically stressed-out real estate woman who drives around town sputtering slogans.

Lester simply cuts himself off from life, angering Carolyn and his teenage daughter, Jane (Birch), who hates him to the extent that she half-seriously discusses killing him with her boyfriend and neighbor, Ricky (Bentley).

Rejuvenation for Lester, such as it is, comes in the form of a crush he develops on Jane's voluptuous teenage friend Angela (Suvari). Suddenly he wants to live and undertakes a vigorous physical makeover.

But as these characters flounder, the film extends them some compassion, laying in some gravity beneath the absurd surfaces.

AMERICAN PSYCHO

Christian Bale, Willem Dafoe, Jared Leto, Reese Witherspoon, Samantha Mathis, Chlöe Sevigny

Directed by Mary Harron
2000. 102 minutes. R.

Trimming fat from Bret Easton Ellis's novel, Harron's film is a sleek, satirical tale of a multiple-personality yuppie for the gluttonous 1980's. By turns an arrogant, preening Wall Street master of the universe, chain-saw-wielding maniac and whimpering crybaby, 27-year-old Patrick Bateman (Bale) may be in part a product of his own imagination.

To the world he is the very model of a perfectly chiseled pneumatic moneymaker, with black-and-white minimalist apartment, teams of girlfriends and their replacements, and a group of reptilian friends for whom designer labels and instant entree to New York's priciest restaurants count for much.

Patrick is also a serial killer, or at least he imagines himself to be. The film plays with the idea that his violent tendencies may be merely the revenge fantasies of a corporate flunky. Real or invented, this side of Patrick results in some beautifully stylized gore.

Or, the killings could be his way of being noticed. Beneath the gleaming armor is a murderous inner child with a steadily increasing bloodlust fanned by an advanced case of 80's-style narcissistic rage. By the end he has become a hysterical wimp in a cinematic satire that trims Easton's excesses into a lean, mean horror comedy classic.

AMERICAN SPLENDOR

Paul Giamatti, Harvey Pekar, Hope Davis, Joyce Brabner,
Earl Billings, James Urbaniak, Judah Friedlander

Directed by Shari Springer Berman and Robert Pulcini
2003. 101 minutes. R.

It takes a several-barreled blast to put Harvey Pekar, the comic-strip writer and famously irascible voice of no-bodies everywhere, on screen. Pekar himself appears to support Giamatti's portrayal of the pessimistic hospital file clerk and aspiring writer from Cleveland who wondered why comics couldn't ever be about little people like himself.

Why not indeed, thought the renowned comics artist Robert Crumb (Urbaniak), whom Pekar met in the 70's. Taken by Pekar's stories, Crumb began to draw the strip *American Splendor*. On screen, bits of documentary, dramatic vignettes and scenes drawn like the comic strip tell the saga of an angry little man from the lower rungs of the ladder whose rants about life took him all the way to David Letterman's show before his verbal excesses got him tossed off.

Though the film doesn't fully portray Pekar's stark bitterness or capture him as a hipster remnant of the Beat era, it does give us a man who wouldn't be beaten down by his circumstances. It took the help of a good woman, Joyce Brabner, maybe the only woman on the planet who could make a match with Harvey. Davis plays her with tart directness, and Brabner is on hand to fill in the cracks.

But don't ask her to clean up Harvey's apartment, so crammed with record albums and jazz 78's that an avalanche seems imminent. A fine soundtrack includes "Ain't That Peculiar," not once but twice.

AMORES PERROS

Vanessa Bauche, Gael García Bernal, Humberto Busto, Emilio Echevarría, Álvaro Guerrero, Rodrigo Murray, Marco Pérez, Jorge Salinas, Goya Toledo

Directed by Alejandro González Iñárritu
2000. 153 minutes. Spanish with English subtitles. No rating.

In what may be one of the first art films to emerge from Mexico since Buñuel, González Iñárritu works from an intricate script by Guillermo Arriaga to weave a riveting tale of an almost mythological suffering that is true to Mexican traditions.

A film full of criminal riffraff and violence, it is reminiscent of *Pulp Fiction* in that episodes in separate segments appear out of sequence, only to dovetail at the end. In fact, the film begins with an incident that occurs in the middle, a car chase through Mexico City with a bleeding dog in the backseat.

Three stories catch characters at a beginning, a middle and an end. In "Octavio and Susana," Octavio (García Bernal) falls for his thuggish brother's wife, Susana (Bauche). Needing money to escape with her to Mexico City, he turns down petty holdups in favor of sending his pet, Cofi, after larger pots in the dog-fighting ring.

Dogs figure in all the segments. ("Amores Perros" could be translated as "Love Is a Dog.") In "Daniel and Valeria," a middle-aged magazine publisher (Guerrero) leaves his wife and children to be with a supermodel (Toledo), who then is struck by a car and badly crippled.

In the last segment, "El Chivo and Maru," a former guerrilla turned hit man (Echevarría) who abandoned his wife and child is struggling to feed his pack of mangy dogs when he finally figures out the value of family.

In his first film, González Iñárritu handles them all with verve and understanding.

ANGELS IN AMERICA

Al Pacino, Meryl Streep, Emma Thompson, Justin Kirk,
Ben Shenkman, Patrick Wilson, Mary-Louise Parker,
Jeffrey Wright

Directed by Mike Nichols
2003. 352 minutes. No rating.

More than a decade after Tony Kushner's two-part epic about love in the age of AIDS became a landmark of theatrical achievement and ambition, Nichols turned it into a truly cinematic event for HBO. It is still a story of extraordinary range. The main characters include Prior Walter (Kirk), a Mayflower descendant who is H.I.V. positive; when he gets sick he is abandoned by his lover, Louis (Shenkman), who hates himself for leaving. Joe Pitt (Wilson) is a married Mormon who tries to resist his own homosexuality.

Most spectacularly, there is Roy Cohn, played by Al Pacino at his best, full of rage and self-delusion. In a hospital, dying of AIDS and still denying he is gay, Cohn talks to the ghost of Ethel Rosenberg (the magnificent Meryl Streep in one of four roles, including Pitt's touchingly confused Mormon mother and, less successfully, an aged rabbi). Emma Thompson plays the angel who appears to Prior Walter, a nurse who cares for him and a homeless person.

Nichols has added visual extravagance to the scenes of dreams and fantasies while capturing the starkness of everyday New York. Most important, he captures the soul of the play, which remains set in the 1980's. It has become a more powerful story of survival with the lapse of time.

The mini-series won a record 11 Emmys, including acting awards to Pacino and Streep, and to Wright as Cohn's nurse and Parker as Pitt's neglected wife. Nichols won for directing and Kushner for his screenplay—all deserved.

THE ANNIVERSARY PARTY

Alan Cumming, Jennifer Jason Leigh, John Benjamin Hickey, Parker Posey, Phoebe Cates, Kevin Kline, Mina Badie, John C. Reilly, Jennifer Beals, Gwyneth Paltrow

Written and directed by Jennifer Jason Leigh and Alan Cumming
2001. 115 minutes. R.

This acutely observant film toys with satire but settles into a realistic, deglamorized tale of Hollywood life among smart, successful movie people in their 30's and 40's faced with the predictable anxieties of career, family and aging.

Married for six years but coming off an extended separation, Sally and Joe Therrian (Jason Leigh and Cumming) throw themselves an anniversary party. Sally, an actress definitely at a precarious time in an active career, is in the kind of stormy frame of mind Leigh does so well. Joe, who is a writer, is a goofily playful type. He also has a vicious side.

Joe's book revealing the tribulations of their marriage is about to be made into a movie. Sally claims not to be overly bothered by that, but she is definitely rattled by Skye Davidson (Ms. Paltrow), the gorgeous young thing chosen to play Sally in the film. Sally can feel the sexual current between Joe and Skye, who appears wreathed in twinkly fair princess smiles and packing enough party drugs for a group of about 30.

The guests are a rich cross-section of Hollywood denizens caught up with star buzz and big money, and fraught with the insecurity of being "in" one minute and "out" the next. Partygoers include the Therrians' crass business manager (Hickey), the bluff, slightly-gone-to-seed star (Kline) who realizes that his George Clooney days are behind him and the macho director (Reilly) who is making Sally's next project, a comedy he knows will flop. Cates and Posey are fine as wives along for the bumpy rides.

In a film of finely woven performances, the best scenes project a convincing illusion of spontaneity.

ANTONIA'S LINE

Willeke van Ammelrooy, Els Dottermans, Jan Decleir, Mil Seghers, Catherine ten Bruggencate, Jan Steen

Directed by Marleen Gorris
1995. 102 minutes. Dutch with English subtitles. No rating.

Gorris's exuberant, quirkily charming film tells of a strong woman and her line of talented female descendants who thrive without men in their lives.

On the day of her death at 90, Antonia (van Ammelrooy) reflects on her life, beginning with her return after World War II to the village where she was born. The film begins with the girlhood of her daughter, Danielle, who shares her mother's appreciation of the magical and her talents for adding friends and offspring to the growing extended family.

When Danielle (Dottermans) decides to have a child, a handsome man is brought on. He doesn't speak, nor do most men in the film unless they have something interesting to add about Plato or Schopenhauer. Various brilliant little girls include Danielle's daughter, Therese, a musical prodigy. As happens to women so blessed, Therese chooses the right mate and makes Antonia a great-grandmother.

The film makes no apologies for its faith in nature and destiny and the strength of its women. "I had never talked about women's lives as happy occasions," Gorris said in an interview. "I decided wouldn't it be nice if they were raised in a kind of harmony with life and death."

ARARAT

David Alpay, Charles Aznavour, Eric Bogosian, Brent Carver, Christopher Plummer, Marie-Josée Croze, Bruce Greenwood

Directed by Atom Egoyan
2002. 116 minutes. R.

Egoyan, a Canadian-Armenian, takes a fascinating, multilayered look at a subject of personal interest: the 1915 massacre of more than one million Armenians by the Turks.

So horrendous was the event that the Turks deny it to this day, even in the face of incontrovertible evidence. Aware of how film and video also distort reality, Egoyan steps back from his movie about the act to make a movie about the making of the movie.

As we watch from this vantage point, atrocities take place that aren't easy to watch. But then the camera pulls away, leaving us with the crew making the behind-the-scenes movie and making us aware that while all film-making is artifice, it carries a responsibility not to distort.

Historical Armenians are plentiful in the film itself, of course, and present-day Armenians are injected into the movie within the movie. A Canadian-Armenian film-maker named Raffi (Alpay) has complicated relationships with his mother, his stepsister and the spirit of Arshile Gorky, the Armenian painter. Later, a Canadian customs official (Plummer) suspects him of smuggling heroin into Canada in cans of film.

At times the film's pieces and complex structure may seem overly contrived, but whatever happens is never less than thought-provoking.

ATLANTIC CITY

Burt Lancaster, Susan Sarandon, Kate Reid, Michel Piccoli,
Hollis McLaren, Robert Joy

Directed by Louis Malle
1980. 105 minutes. R.

Set in the first days of the casino boom, Malle's film, with a screenplay by John Guare and stunning cinematography by Richard Ciupka, creates a place of myth, legend and dreams, most of them not that pretty.

At the start we catch an old mobster's man named Lou (Lancaster) taking a surreptitious look through a tenement window at Sally (Sarandon), who's rubbing her body with a fresh lemon to rid herself of the smell after a night of clam shucking at the seafood bar where she works.

Lou, now a numbers runner in the ghetto, likes to recall the days when gambling was illegal and he was a hit man in the employ of top mob figures. Actually, he never rose above a gangster's gofer and errand boy. Sally, a fresh and direct young woman, is studying to become a casino employee and aspires to become the first female croupier in Monte Carlo.

Theirs is a sweet, longing relationship, at least from his perspective, and she's not about to let the old guy down when he gets the chance to prove himself the man he never was when he was young.

Lou is one of Lancaster's best creations, both stingy and magnanimous. Malle avoids sentimentality by maintaining a detached serenity around these characters. While he allows them brief, unlikely breaks of good fortune, he doesn't grant fates that exceed the reality.

BAD SANTA

Billy Bob Thornton, Tony Cox, Brett Kelly, Bernie Mac, John Ritter, Lauren Graham, Lauren Tom, Cloris Leachman

Directed by Terry Zwigoff
2003. 93 minutes. R.

Rotten characters are rarely as much fun as Willie T. Stokes (Thornton), a hard-drinking safecracker with a slick Christmas scam. Every yuletide Willie pulls on his Santa suit, always with a bottle of booze stashed in his baggy red trousers, and heads off to play a surly, badly hungover St. Nick in some department store or other around the country.

Willie has a partner in holiday cheer, a dwarf in an elf outfit named Marcus (Cox) who gathers the kiddies and brings them to Santa. On Christmas Eve, that blessed day of liberation for these two, Marcus hides in the store after closing and lets in Willie to clean out a safe swollen with seasonal take.

Every few kids or so, Santa clears his lap for a long pull on the bottle, and during breaks he has quickie sex with anyone available. But all isn't sugar plums. Willie attracts a morose, rotund little boy named Thurman (Kelly) who attaches himself to Willie and becomes a kind of Santa groupie.

Zwigoff (*Crumb, Ghost World,* pages 87 and 150) has a feel for lost misfits with a spark of redemption in them after all. Oddly enough, Willie begins to feel compassion for the boy, and here a scabrous (and riotous) comedy that could have been too one-note broadens without spilling into sentimentality.

THE BALLAD OF LITTLE JO

Suzy Amis, David Chung, Rene Auberjonois, Bo Hopkins, Ian McKellen, Carrie Snodgress, Anthony Heald, Sam Robards

Directed by Maggie Greenwald
1993. 120 minutes. R.

In the Old West, Josephine Monaghan (Amis) cuts off her hair, dresses like a man and carves a scar in her cheek, the better to survive in the male world of Ruby City, a grubby mining village. This might sound like a gimmick—a feminist Western about a cross-dressing woman—but the film becomes an intriguing drama because Greenwald and Amis turn Jo into such a distinct individual.

Cast out by her genteel Eastern family after having an illegitimate baby, Josephine has headed out West but soon discovers that is no place to be a woman. As the man called Little Jo, she may be small and talk in an unusually high voice, but she becomes a shepherd, teaches herself to shoot and survives a tough mountain winter. She convinces everyone around her that she is a man, though an odd one; her taciturn manner and lack of interest in sex make her suspicious to the townsmen, who are ready to pounce on anyone who seems weak or different.

Still, Jo befriends a family of Russian immigrants and goes to the aid of a Chinese railroad worker, Tinman Wong (Chung), who is about to be lynched. Before long he discovers her secret, and the two become lovers, smoking opium and clinging together as outcasts in a society that would surely kill them if it uncovered the subterfuge.

Amis illuminates the film with a haunting performance. While the usual trappings of the Western are well handled, the bond between Jo and Tinman move a focused, cool-headed story well beyond the boundaries of the Western genre or, for that matter, the cross-dressing genre.

BAMBOOZLED

Damon Wayans, Savion Glover, Jada Pinkett-Smith, Tommy Davidson, Mos Def, Michael Rapaport

Directed by Spike Lee
2000. 135 minutes. R.

Lee comes up with a nifty concept for a hugely risky comedy and passes it on in the form of a brainstorm in the mind of Pierre Delacroix (Wayans), a debonair Harvard-educated executive at a failing television network. To save the operation, Delacroix comes up with a show called *Mantan: The New Millennium Minstrel Show*, a raucous song-and-dance mixture of *Amos 'n' Andy* and vaudeville starring a couple of homeless street performers renamed Mantan (Glover) and Sleep 'n' Eat (Davidson).

The show is a smash, garnering Emmy Awards, starting a national craze for wearing blackface, inspiring furious protests from the Rev. Al Sharpton and Johnnie Cochran (playing themselves) and a declaration of war by a gun-toting rap collective called the Mau Maus.

Multiracial audiences regard *Mantan* as a hip example of black culture laughing at itself, but Lee's movie goes into riskier territory when it implies that the same conclusion leads hip-hoppers to use the word "nigger" with the same kind of latitude.

The film's target is the white-run television industry, but also black writers and performers who demean themselves through caricature. On a deeper level it asks unanswerable questions about black identity. But since no one knows better than Lee how laughter leads to scary truths, *Bamboozled*, which takes its name from a Malcolm X speech, is best when it's simply being fall-down funny.

BAND OF OUTSIDERS

Anna Karina, Claude Brasseur, Sami Frey

Directed by Jean-Luc Godard
1964. 97 minutes. French with English subtitles.

In Godard's approximation of an American gangster film, three students in Paris more or less playact their way through a robbery as if they have been cast in a movie.

Odile (Karina), Arthur (Brasseur) and Franz (Frey) meet in class and become friends. She says she lives in a villa with a lot of money, which tickles cinematic imaginings in the boys, who are enthusiasts of Hollywood movies and pulp fiction. So the three of them decide to rob the place.

Godard makes them a sad enough trio, caught in life's limitations and their own prospects in a mundane world. Still full of life, they dance and cavort, and at one point, they make a nine-second tour of the Louvre.

The fact that they have committed a crime exerts a certain reality, but Godard isn't as concerned with plot as he is with telling the story, and here he leaves himself free to make references to literature, film and himself.

BARAN

Hossein Abedini, Zahra Bahrami, Mohammad Amir Naji

Directed by Majid Majidi
2001. 94 minutes. Farsi and Dari with English subtitles.
No rating.

Majidi, an Iranian filmmaker, plunges into a difficult and sad reality and, without minimizing its brutality, transforms it into a lyrical and celebratory vision.

In Iran, a young laborer named Latif (Abedini) works

serving tea at a construction site where many of the workers are Afghan émigrés who have fled the Taliban and are working illegally. When one of them is injured, his son takes his place, but the boy is not strong enough to haul the sacks of cement or perform other strenuous tasks.

Realizing that the injured man has a family to feed in the refugee camp, the foreman assigns the boy to Latif's tea duties, which means Latif must get involved in some real work. Resentful at first, Latif uncovers a surprise: the boy is a girl named Baran.

Gender crossovers are common in films of Islamic origin (as in *Osama*, page 297). Majidi has a more romantic, populist streak than many other Iranian filmmakers. At first attracted to the girl with unthinking adolescent ardor, Latif changes from a hotheaded boy into a self-sacrificing man, and as he learns about the privations of others his passion turns to compassion.

Majidi's willingness to portray strong, naïve emotions intensifies the film's realism as he uses the sweet spell of a love story to work a more complex magic.

THE BARBARIAN INVASIONS

Rémy Girard, Stéphane Rousseau, Marie-Josée Croze, Marina Hands, Dorothée Berryman, Yves Jacques, Johanne-Marie Tremblay, Pierre Curzi, Louise Portal, Dominique Michel

Directed by Denys Arcand
2003. 99 minutes. French with English subtitles. No rating.

The humor is broad and the emotions are large and accessible as family and old pals and lovers gather around Rémy (Girard) in Arcand's film, which won an Oscar. A 60ish Montreal history professor and lifelong lefty, Rémy is dying of cancer, which calls for a reunion that goes beyond elegy to become a kind of ideological seminar and long movable feast with much wine and remembrance.

Rémy's son, Sébastien (Rousseau), brings it all together, though at first he is none too keen on attending his father. Sébastien is a finely tuned young money man working in Europe, while Rémy describes himself as a sensual socialist. Nevertheless, Sébastien works through the estrangement and, accompanied by his fiancée, comes to his father's hospital bedside.

The two have words, but Sébastien works through that, too, and starts putting his considerable talent for making things happen to work for his father. The right people are summoned: Rémy's former wife (Berryman), two former lovers and several friends from academic and activist days in the 1960's, when they all celebrated seemingly every "ism" ever invented.

Sébastien arranges private quarters for his father at the hospital and sees to it that he receives satellite-phone messages from his daughter, who is sailing in the Pacific. To ease Rémy's pain, he arranges for heroin doses supplied by an addict named Nathalie (Croze), the daughter of one of Rémy's old lovers, and a haunting presence and powerful attraction to Sébastien.

He next secures a friend's cottage out by Rémy's beloved lake, and all move to the country for feasts on the porch and reflections on their lives and interesting historical times. Finally there is the endgame, which is handled as it should be, with no more dramatics than are called for and no less either.

BARTLEBY

*David Paymer, Crispin Glover, Glenne Headly, Joe Piscopo,
Maury Chaykin, Seymour Cassel, Carrie Snodgress,
Dick Martin*

Directed by Jonathan Parker
2001. 82 minutes. PG-13.

It took the rise of psychoanalysis and literary modernism to get a handle on Herman Melville's *Moby-Dick*, and here modern office culture lends a hand to Parker's adaptation of Melville's novella *Bartleby the Scrivener*, his enigmatic "tale of Wall Street."

Somewhere in a surreal contemporary world, office complexes sit perched above freeways on lonely, grassy plateaus. In one of these places Bartleby (the suitably pallid Glover), a former clerk in the post office's dead-letter office, is hired to file papers regarding whatever. Co-workers, all madly compensating for the deadening tasks they perform, include a flashy would-be wiseguy (Piscopo) and the alliteration-prone office manager (Headly), who is something of a sex kitten.

The overall chief is the Boss (the deadpan, baggy-eyed Paymer), who occupies a shabby office decorated in various shades of avocado, mustard and brown. "I would prefer not to," Bartleby tells the Boss when asked to work. Bartleby, in fact, prefers not to do anything but stand looking at a dusty air-conditioning vent.

His attitude is at once suicidal and heroic, completely irrational and perfectly understandable. "Ah, Bartleby! Ah, humanity!" says the Boss, who's as enigmatic as Bartleby himself. He's only trying to do his job in a nicely realized film that uses literature of the past to make the present look as strange as it really is.

BARTON FINK

John Turturro, John Goodman, Judy Davis, Michael Lerner,
John Mahoney

Directed by Joel Coen
1991. 117 minutes. R.

In their fourth film, the Coen brothers (Ethan Coen wrote the script with Joel) score with a fine dark comedy of flamboyant style and immense though seemingly effortless technique. In *The Times,* Vincent Canby called it "a satire on the life of the mind."

In the 1940's, Barton Fink (Turturro), a prissy playwright dedicated to creating "a living theater of, about and for the Common Man," writes a Broadway hit and succumbs to the lure of big bucks as a screenwriter in Hollywood.

He takes up residence at the Earle, a curious, very L.A. establishment with an Art Deco lobby and rooms done up in Skid Row. Barton hopes "to make a difference" in tinsel town, but his first assignment for Capitol Films is a wrestling movie "for Wally Beery." Barton doesn't do wrestling movies, and, not surprisingly, writer's block sets in along with steadily escalating panic.

Surreal things start happening at the Earle as sifted through Barton's tortured bean. Another Capitol writer (Mahoney), a Southerner in the Faulknerian mode, calls Hollywood "the great salt lick," but to Barton the experience becomes a nightmarish illusion.

The Coens said they created the movie when they were blocked working on *Miller's Crossing.* A vivid, startling film seems to be created whole and seamless, packed with pertinent and priceless detail that can't be brought forth piecemeal. It's an exhilarating original.

THE BATTLE OVER *CITIZEN KANE*

A PBS documentary directed by Thomas Lennon and
Michael Epstein
1995. 108 minutes.

Orson Welles's *Citizen Kane* was about the press baron
William Randolph Hearst, but Lennon and Epstein argue that the film was as much about Welles himself.

Their riveting documentary pits the venerable Hearst,
in his 70's, against the upstart Welles, still in his 20's and
making his first feature, in a behind-the-scenes struggle
between titans from different realms.

Hearst often gathered the Hollywood elite at his San
Simeon estate. Asked why he chose journalism over the
movies, he said, "You can crush a man with journalism,
but not with motion pictures."

Welles was new to Hollywood but well known as a
prodigy and seeker of controversy. Perhaps as a bit of mischief, he cast himself as Charles Foster Kane, modeled after the muckraking Hearst. "For the first time ever, the
methods Hearst had used to lay bare the lives of others
had been used on him," a commentator says in the documentary.

Being portrayed as a brooding, isolated wreck bothered
Hearst, who was actually quite sociable and outgoing.
Welles's depiction of Hearst's companion, the actress Marion Davies, as a feather-brained drunk was going too far.

"I think they thought they could get away with it," says
William Alland, a Welles colleague, referring to Welles and
his screenwriter, Herman Mankiewicz. "If Hearst sued,
that would be great. They'd drive the old man crazy, turn
the town on its ear."

Instead, Hearst, who owned a lot of movie theaters,
tried to suppress the film and even have it destroyed.
Welles's career survived, of course, but it never fully recovered.

BEAUTIFUL PEOPLE

Charlotte Coleman, Charles Kay, Rosalind Ayres, Roger Sloman, Heather Tobias, Danny Nussbaum

Directed by Jasmin Dizdar
1999. 107 minutes. R.

Dizdar's highly successful first film cuts among six disparate and complementary stories to get at the complexity of contemporary urban life. What's more, though the scene is London, he has managed to make a comedy based in large measure on the Bosnian civil war.

Perhaps it would be more accurate to say he has added comedic touches to the Balkan situation as it existed in 1993. So this Serb and Croat walk into a bar—not really, but a Serb and a Croat who got into a brawl on a London bus do wind up in adjacent beds at a hospital.

"So you're a Serb and he's a Croat?" asks a nurse who is trying to determine why one repeatedly tries to disconnect the other's intravenous hookup. No, no, it's the other way around, one of them exclaims: "I am Croat and he is Serb."

In the same hospital a young Bosnian refugee, a victim of gang rape in Bosnia, begs the doctor to kill her baby, who is about to be born. A British journalist back from the Balkans has an acute attack of Bosnian syndrome (an irrational need to identify with the victims of catastrophe) and demands that someone amputate his leg.

Londoners have their own problems, including collapsing marriages and children on drugs. Yet the collage of misery is anything but grim. Dizdar, a naturalized British citizen who grew up in Bosnia, directs with extraordinary exuberance and self-confidence in a style that combines documentary realism with a playful, improvisatory sense of formal possibility.

BEAU TRAVAIL

Grégoire Colin, Denis Lavant, Michel Subor

Directed by Claire Denis
1999. 90 minutes. French with English subtitles. No
rating.

Denis moves Melville's *Billy Budd* to a French Foreign Legion outpost in the East African enclave of Djibouti. But Melville's story about the brutalization of a heroic young recruit by a sadistic officer in the British Navy of 1797 really becomes a pretext for Denis's rapt absorption with an all-male society and its punishing rituals.

In fact, she turns *Billy Budd* into a cinematic military ballet in which rigorous training becomes ecstatic rites of purification. In the hands of another filmmaker, that might be viewed as homoerotic, but Denis is reaching for something deeper and more elusive.

Men become beautiful bodies in motion, sleek machines honed to perfection under the blazing sun, with the harsh landscape imparting its own beauty and desolation and surreally mirroring the life of rugged austerity.

In the *Billy Budd* element, a soldier (Colin) offends his sergeant (Lavant) by rescuing a comrade from a mysterious helicopter crash at sea. Thinking the soldier must have had some devious motive for this act, the sergeant begins to persecute him, but we never have a sense of Melville's tale of good and evil locked in metaphysical struggle or relentless cruelty goaded into viciousness.

In the end Denis chalks the sergeant's behavior to the punishing asceticism of military life. The film is as ravishingly beautiful as it is austere.

BEFORE THE RAIN

Rade Serbedzija, Katrin Cartlidge, Grégoire Colin,
Labina Mitevska

Directed by Milcho Manchevski
1994. 113 minutes. Macedonian, Albanian and English,
with English subtitles. No rating.

Manchevski's devastating film about strife in the Balkans needs three intertwining parts to get at what the movie fully realizes can't be gotten at in a literal sense. Set in a world of hatred and violence where there are no answers or solutions, it has an intuitive feel.

On a beautiful night in Macedonia, gunmen in pursuit of an Albanian girl shatter the life of a beatific young monk who has given her refuge. In London, a horrifyingly senseless shootout tears up a restaurant, and a mercurial Macedonian photojournalist (Serbedzija) prepares to leave his lover (Cartlidge) and return to visit his family in his native village, where he hasn't been in 16 years.

He finds the place virtually destroyed. His armed relatives and friends, Macedonian Christians, are out patrolling for Albanian Moslems, who are on the lookout for Macedonians. A former girlfriend, a Moslem, barely dares to speak to him. Small children tote machine guns.

This is a stunning-looking film, achingly beautiful in places. Manchevski leaves some narrative loose ends, but the film is about symbols more than story. The rain is Bob Dylan's, scouring and hopefully purifying, but don't count on it. The troubles are too intractable, and so it is left.

BEFORE SUNRISE

Ethan Hawke, Julie Delpy

Directed by Richard Linklater
1995. 105 minutes. R.

By now we have reunited with Jesse (Hawke) and Celine (Delpy) in the 2004 film *Before Sunset,* but here it is 10 years earlier when Linklater introduces the monumentally romantic young couple as they first happen upon each other on a train to Vienna and wander off for a night together.

It's his idea. She's French, a student on her way back to Paris; he's American, headed for a flight home from Vienna. He suggests that she get off with him there and resume her trip the next day. Through the afternoon they roam Vienna talking, and it's to Linklater's credit that he keeps the conversational gambits coming.

Jesse suggests that she look at their sojourn as time travel. Years later she may be married to someone else and look back and assess whether Jesse would have been right for her. Now is her chance to find out.

As they begin to feel each other out, there is a forced effervescence, but later the film turns more natural as the actors become less bubbly and more settled into their roles. Hawke gets better still, once he stops grinning at everything Celine says and allows an element of tenderness into his performance. Linklater and his co-writer, Kim Krizan, give him the best lines.

Delpy is more notable for her Botticelli beauty, but then, it's tough being a philosophical free-spirited Frenchwoman in a film like this. One is left with the impression that these two are indeed not right for each other, which is Linklater's intention, but that in no way spoils observing their fascinating rite of passage.

BEHIND ENEMY LINES

Owen Wilson, Gene Hackman, Olek Krupa, Joaquim de Almeida, Gabriel Macht

Directed by John Moore
2001. 106 minutes. PG-13.

While other films in this book—for example, *No Man's Land* and *Before the Rain*—aim at the roots and anguish of Balkan strife, Moore's movie might be called the action flick of the conflict. Not that it takes ethnic violence lightly, but it does stay closer to the conventions of a Hollywood war movie. It does so without patriotic bluster (the film appeared two months after 9/11), but with much cool gadgetry, clipped jargon and offhand machismo that lend an authentic feel.

In the skies over Bosnia, the crew of an F-18 plays a wild losing game of dodge 'em with shoulder-launched missiles fired by a Serbian patrol. Ejected from the stricken aircraft, the pilot (Macht) and navigator, Chris Burnett (Wilson), are deposited deep in enemy territory. The pilot is caught and shot. Burnett escapes and spends the rest of the movie on a frantic scramble to evade a Serbian sniper (Krupa) sent to finish him.

At the command level there is disagreement. It's late in the war and a cease-fire is about to take effect; the plane was in unauthorized airspace. The American admiral (Hackman) has had problems with the rambunctious Burnett but is determined to rescue his boy. Fearing a disruption of the peace arrangement, the admiral's NATO superior (de Almeida) would ignore the incident and let Burnett fend for himself.

BEING JULIA

*Annette Bening, Jeremy Irons, Bruce Greenwood, Shaun
Evans, Lucy Punch, Michael Gambon, Miriam Margolyes*

Directed by István Szabó
2004. 105 minutes. R.

---

ening shines as a slightly aging star of the prewar London theater. At 45, Julia Lambert faces up to certain truths about stars' having passed their peak and fights back with high-spirited charm, both on stage and behind the scenes.

Naturally there's a retinue: her droll director, manager and nominal husband, Michael (Irons); the man she prefers to spend her time with, Sir Charles (Greenwood); and various cast members. Naturally a young lover (Evans) comes along to freshen life, and there's a young rival (Punch) to challenge Julia on the boards.

But this is Bening's diva turn. When matters threaten to dissolve into melodramatic bathos (as they do in her plays), Julia takes her cares right on stage with her and turns them into farce.

BELLE ÉPOQUE

*Jorge Sanz, Fernando Fernán Gómez, Maribel Verdú,
Ariadna Gil, Miriam Díaz Aroca, Penélope Cruz, Mary
Carmen Ramírez, Michel Galabru, Gabino Diego*

Directed by Fernando Trueba
1992. 108 minutes. Spanish with English subtitles. No
rating.

---

rueba's warmly inviting film manages an old and a young view of life in rural Spain in 1931. Civil war is under way, but there is still room for a felicitous friendship between Fernando (Sanz), a whimsical soldier (actually a deserter), and Manolo (Fernán Gómez), an old artist with four beautiful daughters.

After his hasty desertion from the Spanish Army, Fernando is taken in by Manolo, and almost immediately the two form a bond. Then, to the young man's astonishment, they are joined by four nubile young women (Verdú, Gil, Díaz Aroca and Cruz), who arrive on the train from Madrid to see Papa.

In the course of things Fernando will have his way with all of them—or, it's as accurate to say, they with him. Each of the daughters has her gentle agenda. They are free spirits all, as is their flamboyant mother (Ramírez), who drops in with her own lover in tow.

But a film that could have settled for leering sex takes a more suggestive tack with its potentially bawdy elements, setting the right tone for a father's reflection (Fernán Gómez gives a sensitive performance) and a young man's bittersweet experiences as he passes through a chapter in his life. "Love brings pain," one sister tells him, "but you had a good time."

BEST IN SHOW

Christopher Guest, Parker Posey, Michael Hitchcock, Eugene Levy, Catherine O'Hara, Jim Piddock, John Michael Higgins, Michael McKean, Patrick Cranshaw, Fred Willard, Jennifer Coolidge, Bob Balaban

Directed by Christopher Guest
2000. 89 minutes. PG-13.

For Guest fans, *Waiting for Guffman* (see page 446) is hard to top (as is his 2003 film, *A Mighty Wind*), but what has to be one of the most sidesplittingly uproarious exchanges ever filmed takes place here, when two antagonistic television announcers, the erudite Englishman Trevor Beckwith (Piddock) and the loutish Buck Laughlin (Willard), go at it barb-to-barb over the finer points at the Mayflower Kennel Dog Show in Philadelphia.

Contenders for best of breed have dragged their owners, many of them played by Guest regulars, from across the country. The most intense are Hamilton and Meg Swan (Hitchcock and Posey), two lawyers from Illinois whose Weimaraner, Beatrice, has interfered with their sex life and turned them into tantrum-prone monsters.

"God loves the terrier!" exclaims Gerry Fleck (Levy), a haberdashery salesman. Gerry and his wife, Cookie (O'Hara), have brought their own terrier, Winky, from Fern City, Florida. God also loves the bloodhound Hubert, escorted to the show by Harlan Pepper (Guest) of Pine Nut, North Carolina; the standard poodle Rhapsody in White; the shih tzu Miss Agnes.

Behind the scenes, dog handlers wrestle with the jitters in a well-organized and exquisitely nuanced skit comedy. Don't look for deeper patterns. Simply savor a jigsaw puzzle crammed with deliriously funny little bits.

BETTER LUCK TOMORROW

Parry Shen, Jason J. Tobin, Sung Kang, Roger Fan, John Cho, Karin Anna Cheung

Directed by Justin Lin
2002. 98 minutes. R.

The characters in Lin's film may be teenagers, but they take on problems and pressures that make them seem worlds older. At the center is Ben (Shen), an Asian-American academic superachiever who grinds for grades that will land him in the Ivy League. To work off steam, he runs with a couple of petty criminals (Tobin and Sung Kang) who steal a ton of consumer electronics and other gimcrackery.

Along comes Daric (Fan), a lanky rich boy with a scheme that makes better use of Ben's brainpower: devising and selling exam cheat sheets. Now there is all the cash they need for a drug-fueled lifestyle, which includes very hot young women like Stephanie (Cheung), rumored to have been in a porn film. Crimes escalate, and with them violence and murder during a crime gone wrong.

So how did a smart, decent boy like Ben get caught in all this? Lin makes the anxious grasping of all these kids for some kind of emotional turf—their own need to shatter the stereotypes that limit them—the heart of his film, a scenario that keeps the movie's blood racing.

THE BIG HEAT

Glenn Ford, Jocelyn Brando, Gloria Grahame, Alexander Scourby, Lee Marvin, Dorothy Green, Jeanette Nolan

Directed by Fritz Lang
1953. 89 minutes.

Decades after *M* and *Metropolis*, Lang went to Hollywood and cast his light and shadows on film noir in films like *Clash by Night* and *Human Desire*. The best is *The Big Heat*.

A detective of exceptional rigidity and persistence, the incorruptible Dave Bannion (Ford) investigates another detective's suicide and learns that the dead man left a long note incriminating a mob boss, Mike Lagana (Scourby), and that the note is being used by the detective's widow to blackmail Lagana.

Bannion takes his investigations head-on, which costs some people their lives. The dead detective's mistress (Green) has already been killed for telling Bannion about the note. Charging into Lagana's lair, Bannion confronts the mobster and beats up a bodyguard. Later a car bomb kills Bannion's wife.

This is a brutal film, but Lang is concerned not so much with presenting violence as with depicting its consequences on the lives it affects.

BIG NIGHT

Stanley Tucci, Tony Shalhoub, Minnie Driver, Isabella Rossellini, Ian Holm, Campbell Scott

Directed by Stanley Tucci and Campbell Scott
1996. 107 minutes. No rating.

Of all the big food movies (like *Babette's Feast*) this may be the most fun. The actors Stanley Tucci and Campbell Scott teamed up to direct this rambling story set in one all-important day and night in 1950's New Jersey, where two brothers from Italy are struggling to keep their restaurant, the Paradise, in business. Primo (Shalhoub) is a temperamental artist in the kitchen, creating dishes of exquisite lightness and complexity. The smooth-talking Secondo (Tucci) holds to impeccable standards out front. Yet, across the street another Italian restaurant dumps meatballs on spaghetti, makes two-alarm blazes of flambé dishes and gets all the customers. The brothers may have to abandon Paradise.

Then Pascal (Holm), who owns that place across the street with the lounge singer and the celebrity photographs, offers a helpful suggestion. Secondo and Primo should invite Louis Prima and his band to the Paradise and reap the publicity; Pascal can get him there that very night.

Preparations begin, all captured in loving, if antic, detail. There is no describing Primo's devotion to ingredients and the purity of preparation as he puts together a feast that will culminate with his masterpiece, an extravagant drum-shaped pasta dish called a timpano. Since food can't be everything, Secondo busies himself in a flurry of activity, including his affair with Pascal's glamorous girl-friend (Rossellini) and another relationship with his own love interest (Driver). Characters and their nerves are set racing, fates are sealed, the audience's mouth waters. On the big night, who does or doesn't appear fades almost to insignificance in the stream of glories from Primo's kitchen.

BILLY ELLIOT

Jamie Bell, Gary Lewis, Julie Walters, Jamie Draven,
Adam Cooper

Directed by Stephen Daldry
2000. 110 minutes. R.

---

esides an iconoclastic young hero, Daldry's film has
the Father of the Year. It's not every striking coal miner
in the north of England who has a son who wants to be a
ballet dancer, but that appears to be the situation when
Dad (Lewis) walks into the gymnasium where he boxed as
a kid and finds his younger son, Billy (Bell), dancing with a
male friend wearing a tutu.

"Bali?!" shouts Dad. Yes, ballet. Since early childhood,
Billy has pranced around his room and dreamed of being
on stage. That's not the safest aspiration for a boy in this
hardscrabble quarter of the realm, but Billy, sent to the
gym with his grandfather's boxing gloves, surreptitiously
joins a ballet class for local girls taught by the tough but
kindly Miss Wilkinson (Walters).

He has some talent, too. Whether it's enough to qualify for the Royal Ballet School in London is another matter,
but even Dad, fresh from battles on the picket line, gets
behind the boy and helps raise the money. In London they
run into some typical British class antagonism, but by
now Billy has the freedom to be himself, and it makes a
beautiful loosening of frustrations.

BLACK AND WHITE

Scott Caan, Robert Downey Jr., Brooke Shields, Ben Stiller,
Allan Houston, Claudia Schiffer, Bijou Phillips, Oliver
"Power" Grant, Mike Tyson, Method Man, William Lee Scott

Directed by James Toback
1999. 98 minutes. R.

Toback's vibrant, at times chaotic film creates a stew of confused Manhattan white kids and assorted older fringe players. A filmmaker named Sam (Shields) figures the scene is worth a documentary, so that becomes the rack on which to hang a dozen or so characters.

Will (Scott) is "some white boy trying to be black," says Dean (Houston), a black college basketball star. He's typical of other white kids, says Dean's shady friend Rich (Grant). Take Charlie (Phillips), the rich white girl who would like be black for a while but knows she'll get over it. "They think they're gonna get some life force," says Rich.

Then Dean gets trapped in a point-shaving scheme by a jittery cop named Mark (Stiller). Dean's only way out is to betray Rich and set him up. For his part Dean has a traitorous girlfriend, a German supermodel (Schiffer).

Tyson is on hand—he's very good, too—to offer some told-you-so reflections on getting into trouble and lend some advice to the beleaguered Rich.

Downey is very fine as Sam's gay husband, who makes a pass at Tyson. Good luck there. Sam keeps the camera whirring, as does Toback, in a crackling, highly intelligent film that may be about kids but has an adult take on constantly shifting loyalties.

BLIND SHAFT

Li Yixiang, Wang Shuangbao, Wang Baoqiang, An Jing,
Bao Zhenjiang, Sun Wei

Directed by Li Yang
2003. 92 minutes. Mandarin with English subtitles. No
rating.

By mixing a documentary style and fictional characters,
Li Yang can deliver social commentary and spin some
film noir, too.

The title refers to coal mining in China, and as an elevator descends into the blackness, we're preparing for a
real-life look at abused miners at work. Then we're let in
on a brutal little racket.

When a miner dies in an "accident," his "brother," also
a miner, makes a claim against the mine owner. The man
was actually murdered before the accident, which was
staged so that the two racketeers, Song and Tang, can extort money for the death of a "relative."

Song and Tang go from mine to mine, staging accidents. Owners would rather just pay the money than investigate. The film's documentary style enables them to
be interviewed, and when one owner is asked why he
doesn't just have Song and Tang killed, he says it would
take more money to silence the cops.

Times are grim in China, where the economic boom
stops far short of reaching everybody. The film is relentless and tough-minded, deftly directed with airtight ruthlessness. Yet, it wrings some humor out of the pettiness
of the killers, and an engrossing climax spells out what
makes these people the way they are.

BLOOD SIMPLE

John Getz, Frances McDormand, Dan Hedaya, M. Emmet Walsh, Samm-Art Williams

Directed by Joel Coen
1984. 96 minutes. R.

There are other Coen brothers' films listed in this book, but this is the first feature by the pair, with Ethan Coen as co-writer and producer. It's hard to imagine a more entertaining down-and-dirty bit of business.

Out in a grubby stretch of back country, a slimy bar owner (Hedaya) tries to hire a private detective (Walsh) to kill his wife (McDormand). The detective takes the money and then shoots the bar owner, thereby eliminating the one witness to the transaction.

And what of this wife? Actually, she's been having an affair with a bartender (Getz) in her husband's establishment, which has created the problem in the first place.

At this point the film starts doling out misimpressions, and they are formidable. Everybody, it seems, is pretty much mistaken about everybody else, and that gets dangerous, not to mention amusing in the cleverly mischievous, visually playful way we have come to expect from the Coens.

BLOW

Johnny Depp, Franka Potente, Ethan Suplee, Paul Reubens, Ray Liotta, Rachel Griffiths, Jordi Mollà, Penélope Cruz

Directed by Ted Demme
2001. 124 minutes. R.

By his very charisma Depp lifts a hurried script by David McKenna and Nick Cassavetes about a Massachusetts kid who goes out West to make his mark as a drug dealer (a true story, based on a book by Bruce Porter).

In 1968, "Jawdge," as George Jung (Depp) refers to himself in Bostonian, leaves home after his father (Liotta) goes bankrupt and travels to Manhattan Beach, California, where the stewardesses who populate the place are not yet called flight attendants. There he meets Barbara (Potente), his stewardess girlfriend, and a hairdresser named Derek (Reubens), who helps George transport and sell marijuana to kids back East to the tune of $15,000 a week.

Then George gets caught. In jail he meets a Colombian (Mollà) who introduces him to cocaine. Back on the outside, George goes to Colombia and meets the drug lord Pablo Escobar (Curtis), who sets him up as the major supplier of the drug in the United States. There's marriage to a cartel princess (Cruz). Later, after being ratted out by his well-meaning mother (Griffiths), George is sent back to prison for a long stretch (and Depp is sent into heavy prosthetics with liver spots).

But unlike *Traffic* (or the British *Traffik,* page 422), Demme's film isn't a morality tale about the evils and costs of drugs. Instead it's about the fabulous style that money makes possible. Depp is just the fellow for this, and his sheer charisma takes over a film that stays quick and engaging.

THE BLUE PLANET: SEAS OF LIFE

A documentary by the BBC.
2001. Eight 50-minute episodes.

It's not a movie and it does involve four DVDs, but the BBC mini-series plunges into the world's oceans for about as spectacular an adventure as you're likely to encounter on disc.

Thirty-five photographers took years perusing deep seas, arctic seas, coral seas and along the coasts. The results are often so visually stunning and biologically various that it's hard to believe.

The series opens with a 100-foot blue whale, which, viewed from overhead, is as big as a submarine. A mile or so beneath the surface, some creatures turn transparent and others have teeth so large that they can't close their mouths. In the mouth of the Amazon a tidal bore racing at 40 miles per hour uproots trees. And have you ever watched a grizzly shell clams?

BLUE SKY

Jessica Lange, Tommy Lee Jones, Anna Klemp, Amy Locane, Powers Boothe, Chris O'Donnell, Carrie Snodgress

Directed by Tony Richardson
1994. 101 minutes. PG-13.

Richardson may be remembered primarily for *Tom Jones*, but his last film, this powerful portrait of a family imploding, is among his finest work. Because it was caught in distribution chaos before its low-profile release (three years after Richardson's death), it isn't as well known as it should be. Nonetheless, Lange won an Oscar for her strong, subtle performance as the manic-depressive Carly Marshall, an Army officer's wife with fantasies of a Hollywood career.

It is 1962 and Carly imagines herself as a Marilyn Monroe. Bathing topless or treating soldiers to a steamy flamenco isn't the kind of low-profile conduct destined to complement the career of Hank Marshall (Jones), an engineer who studies the effects of nuclear testing.

When Carly's erratic behavior gets Hank transferred from Hawaii to Alabama, she erupts at the sight of their shabby new home and takes off in the family station wagon. "He's blind and she's crazy," says Alex Marshall (Locane), the older of two adolescent daughters.

A hardheaded military man, Hank avoids getting help for his wife, as badly as she needs it, preferring to keep their troubles inside the family. Jones's performance reaches understated depths, but eventually Hank can't stand the strain. When Carly all but sinks to the dance floor in the embrace of his commanding officer, Hank drags her off and throws her into a swimming pool.

In the end, oddly, it's Carly who comes to the rescue of Hank after he's drugged and put in a mental hospital for refusing to keep quiet about deaths caused by military testing. She and Richardson come through with their usual dramatic flair.

BLUE VELVET

Isabella Rossellini, Kyle MacLachlan, Laura Dern, Dennis Hopper

Directed by David Lynch
1986. 120 minutes. R.

___

If everything is so cute and neat in the suburb of Lumberton, who belongs to that severed ear lying in the grass? Lynch mixes kinkiness and deadpan humor as our hero, Jeffrey Beaumont (MacLachlan), and a detective's inquisitive daughter, Sandy Williams (Dern), set out to solve that mystery.

As weird episodes multiply, the trail has all the logic of a bad dream. Sandy says she "hears things, bits and pieces," about the ear. When the search leads to the torch singer Dorothy Valens (Rossellini), Beaumont hides out in her place at the Deep River Apartments and watches as a madman (Hopper) sniffs a narcotic and screams obscenities, then beats and rapes her.

The odd part is that Valens likes this, and there will be other occasions for her to exercise kinkier tendencies. At her invitation, Beaumont discovers that he too has a sadomasochistic side.

Lynch blends elements of 1940's small-town comedy, with the squeaky-clean making their rounds with smiley faces, and a film noir with very weird doings deep out of sight somewhere. In this way the normal becomes de-mented in a film that is as fascinating as it is freakish. As in his later *Mulholland Drive*, Lynch is obsessed with the rot under the scrubbed surface of American life.

BOB ROBERTS

Tim Robbins, Giancarlo Esposito, Ray Wise, Rebecca Jenkins, Harry J. Lennix, John Ottavino, Robert Stanton, Alan Rickman

Directed by Tim Robbins
1992. 102 minutes. R.

Robbins's political satire may be more relevant now than when it was released, with its 1990's references to then-President Bush, Saddam Hussein and Iraq speaking eerily to another President Bush and another face-off with Saddam. Robbins, an outspoken liberal in real life, takes his best revenge on conservatives by playing Bob Roberts, a smoothly ingratiating, guitar-strumming, self-made millionaire who decides to run for the United States Senate from Pennsylvania. Roberts is a narrow-minded ideologue masquerading as a man of the people.

The film takes the form of a documentary being made about Roberts's campaign, from its beginning through the election and its aftermath. On the stump, Roberts sings upbeat campaign songs (written by Robbins and his brother David) like "My Land," "The Times Are Changin' Back" and "Wall Street Rap," and projects a folky 60's protest style even when he's singing about right-wing attempts in the 90's to roll back the freedoms of the 60's.

Roberts's supporters call him a savior; detractors see a crypto-fascist. Either way, there's little room left in this political landscape for the most decent, intelligent candidate, the patrician senator Brickley Paiste, played by Gore Vidal in a shrewd and delightful bit of casting.

As the political conspiracies and melodramas mount,

the mock documentary form wears thin, but the movie is wonderfully funny at exposing the shams of media-made candidates, then and now.

BOILER ROOM

Giovanni Ribisi, Vin Diesel, Nia Long, Ben Affleck, Nicky Katt, Scott Caan, Ron Rifkin, Jamie Kennedy, Taylor Nichols, Bill Sage, Tom Everett Scott

Directed by Ben Younger
2000. 118 minutes. R.

Having no imaginative ideas about what to do with their money or their lives, a gang of pre-bubble-bust stockbrokers in their 20's spend a typical night huddled in the huge, virtually empty stucco mansion belonging to one of their number and watching, yet again, *Wall Street*, Oliver Stone's hymn to avarice and their handbook on how to behave in the world.

By day they jam into a crummy Long Island outfit called J. T. Marlin and work the phones peddling shares in enterprises as risky and dubious as their own. The honcho of the operation is 27-year-old Jim Young (Affleck), who acts as a sort of drill sergeant along the lines of Alec Baldwin's intimidating bosses' man in *Glengarry Glen Ross*.

Diesel, Katt and Caan are very fine as sharky types around the office and in after-hours joints, but the central figure is a comparatively whimsical college dropout named Seth (Ribisi), who runs an illegal 24-hour casino in his Queens apartment.

Seth likes the idea of a Ferrari more than what he's currently driving (his mother's Volvo wagon), but at J. T. Marlin the road to riches leads to rise, fall and redemption.

Seth also has problems with a demanding, disapproving father (Rifkin) and a crush on Marlin's receptionist (Long), a black woman surrounded by white guys trying to act like homeboys.

Avoiding moralism, the film presents a world of lawless, soulless children but also actors and a filmmaker with soul to spare and talent to burn.

BORN ON THE FOURTH OF JULY

Tom Cruise, Kyra Sedgwick, Raymond J. Barry, Caroline Kava

Directed by Oliver Stone
1989. 145 minutes. R.

In a film with enormous visceral power, Cruise is Ron Kovic, all-American boy from a lower-middle-class family who went to Vietnam with patriotic fervor, was paralyzed from the waist down and became one of the most implacable spokesmen for Vietnam Veterans Against the War.

Cruise does the transformation of young men particularly well, though Kovic is far from the pretty boy who learns a thing or two in Cruise films like *Rain Man* and *Vanilla Sky* (pages 329 and 440). Actually born on the Fourth, Kovic was a high school wrestler who wept when he lost and never questioned his country's values or policies.

In Vietnam his spinal cord is severed, leaving him to the vagaries of an outrageously inadequate medical system overwhelmed by the wounded who crowd veterans' hospitals around the country. When he emerges in his wheelchair, his only refuge is home with his parents (Barry and Kava), who are bewildered by his alcoholism and rage (not to mention upset at his use of the word "penis," an organ which is now useless). His old girlfriend (Sedgwick) is struggling with his downward plunge.

Despite ideal looks, Cruise is absolutely right. Watching Kovic's evolution as he comes to terms with a reality for which he was totally unprepared is both harrowing and inspiring.

BOTTLE ROCKET

Luke Wilson, Owen C. Wilson, Ned Dowd, Robert Musgrave,
James Caan, Lumi Cavazos

Directed by Wes Anderson
1996. 92 minutes. R.

Before three flakes of a certain age can take to the road for a crime spree, one of them needs to spring himself from a mental hospital. Actually, Anthony (Luke Wilson) is perfectly free to leave, but his friend, the high-strung Didgnan (Owen C. Wilson), craves drama, so Anthony slips out a back window while Didgnan watches with a pair of binoculars.

Bob Mapplethorpe (Musgrave), a rich boy who raises marijuana, has a car, so he's added to the holdup crew. They aren't aiming at big stakes. Their first heist is at a bookstore. No one takes them seriously, but a heist is a heist, so they hole up at a motel, where Anthony falls in love with a Paraguyan maid (Cavazos) who speaks little English.

Anderson wrote the film with Owen C. Wilson, his friend at the University of Texas. The three roadies are essentially boys playing out their daydreams against a nicely photographed Southwestern backdrop. Caan comes along to lend some comic lunatic spark in the later stages of a film that flags a bit in the middle, when the characters grow introspective, but has a lively beginning and end for those in step with some quirky Generation Xers.

BOUNCE

Gwyneth Paltrow, Ben Affleck, Joe Morton, Natasha Henstridge, Johnny Galecki, Tony Goldwyn

Directed by Don Roos
2000. 106 minutes. PG-13.

F or once, a mainline Hollywood romance presents two complicated, strong-willed individuals in a film that's nowhere near as nervy as Roos's *Opposite of Sex* (page 295), but in its eye for detail and language offers an extremely accurate and slightly chilly portrait of the yuppie class.

Abby Janello (Paltrow), mother of two small boys, has lost her husband in a plane crash. Earlier at O'Hare Airport, Buddy Amaral (Affleck) generously gave his seat to a stranger who turned out to be Abby's husband (Goldwyn). The plane went down. A driven account executive in the cutthroat world of advertising, Amaral is torn by guilt, which activates his problems with alcohol. When he dries out a year later, his 12-step program asks that he make amends to someone.

He chooses Abby and seeks her out. She's a fledgling real estate agent, and as a way of getting to know her, Buddy helps her swing a deal. The two are attracted but extremely wary. He hasn't told her about the plane ticket, and as they hesitantly begin to date, the question becomes how and when he will tell her the truth.

Paltrow is powerfully convincing as a harried mother, and Affleck gives Buddy an understated intensity. As these characters cautiously approach each other, the waves of longing and anxiety crossing their faces reveal how much is at stake.

THE BOXER

Daniel Day-Lewis, Emily Watson, Gerard McSorley, Brian Cox, Ciarán Fitzgerald, Ken Stott

Directed by Jim Sheridan
1997. 113 minutes. R.

At the core of Sheridan's film, Danny Flynn (Day-Lewis) embodies the dynamics of the bloody strife in Northern Ireland. Once a boxer and a firebrand for the Irish Republican Army, he is released from 14 years of very hard prison time wanting only peace and quiet.

At home in Belfast he's again attracted to a childhood sweetheart, Maggie (Watson), who happens to be married to a prisoner still behind bars. The I.R.A. admires Danny for keeping his mouth shut, but as Joe Hamill (Cox), the local I.R.A. leader, warns Maggie, his daughter, you don't mess around with another I.R.A. man's wife.

Joe urges her to stay away from Danny. "You have to get rid of him, or you're going to find him in a pool of blood," he says. That's hard to hear about a man you're falling for (especially if he's Day-Lewis in an amorous mood). Later, Maggie will tell her father that his politics have made her the prisoner.

Danny is happy to be back in the ring again and helps organize a boxing club intended to bring together Protestants and Catholics for some nonsectarian sport. Hatred and suspicion doom the effort, yet, for all the violence and grief, a very fine film holds out hope for love and renewal.

BOYCOTT

Jeffrey Wright, Terrence Howard, CCH Pounder, Carmen Ejogo, Iris Little-Thomas

Directed by Clark Johnson
2001. 118 minutes. No rating.

Portraying the Rev. Dr. Martin Luther King Jr., whose face and voice have become ubiquitous, seems like an impossible job, but Jeffrey Wright pulls it off with understated power in this film made for HBO. The story begins in 1955, when Rosa Parks (Little-Thomas) refuses to give her bus seat to a white man in Montogomery, Alabama, and touches off a 13-month crusade that made a national figure of King, then a young man with a wife, Coretta (Ejogo), and small daughter.

Wright captures the well-known cadences of King's speech: "You know, my friends, there comes a time when people get tired of being trampled by the iron feet of oppression," he says. But he isn't going for mimicry. His approach fits the film's style: controlled, leading to emotional moments that are all the more powerful because they are so modulated. King's strength of character and his philosophy of nonviolence are shaped with stunning clarity.

The rest of the cast shows the same intelligence and restraint. As Parks, Little-Thomas portrays a quiet, gracious woman who knew exactly what she was doing that day in Birmingham. CCH Pounder is Jo Ann Robinson, one of the boycott's leaders. Erik Todd Dellums is the pacifist Bayard Rustin, who has to be smuggled out of town. Everyone involved seems to grasp the film's approach: to preserve the past, *Boycott* must daringly reconceive it.

Johnson may still be better known as an actor on the television series *Homicide* or as the director of the action movie *S.W.A.T.,* but here he creates a film of profound strength and eloquence.

BOYS DON'T CRY

Hilary Swank, Chloë Sevigny, Alison Folland, Alicia Goranson, Matt McGrath, Peter Sarsgaard, Brendan Sexton III

Directed by Kimberly Peirce
1999. 118 minutes. R.

Peirce's emotionally savage film tells the strange and resonant true tabloid tale of Brandon Teena (Swank), named Teena Brandon at birth. As a teenager she determined to change into a young man, ultimately headed for a tragic end in rural Nebraska.

Our sympathies may be with Brandon, portrayed by Swank in a devastatingly real and poignant Oscar-winning performance, but one strength of the film is that it gives a voice to all those around him in the little town of Falls City, where he goes to make a new life. A complicated new family includes Lana (Sevigny), her dissolute mother and Lana's erstwhile boyfriend, John (Sarsgaard), who stills hangs around the house.

Brandon has another girlfriend, but his growing, tender relationship with Lana is obviously leading to trouble with John and his loutish, equally macho friend Tom, neither of whom immediately catches on to Brandon's history. We sense it won't be long.

Until then, Brandon flourishes in his new surroundings and especially with Lana. The end is brutal. "It's not just about two stupid thugs who killed somebody," says one of the film's executive producers on the DVD. "It's about these guys whose world is so tenuous and so fragile that they can't stand to have any of their beliefs shattered."

Nevertheless, Brandon and Lana manage to rise above that, however briefly, in one film about a horrific tragedy that still manages to be full of hope.

BOYZ N THE HOOD

Ice Cube, Cuba Gooding Jr., Larry Fishburne, Morris Chestnut, Angela Bassett, Nia Long, Tyra Ferrell

Directed by John Singleton
1991. 107 minutes. R.

Singleton's film remains one of the most accessible and affecting of ghetto dramas. The characters are believable. The story is direct and powerful. The mood is matter-of-fact. Feelings and emotions are strong but unvarnished.

It's a family story. When the teenage Tre Styles (Gooding) drifts toward trouble, his mother, Reva (Bassett), decides the boy would do better under the firm guidance of his father, Furious Styles (Fishburne, who was Larry then). To the film's great credit, here are divorced parents acting wisely in the interests of the child they love.

Furious sets up strict guidelines for his son, then steps back to worry and keep watch. Across the street, the hot-tempered Doughboy (Ice Cube) heads deeper into confrontation with street gangs and drive-by shooters while his half-brother, Ricky (Chestnut), a football hero who is already a father, struggles to stay above the violence around him.

Police helicopters are so numerous that Tre's girlfriend, Brandi (Long), has trouble doing her homework. "Can't we have one night where there ain't no fight and nobody gets shot?" somebody asks. Tragedy can't be avoided, but Singleton leaves room for hope and growth.

BREAD AND ROSES

Pilar Padilla, Adrien Brody, Elpidia Carrillo, George Lopez

Directed by Ken Loach
2001. 110 minutes. R.

The slogan on T-shirts reads JUSTICE FOR JANITORS, but Loach's film about a nascent labor movement to redress workers' grievances escapes didacticism to become a vital and complex piece of political art.

In Los Angeles an illegal Mexican immigrant named Maya (Padilla) goes to work for Angel Cleaning Services, owned by an impersonal corporate entity that uses intimidation to keep workers' wages at a minimum and union representation at bay. Spurred on by an outside organizer named Sam (Brody), the spirited Maya fans the first flames of militancy among the cleaners in her building.

This alarms her sister Rosa (Carrillo), who helped Maya come to California and got her the job but now fears that agitation could cost them their jobs. But Sam is confrontational and persistent, and the notion of standing up for themselves starts to take hold with the workers.

Clandestine planning brings them together for such thrilling acts of subversion as crashing a corporate party with roaring vacuum cleaners. Bonds and loyalties slowly form, and an occasionally festive air breaks out. But there is also the stress of firings and workplace abuse.

Loach has championed the downtrodden for almost 40 years, and he and his screenwriter, Paul Laverty, share a pedagogical impulse. Here, their fine-grained realism helps political engagement grow from the ground sustained by generosity, humor and fellow-feeling.

BRIAN WILSON: I JUST WASN'T MADE FOR THESE TIMES

Brian Wilson, Tom Petty, Lindsey Buckingham, Thurston Moore, David Crosby, Graham Nash, Linda Ronstadt

Directed by Don Was
1995. 69 minutes. No rating.

As Janet Maslin put it in *The New York Times*, Was's documentary about Brian Wilson of the Beach Boys "ought to fascinate anyone who's ever turned on a car radio in America." Wilson himself is on hand to talk about himself and his work, which he has always done sparingly, and there's plenty of help to fill in any gaps.

Was, a record producer who has worked with Bob Dylan, Bonnie Raitt and the Rolling Stones, generates tremendous enthusiasm for the story of a man who parlayed his much-publicized personal troubles and torment into a rich musical legacy.

Brian lights up at the mention of the Four Freshmen, who strongly influenced him, but when he can't easily express where his music took him, Was turns to others to explain. Ronstadt and Petty talk about complex arrangements and elaborate orchestration. A professor at the Eastman School of Music demonstrates what was so different and influential about certain Beach Boys songs.

The music is at the center of "I Just Wasn't Made for These Times." The film also looks at Wilson's famously antic side; not mentioned are his battles with band members and some of the darker personal elements of his life. But there's something honest and uplifting about the celebration of music as a man's salvation.

BRIDESHEAD REVISITED

Jeremy Irons, Anthony Andrews, Claire Bloom, Laurence Olivier, Simon Jones, Diana Quick, Phoebe Nicholls, Stéphane Audran

Directed by Michael Lindsay-Hogg and Charles Sturridge 1981. Eleven 60-minute episodes. No rating.

Quite simply one of the best mini-series ever made, this television adaptation of Evelyn Waugh's novel remains an unparalleled evocation of time and place—from Oxford in the 1920's to World War II and its aftermath—filmed in wonderfully observed detail, with richly nuanced characters and magnificent actors at the start and the end of brilliant careers.

At Oxford the conventional, upper-middle-class Charles Ryder (Irons) is swept into the circle of Sebastian Flyte (Andrews), a flamboyant aristocrat who wanders the campus carrying a stuffed bear named Aloysius. Sebastian takes Charles home to Brideshead, the family estate ruled by his imperious and devoutly Catholic mother, Lady Marchmain (Bloom). Brideshead is also home to Sebastian's three colorful siblings: the fussy heir, Bridey (Jones), the beautiful Julia (Quick) and the good, perfectly named Cordelia (Nicholls). Their father, Lord Marchmain (Olivier) long ago retreated to Italy and a glamorous mistress (Audran), who notices that Charles and Sebastian have one of those "romantic friendships" so many Englishmen have and grow out of.

Such an idyll can't last. Picking up the story years later, we find that Sebastian is lost to alcoholism, and the married Charles falls passionately in love with the miserably married Julia. These later episodes are as fraught with pained emotions as the early ones are filled with sunny innocence and discovery.

The series made Irons a star, and Lord Marchmain's death scene is one of the highlights of Olivier's later career.

BRING IT ON

Kirsten Dunst, Eliza Dushku, Jesse Bradford, Gabrielle Union, Clare Kramer, Richard Hillman, Lindsay Sloane

Directed by Peyton Reed
2000. 98 minutes. PG-13.

A sleeper of a high school movie offers a change of pace, though at first glance you'd never know it. Since the subject is cheerleaders, the views are predictable: skimpy uniforms on the field and skimpier outfits off it. From there, though, Reed's film manages to be at least somewhat substantial.

Never mind the football team (awful); cheerleading competitions are getting the airtime on ESPN. At Rancho Grande High School, the very white, very Southern California yell team, called the Toros, is a five-time national champion. They are also cheats, or so it is alleged by the East Compton Clovers, a largely black squad from the city.

It seems that the Toros stole a winning cheerleading routine from the Clovers, who, truth be told, can outsizzle the Toros in any leap or crotch thrust you want to mention. Most of the Toros scoff at the accusation, but it does upset Torrance (Dunst), the new team captain, who insists that the Toros start again from scratch with an entirely new routine.

Torrance and her sense of morality take a lot of grief, but she sticks to her standards. "My whole cheerleading career is based on a lie," she laments when she learns of the theft, and the film is at its most interesting, if that's the word, when it deals with the consequences and her efforts to reach out to the Clovers and Iris (Union), their proud captain.

Then relax and enjoy Dunst, a terrific comic actress with great expressive range.

LA BÛCHE

Sabine Azéma, Emmanuelle Béart, Charlotte Gainsbourg, Françoise Fabian, Jean-Pierre Darroussin, Christopher Thompson, Claude Rich

Directed by Danièle Thompson
1999. 106 minutes. French with English subtitles. No rating.

Films set around Christmas bustle automatically and sound the effervescence alarm, but Thompson's navigates the season by substituting deft insight and complex, understated emotions for oversentimentality and forced good cheer.

We may begin with mobbed department stores and gold tinsel, but we quickly move on to a funeral montage and the inevitable cell phone going off in someone's pocket. Only in this case the phone is inside the coffin. The caller is the deceased's widow, who obviously hasn't been kept in the loop.

This is a complicated family situation, what with two rival violinists, one of whom is in the coffin; his widow, Yvette (Fabian); her three daughters (Béart, Azéma and Gainsbourg); and Yvette's first husband, the bohemian, impulsive Claude (Rich). Stir in a large supporting cast of parents, lovers and husbands.

They all have secrets, but their lives are much too complicated to summarize, especially in a film whose pleasures lie in getting to know them over time. Suffice it to say that, busy as it is with the making and unmaking of marriages and friendships, *La Bûche* unfolds with the verve and clarity of a piece of music carefully composed and passionately played.

BULWORTH

Warren Beatty, Halle Berry, Oliver Platt, Christine Baranski,
Amiri Baraka, Don Cheadle

Directed by Warren Beatty
1998. 108 minutes. R.

Warren Beatty's acerbic view of the political system is given a comic spin here as he plays a senator who has had enough—enough of his career and enough of his life. So Bulworth hires a hit man to polish himself off so that his family can collect his insurance money, then heads home to California.

With three days to live, why not use the time to break loose? With no incumbency to protect any longer, he can at last shake off phony propriety and deliver some speeches that tell the truth. Suddenly he's saying anything that comes into his mind and rapping political messages, like, "One man, one vote, is that really real? The name of our game is let's make a deal." Beatty makes an intentionally ridiculous, unconvincing rapper, but he's a hilarious breath of political fresh air.

When he tells black churchgoers they'll never have power until they buy it like everybody else does, his horrified campaign manager (Platt) hits the fire alarm to empty the premises.

Naturally, there has to be a romance, and here the movie goes unintentionally haywire as Bulworth falls for Nina (Berry), a young observer who hangs on the fringes. And of course, with a new reason to live, Bulworth has to find a way to call off the best hit men his ill-gotten money could buy.

Despite being sidetracked, the film is worth seeing for its shrewd and funny portrait of the chaos that might result if a fed-up politician dared to tell the truth.

THE BUSINESS OF STRANGERS

Stockard Channing, Julia Stiles, Frederick Weller

Directed by Patrick Stettner
2001. 84 minutes. R.

Tables are turned in a battle of the sexes that lets women dish out some abuse for once. Being pretty smart women, they use the experience to make self-discoveries that would never occur to most men.

On the road for a presentation (as always), a hard-boiled executive named Julie Styron (Channing) hears that her boss is flying in for a personal meeting and assumes she'll be fired. On top of this, a young assistant, Paula Murphy (Stiles), is late with presentation materials. So Julie fires Paula.

As it turns out, Julie is promoted, not dismissed, which puts her in a forgiving mood. She and Paula, a tattooed Dartmouth graduate who would rather be a writer, get together for a lot of drinks in a hotel bar and decide to wreak some sexual vengeance on a slippery corporate recruiter named Nick (Weller).

Paula says Nick once raped her best friend, which outrages Julie. Booze-fueled revenge escalates into pent-up rage at male-dominated corporate culture. But doubts arise about Paula, who takes on the kind of craziness that transformed Glenn Close's stalker in *Fatal Attraction*. Here there is a very different sexual agenda, but Stiles gives Paula a frightening bravado.

Channing's complicated performance adds layers to a character who might have remained the lonely, hardened career woman. Far from a corporate stick (or a man-hater), Julie has a fully developed, self-respecting sense of her life and accomplishments.

The film's conclusion gets unwieldy, but its fine performances add blood and soul and a kind of weird fascination to its stark corporate landscape.

BUTTERFLY

Fernando Fernán Gómez, Manuel Lozano, Uxía Blanco,
Gonzalo Uriarte, Alexis de los Santos, Jesús Castejón

Directed by José Luis Cuerda
2000. 96 minutes. Spanish with English subtitles. R.

Cuerda's delicate, quietly devastating film is doubly nostalgic in that it filters the cataclysm of the Spanish Civil War through the eyes of a child, thereby softening the hurts of one with the bittersweet memories of the other.

Moncho (Lozano), a bright, sensitive boy of 8, is living in a Galician town on the eve of the conflict in 1936 when he is taken under the wing of a freethinking schoolmaster, Don Gregorio (Fernán Gómez), who recognizes Moncho's potential.

Don Gregorio embodies the faltering, slightly comic dignity of the faltering republic. His unorthodox views about pedagogy and discipline (to say nothing of religion and politics) make him a suspect, if revered, figure in the town.

As fascism seeps in, the wide-eyed Moncho is more consumed by the physiology and mechanics of human sex, which he observes while spying on a hayloft romp. Inevitably he faces a loss of innocence made all the more devastating by the conflict, but through the eyes of a child the film looks at the war from a consoling distance.

CAPTURING THE FRIEDMANS

The Friedman family: Arnold, Elaine, Jesse, David and Howard; John McDermott, Detective Frances Galasso and other detectives of the Nassau County Police Department; Judge Abbey Boklan

Directed by Andrew Jarecki
2003. 107 minutes. No rating.

The famous Long Island child-molestation case of the late 1980's receives an engrossing examination in Jarecki's Oscar-nominated documentary.

The film hits a motherlode. Not only were Arnold Friedman, a high school teacher in Great Neck, and his son Jesse separately convicted of molesting young computer students in the Friedmans' basement, but most of the Friedman family talks about its calamity bluntly and at length in home videos made by David Friedman, one of the brothers, before, during and after the two cases.

So for the most part Jarecki lets the Friedmans do the talking. Each has a distinctive profile. Arnold, an admitted pedophile who died in prison, admits nothing but seems resigned. Elaine, the mother, feels excluded in a family of close-knit males. Jesse, the youngest son, who was accused of abetting his father and who served 13 years in prison, talks convincingly about his innocence. David, the eldest brother, who is New York's leading party clown, is the angriest about the destruction of his family.

Always there is the question of guilt or innocence. In the film, detectives defend their methods of child interrogation that led to the convictions. Others attack those methods and point to a kind of community hysteria that may have gripped Great Neck.

At screenings there were heated discussions between the filmmakers and those involved with the case. When the movie opened in theaters, audiences remained in their seats to discuss and argue the merits of both sides. It infects everyone that way; it is impossible not to discuss this movie.

CARNAGE

Chiara Mastroianni, Ángela Molina, Lio, Lucia Sanchez,
Esther Gorintin, Marilyne Even, Jacques Gamblin,
Bernard Sens

Directed by Delphine Gleize
2002. 130 minutes. French and Spanish with English
subtitles. No rating.

Through a series of oblique, half-comic scenes and meticulous, rhyming visual compositions, Gleize's film offers up an elegant, discursive essay on carnality and carnivorousness—on sex, death, meat and the ravening hunger for companionship.

Gleize proceeds in European fashion, replacing linear narrative with chains of association and coincidence. Begin with death and meat as a five-year-old girl witnesses the goring of a bullfighter on television. He lies in a coma while the bull is butchered and distributed across Europe.

The eyeballs go to a veterinary researcher (Gamblin) who is increasingly estranged from his pregnant wife (Lio). Some sirloin is served to a depressive Spanish woman (Molina) whose daughter is the five-year-old's kindergarten teacher. Horns go to an antisocial taxidermist who lives in a trailer with his mother.

Intricacies of relationships are revealed if not always clarified, which can be annoying, and births, deaths and other occasions register as logical results of chance, coincidence and fate. But though Geize's intellectual ambitions are large and sometimes vague, her cinematic self-confidence is as bracing as her eye is meticulous.

CARRINGTON

Jonathan Pryce, Emma Thompson, Steven Waddington, Samuel West, Rufus Sewell, Penelope Wilton, Janet McTeer

Directed by Christopher Hampton
1995. 123 minutes. R.

Hampton's film has a fine time watching the gay writer and intellectual Lytton Strachey (Pryce) and his Bloomsbury cohorts playing their sexual games—or seeking "a great deal of a great many kinds of love," as the arch Strachey put it.

When he first spied the young artist Dora Carrington (Thompson), 17 years his junior, Strachey thought she was a boy. That would have been fine with him, and thereafter Carrington (who stopped calling herself Dora) affected a cropped haircut and mannish attire.

Actually, Carrington attracted many lovers, some of whom she passed along to Strachey. If that has an unsavory flavor, be assured that Pryce and the film make all of it utterly charming. Strachey's rapier wit never fails him, and Carrington is the perfect devoted soul mate to a figure whose social and literary influence helped define an age (or one corner of an age).

The film bursts with summery English landscapes, ideal for languid walks and picnics as Strachey and Carrington handle each new sexual threat to their delicately balanced relationship. Not many would survive such games, but they did so for 17 years before his death in 1932. As for Hampton's sparkling if slender picture, captivating is the word.

CASA DE LOS BABYS

Maggie Gyllenhaal, Marcia Gay Harden, Daryl Hannah, Susan Lynch, Vanessa Martinez, Rita Moreno, Mary Steenburgen, Lili Taylor

Directed by John Sayles
2003. 95 minutes. R.

In another of his social mosaics, Sayles goes to an unnamed Latin American country where six white American women are waiting out the residency requirements before they can return home with babies adopted from an orphanage.

As in all Sayles films, matters of money, class and ethnicity shape the point of view. Nan (Harden), a bullying ugly American, tries bribery to force her application to the top of the pile. Jennifer (Gyllenhaal) is a wistful young woman with an aggressive husband back home who wants to dictate the process. An athletic Colorado golden girl and fitness freak, Skipper (Hannah) is adopting after losing three babies of her own. Gayle (Steenburgen) is a recovering alcoholic who speaks Spanish and attends 12-step meetings as she waits. Leslie (Taylor), a hardheaded single New Yorker, has no grand illusions about motherhood, while Eileen (Lynch), an Irish-American from Boston, dreams about spending a snow day with her new daughter.

The film goes out into the countryside to mingle with a dirt-poor population able and willing to provide what the rich and powerful lack and so desperately want. Back at the casa on the beach, the women are unaware of the poverty and hardship, adding another element of authenticity to a neutral portrayal of two cultures transacting the most personal of business.

THE CELEBRATION

Ulrich Thomsen, Henning Moritzen, Thomas Bo Larsen,
Paprika Steen

Directed by Thomas Vinterberg
1998. 106 minutes. Danish with English subtitles. No
rating.

Filling up his family-owned chateau-hotel with relatives and friends, a prosperous patriarch named Helge
(Moritzen) gives himself a lavish 60th-birthday party. Perhaps he should have thought twice.

Rote gentility is blown sky high with the arrival of
Helge's son, Christian (Thomsen), who's on a mission to
let one and all in on just what life with father was like.
Rising to clink his knife on glass, Helge prepares to tell
the audience—which includes his black-sheep brother,
Michael (Larsen), and loose-cannon sister, Helene (Steen)—
that Helge sexually abused him and was responsible for
the death of Christian's twin sister.

To his surprise, the gathering is ruffled but not as
shocked as one would think.

"It's quite a job being toastmaster tonight," says one
guest.

Around this core of bile swirls a large, credible cast of
patrician guests, flirtatious waitresses and vengeful
kitchen staff. Helene's African-American boyfriend brings
out the worst in the family.

Vinterberg's stripped-down Dogma 95 directorial style
makes it all work beautifully. The camera work is agile;
the jump cuts are nimble; and savvy editing juxtaposi-
tions maintain the momentum.

CHANGING LANES

Ben Affleck, Samuel L. Jackson, Kim Staunton, Amanda Peet, Toni Collette

Directed by Roger Michell
2002. 99 minutes. R.

A fender-bender on an expressway throws two protagonists from opposite worlds into a harrowing conflict and parallel journeys of self-discovery. When the Mercedes belonging to the lawyer Gavin Banek (Affleck) sideswipes the Toyota belonging to the recovering alcoholic Doyle Gibson (Jackson), papers are exchanged and Gavin races off, leaving Doyle with a flat tire and the good wish, "Better luck next time."

Gavin is in a hurry to get to court to file papers in a case that spells life or death to a budding career as a new partner in a big law firm. Doyle is in a hurry to get to court, too, so he can impress upon a judge that he has straightened himself out and deserves visiting rights with his children.

Doyle misses that appointment and with it a chance to stop his wife (Staunton) from moving to Oregon with the kids. Gavin has a problem as well. In his haste to exit the accident scene, he has left his papers with Doyle, who faxes him a sheet with the inscription, "Better luck next time."

That precipitates a nasty conflict between the two, but it also starts them thinking about their own lives. Gavin has doubts about his willingness to abide the ethical compromises that go along with a big-time law career. Doyle has to face a wife worn down by his excesses and face the truth about himself and their relationship.

Great performances help us care about these men, who they are, what motivates them and where they're headed.

CHASING AMY

Ben Affleck, Joey Lauren Adams, Jason Lee, Dwight Ewell,
Jason Mewes, Kevin Smith

Directed by Kevin Smith
1997. 111 minutes. R.

Hailed as a virtual minor masterpiece in its day (way back in the late 1990's), Smith's film acts and speaks exactly as it pleases, which can be refreshing, not to say a little alarming, when the subject is sex. Not many movies intended for general consumption would sit down two comic-book artists, Banky (Lee) and Alyssa (Adams), and let them trade explicit war stories about injuries they received in the throes of oral sex.

Banky's fellow comics creator, Holden (Affleck), discourses on a somewhat higher level in his pursuit of Alyssa, a pretty blonde with a crinkly voice and breezy delivery that suggests Holden has very little to divulge that she doesn't already know. What he doesn't realize at first is that she's gay, which would send a boy like Banky fleeing into the wilds of Smith's beloved New Jersey. Holden, however, is attracted, and so in a way is Alyssa. Perhaps "intrigued" is more the word.

Smith's sharp, ever candid repartee turns the subject to penetration. How, Alyssa wants to know, does a bright fellow like Holden still have the notion that penetration defines sex? The two feel each other out (figuratively speaking, of course) in many frank and cute discussions that grow a little strident by the end of the film. By then, Smith's traveling sideshow, Jay (Mewes) and Silent Bob (Smith), has arrived to lighten things up in a film that thrives on Smith's dry, deadpan direction.

CHICKEN RUN

The voices of Julia Sawalha, Phil Daniels, Mel Gibson, Tony Haygarth, Jane Horrocks, Miranda Richardson, Timothy Spall, Imelda Staunton, Benjamin Whitrow

Directed by Peter Lord and Nick Park
2000. 84 minutes. G.

Park, a master of the Claymation style, tells edgy animated tales (*Wallace and Gromit*), and here he lands scores of chickens in a setting that is more *Stalag 17* than barnyard. At the Tweedy farm, run by the fearsomely demanding Mrs. Tweedy, their duty is egg production. "We lay day in and day out, and when we don't lay enough, they kill us," says one hen.

While nonperformance can be a ticket to the Tweedy dinner table, the mood stays feisty and as upbeat as possible. True, the ax falls discreetly now and then, but, under the leadership of a spirited hen named Ginger (Sawalha), plans are always afoot for the great escape.

Flightless birds have to tunnel like the rest of us; either that, Ginger figures, or they might be propelled out of the place by catapult or slingshot. None of this proves workable, which is why the airborne arrival of a high-flying, big-talking rooster named Rocky (Gibson in a nice semiparody of some other Gibson characters) holds such promise. Flattered by the attention of several hundred hens, Rocky promises to train everybody to fly. Later it's learned that his own takeoff was from the mouth of a cannon at a local carnival.

Meanwhile, Mrs. Tweedy decides that the hens might be more profitable in pot pies. Industrial equipment arrives by truck and is assembled. Could that happen to a nice bunch of chickens?

CHILDREN OF THE REVOLUTION

*Judy Davis, Sam Neill, F. Murray Abraham, Richard
Roxburgh, Rachel Griffiths, Geoffrey Rush*

Directed by Peter Duncan
1996. 101 minutes. R.

A brash performance by Davis meshes perfectly with a
brazen notion by Duncan, a lawyer turned filmmaker.
Finish off Stalin (a madly antic F. Murray Abraham) while
he's having sex with a worshipful Australian activist
named Joan (Davis), leaving her to bear a son she names
Joe (Roxburgh).

Of course, Joe also could well be the son of an
Australian-Russian agent called Nine (Neill), with whom
Joan also shared a bed on the evening in question. Back in
Australia, the fiery Joan has a loyal ally in Welch (Rush), a
fellow communist who tolerates her political diatribes,
marries her and raises the boy as his own.

But there's too much Russian in Joe, who is a natural
Stalin expert from his early youth. "You were marching
before you could walk," Joan tells him. Later he grows a
mustache and learns you don't have to be Stalin to be
Stalin in a splendidly irreverent comedy that rises on
sheer chutzpah and first-rate performances.

CHRIS ROCK: BRING THE PAIN

1996. 70 minutes. No rating.

This is the stand-up special that catapulted Rock into
the front ranks of smart, socially aware, endlessly
funny comedians. Up to that point, he says in a compre-
hensive interview on the DVD, he was a "hack comic," doing clubs and colleges (although some of us remember
him as an underused cast member on *Saturday Night*

Live). "My career was kind of over," he says, so he trained like a boxer for the HBO special. Andrew Dice Clay advised him to watch *Rocky*.

"Maybe I could have cursed less," he says now, but we don't think he means it. There is some rough humor; don't ask about the "tossed salad man" routine about prison sex unless you really want to know.

But his high-risk humor is worth it, especially when he analyzes racial preconceptions among both blacks and whites. This leads him to assessing Colin Powell's prospects for being the first black president (he'd have a better chance of winning women's gymnastics) and reactions to the O. J. Simpson verdict (black people are too happy, whites too mad). In the interview he salutes hip-hop and how it allowed him to say anything and make money. More than that, he says, it showed how he "could be a black artist in the truest sense and not compromise my art." That's something he really means, and it has made him quite possibly the best and funniest comedian working today, an edgy social commentator in a bland sit-com world.

CHUCK & BUCK

Mike White, Chris Weitz, Lupe Ontiveros, Beth Colt, Maya Rudolph, Paul Weitz

Directed by Miguel Arteta
2000. 95 minutes. R.

A strange, intense film about friendship departs from the usual diet of lazy movie nostalgia for the innocence of childhood.

Buck (White), in fact, may be a friend from hell. He and Charlie Sitter (Chris Weitz) were boyhood friends, but whereas Charlie, whom Buck calls Chuck, grew up and moved on to Los Angeles, Buck stayed stuck at home as a perpetual 12-year-old. When Buck's mother dies, Charlie goes back to attend the funeral and afterward rebuffs Buck's fumbling sexual pass.

As a gesture, Charlie makes the mistake of inviting Buck to visit him if he's ever in L.A. Buck does just that and, along with his toys and a supply of lollipops, camps out in a motel and begins a weird stalking operation.

White's performance is an uncanny embodiment of arrested development. Charlie goes into full avoidance mode, but his fiancée (Colt) offers Buck maternal solicitude, as does the manager of a local theater (Ontiveros). Buck even writes a play, *Hank and Frank,* to remind Charlie of the old days in a film that is neither cute nor heartwarming about its view of childhood but offers an intimate, creepy, sometimes funny look at loneliness and need.

THE CIDER HOUSE RULES

Tobey Maguire, Michael Caine, Paul Rudd, Charlize Theron, Delroy Lindo, Jane Alexander, Kathy Baker, Kieran Culkin, Kate Nelligan, Erykah Badu, Heavy D

Directed by Lasse Hallström
1999. 125 minutes. PG-13.

Adapted by John Irving from part of his novel, Hallström's film lends warm compassion to the author's sense of the fantastical. The scene is Maine in golden autumn during World War II. At St. Cloud's orphanage the good-hearted Dr. Wilbur Larch (Caine), a quiet upstart if ever there was one, delivers the babies of unwed mothers and performs abortions on request.

Babies born at St. Cloud's grow up there, ever hoping to be adopted by prospective parents who come to look them over. Among the unchosen is Homer Wells (Maguire), who has grown into his teens at the orphanage.

In a film with a Dickensian flavor, *David Copperfield* is read to the children at bedtime. Homer, a favorite of

Dr. Larch, has learned to assist in medical procedures. On a rare excursion away from St. Cloud's he is taken for a ride in a red convertible by Wally Worthington (Rudd), an Army pilot, whose beautiful blond fiancée, Candy (Theron), has had an abortion.

Freed of St. Cloud's, Homer takes a job on Wally's father's apple farm, and, with Wally back at war, he and Candy fall in love. At the farm he also is involved in the lives of migrant workers and has an opportunity to apply life lessons he has learned from Dr. Larch.

There is an epochal feel to all this, a slightly mythical quality. Caine is superb as a man of compassion, albeit one who continually numbs himself with an ether addiction. Irving's screenplay is subtly literary, Hallström's vision warm and soft-hearted.

THE CIRCLE

Maryiam Palvin Almani, Nargess Mamizadeh, Fereshteh Sadr Orfani, Monir Arab, Elham Saboktakin

Directed by Jafar Panahi
2000. 91 minutes. Farsi with English subtitles. No rating.

Four Iranian women are forced into a more or less outlaw existence for having committed the same offense: being women. At the start, an older woman reacts to her granddaughter's birth. "The ultrasound said it was going to be a boy," she says. "Now the in-laws will insist on a divorce."

Outside the hospital she happens upon three younger women with chadors thrown over their heads, all seemingly in flight from something. We learn that all of them have spent time in prison, but we never find out why.

Without ever resorting to melodrama, Panahi looks at the problems faced by Iranian women, widening the view to taboo subjects affecting women in any society: abortion, prostitution, family violence, the abandonment of children. But you never feel he is making an argument. His film, which was banned in Iran, is investigative rather than didactic, and his bravery stems from his conviction that it is necessary and possible for an artist simply to tell the truth.

Or maybe not so simply. One of the deepest impressions the film leaves is of the terrifying yet thrilling complexity of life, however one views its conditions.

CITIZEN RUTH

Laura Dern, Swoosie Kurtz, Kurtwood Smith, Mary Kay Place, Alicia Witt, Kelly Preston, Tippi Hedren, Burt Reynolds

Directed by Alexander Payne
1996. 102 minutes. R.

The first film by Alexander Payne, who would go on to make the more extravagantly praised *Election* (page 124) and *Sideways,* deserves to be rediscovered for its wit and its timelier-than-ever take on the abortion issue.

Ruth Stoops (Dern) is a glue-sniffing derelict with four children she doesn't like and a fifth on the way. She may be the most sidesplittingly unfit negligent Mother of the Year, and the abortion forces—pro and anti—can't wait to get their claws into her. Payne hilariously spoofs both sides as they engage in a tug-of-war to make Ruth their poster girl.

After she's clapped in jail on yet another charge of vapor inhalation and the judge insists she have an abortion, a Christian women's group is determined to keep her out of the hands of an abortionist. But her stint in the overly happy home of Norm and Gail Stoney (Smith and Place) doesn't work out after Ruth gets into their son's airplane glue and attracts the not-so-wholesome attentions of Norm.

Rid of the Stoneys, she is next taken in by a household

of stern lesbians (Kurtz and Preston), who sing hymns to the moon goddess. Ruth may now wear a Frida Kahlo T-shirt, but she's still the pawn in a battle even crazier after both sides start to bribe her.

In later films, Payne's satire becomes gentler. Here is a chance to catch him at his most scathing.

CITY OF GOD

Seu Jorge, Alexandre Rodrigues, Leandro Firmino da Hora, Phellipe Haagensen, Douglas Silva, Darlan Cunha

Directed by Fernando Meirelles
2002. 130 minutes. Portuguese with English subtitles. R.

With guns blazing and blades flashing, Meirelles's feverish film surveys three decades of street-gang warfare raging in and around Cidade de Deus, a huge housing project built in the 1960's on the outskirts of Rio de Janeiro.

Drugs and poverty fuel the crime. The police show up now and then, but this is a free-for-all, an all-out war fought nonstop by boys who aren't odds-on favorites to make it to manhood.

When Li'l Dice (Silva) first gets his hands on a gun as a small boy, he blasts people with wanton glee, just for the fun of it. Later he'll become Li'l Zé (Firmino da Hora), a trigger-happy drug lord. Meirelles's film contrasts him with Rocket (Rodrigues), who could have taken the same route but is set on a more favorable path by his determination to be a photographer.

Rocket narrates the film, which begins with his recollections of the 60's, then jumps to the 70's and Li'l Zé's reign of terror. In the 80's his empire is threatened by the Runts, the next wave of preteenage gangsters, some 9 and 10 years old. Finally, Li'l Zé's crew takes on the vengeful Knockout Ned (Jorge) and his band.

Meanwhile, Rocket's photo of Li'l Zé and his posse

makes it onto the front page of a newspaper. That might have gotten him killed, but, there being no such thing as bad publicity, the gangster hires him as a kind of staff photographer. With its own handheld cameras, Mereilles's film has the authenticity of a cinema verité scrapbook.

THE CLAIM

Peter Mullan, Wes Bentley, Milla Jovovich, Nastassja Kinski, Sarah Polley

Directed by Michael Winterbottom
2000. 120 minutes. R.

Transferring Thomas Hardy's *Mayor of Casterbridge* to the California gold rush turns out be an inspired idea in Winterbottom's moody, visually stunning drama. The year is 1867, and stakes are high for the mining town of Kingdom Come in the High Sierras. The gold has to keep coming, but so does the Central Pacific Railroad. If its tracks take a lower, easier route, the town will have no future.

The man with the largest stake is the mayor, Daniel Dillon (Mullan). A self-invented figure with a murky past, Dillon has set up life the way he likes it in Kingdom Come, down to moving his large three-story house from one site to another. Peaceable enough as a rule, Dillon insists that visitors shed their firearms, though he keeps his own sharpshooters at the ready. Among the more important visitors is a man named Daglish (Bentley), the railroad surveyor who will make the decision about Kingdom Come.

The town's other new arrival is even more disturbing. Nastassja Kinski plays the wife Dillon sold to a miner in exchange for the claim that made him rich, and Sarah Polley is the grown daughter who was then an infant. Now the two are back in need of his help. Dillon takes them in, which can lead only to an explosive ending for them and for the town, and Winterbottom doesn't hold back.

Mullan's exceptional performance captures the tortured soul of a man who is not unfeeling, and certainly not exempt from guilt. True to the spirit of Hardy, Winterbottom tells of the tragic fall of a complicated, self-styled king.

CLOSE-UP

Hossain Sabzian, Mohsen Makhmalbaf and Abbas Kiarostami as themselves; Abolfazl Ahankhah, Hossain Farazmand

Directed by Abbas Kiarostami
1990. 100 minutes. Farsi with English subtitles. No rating.

To deflect censors, Iranian films have taken a child's-eye view of suppression and injustice, thereby softening the kind of direct social criticism that invites repression. Here, Kiarostami takes a different tack and edges toward issues like poverty and inequality by wrapping his film not in children but in the great cause of art, in this case movie-making.

Kiarostami's pensive tone and deliberate pace take some getting used to, but there's great reward in settling into his mood and rhythms. Taking the form of a documentary, the film recounts the real-life case of Hossain Sabzian (playing himself), a young man put on trial for impersonating the renowned Iranian film director Mohsen Makhmalbaf.

It all starts on a bus when Sabzian is reading Makhmalbaf's book *The Cyclist* and strikes up a conversation with the well-to-do Mrs. Ahankhah. Identifying himself as Makhmalbaf, he talks himself into the prosperous Ahankhah household by telling her he plans to make a film about the family.

Such is not the case, of course, and Sabzian ends up in

court, where he says he is really a down-and-out divorced father inspired by Makhmalbaf's view of the human condition as expressed in his art. Case more or less dismissed. Makhmalbaf himself shows up on his motorbike and gives Sabzian a lift to the Ahankhahs' house, where everybody exchanges kisses on the cheek.

COLD COMFORT FARM

Kate Beckinsale, Rufus Sewell, Ian McKellen, Stephen Fry, Ivan Kaye, Eileen Atkins, Christopher Bowen, Joanna Lumley, Sheila Burrell, Freddie Jones, Maria Miles

Directed by John Schlesinger
1995. 95 minutes. PG.

Made for the BBC, Schlesinger's film gets Stella Gibbons's sly 1932 satirical novel just right. This is a frothy, comic trifle that plays as if all English eccentricity had gathered under one roof (badly in need of reshingling) in the Sussex countryside, home of the rural curiosities aptly named Starkadder.

Back in London, a pretty, young distant cousin named Flora Poste (Beckinsale, back when she was playing sweet young things) finds herself financially strapped and obliged to throw herself on the mercy of family. To the horror of friends, she chooses to go to the country and cast her lot with people who probably haven't bathed in a while and name their cows Feckless and Pointless.

Flora, a bright, snippy young woman with literary ambitions, notes that every farm has its highly sexed sons, invariably named Seth and Reuben. On her arrival the dark, sensual Seth (Sewell), the Starkadders' answer to D. H. Lawrence's gamekeeper, and Reuben (Kaye) drool over the new tenant.

Meanwhile, the ancient grandmother, Ada Doom (Burrell), is holed up in the attic, ranting on about the murky terrors that drove her into hiding decades ago, while a floor below the rheumy-eyed Judith Starkadder (the incomparable Atkins) anguishes over the departed and the hopelessness inflicted on the remaining. Flora is determined to straighten out their poor country lives—the highest calling of a city cousin, after all—and proves herself unexpectedly wise.

COLLATERAL

Tom Cruise, Jamie Foxx, Jada Pinkett Smith

Directed by Michael Mann
2004. 120 minutes. R.

Cruise may be underrated by some, but leave him to his own devices and he comes through very well indeed. A twitchy, highly physical person, he reveals his characters from the outside in, and so it is in Mann's edgy thriller about a contract killer named Vincent who sets out one evening to wipe out five people in Los Angeles.

As a hit man, Cruise is gunmetal gray in attire and hair color, which suits Mann's harshly lighted, smokily treacherous L.A. night. Needing to kill five people and get to the airport, the efficient Vincent hires a cab to convey him from shooting to shooting. The driver, a kindly dreamer named Max (Foxx), doesn't think he can keep the meter running, but the promise of a $600 fee keeps him rolling.

Vincent is superb at what he does, but this is a night's work that will come to no good end. Thinking his passenger is a regular businessman on his rounds, Max learns what he's in for when Vincent's first victim comes flying out a window and lands *kersplat* on top of his cab.

As an employer, Vincent is civil in a deadly kind of way, probing, tightly wound. The two men feel each other out, one a trained predator with little hope, the other a nice guy with all the hope in the world who wants to start a limousine service. The violence escalates. Mann's films are about men doing their work; the look and feel convey meaning. In a supporting role (some would say the lead), Los Angeles has never been better.

THE COMMITMENTS

Robert Arkins, Michael Aherne, Angeline Ball, Maria Doyle, Dave Finnegan, Bronagh Gallagher

Directed by Alan Parker
1991. 118 minutes. R.

Dropping in on pop-obsessed North Dublin, Parker's film does what he does best: assemble a group of talented newcomers and piece together high-energy snippets to tell how a music group was formed.

The music is American soul, an odd passion for an all-white band, but everybody from priests to street kids lives by the memory of Presley and the sounds of the 60's. When the Commitments belie their working-class roots by wearing evening dress and black tie, it's pointed out that the Motown brothers also wore suits.

There is the cute, predictable bad-audition montage, with the fledgling impresario Jimmy Rabbitte (Arkins) screening aspirants. Talent turns up in unexpected places. Jimmy practices giving interviews in the shower.

Music and talk about music saturate North Dublin, with everybody singing along, or so it seems. That can get a little too adorable at times, but again the energy of performance overcomes the cuteness.

With so much emphasis on the group's stage show, romances and other personal matters never get too far off the ground. It's all about the music.

CONCERT FOR GEORGE

Eric Clapton, Ringo Starr, Paul McCartney, Olivia Harrison,
Ray Cooper, Billy Preston, Jeff Lynne, Tom Petty

Directed by David Leland
2003. 146 minutes. PG-13.

***

Leland's documentary of the concert at Royal Albert Hall in London to celebrate the life and art of George Harrison reflects the contemplative quality of music emanating from a spiritually heady segment of hippie culture.

Believing music to be a universal language that could help heal the world, Harrison gave even his lighter songs a hybrid East-West flavor that came from his slide guitar and echoed the sitar of his mentor Ravi Shankar.

Adapting the mantric drone and modal angularity of Hindu devotion into highly melodic pop, Harrison's best-known songs now have a nostalgic ring. Among them here are "If I Needed Someone," "Taxman," "Isn't It a Pity," "Something," "Beware of Darkness" and "All Things Must Pass."

Interspersed are recollections from Clapton, McCartney, Starr, Petty, Lynne, Preston and other lifelong musical friends. Tom Hanks joins the chorus line of Canadian Mounties as the Monty Python troupe, who Harrison thought inherited the Beatles' spiritual mantle, renders "The Lumberjack Song." Shankar remembers Harrison as being like a son.

The most joyful moment is Starr's rousing version of "Photograph," which he wrote with Harrison. It stands as a moving reminder of the communal ideals that the Beatles embodied for a generation now in its 50's.

CONFESSIONS OF A DANGEROUS MIND

Sam Rockwell, Drew Barrymore, George Clooney, Rutger Hauer

Directed by George Clooney
2002. 113 minutes. R.

Long after becoming famous as the creator of tacky but spectacularly successful game shows (*The Gong Show, The Dating Game*), Chuck Barris wrote a book in which he said he had been a hit man for the C.I.A. True or not, that story is the basis for this clever, edgy film, smartly directed by George Clooney (yes, the *Ocean's Eleven* hunk) and written by the always imaginative Charlie Kaufman (*Being John Malkovich*).

Rockwell plays Barris as a raving egomaniac but also captures his total confusion. Talk about an identity crisis. When Barris chaperoned a *Dating Game* couple on a prize trip to, say, Helsinki in the dead of winter, did he drift off unnoticed to commit a government-sanctioned rubout? No wonder this little sideline led to depression, drinking and barricading himself in a room for days at a time.

Barrymore is at her most appealing as Barris's spacy on-again, off-again girlfriend, who genuinely loves him and tries to save him from himself. And the supporting roles are great fun to watch. Clooney plays Barris's C.I.A. recruiter and handler in an especially wry, tongue-in-cheek scene. Julia Roberts puts in an appearance as a vampy agent who seems drawn to Barris—or is this mystery woman simply doing her job?

In his first film, Clooney shows sophisticated comic flair and keeps the movie from running away with its overload of wacky ideas.

CONTEMPT

Brigitte Bardot, Michel Piccoli, Jack Palance, Fritz Lang

Directed by Jean-Luc Godard
1963. 102 minutes. French with English subtitles.

An adaptation of Alberto Moravia's novel *A Ghost at Noon,* Godard's film concerns itself with adapting literature to the screen. Here it's a question of art versus commerce.

A screenwriter named Paul Javal (Piccoli) is hired by a crass American producer, Jerry Prokosch (Palance), to work on a film to be directed by the great Fritz Lang (playing himself). In the middle is Javal's wife, Camille (Bardot), who is impatient with Javal's fitful career to begin with and put off when he voices no objections after Prokosch makes a pass at her.

Prokosch and Lang's movie is supposedly modeled after *The Odyssey,* though it probably has more direct relation to Godard's own adventures with *Contempt* and his relations with the producers Joseph E. Levine and Carlo Ponti. Casting suggestions ran from Frank Sinatra and Kim Novak to Sophia Loren and Marcello Mastroianni. To appease the Americans, who found the project too artsy, Godard added a scene with Bardot's clothes off.

On screen, Prokosch throws a tantrum when Lang's movie isn't what the producer expected. Javal and Camille argue for a long while. Lang has his moments of exasperation (Godard plays his assistant director) but carries on wonderfully in a brilliant reflection on the filmmaking process.

COOKIE'S FORTUNE

Glenn Close, Patricia Neal, Julianne Moore, Liv Tyler,
Charles S. Dutton, Ned Beatty, Courtney B. Vance, Donald
Moffat, Lyle Lovett, Ruby Wilson, Chris O'Donnell

Directed by Robert Altman
1999. 118 minutes. PG-13.

One of Altman's more flavorful ensembles comes together in Holly Springs, Mississippi, a town that manages to be both a hotbed of grudges, family secrets and power struggles and a place where little or nothing appears to be happening.

As the film hunts for mischief, it notices racial contrasts. A sultry black singer (Wilson) performs at a blues club, while in a church basement white folks rehearse a play about Salome and John the Baptist, directed by the control-obsessed Camille Dixon (Close), who insists on sharing a writing credit for the work with Oscar Wilde.

There is a beautiful friendship between the good-hearted Willis Richland (Dutton) and Camille's aunt, the prickly Jewell Mae Orcutt, called Cookie (Neal). Cookie's wealth annoys Camille mightily, as do Cookie's dizzy sister Cora (Moore) and Cora's free-spirited daughter, Emma (Tyler), who likes working with catfish and turns the heads of a rookie cop (O'Donnell) and the local peeping Tom (Lovett).

Eventually matters turn nasty when Camille's vindictive meddling results in Willis Richland's being charged with Cookie's murder, actually a suicide. This tests everyone's mettle.

Altman has a lot of balls in the air, but he avoids the vagueness that has plagued some of his other smaller works. The film is tighter and more direct, and in that spirit of tidiness, everybody gets exactly what he or she deserves.

THE COOLER

*William H. Macy, Alec Baldwin, Shawn Hatosy, Maria Bello,
Ron Livingston, Paul Sorvino*

Directed by Wayne Kramer
2003. 101 minutes. R.

Macy's Bernie Lootz is a man with unluckiness to spare,
which makes him a valuable man around the casino
in a film that gives Macy plenty of room to work and does
nothing to hurt Baldwin's reputation as one of the best
character actors at work today.

A morose little sad sack, Bernie has such bad luck that
it actually seems to rub off on anyone in his proximity. In
Las Vegas he works for Shelly Kaplow (Baldwin), owner of
the Shangri-La, who employs him to cool off big winners
at the tables merely by standing near them.

But a problem arises when, for some reason, Bernie attracts a good-looking cocktail waitress named Natalie
(Bello). A Bernie ecstatically in love isn't good medicine for
Bernie the glum cooler, who turns completely ineffective
under the influence of a positive attitude.

This displeases Shelly, who, as portrayed by Baldwin,
turns as scarily nasty as any character in memory. It's definitely not advisable to rile Shelly, as Bernie's smart-
mouthed, card-counting son (Hatosy) discovers. But
Kaplow has a mellower side, reflected in his appreciation
of Sinatra and determination to keep the Shangri-La doing business the old-fashioned way.

Kramer's film may fall back on noirish Vegas conventions, but it is skillfully made and certainly knows better
than to interfere with the superb performances.

COP LAND

Sylvester Stallone, Robert De Niro, Harvey Keitel, Ray Liotta, Michael Rapaport, Cathy Moriarty, Janeane Garofalo, Annabella Sciorra

Directed by James Mangold
1997. 105 minutes. R.

If you think Stallone could never hold his own on screen against the likes of De Niro and Keitel, guess again. As the overweight Freddy Heflin, he leaves Rambo and even Rocky Balboa far in his wake.

Stallone gained 40 pounds to play the ridiculed sheriff of Garrison, New Jersey, a small town just across the George Washington Bridge that serves as a bedroom for New York City cops and their families.

On the George one night, a stressed-out New York City police officer and Garrison resident (Rapaport) has a traffic altercation and shoots two people. Not wanting New York's finest besmirched, his uncle Ray (Keitel), also a cop, hustles him off the bridge and engineers a cover-up.

Enter Moe Tilden (De Niro) from the N.Y.P.D.'s internal affairs division. Moe starts poking around Garrison, leading to a confrontation with Ray. Meanwhile, Freddy borrows quarters from parking meters to play pinball and serves as the passive local schlump who's there to write parking tickets and stay out of the big boys' way. But all that changes quite remarkably when Freddy finally asserts himself, and Stallone earns his wings among high-flying talent.

CROUPIER

Clive Owen, Kate Hardie, Alex Kingston, Gina McKee, Alexander Morton, Nick Reding

Directed by Mike Hodges
1998. 89 minutes. R.

Considering his manner and appearance, the taciturn Owen was handed just about the perfect vehicle in Hodges's whip-smart suspense thriller about the gaming business and what it does to people.

As Jack Manfred, Owen deals cards and rakes in chips at a posh London casino. Behind glittering blue eyes, a languidly impenetrable expression suggests detached contempt for the high rollers throwing their money away. By the end of the evening, though, accumulated tension leaves Jack a quivering wreck.

Beyond its thrillerish aspects, Hodges's film is a breezy meditation on life as a game of chance. Jack, the son of a South African casino owner, is no gambler himself, at least at the tables. He fancies himself a budding novelist, which he supposes is just as big a crap shoot. One needs the right subject matter, and then just the right title.

Needing money, he sticks to his job at the casino, where he starts to gamble with house rules against dating fellow staff members and socializing with the clientele. There's an affair with a waitress (Hardie) and a scheme hatched by an amoral, glamorous gambler (Kingston) whom Jack escorts to a debauched weekend at a country estate.

Jack rationalizes these ethical lapses as the story builds to a climax with an unexpected sideways turn. In the end, Hodges's film suggests a less stylized British answer to David Mamet's *House of Games*, which also played a joke on the audience, but here the mood is more whimsical than vengeful.

THE CRUCIBLE

Daniel Day-Lewis, Winona Ryder, Joan Allen, Paul Scofield,
Bruce Davison, Charlayne Woodard, Karron Graves,
Jeffrey Jones

Directed by Nicholas Hytner
1996. 123 minutes. PG-13.

By anchoring itself so firmly in the Salem, Massachusetts, of 1692, Hytner's vibrant film, adapted by Arthur Miller from his 1953 play, has a base from which to transcend time and space. Miller originally set the work against a background of the McCarthy era, but whatever the period the seed of mass paranoia always awaits the manipulators.

In the Salem witch trials paranoia is fanned into outright hysteria. When lovestruck young girls cavort and dance naked in the woods, two of them fall into a coma-like state. Witchcraft is charged, greatly riling the town and creating an opportunity for the girls' scheming leader, Abigail Williams (Ryder). Her affair with the charismatic John Proctor (Day-Lewis) is over, but Abigail refuses to accept this. She sees a way to implicate Proctor's wife (Allen) in the growing furor and, since he continues to resist her advances, eventually bring down Proctor himself.

Judges arrive in Salem to assess righteousness, and they make perfect prey for the wily, treacherous Abigail, convincingly played by Ryder, whose maneuvering sends matters out of control in an agile film that suggests such a situation could arise anywhere at any time.

CRUMB

Robert Crumb, Beatrice Crumb, Charles Crumb, Max Crumb, Dana Morgan, Robert Hughes, Aline Kominsky

Directed by Terry Zwigoff
1994. 119 minutes. No rating.

Zwigoff's film about the cartoonist Robert Crumb would have exerted a gothic sort of appeal if it had just profiled Crumb and his spectacularly troubled family, but it goes much further by showing how Crumb's psychic wounds goaded him into turning personal pain into garish visual satire.

Crumb's major gripes are against his father, a former Marine of classic rigidity, and American society in general. Here he freely acknowledges that his desire to succeed was motivated by a desire for revenge.

Not that he stood as a model of someone to emulate. As a boy, he says in Zwigoff's documentary, he was sexually attracted to Bugs Bunny and later to the television character Sheena, Queen of the Jungle. Though he created such famous characters as Fritz the Cat and Mr. Natural and helped start the underground-comics movement, remnants of Bugs and Sheena turned up in work that is savagely misogynistic and pornographically explicit.

Much of the film is devoted to relatives, including a long look at Crumb's talented, mentally disturbed brother, Charles, who recalls homicidal feelings he had for Robert and who committed suicide before the film was released. Another brother, Max, a self-punishing ascetic, is shown lying bare-backed on a bed of nails while preparing to meditate.

Amazingly candid interviews with them and current and former wives shed some light on the work, but nothing reveals what enabled Crumb to leap from neurosis to artistic brilliance. It's still one of the most revealing documentary portraits of an artist ever filmed.

THE CRYING GAME

Stephen Rea, Jaye Davidson, Miranda Richardson, Adrian Dunbar, Forest Whitaker, Jim Broadbent

Directed by Neil Jordan
1992. 112 minutes. R.

Jordan's films play with love, but seldom as trickily as in the twisty story of a naïve, sweet-tempered I.R.A. man named Fergus (Rea), who falls for a furtive London hairstylist named Dil (Davidson). The movie also has other things on its mind.

Everyone wears a mask, including Fergus, who is hiding out in England under an assumed name after a botched kidnapping in Northern Ireland. He's never met someone like the witty, glamorous Dil, a vision in a spangled dress who climbs onto the stage at her favorite pub to sing the title song.

Love flares but as quickly flickers upon the arrival of Fergus's I.R.A. cohorts, who threaten to harm the unsuspecting Dil if Fergus doesn't help them assassinate an English judge. And, of course, Dil has a surprise of her own—quite a shocker, in fact, when the film was released but perhaps less so now.

The film also believes in redemption, which leaves Fergus in torment over the snatching of an English soldier (Whitaker) he comes to know and respect and other brutal acts aided and abetted by I.R.A. operatives like his girlfriend (Richardson). Beyond Fergus and Dil, Jordan's screenplay reaches for matters like the strength of political commitment and the shiftiness of life's fugitives.

THE DANCER UPSTAIRS

Javier Bardem, Laura Morante, Juan Diego Botto, Abel Folk

Directed by John Malkovich
2002. 133 minutes. R.

Malkovich (who does not appear on screen) creates a languorous but riveting story, shot in Ecuador, of a people caught in a cycle of violence that seems to have no end. He is greatly aided by Bardem, whose performance brings star presence to a political story that may seem murky to some viewers.

The film watches a terrorist organization through the eyes of Rejas (Bardem), a former lawyer and now a police official assigned to track down the group's leader, known as Ezequiel (Folk) and modeled after Abimael Guzmán, the leader of the Shining Path terrorist group in Peru. In fact, Rejas is the film's true subject. Five years earlier, he encountered Ezequiel during another bloody incident (one of the film's memorable set pieces) and learned that the best way to approach the prey was quietly, methodically, without emotional involvement. The film's chilling understated style reflects Rejas's approach of detachment and unwavering pursuit to the point of obsession.

There are glimpses of Rejas's home life: his wife prattles on about the virtues of cosmetic surgery and *The Bridges of Madison County,* which her book club is studying. His one bit of relief comes from his daughter, and through her he is ultimately drawn to an attractive dance instructor named Yolanda (Morante) who leads him to unexpected knowledge and fresh betrayals in a film whose secrets may be revealed slowly but also have a haunting, lingering power.

DANGEROUS LIAISONS

Glenn Close, John Malkovich, Michelle Pfeiffer, Swoosie Kurtz, Uma Thurman, Keanu Reeves, Mildred Natwick

Directed by Stephen Frears
1988. 118 minutes. R.

Frears's good-looking, intelligent adaptation of Christopher Hampton's play *Les Liaisons Dangereuses*, itself based on the 18th-century epistolary novel by Choderlos de Laclos, makes a witty and entertaining study of decadence, topped by a performance by Close that is as savage as her spurned mistress in *Fatal Attraction*.

About to erupt from a cinched bodice, the Marquise de Merteuil (Close) plots sexual games of devilish cruelty with her former lover and near equal in such matters, the Vicomte de Valmont (Malkovich). To pay back another lover who left her, the Marquise would have Valmont seduce the man's virginal bride-to-be (Thurman).

But Valmont appears more interested in seducing the faithful wife (Pfeiffer) of an officer serving abroad. To bring him around to her own mission of seduction, the Marquise agrees to spend a night with Valmont, provided he can prove that he has succeeded with the officer's spouse.

So what does Valmont do but fall in love. Reviews of the film at the time it appeared noted Malkovich's American appearance and speech ("more like 20th-century Pittsburgh than 18th-century Paris," Vincent Canby wrote in *The Times*), but it's hard to imagine such a criticism 16 years later. Even then, Canby noted, Malkovich's strength and intelligence shaped the audience's response to him.

Close does full justice to a beautifully written role of classical proportions that allows her a full measure of richness and comic delicacy.

Hampton wrote the screenplay, and although it takes a while to get used to the stylized dialogue and mannerisms, the strangeness wears off as the film takes off in mad pursuit of its seducers.

THE DANGEROUS LIVES OF ALTAR BOYS

Kieran Culkin, Jena Malone, Emile Hirsch, Vincent D'Onofrio, Jodie Foster

Directed by Peter Care
2002. 105 minutes. R.

Care's film, adapted from Chris Fuhrman's novel, takes a wonderfully fresh leap into the flaming recesses of the adolescent mind.

To up the ante facing any group of rambunctious teenagers, the ribald chicanery takes place within the moral parameters of a tightly lashed-down Catholic high school in the 1970's. To stir the waters, Francis (Hirsch) and Tim (Culkin) collaborate on a wild action-adventure comic book in which they imagine themselves as superheroes battling a repressive school regime headed by the eagle-eyed, tight-lipped Sister Assumpta (Foster), who wears a prosthetic leg.

A small, heartfelt film brilliantly integrates some lively animated sequences. Not too surprisingly, the headmistress engages in kinky sex with Father Casey (D'Onofrio), the parish priest and soccer coach, and then metamorphoses into Nunzilla, a motorcycle-riding savage and kind of heavy-metal Wicked Witch of the West.

Away from the fantasy, Francis starts a romance with Margie Flynn (Malone), a classmate with an agonizing personal secret so tantalizing that Francis can't keep it one second longer. And there are lots of pranks, not the least of which involves drugging a cougar with a quart of NyQuil and later turning it loose in school to terrify Sister Assumpta.

But maybe the best part of this film is that it removes these kids from the jaded Hollywood brats of most high school films and recognizes that there are no shortcuts to adulthood.

DAVE

Kevin Kline, Sigourney Weaver, Frank Langella, Kevin Dunn, Ving Rhames, Ben Kingsley

Directed by Ivan Reitman
1993. 110 minutes. PG-13.

Reitman's film has good fun with a presidential look-alike who is brought on board to stand in for the chief executive at ceremonial events but is then pressed into actually taking over the Oval Office when the legitimate occupant suffers, as the president's spinmeisters describe it, "a minor circulatory problem of the head."

Kevin Kline is Dave, who takes all kinds of gigs impersonating President Bill Mitchell at openings of car dealerships and the like, but he is shocked when approached by the White House to make himself available to be Mitchell when glad-handing visiting dignitaries and kissing babies.

Kline is most entertaining as a plain-vanilla guy who can sing "Oklahoma!" and is thrilled to be on his wide-eyed own, sort of, in the halls of power. Then, amid sexual exertion with a favored aide, Mitchell suffers a stroke that leaves him comatose.

Anxious to conceal that fact at all costs, the scheming chief of staff (Langella) describes the ailment as minor and slips Dave into office, so to speak. Even Mitchell's embittered wife (Weaver) is fooled. "Why can't you die from a stroke like everybody else?" she asks Dave.

Not surprisingly, Dave imparts much of his natural sweetness and nobility to his duties, not to mention an independent streak that is vastly annoying and alarming to the chief of staff. The film may flag a little in these latter stages, but by then Kline, Langella and Weaver have built up nice momentum.

DAY FOR NIGHT

*François Truffaut, Jacqueline Bisset, Jean-Pierre Léaud,
Valentina Cortese, Jean-Pierre Aumont, Dani, Alexandra
Stewart, Jean Champion*

Directed by François Truffaut
1973. 115 minutes. French with English subtitles. No
rating.

There are many movies about the movies, but to quote
the film scholar Annette Insdorf, this is "the one."

We are on the set with Ferrand (Truffaut), a director
with limitless reserves of equanimity, which is good because things aren't going well with his new movie, *Meet
Pamela*. For one thing, there may well be no Pamela, since
the actress hired for the role, the beautiful and celebrated
Julie (Bisset), is still in the throes of her latest emotional
upset and hasn't shown up. (Julie has just married her
doctor, and the hope is that her health will improve.)

Another of Ferrand's stars, the mercurial Alphonse
(Léaud, star of Truffaut's Antoine Doinel films), is a hand-
ful, and the older leading man (Aumont) is at last dealing
with the fact that he is a homosexual.

And there is the inevitable run of production glitches,
all of which are taken in stride by Ferrand, who in some
ways is a throwback to the days when studios ground out
a film a week. As a filmmaker, he is more in love with the
nuts and bolts of making a movie than with the movie he
happens to making.

To Ferrand a movie is like a stagecoach journey that
could go one way or the other. "At first you hope for a
pleasant trip," he says. "Then you simply hope to reach
your destination." That established, he settles in to show
us how movies are made, and what fun that is for everybody involved.

DAYS OF HEAVEN

Richard Gere, Brooke Adams, Linda Manz, Sam Shepard

Directed by Terrence Malick
1978. 95 minutes. PG.

The cinematographer Néstor Almendros won the Oscar for the stunning vistas, and Malick does credibly as he reaches for echoes of American myth, biblical connections and elements of Greek tragedy.

In the early 1900's a hotheaded blast-furnace worker named Bill (Gere) kills a foreman in a labor dispute and flees west with his lover, Abby (Adams), and little sister, Linda (Manz). After joining a caravan of migrants looking for work, they find employment with a wealthy Texas wheat farmer (Shepard), referred to only as "the farmer," who lives alone in a huge mansion.

The farmer appears to have a fatal illness of some kind and stays by the house, but, as Pharaoh did Sarah in the Old Testament, he admires Abby at work in the fields and imagines her as his queen. That gives Bill an idea. If Abby were to marry the fellow, she would come into possession of his spread when he dies.

But after the wedding Abby develops a growing fondness for the farmer. Bill goes back to the city to earn some money to spring the three of them from this situation, but on his return the farmer realizes the relationship between Bill and Abby, which leads to a tragic struggle.

The most talkative character is Linda, the little sister, who serves as narrator. Otherwise everyone stays fairly mute in a film that communicates by pictorial effects and its sound and score, both nominated for Oscars.

DEAD CALM

Nicole Kidman, Sam Neill, Billy Zane

Directed by Phillip Noyce
1989. 95 minutes. R.

Noyce, an Australian, has a couple of other dramas listed in this book, one languorously atmospheric (*The Quiet American,* page 325), the other stirring (*Rabbit-Proof Fence,* page 327). Here, he's more in the white-knuckle mode of later films like *Patriot Games* and *The Bone Collector*.

Rae and John Ingram (Kidman and Neill) are on a long sail on a leased yacht, trying to deal with the death of their child, when they come across a sinking schooner dead in the water. A man in a dinghy rows toward them.

Hughie (Zane) is a slightly daffy name for the fairly menacing-looking character, who says that the schooner's crew has succumbed to food poisoning and he is the lone survivor. John rows over to the stricken vessel to see for himself, finds evidence of a grisly slaughter and spends the rest of the film fighting for his life.

Aboard the Ingrams' boat, the game but unpracticed Rae is left to fend for herself against a homicidal maniac. She has her chances but fails to sink the knife (and never tie up someone with the knots in front). Meanwhile, John struggles to stay afloat as Hughie gains the upper hand.

All this has a slightly sleazy exploitative feel, and that applies to the slasher-film-style ending. But the tension is never less than gripping, and the performances are very fine.

DEAD MAN WALKING

Sean Penn, Susan Sarandon, Robert Prosky, Raymond J. Barry, R. Lee Ermey

Directed by Tim Robbins
1995. 120 minutes. R.

Based on a memoir by Sister Helen Prejean, a nun from Louisiana, Robbins's hard look at death row comes furiously alive without sentimentalizing. Much of its power comes from Penn's stern, uncompromising performance as Matthew Poncelet, sentenced to death for murdering two teenagers. He is matched by Sarandon, who won an Oscar for her role as Sister Helen, whom she plays with a calm resolve, rock-bottom decency and an open mind.

Asked why she would come to the aid of such a despised figure, Sister Helen responds, "Every person deserves respect." She becomes Poncelet's pen pal and eventually goes to visit him on death row. Nothing about the sullen, heavy-lidded convict suggests innocence, but his magnetism make him hard to ignore. Repelled and alarmed by him, Sister Helen is determined to reach and help him nevertheless, and she sets about the task of becoming his spiritual adviser.

She also has an agonizing encounter with the family of one of Poncelet's victims, and scenes like that raise the film above the level of polemic. Although its point of view is decidedly against the death penalty, this is a thoughtful consideration of the issue and a profound study of two thoroughly opposite characters.

Robbins and Penn were also deservedly nominated for Oscars. Robbins's direction is graceful and finally devastating as the film moves toward its agonizing conclusion.

THE DEEP END

Tilda Swinton, Jonathan Tucker, Goran Visnjic, Peter Donat, Josh Lucas

Directed by Scott McGehee and David Siegel
2001. 101 minutes. R.

A great-looking thriller with polish and sophistication plays some nice tricks on its unordinary protagonists.

When Margaret Hall (Swinton), the mother of three living in a fine rustic setting by Lake Tahoe, learns that her eldest son, Beau (Tucker), is involved with a predatory homosexual named Darby (Lucas), she tries to cut off the liaison. Darby says fine, but he wants $5,000.

Then Darby turns up dead on the Halls' waterfront. Margaret assumes Beau is responsible and, being a good mom, disposes of the body. Beau, on the other hand, presumes his mother was involved. There's a police investigation to parry—and another blackmailer, Alek (Visnjic), who suddenly appears bearing a videotape supposedly of Beau having relations with Darby. Alek wants $50,000.

With her husband away in the Navy, Margaret spends the rest of the film in a gripping battle to protect her son (and keep up with the housework). Swinton, who has shone in more rarefied fare, is very fine at conveying Margaret's desperate devotion. Nothing good will come of this, she knows, but she has to follow through, and a smart film finally allows her a place to rest her trust.

LES DESTINÉES

Emmanuelle Béart, Charles Berling, Isabelle Huppert

Directed by Olivier Assayas
2000. 180 minutes. French with English subtitles.
No rating.

Assayas's ambitious, nicely realized film depicts a scrupulously defined slice of early 20th-century French provincial life. At the core is Jean Barney (Berling), the scion of a porcelain-company family, who tries to make his way in the modern world from about 1900 through the Depression.

Barney goes through several transformations geared to an era of war and upheaval. In 1900 he is a pastor in a small Protestant community. His marriage to the severe Nathalie (Huppert) is collapsing, taking with it his beloved daughter and his vocation. Next on the scene is the warmly sensual Pauline (Béart), an orphan newly arrived from England, who will become his second wife. That union lasts, but it won't be easy.

Jean's two wives—one a moralist, the other a sensualist—are at the poles of his temperament. At the start he is a man of God. With Pauline he becomes a man of feeling. During World War I, life in the trenches turns him into a relative primitive. Back home after the death of his father, he takes over the family business and finds fulfillment in the material world.

Like a good novel, *Les Destinées* is many things: a family chronicle, a series of psychological portraits, a sumptuous re-creation of the past. At its best, the film displays a commitment to the fine grain of its story that is nothing less than thrilling.

DEVIL IN A BLUE DRESS

Denzel Washington, Tom Sizemore, Jennifer Beals,
Don Cheadle, Maury Chaykin, Terry Kinney

Directed by Carl Franklin
1995. 102 minutes. R.

In one of his better performances, Washington is Easy Rawlins, reluctant private eye, in one of Franklin's better films, adapted from the Walter Mosley novel. The scene is Los Angeles in 1948, where a richly defined black culture had a good sense of itself and how things worked in a segregated society. The texture and mood is silky noir, a Franklin strength.

Trouble crosses racial boundaries when Easy is hired by a white hoodlum, Dewitt Albright (Sizemore), to find the white woman of the title (Beals), who may be the girl-friend of the richest man in L.A. (Kinney) but is said to prefer black men. Behind on the payments on his neat little house, Easy could use the cash.

Albright helps Easy avoid a brawl with racists early on, but he's nasty and unpredictable on all fronts. Easy doesn't own a gun, but like all Washington characters he's adept at handling himself. He's not the only man looking for Daphne Monet. There are a couple of murders, a lot of money passing hands and some dirty and deadly politics.

Easy's wary intelligence fits the racial climate of the times. Franklin allows him and the film a certain geniality. For all the dirty business, these are characters who know how to relax and enjoy one another's company.

THE DEVIL'S BACKBONE

Eduardo Noriega, Marisa Paredes, Federico Luppi, Íñigo Garcés, Fernando Tielve, Irene Visedo, Berta Ojea

Directed by Guillermo del Toro
2001. 106 minutes. Spanish with English subtitles. No rating.

Provoking some screams and shudders, del Toro's film also keeps political and metaphorical balls in the air to good effect. The setting, a voluptuously scary one, is a lonely boarding school during the late stages of the Spanish Civil War. The place is now an orphanage for the sons of dead Republicans, and in the courtyard, protruding from the ground like a piece of sculpture, is an unexploded fascist bomb.

Two old leftist stoics (Luppi and Paredes) run the school. Both are affected by disabilities that reflect the futility of their political stance. Of course, there is a crumbling garden and in the garden a snake in the person of the sadistic, deceitful Jacinto (Noriega), a former student and now the caretaker, to introduce villainy.

It's left to a young boy named Carlos (Tielve) to serve as narrator and go exploring his weird surroundings in the dead of night. An apparition with a half-crushed skull belongs to a boy killed the night the bomb fell into the courtyard, and the ghost's attempts to communicate with Carlos are meant either to frighten or to deliver a warning.

By day we witness the turmoil of the adult world, the source of the nightmares that emerge once the sun has gone down. Del Toro's allegorical intentions become increasingly overt as the boys must band against their oppressor in a film that moves beyond horror into heartbreak.

DICK

Kirsten Dunst, Michelle Williams, Dan Hedaya, Jim Breuer, Will Ferrell, Dave Foley, Teri Garr, Bruce McCulloch, Harry Shearer

Directed by Andrew Fleming
1999. 94 minutes. PG-13.

Bill Clinton had his problems with Monica Lewinsky, but did you realize that Dick Nixon (Hedaya, in a priceless shoulder-scrunching impersonation) had his own difficulties with a couple of teenage girls who infiltrated the White House back in the days when the country was caught up in the Watergate flap?

It all starts when Betsy Jobs (Dunst) and Arlene Lorenzo (Williams) encounter G. Gordon Liddy (Shearer) as he's skulking about the Watergate apartment complex, where the girls live. Later, on a school trip to the White House, they run into Liddy again and discover a secret list of political donors to the Committee to Re-Elect the President.

They also meet Checkers, Nixon's spaniel, and the president himself, who patronizingly appoints them official dog walkers. When Arlene uses the occasion to dress down Nixon for the Vietnam War and other matters, he seems to understand.

That's enough for Arlene, who develops a wild crush on the president. Now, with regular access to the White House, the girls come across large paper-shredding operations and big piles of cash. Informed of their discoveries, Nixon promotes them to the rank of secret youth adviser.

But then there's all that business with Nixon's tape recorder. While leaving an unsolicited declaration of passion on the machine, Arlene inadvertently plays back excerpts of Nixon using foul language and being mean to Checkers. From there we're on to Deep Throat in a film with just enough funny business to sustain the fizz.

DICK TRACY

Warren Beatty, Al Pacino, Madonna, Dustin Hoffman,
Glenne Headly, Charlie Korsmo

Directed by Warren Beatty
1990. 103 minutes. PG.

You have to like a movie, drawn from Chester Gould's comic strip, that calls the daily paper The Daily Paper. (GANGLAND TOUGHS BREAK ARMS OF NEWS DEALER, screams one headline.) Beatty's stylish, intelligently constructed film has everything required of an extravaganza: a splendid cast, great songs by Stephen Sondheim, technological wizardry, a screenplay that knows how to separate comedy from camp.

A film about the jut-jawed detective (Beatty) breaks into a "great uninterrupted grin," Vincent Canby wrote in *The Times*. Vibrant colors are so wildly mismatched that they seem almost to go together. As for plot, the movie asks the question: Will Tracy's girlfriend, Tess Trueheart (Headly), be rescued before she's recycled into mincemeat at the power plant?

The violence is pronounced but artful. When Tracy slugs it out with a tough guy in a waterfront shack, the building sways back and forth.

Beatty had a dozen yellow raincoats to keep Tracy looking dapper and snap-brimmed. Pacino is all growling, mercurial comic menace as Big Boy Caprice, the squinchy hunchback mobster who threatens to take over the city but goes almost crazy whipping a group of clumsy chorines into shape for a nightclub act.

Madonna is glorious as Breathless Mahoney, the steamy vamp who comes close to making Tracy blow all reserve. "You don't know whether you want to hit me or kiss me," she says. "I get a lot of that."

THE DINNER GAME

Jacques Villeret, Thierry Lhermitte, Francis Huster

Directed by Francis Veber
1998. 80 minutes. French with English subtitles. No
rating.

Just how stupid can one dinner guest be? A mean-spirited game, in which a group of friends engage in a contest to see who can bring the biggest idiot to dinner, becomes French farce in Veber's delightful film.

The host is Pierre Brochant (Lhermitte), a smug publisher and the very model of arrogant middle-aged success. Normally Pierre wouldn't stoop to recruit such a fool himself, but he decides to submit an entry after encountering a boring clown named Pignon (Villeret), who is fond of making little buildings out of matchsticks and should make Pierre an easy winner in the idiot-guest competition.

Pignon actually goes beyond idiocy in that he's really too stupid to be easily gotten rid of. When Pierre can't go to the dinner after all, there's no deterring Pignon, and he hangs around to be useful any way he can. This includes mixing up Pierre's wife with his girlfriend. Later he invites a tax inspector into Pierre's apartment, where a lot of undeclared artwork has to be covered up fast.

Eventually, Pierre comes to understand just who is the idiot, and Veber's film uses some funny and diabolical means to help him reach that conclusion.

DIRTY PRETTY THINGS

Chiwetel Ejiofor, Audrey Tautou, Benedict Wong, Sophie Okonedo, Sergi López

Directed by Stephen Frears
2002. 97 minutes. R.

Like *Blind Shaft* (page 38), Frears's sure, understated film doubles as an indictment of societal conditions and a noirish yarn with some nice thriller twists.

In London an exiled Nigerian doctor named Okwe (Ejiofor) drives a cab and works as a porter in a hotel. We don't know why he's in these straits, but he sorely misses his wife and daughter. To save money, he rents a couch from a Turkish maid, Senay (Tautou), who also works at the hotel.

One day on his rounds Okwe finds a toilet blocked by a large object that turns out to be a human heart. The night manager, a slippery customer named Slinky (López), in effect tells Okwe not to worry about it and to keep his mouth shut.

Here begins a taut game of cat and mouse that pits the hotel management against the maids, porters, doormen and others from the lowest rungs, including prostitutes, who perform the dirty work for a society that doesn't know or care that they're alive.

A splendid turning of the tables on Slinky is very satisfying, but Frears's low-key curiosity about what drives people like Okwe and Senay lubricates the tough, involving narrative.

DIRTY ROTTEN SCOUNDRELS

Michael Caine, Steve Martin, Glenne Headly, Anton Rodgers, Barbara Harris, Ian McDiarmid, Dana Ivey

Directed by Frank Oz
1988. 110 minutes. PG.

David Niven and Marlon Brando had these roles in the 1964 comedy *Bedtime Story*, but they weren't as funny as Michael Caine and Steve Martin as an odd couple of con artists loose in the Riviera town of Beaumont-sur-Mer.

Targeting rich widows, the elegant clotheshorse Lawrence Jamieson (Caine) tells them he's a deposed royal looking for contributions to free his motherland from communism. Freddy Benson (Martin), more the T-shirt and baggy trousers type, just says his grandmother needs an operation.

After Freddy makes the mistake of settling on Lawrence's turf, the two bicker awhile before Freddy gains some leverage and blackmails Lawrence into teaching him a few tricks. They set up a challenge: The first to relieve a mark of $50,000 can keep the money and take over the territory.

Lawrence says he never victimizes the poor or the virtuous. Freddy prefers sitting targets. The two choose a gullible young soap heiress (Headly). Freddy tells her he's been unable to walk since his fiancée ran off with the host of the television show *Dance U.S.A.* Lawrence, a famous Viennese psychiatrist on this assignment, tells her he can cure Freddy.

Harris is a husky-voiced Nebraska widow, Ivey an Oklahoma millionaire. Everybody is a delight in this film, particularly Caine and Martin, who work together easily and exuberantly.

DIVA

Frédéric Andréi, Richard Bohringer, Thuy An Luu,
Wilhelmenia Wiggins Fernandez, Jacques Fabbri

Directed by Jean-Jacques Beineix
1981. 123 minutes. French with English subtitles. No
rating.

C ritics sometimes jump on this film as merely a piece
of stylishness, but in this case that's not a bad thing.
Throw in two intriguing Parisian living spaces, some ridiculous heavies, a vain but nice soprano and a great chase
scene in and out of subway cars.

And don't take it seriously. A winning young protagonist tries to but can't, despite being in great peril. He's just
not the type. A relaxed young fellow, Jules (Andréi) makes
deliveries by motorbike, which he rides right into his
large, cluttered abode, a cross between a garage and a receptacle for all manner of items having to do with pop
culture, especially music.

Jules also is an opera fan, particularly devoted to a
striking American concert singer named Cynthia (Fernandez). For reasons having to do with artistic integrity, Cynthia refuses to make recordings. So Jules smuggles a tape
recorder into her performance and comes away with a
souvenir he listens to in rapture back at his place.

A record company will kill, or at least steal, for that
tape. And there's another tape, this one implicating people in a white-slavery ring. After it is dropped into the basket on Jules's motorbike, he has another set of heavies to
contend with.

Most of the time, though, he hangs out with a meditating dilettante named Gorodish (Bohringer) in the latter's stupendous loft. With only a freestanding tub and a
bed to mar the loft's vast spaces, Gorodish's girlfriend
(Thuy An Luu), a daffy Vietnamese bonbon in virtually
nonexistent miniskirts, has plenty of room to roller skate.

DR. T & THE WOMEN

Richard Gere, Helen Hunt, Farrah Fawcett, Laura Dern,
Shelley Long, Tara Reid, Kate Hudson, Liv Tyler

Directed by Robert Altman
2000. 122 minutes. R.

No one knows women like Sully Travis (Gere), who attends to a stream of them daily as the most popular ob-gyn in Dallas. "Women are sacred and should be treated as such," he tells his hunting buddies. And he sincerely practices what he preaches as he moves from examining room to examining room amid the chic clamor in his always overcrowded office.

Sully is caramel smooth, as he needs to be with a pampered clientele fresh from the shopping fields of a garishly opulent Dallas. They all require his attention desperately, and Sully is always there with warm assurances.

At home he is devoted to his own three women, his wife (Fawcett) and two daughters, one of whom is about to be married. Out at the golf course he has a crush on the new pro (Hunt). Every woman is unique, he tells her. He should know, she replies.

Now and then some of these women get out of hand, as when his recently divorced sister-in-law (Dern) takes off all her clothes for a splash in a mall fountain and is institutionalized. Then the engaged daughter, Dee Dee (Hudson), seems to be attracted to her maid of honor (Tyler).

But Sully skates through. Altman has been hard on women in many of his films, but here he's inclined to forgive them their foibles as he perceives them. And if anyone could play Sully without sentimentality or sleaze, it's Gere. For much of his career he has coasted on his easy charm, but here he truly is a sensitive masculine presence.

DOGMA

Ben Affleck, Matt Damon, George Carlin, Linda Fiorentino,
Janeane Garofalo, Salma Hayek, Jason Lee, Jay Mewes,
Alan Rickman, Chris Rock, Kevin Smith, Alanis Morissette

Directed by Kevin Smith
1999. 130 minutes. R.

As freewheeling and irreverent as most of Smith's films, this one is even more pointed. To appreciate his take on religion, you have to accept the idea that Morissette is God and Affleck and Damon are angels. It makes things a little more credible to know that they are banished angels who want back into heaven. They see their chance when Cardinal Glick (Carlin) kicks off a public relations campaign to promote a church rededication in Red Bank, New Jersey.

Glick wants to rally his flock with images of the "buddy Christ," who will wink and give a thumbs-up. To the fallen angels, the cardinal and the rededication offer an opportunity to re-enter the pearly gates and spring their plan—refuting God's infallibility and indeed negating all existence.

There is a heroine from the earthly ranks, Bethany (Fiorentino), a soul-weary worker at an abortion clinic who tithes part of her salary from Planned Parenthood to the Roman Catholic Church. Rickman portrays an angel who delivers God's message with an English accent. Chris Rock is a 13th apostle, Hayek a stripper-muse. And, this being a Smith invention, of course there are Jay (Mewes) and Silent Bob (Smith), who think an abortion clinic is a good place to hang out and meet women.

Smith's scattershot style has never been more scattered; that's what happens when you load a film with big names in small parts. But the film is daring and always immense fun to watch.

DOGTOWN AND Z-BOYS

Sean Penn (narrator), Stacy Peralta, Jay Adams, Tony Alva
and various former members of the Z-Boys

Directed by Stacy Peralta
2001. 90 minutes. PG-13.

Peralta's thrilling rock 'n' roll history of skateboarding in Southern California in the 1970's has the advantage of being made by people who are legends in the world celebrated by their movie.

Expert in the bad-boy style of boarding called Dogtown, Peralta moved on to skateboard manufacturing, videos and team sponsorship as the sport became huge in the 80's. Craig Stecyk, who wrote the film with Peralta, helped put together the Zephyr Skateboard team with local teenagers and others from the daredevil surf culture that formed in the blighted area of Santa Monica and Venice also called Dogtown.

"We were punk kids, tough kids," says one former Dogtowner, one of a dozen or so veterans of the era who remain as outspoken and insistently prideful in the film as they were when they rode waves through the piers of a rotting amusement park.

They also took to riding boards on wheels. Dismissed as a kiddie fad in the 60's, skateboarding took off a decade later with the urethane wheel. Dogtowners raced around the asphalt wastelands surrounding grade schools, and when drought emptied Los Angeles swimming pools, they rode those, too, caroming around the bowls and shooting over the lips.

The Zephyr competed nationally in 1975, and a galaxy of skateboarding stars gained national prominence. Many are in a film that resurrects those days in explosive, freewheeling montages.

DON JUAN DEMARCO

Marlon Brando, Johnny Depp, Faye Dunaway,
Géraldine Pailhas

Directed by Jeremy Leven
1995. 97 minutes. PG-13.

Watching late Brando is a treat because we see him playing Brando, which he does with a wink and an eye to the money. In *The Freshman* (page 144), he delivers a very nicely handled parody of himself as a mob boss. But here he's in about the last guise you would expect: Brando as a happily married suburbanite who is about to retire from a hospital where he's hailed as "the best damn clinician this place has ever seen."

Brando's Jack Mickler is a hugely overweight shrink out on a limb, so to speak, when he is forced to the top of a billboard to talk Don Juan (Depp) out of killing himself. Don Juan (last name DeMarco) has asked the police to send a swordfighter who might end his life in a duel. Mickler strikes him a poor substitute, but later at Woodhaven State Hospital, where DeMarco is sent for observation, the two wind up as doctor and patient.

At 21, Don Juan says he has made love to more than 1,500 women, indications of which we see when he is allowed to pick up a woman to prove his prowess. Mickler, now calling himself Don Octavio de Flores to better accommodate his patient's fantasy, is a warm, compassionate man, and he plays along with these delusions as he feels the young man out.

Gradually, though, he discovers that Don Juan's insistent and enthusiastic accounts are having an effect on his own life, particularly in bed with the missus (Dunaway). Fortunately, the camera averts its eye at the point of consummation.

Should Don Juan be encouraged? At bottom, the reality doesn't matter as much as the spirit.

DONNIE BRASCO

Al Pacino, Johnny Depp, Michael Madsen, Bruno Kirby,
James Russo, Anne Heche.

Directed by Mike Newell
1997. 127 minutes. R.

A mobster and an F.B.I. undercover informant play cat and mouse in an exceptionally well-realized film from a director (*Four Weddings and a Funeral*) who may seem out of his element in a gangster story but gets the most from sharp performances and good conversation.

Pacino is Lefty Ruggiero, a fading hit man who has lost his clout with the bosses. Depp is Donnie, modeled after a real-life F.B.I. plant named Joe Pistone, who infiltrated the Bonnano family in the 1970's.

Donnie uses Lefty to work his way into the mob, but there is a set of special complications. Thinking he has a young protégé, the needy Lefty adopts Donnie and schools him in the ways of the family. In the process the pupil becomes fond of the teacher, and his knowing that he will have to betray Lefty when he pulls out adds dramatic tension. Realizing that he could be exposed himself at any moment doesn't add to Donnie's peace of mind, and on several occasions the band of wise guys seems to come close.

Gangland color is plentiful and worthy of *Goodfellas*. A bloody conclusion doesn't add to the life and feelings of humanity in the film, but it doesn't kill them either.

DONNIE DARKO

Jake Gyllenhaal, Jena Malone, Drew Barrymore, Mary McDonnell, Katharine Ross, Patrick Swayze, Maggie Gyllenhaal

Directed by Richard Kelly
2001. 113 minutes. R.

Kelly's film weaves an intriguing tangle around a schizophrenic teenager (Jake Gyllenhaal), but perhaps it's better just to ponder the puzzle rather than to try to solve it completely. Donnie himself has no certain idea.

"How does it feel to have a wacko for a son?" he asks his patiently loving mother (McDonnell). Donnie lives in suburbia with his parents and his testy older sister (Maggie Gyllenhaal). At night he is visited by visions brought to him by a six-foot rabbit.

The rabbit takes him sleepwalking and leaves him with premonitions of the apocalypse. One night a jet engine from an airplane crashes through the roof of the house. That's real enough, as the neighbors can attest.

Donnie's therapist (Ross) uses hypnosis to meet the rabbit and get at some of Donnie's sexual proclivities, which, oddly for a therapist, seem to throw her. But there's no explaining Donnie. An unhappy home can't be blamed. Aside from some sisterly rivalry, Donnie's home is fairly normal, or at least trying to be under the circumstances.

Donnie can see into the future, led by rivulets of silvery liquid. And there is a book, *The Philosophy of Time Travel*, written by a 100-year-old neighbor who is going to be run over if she doesn't stop standing in the middle of the road.

In a weird but compelling film, the world is just as irrational as Donnie's fantasies.

DON'T LOOK NOW

Donald Sutherland, Julie Christie

Directed by Nicolas Roeg
1973. 110 minutes. R.

As in his film *Walkabout* (page 449), Roeg leans to symbols and the supernatural, and here he applies them wonderfully to a Daphne du Maurier story of the occult. In Venice, an art restorer named John Baxter (Sutherland) explains his predicament to an official who notes the tale dutifully but has nothing to suggest. There is no earthly way to approach what has happened.

Earlier, Baxter and his wife, Laura, lost their young daughter in a drowning accident in England. Now they find themselves still burdened by their grief during a misty Venetian winter. The atmospherics are haunting in this film, with Roeg's camera (before directing, he was a cinematographer) turning the city even more beautiful and intriguingly decayed. Water is everywhere, reflecting and revealing the way it did in the pond where their daughter died. So is the color red—the color of the coat the girl was wearing, the wine John spills and the blood he will shed.

A blind woman, a psychic, tells Laura that she has seen the little girl and the child is happy. Laura is a believer and passes the news on to John, but he can't comprehend such a thing. In the hands of Christie and Sutherland, this is a most believable couple, clinging to each other yet estranged by their trauma.

Sex, probably the first they've had in a while, is still among the best ever filmed. But the psychic has grave fears for John, who is subjected to strange signs and incidents, one of them nearly fatal. If he could only see and hear, which, of course, he can't.

DOOR TO DOOR

William H. Macy, Kyra Sedgwick, Helen Mirren, Kathy Baker

Directed by Steven Schachter
2002. 90 minutes. No rating.

In this warmhearted yet unsentimental drama (first shown on TNT), based on a true story, Bill Porter (Macy) goes door-to-door in Portland, Oregon, selling cleaning products. It's a particularly unlikely occupation for someone with cerebral palsy. Bill limps along 8 to 10 miles a day. Not only does he walk crazily, but his speech is funny, a combination that gets a lot of doors slammed in his face. What's more, he does this, successfully, for 40 years.

With enormous jug ears and a goofy grin, Macy looks like Howdy Doody come to life. "Some scary guy," a prospective customer is heard saying as he slams the door. That's an irreverent association, but the irreverence suits the tone of this film and of this character, who never asks for sympathy.

"It takes people a wee bit longer to warm up to you," says his shrewd, unflappable mother (Mirren). "Just be patient. Patient and persistent."

Bill volunteers to take the worst route the Watkins Company has to offer and gradually builds a clientele among people who are friendly but never become his friends. Baker plays a longtime customer. Mirren is touching and feisty as a character who finally succumbs to Alzheimer's disease. Sedgwick plays a spirited young woman in the 1970's who befriends Bill and sticks with him during the film's eloquent, tough-minded late stages, when he turns old and cranky at the emergence of telephone and Internet selling.

But it is Mr. Macy's wonderfully rich, controlled performance as a man who approaches his difficulties with wit and determination that holds the film together.

DOWN AND OUT IN BEVERLY HILLS

Nick Nolte, Bette Midler, Richard Dreyfuss, Little Richard,
Tracy Nelson, Elizabeth Peña

Directed by Paul Mazursky
1986. 103 minutes. R.

Mazursky's keen comedy of manners finds friendship in the craziest places. "Barbara, is that the new pool man?" Dave Whiteman (Dreyfuss) asks his wife (Midler). Actually, Jerry Baskin (Nolte), the disheveled wreck of a man in backyard of the Whitemans' peach-colored manse, has filled his pockets with rocks and is about to sink himself in the chlorinated depths.

The film is inspired by Jean Renoir's *Boudu Saved from Drowning*, based on a play by René Fauchois, about a prosperous Paris bookseller who rescues a suicidal bum from the Seine. Like Boudu, Jerry has been wandering around the area, scaring the locals, which in Beverly Hills raises the security-alert level from orange to red.

Dave and Barbara, whose alarm system could summon a SWAT team, gaze down from their boudoir with his-and-hers pastel refrigerators. Barbara isn't the nicest person, but she and Dave, a coat-hanger manufacturer, are into matters concerning salvation.

So Dave saves Jerry, who is not the least bit appreciative but quickly figures that it pays to tell the Whitemans the kind of things they want to hear. In reality Jerry hit bottom after he lost his dog, but he says he's been jilted by a beautiful woman in his acting class. "Linda Evans, between *The Big Valley* and *Dynasty*—you know, that period," he tells Dave.

Jerry will change Dave's life. Mazursky has an obvious fondness for his characters and observes them closely. Midler is bold enough to make Barbara thoroughly unpleasant in a lifelike way. Dreyfuss captures Dave's silliness and poignancy when he comes to realize that poverty has its own authenticity.

DRACULA: PAGES FROM A VIRGIN'S DIARY

Zhang Wei-Qiang, Tara Birtwhistle, David Moroni, CindyMarie Small, Johnny Wright

Directed by Guy Maddin
2002. 73 minutes. No rating.

A brave man's blood is the best thing for a woman in trouble," Dr. Van Helsing (Moroni) tells a donor as he hooks up transfusion equipment to Lucy Westenra (Birtwhistle). And Lucy is certainly at risk, having been infected not once but twice by the fanged count (Zhang).

Dracula has often struck on screen, but never more imaginatively than in this visionary interpretation. Maddin, a Canadian and cult favorite, makes mostly silent films that re-create the flickering, melodramatic ambience of early movies. With a look and feel from about 1910, they also impart a puckish sense of humor and a winking postmodern knowingness. Made for the CBC, this *Dracula* is in collaboration with the Royal Winnipeg Ballet, which unveiled a full-length adaptation of Bram Stoker's novel six years ago.

Finished with poor Lucy, who's beyond salvation, the count moves on to Mina (Small), who has only her love, Harker (Wright), and Van Helsing ("M.D., Ph.D., D.Litt, etc."), to save her. Full of visual eccentricities and quirks, the film unfolds in the wild-eyed tradition of silent melodrama.

All lithe, sadistic sexuality, Zhang's performance fans the demonic hysteria that grips Victorian England. Subtitles and intertitles ("Death is only the beginning") are used sparingly to clarify the narrative and announce themes. Pantomime, silhouette, slow-motion and much fog give a sometimes campy Gothic feel.

There are also flashes of color. Currency is bright green, and Dracula, an avaricious fellow, seems to be stuffed with gold coins. And, wittily enough, there are a few attendant sounds, as when Van Helsing and helpers unpack their tools to pry open a coffin or two.

THE DREAMERS

Michael Pitt, Eva Green, Louis Garrel, Robin Renucci, Anna Chancellor

Directed by Bernardo Bertolucci
2003. 115 minutes. NC-17.

Long preoccupied with passive characters inadvertently caught in great social moments and matters of sexual intimacy, Bertolucci fashions a tale fusing sexual discovery and political tumult shot through with a heady youthful romanticism.

Paris in 1968 is in turmoil as Matthew (Pitt) is taken in by Isabelle (Green) and Theo (Garrel), brother and sister, whose huge apartment is theirs for a month while their parents are away. Outside, the city is in the throes of a revolt that began with the dismissal of Henri Langlois, founder of the Cinémathèque Français. The French, especially young French, take their cinema seriously, and no one is more raptly steeped in the subject of film than Isabelle and Theo.

The three 20-year-olds endlessly and intensely engage one another, arguing matters from Jimi Hendrix to Buster Keaton to Chairman Mao, and reveling in film analysis seasoned by Bertolucci's selection of clips of Dietrich, Garbo, Robert Bresson, Samuel Fuller and the like, set to well-chosen songs by Hendrix, the Doors and Françoise Hardy.

Naturally, in such a hothouse atmosphere sex comes to the fore. Using movies as reference points, Isabelle and Theo invent a sex game with psychologically sadistic undertones and seduce Matthew into playing along. As measured by the time they spend out of their clothes, the film exceeds Bertolucci's *Last Tango in Paris*, but there is an Edenic quality to the nakedness.

For Bertolucci, sexuality is a part of natural human vitality, and the director plunges into his art with a reckless, confident ardor.

DRUGSTORE COWBOY

Matt Dillon, Kelly Lynch, James Le Gros, Heather Graham, Grace Zabriskie, William S. Burroughs

Directed by Gus Van Sant
1989. 100 minutes. R.

Set in 1971 in Portland, Oregon, Van Sant's first major feature offers a cool-eyed vision of young heroin addicts adrift during the twilight of the counterculture when drug-taking still had an aura of hipness.

Two couples roam the Pacific Northwest, suspended between somnolent periods under the influence and ferocious spasms of violence and paranoia. As leader of the pack, Bob Hughes (Dillon) brings a swaggering savvy to the job of looting drugstores to supply himself, his arrogant wife, Dianne (Lynch), his dumb sidekick, Rick (Le Gros), and Rick's teenage girlfriend, Nadine (Graham).

Together they make a sorry, fascinating spectacle, creating diversions so that they can clean out pharmacies of whatever drugs they can use. Otherwise they stay high, watch TV and mark time before moving on to replenish their drugs and repeat the cycle.

There are graphic scenes of the group shooting up and being carried off on waves of euphoria. We feel the texture of their shabby, transient world with its scary thrills and bleak, fatalistic uncertainty. When Nadine dies from an overdose, Bob decides he has had enough and heads home to try to straighten himself out.

Such self-absorbed, unproductive excess has an element of comic absurdity. When Nadine dies in a motel full of deputy sheriffs, there's the problem of how to remove the body. Careful not to overplay the situation, Van Sant treats it as deadpan black comedy.

DRUMLINE

Nick Cannon, Zoë Saldana, Orlando Jones, Leonard Roberts, GQ, Jason Weaver

Directed by Charles Stone III
2002. 119 minutes. PG-13.

Honing an appreciation for marching bands may not be at the top of the to-do list, but Stone's film makes a bouncy, boisterous case for an irresistible, quite astonishing art form.

The plot is plugged into the handiest formula. At historically black colleges like Atlanta A&T, competition between "show style" marching bands makes football something of an afterthought. Devon Miles (Cannon), a talented, headstrong young drummer, has problems with A&T's strict regimentation. A buttoned-up old-school band director (Jones) is after another national championship.

Devon has a troubled family background and a cheerleader for a girlfriend. Stock secondary characters (nerdy guy to bulky tuba player) are around for comic relief.

Then stand back for rousing scenes of rhythmic invention, including both large-scale stadium-shaking production numbers and sharp, intense episodes of hand-to-hand musical combat in an ebullient stew of musical influences that include hip-hop, jazz improvisation and classic funk.

THE DUELLISTS

Keith Carradine, Harvey Keitel, Albert Finney, Edward Fox, Cristina Raines, Robert Stephens, Tom Conti

Directed by Ridley Scott
1977. 101 minutes. PG.

Scott's first film, adapted from a Joseph Conrad story, is an arresting tale of obsession, but it's most notable for the way it bathes the French countryside in glorious color and light. Considering that it rained for 56 of the 58 days the film was on location, the extraordinary shimmering beauty is all the more remarkable.

What sun gets through is caught in brilliant slashes here and there, which makes it all the more pronounced in the mind's eye. "People don't realize how overcast can help," Scott said in a *Times* interview.

Cinematography is the hallmark of all Scott films, of course, this one made with little fuss for $900,000 using no built sets. Sharing the screen with the natural splendor are two French officers of the Napoleonic era, D'Hubert (Carradine) and Feraud (Keitel), who fight a series of ferocious duels over 15 years. D'Hubert would as soon forget the matter, but Feraud carries the memory of some imagined slight or other inside him with unabated fury.

Crossing paths with Feraud every several years on one military posting or another, D'Hubert tries to avoid confrontation but each time feels honor-bound to take up sword and pistol. Feraud is unavoidable and unappeasable, nothing short of psychotic. And so the two keep taking chunks out of each other, whittling each other down, so to speak.

Carradine and Keitel hold their own with Finney, Fox and others in a splendid cast, but the film belongs to Scott's visual images and their evocation of time and space.

EAST-WEST

Sandrine Bonnaire, Oleg Menchikov, Catherine Deneuve, Sergueï Bodrov Jr., Ruben Tapiero, Erwan Baynaud

Directed by Régis Wargnier
1999. 121 minutes. Russian with English subtitles. No rating.

Wargnier's sumptuous, moving film captures the hope and betrayal of Russian émigrés invited home by Stalin and the Soviet government after World War II. In this scenario, a voyage on an elegant steamship, complete with vodka toasts and patriotic songs, leads to the grim reality of life and death in a police state.

Aleksei (Menchikov), a doctor, and his French wife, Marie (Bonnaire), and their young son are assigned to a communal apartment in Kiev, where they are roommates with assorted New Socialist snoops, black marketers and drunkards.

The spirited Marie is miserable, and her husband, convinced that good behavior is the best way to protect his family, doesn't offer much consolation. But if Stalinism is monstrous, those caught in it have redeeming human qualities.

A military officer is kind to Marie; a hospital bureaucrat recognizes Aleksei's talent and dedication. A fierce, unyielding martyr, Marie is no saint herself, often seeming haughty, selfish and capricious.

Wargnier's historical pageant is full of grandeur and detail, but it's also a portrait of a marriage under extreme pressure. Marie finds relief from her husband's conventionality in the arms of a young swimmer, and Aleksei has an affair of his own. Menchikov is a subtle, generous actor, but this is a woman's picture in the best Old Hollywood sense, and Bonnaire burns with a moral, erotic fervor as if inhabited by the spirit of Ingrid Bergman.

EAT DRINK MAN WOMAN

Sihung Lung, Chien-lien Wu, Kuei-Mei Yang, Yu-Wen Wang, Winston Chao

Directed by Ang Lee
1994. 123 minutes. Chinese with English subtitles. No rating.

Food and sex, as the title implies, are natural companions in Lee's warmly engaging tale of a widowed father (Sihung Lung) who has three daughters with romantic problems.

Family dinners are so racked with tensions that it's hard to eat, which is a sorry state of affairs for Mr. Chu, the greatest chef in Taipei. At home he primarily cooks elaborate school lunches for a little girl, the daughter of a family friend. His own daughters see him as unhappy, remote and reluctant to engage in life, which they feel relates to their own unhappiness. The most beautiful of the daughters, a chilly executive, has impersonal sex with a former lover and dreams of a pad in a sleek new high-rise. The eldest daughter, a straitlaced schoolteacher, has never recovered from a bad affair.

The youngest strikes at her father in another way: she's a clerk at Wendy's. But she has a boyfriend who reads Dostoyevsky and rides a motorcycle. "I want to end this addiction to love, but I'm too weak," he says.

Mood, a gentle pace and nice small touches mark a delightful little film. Lee intermingles a sexual episode with a look at Mr. Chu blowing air into a duck and otherwise keeps things interesting with some last-minute surprises.

EDDIE IZZARD: DRESS TO KILL

A one-man show with Eddie Izzard

1999. 110 minutes. No rating.

Some stand-up routines are so rich and funny that they never seem tired, and this is one of them. Izzard describes himself as "an executive transvestite," and he appears on this HBO special with blue eye shadow, an embroidered Chinese tunic and platform shoes. But how he dresses is nothing next to how smart and hilarious he is as he offers observations about history, movies, language and the gap between British and American cultures.

There are the Druids to consider—but why stop there? Within minutes he has covered Pol Pot, squirrels, gun control, Scooby-Doo, perjury and the Austro-Hungarian Empire. The British may be so overly regimented and detail-oriented that they'll never get it together to make an action movie like *The Great Escape,* but the Americans can't decipher what's going on in their own national anthem. He does a good imitation of God, who sounds like James Mason. And there is his priceless account of a trip to Paris and an attempt to use schoolboy French. ("The monkey is in the tree.")

What at first seem to be random, unconnected riffs eventually come together as he weaves back to an earlier joke, in a show that feels laid-back but is as sharp and carefully thought through as comedy gets.

ELECTION

Reese Witherspoon, Matthew Broderick, Chris Klein, Phil Reeves, Mark Harelik

Directed by Alexander Payne
1999. 103 minutes. R.

Canny, malevolent humor flows through Payne's dark, deft film, as it did through his *Citizen Ruth* (page 72). This is one of the two or three finest American comedies of the last 20 years.

When Tracy Flick (Witherspoon) asks God for help in winning the student-government presidency at her Omaha high school, she's not really asking. "I really must insist," she says. Winning, in fact, is not at all negotiable for the ferociously ambitious Tracy, who stamps out her own campaign buttons, goes berserk when one of her banners is torn and bakes a cupcake for every potential voter on election day.

Witherspoon perfects the mannerisms of a character who continually furrows her brow, stamps her foot and lifts her voice in fierce little blasts of determination. Fearing that the school has a budding monster on its hands, Jim McAllister (Broderick), a meddlesome geometry teacher, induces the school's top jock (Klein) to run against her.

McAllister is both attracted to and wary of Tracy. She already has had an affair with one teacher, and that poor fellow, having lost his job and his wife, is last seen slapping price stickers on products in a Milwaukee supermarket. Broderick is very good at making a gentle fool of McAllister, and Witherspoon ascends to true comic monstrosity in a film that could have succumbed to broad gags but keeps it chillier.

ELIZABETH

Cate Blanchett, Geoffrey Rush, Christopher Eccleston,
Joseph Fiennes, Richard Attenborough, John Gielgud,
Vincent Cassel, Fanny Ardant, Kathy Burke

Directed by Shekhar Kapur
1998. 124 minutes. R.

Blanchett makes an activist Elizabeth I, perhaps by way of Woodstock, in Kapur's highly entertaining film. In 1554, the young daughter of Henry VIII and Anne Boleyn is dancing and frolicking in the meadows with her lover, Robert Dudley, Earl of Leicester (Fiennes), and a circle of gushy attendants when she is presented the ring of her freshly deceased half-sister, Mary Tudor, and sourly hailed as queen.

Prospects are unpromising for a fairly secular new monarch in a country torn between Roman Catholics and Protestants. The pope (Gielgud) dispatches assassins; Elizabeth's armies are weak; her enemies are massing troops in the north; her coffers are empty; her advisers full of bad counsel. The Duke of Norfolk (Eccleston), a Catholic zealot, wishes her dead and has her rush into a Bay of Pigs–style situation in Scotland. A gentler adviser, Sir William Cecil (Attenborough), would have her marry out of her difficulties, first with the French, then, after the duke suggested for that union proves to be a cross-dressing lunatic, the Spanish.

Torn this way and that, Elizabeth has another idea: she chops off her hair, adopts whiteface and marries England.

EMMA

Kate Beckinsale, Mark Strong, Bernard Hepton, Samantha Morton, Samantha Bond, James Hazeldine, Raymond Coulthard

Directed by Diarmuid Lawrence
1997. 107 minutes. No rating.

In a runoff, this *Emma* easily beats the Gwyneth Paltrow version, in quality if not in recognition. Here, Emma (Beckinsale), Jane Austen's matchmaking busybody, is plainer-looking and sharper-speaking than Paltrow's graceful blond princess in Doug McGrath's film a year earlier. That is, she's more the way Austen made her. Lawrence's film, made for British television and shown on A&E, has the most in common with Roger Michell's adaptation of Austen's *Persuasion* (page 312), sharing a smaller scale, a darker tone and a focus on psychological nuance.

Beckinsale's Emma is practical, funny and believable, and she is good partner for Mr. Knightley (Strong), who also doesn't have movie-star looks. The two are natural verbal sparring partners, vehemently matching wits and social observations.

The screenplay by Andrew Davies does a deft job of letting viewers pick up the social clues Emma misses as she so assuredly goes about determining who is best suited for whom. We see, as she should, the glances between the handsome, eligible Frank Churchill and the poor Jane Fairfax, and we can guess that the clergyman Mr. Elton has designs on Emma and her dowry, not on her penniless friend Harriet (Morton).

Sue Birtwistle, the producer, calls the tale a psychological detective story, and a brilliant one. Austen herself might have admired this sly, understated interpretation loaded with a sense that even a society as well ordered as Emma's leaves room for comic misjudgments and happy endings.

THE END OF THE AFFAIR

Ralph Fiennes, Julianne Moore, Stephen Rea

Directed by Neil Jordan
1999. 102 minutes. R.

Jordan's intoxicating version of Graham Greene's 1951 novel about illicit romance is a gripping story of passion and its renunciation, the most graceful Greene adaptation since *The Third Man*.

Ralph Fiennes is Maurice Bendrix, the Greene stand-in, a writer in London who has an affair with Sarah Miles (Moore), wife of a nondescript civil servant named Henry (Rea). For a while, Bendrix and Sarah are shown in dreamily voluptuous union. But while they are making love one day during the war, an explosion appears to kill Bendrix. On regaining consciousness, he finds Sarah in prayer, and the story turns to its real concern: an agonizing tug-of-war between religious faith and adulterous love. Sarah believes in a God she can bargain with, while Bendrix believes only in his own writing and in Sarah.

This story is told in flashback, and an air of sadness haunts the film because the affair has so clearly come to an agonized end. Fiennes and Moore breathe life into the story with a dreamy intensity. Rea is superb as the colorless but thoroughly decent Henry, who forms a bond of his own with Bendrix. And Jordan, who also wrote the screenplay, creates a seamlessly engrossing film that does justice to the book's depth of thought and feeling, and also vividly captures the music and fraught atmosphere of London just before and after the war.

THE END OF VIOLENCE

Bill Pullman, Andie MacDowell, Rosalind Chao, Gabriel Byrne, Traci Lind, Daniel Benzali, Loren Dean, Marisol Padilla Sánchez

Directed by Wim Wenders
1997. 122 minutes. R.

___

Wenders puts together a brilliant puzzle in a film that both speculates about technology and the effects of mass media and functions nicely as a European-style art film of the 1960's.

In Los Angeles an abrasive producer of action films named Mike Max (Pullman) finds a 400-page document about a government surveillance program in his e-mail. The government, it seems, plans to scan city streets with such thorough surveillance that it will put "an end to violence."

A man named Ray (Byrne) runs the program from an observatory above the city. When Max is kidnapped by a pair of thugs, Ray's system videotapes the whole thing, but the more he enlarges the images, the more they blur.

It develops that Max evidently has escaped his kidnappers, who turn up dead. In any event, he is found in a state of shock by a group of Chicano gardeners, who take him home and restore him to health.

Max, a changed man, stays undercover as the world loses track of him, and Wenders's movie, filmed by Pascal Rabaud with a keen feel for the soul of L.A., spins fascinating paranoid fantasies with a free-spirited sense that all this could be possible.

ENIGMA

Dougray Scott, Kate Winslet, Jeremy Northam,
Saffron Burrows

Directed by Michael Apted
2001. 117 minutes. R.

The story of the British effort to crack the Enigma code that the German forces lived by in World War II is turned into an intense thriller, thanks partly to its behind-the-scenes pedigree. Tom Stoppard wrote the screenplay (from Robert Harris's novel) and Michael Apted directed with taut focus. On camera, the cast—including Winslet and Northam—hides its natural glamour in drab wartime costumes, but sacrifices not a bit of the story's romance and intrigue.

With Nazi U-boats threatening to close Allied shipping lanes, code-cracking takes on extreme urgency at Bletchley Park, the English country estate where the code breakers have been gathered. Here, a knack for getting to the bottom of trillions of numeric permutations amounts to heroic action. Tom Jericho (Scott) fits right in with the raggedy band of Bolsheviks, stammerers and assorted oddballs brought to Bletchley by a British command more attuned to fighter pilots.

Fresh back from a leave after a nervous breakdown, the pasty, haggard Tom is brilliant and intuitive, but he often rambles off into longing for Claire (Burrows), the willowy, mischievous blond file clerk who threw him over and disappeared after he wouldn't share some mathematical findings with her. Is she a German spy? British intelligence, represented by a snide, ruthless agent named Wigram (Northam), thinks Tom could be of assistance here, and the two begin a movie-long duel. Tom's bout with Wigram connects him with the much sweeter Hester (Winslet, once more demonstrating her great range).

With its many subplots and political twists, the film itself is a wonderfully enigmatic puzzle.

ETERNAL SUNSHINE OF THE SPOTLESS MIND

Jim Carrey, Kate Winslet, Kirsten Dunst, Mark Ruffalo, Elijah Wood, Tom Wilkinson

Directed by Michel Gondry
2004. 108 minutes. R.

Always on the lookout for brittle bourgeois psyches (see *Adaptation*, page 2) to torment, the screenwriter Charlie Kaufman invents Joel Barish, played by Jim Carrey with all the wattage drained from his face.

For Joel life has ground to a virtual halt. Finding his car scuffed up one morning, he plays hooky from work and meets a girl who may or may not be good for him. Clementine Kruczynski (Winslet) is a bit on the crazy side for staid Joel, but he falls hard, as does she, at least for a bit. But tensions arise. He's too boring; she's too needy. Then one day Clem simply doesn't recognize him at all. It seems that she's been to a certain Dr. Mierzwiak (Wilkinson), who has erased her memory of Joel.

He's crushed, but two can play that game, and Joel goes to the doctor to cleanse his brain of Clementine. But after Mierzwiak and his flaky aides (Ruffalo and Wood) botch the procedure, Joel decides he doesn't want to disconnect after all. The chase is on, with Dr. Mierzwiak erasing as fast as he can and Joel and Clem racing ahead as everything they ever knew together evaporates behind them.

As they flee, they rediscover each other in an intelligent romantic comedy that borrows its title from a poem by Alexander Pope. Stripped of his lunatic extremes, Carrey seems deflated at times. Winslet, on the other hand, soars as a woman ready for whatever comes.

EUROPA EUROPA

Marco Hofschneider, René Hofschneider, Piotr Kozlowski, Julie Delpy

Directed by Agnieszka Holland
1991. 115 minutes. German with English subtitles. R.

Holland's film does what every film about the Holocaust seeks to accomplish: bring new immediacy to a much-told story by adding details that transcend cliché.

The story is based on the memoirs of Solomon Perel, called Solly (Marco Hofschneider) in the film, who as a young Jew survived the Nazis by posing as a Nazi himself. In one of many strong ironies, Holland maintains a blithe directorial style and gives the film the pretty, sensitive look of a pastoral French romance as Solly flees a German city in 1938 and eventually winds up in a Soviet orphanage.

A good-looking, smart young fellow, Solly appeals to everybody he comes across. The Russians love him, and so do the German soldiers he necessarily falls in with after the orphanage is bombed. One of his major problems is concealing his circumcision in the shower.

After happenstance makes him a hero in battle, a fresh-faced German girl (Delpy) admires him but eventually tells him that if she ever caught a Jew, she would cut his throat. So much for romance. Given his personal copy of *Mein Kampf,* Solly becomes a respected member of Hitler Youth, but the guilt of maintaining the subterfuge, no matter how justified, gradually becomes unbearable.

Here Holland's film is not as effective as it is with Solly on the run and playing the game. Similarly, Hofschneider conveys Solly's raw panic and confusion more effectively than the crisis of confidence that follows, but it is an impassioned performance nonetheless.

EXOTICA

Mia Kirshner, Elias Koteas, Bruce Greenwood, Arsinée Khanjian, Don McKellar

Directed by Atom Egoyan
1994. 103 minutes. R.

As Egoyan did with mordant characters in earlier films, he throws several pretty strange cases into a tale of eroticism, secrecy and deceptive appearances. In his skewed way of looking at things, nothing is what it seems.

Exotica is a strip club, more eerie than erotic. Eric (Koteas), a disc jockey, introduces Christina (Kirshner), a "sassy bit of jailbait" who will dance at your table for five dollars. Christina dances and dances for the handsome, sad-looking Francis (Greenwood), who repeatedly asks, "How could anyone hurt you?"

Eric and Christina have been lovers, and he has a contract to impregnate Zoe (Khanjian), the club's owner, who is so obsessed with taking over her dead mother's role as hostess that she wears her wigs and clothes.

But who is Francis? Eric is jealous of Christina's devotion to him. Was she hurt, and by whom? Francis is seen in his car giving money to a young woman whom we assume to be a child prostitute, but that's not the case. There's another disturbing explanation.

We see Francis in an exotic pet shop owned by Thomas (McKellar), a smuggler of rare, valuable birds' eggs. Francis examines his financial records. Is he a black marketer or a tax auditor?

At the heart of the story is Francis's relationship with Christina, pursued with a mixture of sexuality and innocence. There is a reference to the death of Francis's young daughter. If nothing comes entirely clear, Egoyan doesn't spread confusion for its own sake. In the film's dreamy atmosphere, we are left to reflect on the fragmented way we think about people.

FAST, CHEAP & OUT OF CONTROL

A documentary by Errol Morris
1997. 82 minutes. No rating.

Morris's captivating film pokes into corners of science, philosophy and animal behavior through the thoughts of four visionaries: a topiary gardener, a lion tamer, a robot scientist and a man who studies the ways of tiny, hairless mole rats.

As George Mendoca forms bushes into the shapes of animals, he learns about nature's design and process. "This is all from memory," he says as he shaves and shapes a small tree into a giraffe or other creature.

Dave Hoover says that you have to know what lions are thinking to put a cage full of them through their paces. Control is paramount, as is evidenced by the singed fur on three animals who leap through fiery hoops for Dave. Lions are quick. "They can nail you before you say oops," he says. And don't wear a wristwatch in the cage. Once a lion took a swipe, caught a claw in Dave's watch strap and almost dragged him to death.

Rodney Brooks, an M.I.T. scientist, studies ants' communal efforts as he designs tiny robots that scurry around his laboratory. Ray Mendez ponders the mole rat in an underground colony, where it is considered perfectly fine to sacrifice one of their number for the salvation of the rest.

Morris, director of the highly recommended *Fog of War,* about Robert McNamara, brings them all together into an inquisitive, enlightening overview of man and beast.

THE FAST RUNNER

Natar Ungalaaq, Sylvia Ivalu, Peter-Henry Arnatsiaq,
Lucy Tulugarjuk

Directed by Zacharias Kunuk
2001. 172 minutes. Inuktitut with English subtitles. No
rating.

Not only does this film (the first one in Inuktitut) immerse us in a radically different cultural point of view, but it is a work of superlative narrative sweep and visual beauty.

Working with Inuit actors and a widescreen digital video camera, Kunuk takes us out onto the Arctic ice, where a nomadic tribal society chafes under the pressures of its complex ideas of honor and loyalty.

The people of Igloolik fall under a shamanic curse when a young hunter falls in love with a woman who has been promised to the chief's son, an arrogant, unstable hothead. Because different factions must depend on one another for survival, their violent rivalry is disruptive, particularly when it goes on for years.

Visually remarkable from smoky igloo interiors to vast icy vistas (in several shades of white and blue), Kunuk's film is most astonishing for one episode of treachery that almost has to be seen to be believed. Stalking their enemy, hunters creep up on the skin tent where he is sleeping and spear it repeatedly. But they miss, and the quarry bolts from the shelter and leads them on a chase for miles across the ice. He is barefoot and stark naked.

FEMME FATALE

Rebecca Romijn-Stamos, Antonio Banderas, Peter Coyote, Rie Rasmussen, Gregg Henry, Edouard Montoute, Eriq Ebouaney, Régis Wargnier

Directed by Brian De Palma
2002. 114 minutes. R.

Style is about everything in De Palma's dazzling exercise of illusion and double cross, proof positive that a film can flourish on supple moves and sheer visual imagination. (A cool score helps, this one by Ryuichi Sakamoto.)

Narrative flies off the road around the twists and switchbacks, and don't look too hard for substantial characters to hang on to; you'll be involved enough just taking in the sights.

Nominally, there is some kind of story involving a beautiful jewel thief (Romijn-Stamos) who lifts a priceless necklace right off a model at the Cannes Inernational Film Festival, double-crosses two partners and disappears. Years later she re-emerges as the sedate wife of the American ambassador (Coyote) and is recognized by a paparazzo.

This being De Palma, stir in plenty of voyeurism and paranoia, with allusions to *Dressed to Kill*, *Blow Out* and *Body Double*. Who knows if all the visual clues, most of them stunning, mean anything. But then, what does it matter?

FESTIVAL EXPRESS

A documentary by Bob Smeaton
2003. 90 minutes. R.

In the summer of 1970 a planned five-day rock tour organized by a pair of Canadian promoters jammed itself on a train and headed west from Toronto toward dates in

Winnipeg and Calgary. Charging audiences $14 a head, the tour was boycotted and flopped, leaving a trainload of talent with nothing better to do than tear it up in one long drug- and alcohol-fueled jam session as it rolled along.

Janis Joplin, at the height of her powers, was aboard, as were Jerry Garcia and the Grateful Dead, the Band, the Flying Burrito Brothers, Delaney and Bonnie, Ian and Sylvia, Buddy Guy, Great Speckled Bird and New Riders of the Purple Sage.

For decades a fight between the promoters and film-makers kept *Festival Express* in limbo, but now it has been cleaned up and released by the Canadian National Archives in Ottawa. Here are the biggest stars of the 1960's and 70's, in close social contact without publicists or security to screen them. Plenty of Canadian Club is passed around. Two months before her death, Joplin rips her heart out with renditions of "Cry Baby," "Tell Mama" and "Me and Bobby McGee."

FIGHT CLUB

Brad Pitt, Edward Norton, Helena Bonham Carter,
Meat Loaf Aday, Jared Leto

Directed by David Fincher
1999. 139 minutes. R.

A visionary film hurls convention into a kinetic stew of violent trial and struggle for lost male identity. Deadened by insomnia, a dull job and his own materialism, the nameless narrator (Norton) has taken to wandering into 12-step meetings, where he can at least cry. There he finds Marla (Bonham Carter), a witchy, sensual 12-step addict. Then, after an airline loses his luggage and an explosion destroys all his belongings, he encounters Tyler Durden (Pitt), a man on a mission to shake things up.

Durden is bent on driving young men like the narrator,

whom Tyler labels "Ikea Boy," out of their shells of complacency and into a new sense of identity. He takes the narrator into a chaotic world he has carved for himself in a dilapidated, abandoned mansion. And, to get him out of his shell and get the blood flowing (literally), he teaches him to fistfight.

Their fights are addictive, as is riotously ardent sex with Marla. Soon a group of men, all converts to Durden's views and subject to his charisma, are slugging it out in Tyler's fight club, which evolves into a secret society.

That sort of power corrupts as much as any other, and eventually Durden is channeling his rhetoric into the kind of paramilitary project Ayn Rand might have admired.

Though the story, based on Chuck Palahniuk's novel, may offend some, this is a visually striking film, expertly shot, spiked with clever computer-generated surprises and unfolding like a fever dream. Exploring violence in a dehumanized society is bound to step on a few toes.

THE FISHER KING

Jeff Bridges, Robin Williams, Mercedes Ruehl, Amanda Plummer, Michael Jeter

Directed by Terry Gilliam
1991. 137 minutes. R.

With a plethora of whimsy, mythology and romance swirling around Richard LaGravenese's loose-knit screenplay, Gilliam's film could have flown off into the beyond. Instead, it usually manages to channel those impulses into small, comic encounters in a down-to-earth mode.

An arrogant, abusive radio D.J. named Jack Lucas (Bridges) is grinding the world under his heel when he makes some remarks on the air that prompt a deranged caller to commit mass murder in a yuppie bar. Thrown off his show and into rapid decline, Jack sinks into a dispirited void. Three years later, a disheveled shadow of his formerly sleek, mean-spirited self, he lives with the one person who still cares for him, a sweetly flamboyant video-store owner named Anne (Ruehl).

At the end of his rope, Jack meets a colorful derelict named Parry (Williams), who answers to "hundreds of the cutest little fat people floating right in front of me." Parry is the kind of person the old Jack would have sneered at from behind his dark glasses, but when the chastened Jack learns that the derelict is a casualty of the yuppie tragedy, he sees the possibility of redemption.

Jack devotes himself to Parry's rehabilitation, a mission with two goals. He must help Parry win the sweet, shy woman he loves (Plummer), and he has to help reclaim the Holy Grail from the place, given the pecuniary ways of the world, Parry is sure it must reside: in a billionaire's apartment on the Upper East Side of Manhattan.

Gilliam being Gilliam, the flights of fancy begin to derail the story line, which can be disconcerting. Luckily, a clever premise and lively, unpredictable performances transcend the confusion.

FLIRTING

Noah Taylor, Thandie Newton, Nicole Kidman, Bartholomew Rose, Felix Nobis

Directed by John Duigan
1991. 100 minutes. No rating.

Here's a very rare bird indeed: a romance between high school kids with more nuance and heft than most so-called adult screen relationships.

Danny Embling (Taylor) is a very bright kid who immediately gets the hang of the Australian boarding school he's been packed off to by his parents. "You're surrounded 24 hours a day," he says. "Either you become a herd animal or you dig a cave deep inside your head." Then he meets

Thandiwe (Newton), a very bright student at the girls' school across the lake, who is from Uganda.

A very tentative love affair strikes up between two kids who realize that each is different in ways that connect them. By virtue of intellectual gifts and racial background, they are outsiders at school. Danny, a stammerer as well as brilliant student, likes being thought of as an outsider, and Thandiwe, who also feels disassociated, can live with her ethnic distinction. On this footing they proceed into a gentle, probing relationship between soul mates in a film that bears Duigan's special touch.

FLIRTING WITH DISASTER

Ben Stiller, Patricia Arquette, Téa Leoni, Mary Tyler Moore, George Segal, Alan Alda, Lily Tomlin, Richard Jenkins, Celia Weston, Josh Brolin

Directed by David O. Russell
1996. 92 minutes. R.

The title may be a little demure for a sidesplitting comedy that dives into more than a little craziness.

Mel Coplin (Stiller) is a new father who thinks he can't name his son until and unless he meets his own birth parents. Hold everything while Mel conducts a nationwide search.

The idea appeals to Tina (Leoni), a shapely official at the adoption agency where Mel presents his problem. Tina makes it her mission to help Mel, and she'll even go along to chronicle the search. Tina, she also lets it be known, is recently divorced and not at all against the idea of becoming impregnated by an intelligent man.

Naturally that's just what Mel's wife, Nancy (Arquette), wants to hear now that she's beginning to regain her sexual appeal after delivering a baby. Still, she's obliged to co-operate with Mel, so they take Tina along to meet Mel's adoptive parents, played hilariously by Moore and Segal.

Mel's mother nags a lot and is not a little proud of her own body. "I want you to consider my age and ask yourself how I maintain this," she announces, lifting her sweater.

She thinks little of Mel's quest, and that includes Tina. "This woman strikes me as being very dangerous," she says. But nothing stops Mel, even after the quest turns up a mother who really isn't and an assortment of characters and situations that get more uproarious by the mile.

FOCUS

William H. Macy, Laura Dern, David Paymer, Meat Loaf Aday, Kenneth Welsh

Directed by Neal Slavin
2001. 106 minutes. PG-13.

Slavin's film, based on a novel by Arthur Miller, drops in on a very ordinary suburban-style neighborhood for a surreal look at fear and nonconformism in 1940's America. The country is held in thrall by a Father Crighton (Welsh), a demagogic radio commentator who, like Father Charles Coughlin in life, peppered his incendiary speeches with coded anti-Semitic language to blame the Jews for World War II.

Observing from the sidelines, more or less accepting Crighton's bile if not embracing it, is a mild-mannered milquetoast of a man, Lawrence Newman (Macy), who lives with his mother and works as a personnel manager at a local company. When Gertrude Hart (Dern), a sexy lady in a red dress, applies for a job, he turns her down because he suspects she could be Jewish.

Gradually, though, Lawrence becomes a fighter. He and Gertrude marry, and Lawrence deliberately keeps wearing glasses that make him appear Jewish. Raising animosity further, he declines to attend neighborhood meetings to plot strategy against a Jewish storekeeper named Finkelstein (Paymer) who has opened a newsstand in the neighborhood.

He and Gertrude are now targets of anti-Semitic discrimination everywhere they turn. Gertrude urges him to save himself and join a fascistic organization called the Union Crusaders, but it's too late.

If there's a preposterousness to all this, the film's surreal quality and Macy's and Dern's finely shaded caricatures catch the tenor and mood of those times and pass a warning to our own.

FRANCES

Jessica Lange, Sam Shepard, Kim Stanley, Jeffrey DeMunn, Bart Burns, Jordan Charney

Directed by Graeme Clifford
1982. 139 minutes. R.

***

After becoming a star in movies like *King Kong*, Jessica Lange emerges as a superb, serious actress with this brave, humane performance (which sets her on the path toward similarly intelligent roles in films like *Blue Sky*; see page 41). Clifford's film is based on the life of Francis Farmer (Lange), the Seattle high school girl who earned a measure of Hollywood fame in the 1930's. By the early 40's she had crashed physically and emotionally to the point where the most radical treatment imaginable, a transorbital lobotomy, was considered her last hope.

As Lange goes from stubborn teenager to troubled, disillusioned woman, the pain of her struggle to overcome her problems is as evident as the trajectory of her inevitable downfall. After the lobotomy, she emerges a strangely placid figure who lives for quite a while and spends her final years as the hostess of an afternoon television program.

Stanley is her ambitious mother, who consents to the lobotomy.

Sam Shepard is the man who loves her and tries to save her. And although the film doesn't say so, the saddest aspect of the story is that his character was invented; there was no knight in shining armor in Frances's life.

FREAKS

Olga Baclanova, Leila Hyams, Wallace Ford, Henry Victor, Harry Earles

Directed by Tod Browning
1932. 64 minutes.

Attracted by the horror-film revenue stream at rival Universal, Irving Thalberg, the head of MGM, jumped into the genre with Browning's bizarre classic about a group of misshapen circus folk who turn the tables and then some on a normal-size trapeze artist (Baclanova) who has married a midget (Earles) for his money.

The film is so bizarre that it took decades to find an audience. Browning scoured the circuses of the United States and Europe for his cast, which includes the legless Johnny Eck and the conjoined twins Violet and Daisy Hilton, among many others.

When the aerialist Cleopatra (Baclanova) learns that the midget named Hans (Earles) has inherited a fortune, she conspires with Hercules the strong man (Victor) to steal the money by marrying the little one and then poisoning him.

Other unusually formed folk gradually get wind of the plan and, suffice it to say, carry out certain alterations to Cleopatra that enable her to fit right in to their deformed ranks. The climactic sequence is astonishing as the vengeful figures advance on their screaming victim.

MGM had Browning try for a happy ending, with Hans reunited with his suitably sized true love. After some tests this scene was tossed out, clearing the way for a dark American classic.

FREAKY FRIDAY

Jamie Lee Curtis, Lindsay Lohan, Mark Harmon, Harold Gould, Chad Michael Murray, Stephen Tobolowsky

Directed by Mark S. Waters
2003. 97 minutes. PG.

———————————————————————————

Curtis and Lohan do a fine job with the mother-daughter dynamic in a very lively film, adapted from Mary Rodgers's novel, that has them swap roles to see what the other is going through.

Tess Coleman (Curtis) doesn't understand why her teenage daughter, Anna (Lohan), is having problems at school. Anna thinks her mother, a psychiatrist, is too pre-occupied with her fiancé (Harmon) and promoting her new book, *Through the Looking Glass: Senescence in Retrograde*. Communications are at a standstill.

Then, after they eat some weird cookies at a Chinese restaurant, Anna wakes up as Tess and Tess as Anna. "I'm like the crypt keeper," Anna shouts as she looks in the mirror and see her mother.

Each must portray the other during crucial periods in their lives. Curtis is most entertaining as she cuts off her hair, shortens her skirts, starts driving like a Nascar competitor and carries on a flirtation with a cute boy at school. Lohan shows that teenage wisdom has a place in the body of an older woman.

After a while Anna comes to realize that her mother puts her children first, and Tess discovers it's not easy being a teenager. Now can they change back, please?

FREDDY GOT FINGERED

Tom Green, Rip Torn, Harland Williams, Julie Hagerty,
Marisa Coughlan, Eddie Kaye Thomas

Directed by Tom Green
2001. 87 minutes. R.

Admittedly, stimulating an elephant into full sexual cry and crawling into the bloody hide of a road-kill deer aren't for everybody, but tolerate or otherwise get by Green's grosser excesses (which is to say all of them) and you have a work of unbridled (yes, there are acts involving horses) originality. Like it or not, the man is an artist.

Green's humor is regressive, but so was Fatty Arbuckle's when he appeared in diapers. Green forsakes the fields of infantile narcissism for the fertile, frightening ground of middle childhood occupied by a young wild man named Gord Brody (Green). Though he'd like to be an animator, Gord is more a performance artist, as witnessed by loopy, chaotic and brilliant happenings that might have qualified him for a grant from some perverse National Endowment of the Arts.

Say what you will, Green never stoops to the winking pseudo-ironies of second-rate pop culture. *Freddy* is scarier than *Scary Movie* and funnier, too.

THE FRESHMAN

Marlon Brando, Matthew Broderick, Maximilian Schell,
Bruno Kirby, Penelope Ann Miller

Directed by Andrew Bergman
1990. 102 minutes. PG.

Brando turns up as a kind of satirical late-career extension of himself in films like *Don Juan DeMarco* (page 110), and in Bergman's warmly engaging comedy he takes on a familiar old-mobster's mantle as the hoarse-voiced Carmine Sabitini, éminence grise of the Old World Social Club.

A well-modulated old operator in a number of unknown activities, Carmine holds out a helping hand to a first-year film student from Vermont named Clark Kellogg (Broderick), who is robbed of all his money on his first day in New York City.

Helpfully enough, the thief (Kirby) suggests that Clark take a job with Sabitini, who is his uncle. Life around the drowsy-eyed Uncle Carmine assumes a lunatic pitch. Brando goes ice skating at one point. The *Mona Lisa* is involved (and you thought the real one was in the Louvre). So is a seven-foot lizard, which Clark is asked to pick up at the airport.

Miller plays Carmine's sexy, vivacious daughter, Tina. Schell is wonderful as a demented chef-scientist-entrepreneur.

FRIDA

Salma Hayek, Alfred Molina, Geoffrey Rush, Ashley Judd, Saffron Burrows

Directed by Julie Taymor
2002. 122 minutes. R.

Movie biographies of artists tend to succumb to the dutiful and decorous, but Taymor's teeming, color-soaked portrait of Frida Kahlo (Hayek) comes close to transcending those limitations.

While certain important events are passed over without much insight or feeling, Hayek's explosive performance (nominated for an Oscar) liberates a film bursting with color, imagination, music, sex and over-the-top theatricality.

We meet Frida as a headstrong teenager intoxicated by art, sex, left-wing politics and, a little later, the muralist

Diego Rivera (Molina). The first great catastrophe of her life is a bus accident that crushes her pelvis and back; the second, she says, is Rivera. Twenty-one years her senior and, if Hayek and Molina are an indication, twice her size, Rivera offers a volatile relationship that blends political fervor, professional respect and sexual ardor.

He also needs a variety of women (his first wife still lives upstairs), and Frida moves along to an impressive array of lovers, male and female, including Leon Trotsky (Rush), Josephine Baker and a New Yorker (Burrows) who had also been one of Rivera's conquests.

Frida is best when it strays from sober convention and gives free rein to Taymor's visual flamboyance, and to a parade of celebrities played by movie stars (Judd and Rush, for example) trying out silly accents in a film that's not interested in realism.

GARDEN STATE

Zach Braff, Ian Holm, Natalie Portman, Ron Liebman, Peter Sarsgaard, Method Man, Denis O'Hare

Directed by Zach Braff
2004. 109 minutes. R.

Braff's smart, off-kilter comedy extracts spiritual gold from the suburban New Jersey landscape when an emotionally numbed 26-year-old named Andrew (Braff) returns home after years of living in a chemical stupor in Los Angeles. With prescriptions supplied by his father (Holm), a pompous psychiatrist, the troubled Andrew has been spared his darker feelings by a range of pharmaceuticals. Now drug-free, he dreads returning to what he assumes is a soulless wasteland.

His mother's death brings him home. His father blames Andrew for a freak accident that made her a paraplegic, and psychiatrist and son have never confronted the layers of guilt concealed by the prescribed medications.

The film presents itself as *The Graduate of 2004*, with drugs taking the place of the 1967 film's job in plastics. But Andrew now has to find new comforts and solutions. A neurologist (Liebman) suggests that for starters he change psychiatrists. In the doctor's waiting room Andrew meets Sam (Portman), a captivating chatterbox who offers the beginnings of a relationship.

Other characters are aggressively quirky. Andrew's best friend from high school (Sarsgaard), a gravedigger and pothead, introduces Andrew and Sam to a bohemian couple who live on a boat in a quarry. Another friend (O'Hare) has made millions by inventing a noiseless Velcro.

If the film becomes a little too scatterbrained, it does allow Andrew to gather himself.

THE GENERAL

Brendan Gleeson, Maria Doyle Kennedy, Angeline Ball, Eamonn Owens, Jon Voight

Directed by John Boorman
1998. 125 minutes. R.

In real life the legendary Irish thief Martin Cahill once broke into Boorman's home—inspiration enough for the director to tell the story of the bandit nicknamed after Gen. Douglas MacArthur. So rich are the black-and-white tones that the film has the visual sharpness of a photo essay.

Played superbly by Gleeson, Cahill develops as a sly, mischievous fellow with a trademark style who stole about everything but preferred jewelry, art and other big-ticket items. His total take was estimated at $60 million.

The police chase him endlessly and fruitlessly, led by the dogged Ned Kenny (Voight). After a particularly slick jewelry heist, Kenny tells him that he may be a good thief, but he's put 100 jewelry-company employees out of work.

Cahill was a mass of contradictions. After viciously nailing a suspected informer's hand to a table, he takes him to a hospital. Gleeson gives his man plenty of charm. (At home, Cahill sleeps with both his wife and her sister.) The police never caught up to him, but after a deal went bad, the Irish Republican Army did.

GEORGE WASHINGTON

Donald Holden, Candace Evanofski, Curtis Cotton III, Eddie Rouse, Paul Schneider

Directed by David Gordon Green
2000. 89 minutes. No rating.

Green's acclaimed film takes us into a languorous North Carolina summer so green and still and hot that we can feel the humidity and hear the insects. There is trouble here, but like everything else it's in no hurry.

A group of black kids about 13 interact with some white kids with no notable ill effect. Boys and girls get up in the morning and meander through their days without much purpose or energy. It's too hot, and there's not much to do in a town that, as evidenced by the rusting rails running through the greenery, has lost much of its livelihood and slipped into hard times.

Gordon recruited his actors from teenage hangouts around Winston-Salem, and they make whimsical, philosophical and in some cases world-weary characters. One stands in a decrepit auditorium wearing a dinosaur mask and delivering a soliloquy. A scruffy loner named George (Holden), who must wear a helmet because of an old head injury, has a mysterious air, which attracts Nasia (Evanofski). They and others less smart or articulate have a need to express their feelings and philosophies.

At risk to his damaged skull, George rescues someone and starts wearing a Superman cape. Nasia believes he's the key to the world's future and starts calling him George Washington. "I hope you live forever," she tells him.

GET SHORTY

John Travolta, Gene Hackman, Rene Russo, Danny DeVito, Dennis Farina, Delroy Lindo, James Gandolfini, David Paymer, Bette Midler

Directed by Barry Sonnenfeld
1995. 105 minutes. R.

Travolta plays Elmore Leonard's debt collector Chili Palmer to perfection in Sonnenfeld's film, which uses bright colors to set a jaunty tone. After a boozy dry cleaner (Paymer) botches an airline insurance scam, the Miami-based Chili heads to Los Angeles to recover $300,000 involved in the fraud. While he's there, he might as well pitch a movie to the sleazeball producer Harry Zimm (Hackman).

With hustlers pressing him for results, Zimm could use some fresh schlock. Chili, however, is a film noir buff, and his idea takes a higher plane, more character-driven. That attracts the actor Martin Weir, a very big name played by DeVito in high satirical gear.

Travolta is very smooth as the suave Chili. Hackman has great fun throwing around terms like "back story" as the trashy Zimm, and Scott Frank's sharp script lends plenty of comic punch.

GHOST WORLD

Thora Birch, Scarlett Johannson, Steve Buscemi, Brad Renfro, Bob Balaban, Illeana Douglas, Teri Garr

Directed by Terry Zwigoff
2000. 111 minutes. R.

Zwigoff, who directed the documentary *Crumb*, turns a graphic novel by Daniel Clowes into a sharp picture of two eccentric, creative teenage girls, played by Scarlett Johannson and Thora Birch before anyone knew who they were. For Enid (Birch) and Rebecca (Johannson), boredom and disdain are already an art form. Recently graduated from high school, they skulk off to the hip end of town, where they plan to work if they have to but otherwise live in splendid ennui until something halfway involving comes along, not that it will.

Eventually, Rebecca shows signs of wanting to join the rest of the world. To Enid, that is simply compromise. In her own continuing search for authenticity amid the phoniness around her, she meets a middle-aged record collector named Seymour (wonderfully played by Buscemi), whose own loneliness and contempt for most of humanity matches her own. Seymour is both excited by his friendship with Enid and able to see its end before it even starts.

In the alienated Seymour, 17-year-old Enid—funny-looking in her retro clothes and jet-black hair—sees a grown-up version of herself. But he's not much of a role model. The film is interested not in telling us what happens to Enid but in depicting that turning point in her life when she will either give up and become conventional or walk into an unknown, mysterious future that she'll have to make up as she goes along.

GIRL WITH A PEARL EARRING

Scarlett Johansson, Colin Firth, Tom Wilkinson, Judy Parfitt,
Cillian Murphy, Essie Davis

Directed by Peter Webber
2003. 99 minutes. PG-13.

Since relatively little is known about the life of Vermeer, Webber's sumptuous film wisely avoids too much narrative in favor of re-creating the rich visual beauty of the setting and the mysterious young woman who peers over her shoulder in one of the more famous of Vermeer's credited 35 paintings.

But the servant girl named Griet (Johansson) causes more than a ripple in Vermeer's household, which is ruled by his manipulative mother-in-law (Parfitt). Assigned to kitchen and laundry, Griet soon works her way up into the painter's studio, where she becomes fascinated with paints and props and other tools of his trade.

Vermeer (Firth) watches her unobserved and, seeing her interest, gradually lets her into his world. He shows her the camera obscura and has her mix his colors. There are feelings between them, but Vermeer remains a brooding figure who never acts on his urges. Not so his patron, the brash, offensive van Ruijven (Wilkinson), who fondles the girl and suggests her as Vermeer's next subject.

Vermeer's wife (Davis) is none too pleased with that idea.

THE GLEANERS AND I

Varda, Bodan Litnanski, François Wertheimer

A documentary by Agnès Varda
2000. 82 minutes. French with English subtitles. No
rating.

A warm, intrepid woman in her 70's, Varda celebrates
the French habit most famously depicted in Jean-
François Millet's 1867 painting of women gathering
sheaves and kernels left after the harvest. These days, as
Varda shows, the practice extends all the way to mall
Dumpsters.

With a handheld video camera and a small production
crew, Varda crisscrosses the French countryside catching
people in an act of collection first approved by King Henry
IV in 1554. They scavenge fields, orchards, vineyards, urban
markets, curbside trash depositories. They glean out of
need, disgust at wastefulness, the compulsion to make
art out of found objects.

An indefatigably curious, skeptical and sympathetic
observer, Varda becomes a gleaner of gleaners in both a
diary and a kind of extended essay on poverty, thrift and
the curious place of scavenging in French history.

GLENGARRY GLEN ROSS

*Alec Baldwin, Al Pacino, Jack Lemmon, Ed Harris, Alan
Arkin, Kevin Spacey, Jonathan Pryce*

Directed by James Foley
1992. 100 minutes. R.

Steeped in the pitch-perfect dialogue of David Mamet,
who wrote the screenplay adapted from his Broadway
play, Foley's film follows a half-dozen real estate salesmen
on the north side of Chicago as they try to peddle

second-rate home sites in Florida and Arizona. It's not a pretty picture. Actually, it's not an entirely tragic picture, either. There are some lighter moments in a story that has elements of classic farce.

Yet, the stakes are high and the consequences dire for those who don't measure up to the challenge thrown like a gauntlet slap to the face by Blake (Baldwin), the very nasty honcho sent from the home office to light a fire under a sales force that has delivered in good times but comes up empty when the economy goes slack.

Feast or famine, the salesmen are all the same to Blake: lazy, stupid, old and tired. Finish first or second in a contest, he tells them, and they will win a Cadillac Eldorado or a set of steak knives. Finish lower and they win a pink slip.

Ricky Roma (Pacino), slickest of operators, is the least worried. The most concerned, close to panic, is Shelley Levene, the perfect embodiment of the desperately pressed character that was a Lemmon specialty.

With contemporary plays set in restricted confines, the trick is to open them up without losing the theatrical life. In a vivid, loving film, Foley and Mamet do this gently, with extreme care and intelligence.

GO

Sarah Polley, Desmond Askew, Taye Diggs, William Fichtner, Timothy Olyphant, Katie Holmes, Jane Krakowski, Jay Mohr, Scott Wolf

Directed by Doug Liman
1999. 103 minutes. R.

A quick-witted cast full of attitude inhabits Liman's grunge wonderland. Three interrelated sections with multiple characters shuffle together and come back to the start in the manner of *Pulp Fiction,* but the film has a powerful personality of its own.

When a supermarket checkout clerk named Ronna (Polley) agrees to help out a co-worker and take part in a drug transaction, it gets her in trouble with a colorfully menacing dealer (Olyphant), who holds her friend Claire (Holmes) hostage as a form of collateral.

Without drugs, Ronna sells baby aspirin to teenagers who expect something stronger. Meanwhile, Simon (Askew) and some friends get into trouble with some hoods in Las Vegas and are chased back to Los Angeles.

And while that's going on, Zack (Mohr) and Adam (Wolf), a gay couple, are part of a police sting supervised by an officer who is also trying to recruit them as salesmen for Confederated Products, an Amway-type operation.

Suffice it to say that Ronna winds up back at her checkout counter in a film with a nicely sardonic sense of adventure. Liman is his own cinematographer, and by manipulating speed, light, editing and point of view, he makes a film that lives up to the momentum implied by its title. Not much more is needed.

GODS AND MONSTERS

Ian McKellen, Brendan Fraser, Lynn Redgrave, Lolita Davidovich

Directed by Bill Condon
1998. 105 minutes. No rating.

McKellen is wonderfully in character as James Whale, the English homosexual who directed the first two Frankenstein movies, as he lives out his last days in the still-grand Hollywood of 1957.

Taking off from the complex and mysterious circumstances surrounding Whale's death, Condon's film adapts Christopher Bram's hypothetical novel about the filmmaker into an immensely touching character study. After suffering a small stroke, Whale emerges as wittily urbane as ever but is bothered by painful thoughts of the past.

Then an attractive gardener named Clayton Boone (Fraser) appears in his yard.

Boone is exactly what Whale needs at the moment. "Suppose we say phooey to the hedges," he says, and asks Boone if he will sit so he can draw him. A far more multidimensional figure than expected, Boone is suspicious at first but intrigued enough by Whale to allow himself to be drawn in.

Sexual excitement isn't the object here, though it plays around the edges. Whale needs a sounding board for his feelings and remembrances, and the young man makes a convenient and suitable enough tool for the moment. Condon impressively weaves their peculiar bond into the spirit of the Frankenstein movies and segues deftly through memory into the moviemaking process itself.

Real Hollywood figures are ably impersonated, especially George Cukor, an emblematic figure in the Hollywood gay subculture of the time. Davidovich and Redgrave are fine as Boone's girlfriend and Whale's devoted housekeeper, respectively, but it's the razor-sharp cleverness of McKellen's performance that elevates the film and brings fullness and feeling to a most unusual man.

THE GOOD GIRL

Jennifer Aniston, Jake Gyllenhaal, Zooey Deschanel, John C. Reilly, John Carroll Lynch, Tim Blake Nelson, Deborah Rush, Mike White

Directed by Miguel Arteta
2002. 93 minutes. R.

Taking a break from *Friends,* Jennifer Aniston pulled her hair back, put on a Texas accent and triumphed in this quietly moving little film about a youngish woman who surprises herself by finding a spark of life in her drab, working-class existence. Justine (Aniston) is terminally bored by her job at a Texas merchandise mart called Retail Rodeo. At home there is her husband, Phil (Reilly), a house painter who spends his free time getting stoned with his pal Bubba (Nelson) and watching TV. Beyond that, there is nothing.

Then she meets a co-worker named Holden (Gyllenhaal), a 22-year-old college dropout with aspirations to be a writer, and starts an affair that is both joyful and guilt-ridden. Holden has named himself after J. D. Salinger's character (his "slave" name, the one his parents gave him, is Tom), and in Justine he sees a character who, like him, hates the world.

There is no good way out of Justine's dilemma. And what likelihood is there that this 30-year-old woman and her 22-year-old boyfriend have a real future?

Gyllenhaal makes Holden both appealing and exasperating, but this is Aniston's film. She lifts it all with a gentle, thoughtful performance as a woman who finds reserves she never knew existed.

The Good Girl is Arteta's second collaboration (after the bizarre *Chuck & Buck,* page 69) with the writer Mike White, who plays a small role here as a creepy Retail Rodeo co-worker who tries to get Justine to accept God.

THE GOOD THIEF

Nick Nolte, Nutsa Kukhianidze, Tchéky Karyo, Gérard Darmon, Ouassini Embarek

Directed by Neil Jordan
2002. 108 minutes. R.

Jordan's films usually incline toward darker, more serious stuff (see *The End of the Affair,* page 127), but this is a stylish heist caper, full of colorful types. Nolte plays the unflappable gambler Bob, based on the character Bob Le Flambeur in the 1955 French film of that name.

When some old acquaintances try to lure him into the casino heist of casino heists, Bob resists. But as a legend of the Nice demimonde, he almost has no choice. A hulking gambler and addict in a black suit, he rumbles around carefully selected noirish nooks and crannies of his private shadowy world, avoiding contact with the unwanted and steeping himself and his reputation in smoky, jazzy cool.

That kind of mystique intensely appeals to Anne (Kukhianidze), the teenage Russian émigrée and hooker who works in Bob's favorite seedy boîte when she isn't hanging out with him out there somewhere in the underworldly mists. But others know where they can find Bob, too, and before long thugs force him into the casino job, which comes with its own double-dealing twists that are fun to watch even if you can see them coming.

The supporting cast adds to the playful atmosphere, with Karyo as the cop who is both Bob's friend and his pursuer, and a small appearance by Ralph Fiennes as a sinister art dealer.

GOOD WILL HUNTING

Matt Damon, Robin Williams, Ben Affleck, Stellan Skarsgard, Minnie Driver, Casey Affleck, Cole Hauser, George Plimpton

Directed by Gus Van Sant
1997. 125 minutes. R.

A restless young character finally comes to terms with himself in a film with both brain and heart. At first, though, Will Hunting (Damon) is at odds with himself at the end of the broom he pushes as a janitor at the Massachusetts Institute of Technology. Not many other janitors can dash off answers to complex mathematical problems on the blackboards of the classrooms he cleans.

Will's fusion of brilliance and angry self-denial have

plagued him since he was abused and shunted off to foster homes as a child. By age 21, a hot temper and destructive behavior have landed him in jail.

By then, too, his talents have been spotted by a professor (Skarsgard) who gets him released on condition that he see a therapist. Not many shrinks can handle Will's combination of smarts and ridicule, but Sean McGuire (Williams) waits out the initial resistance and starts to get through.

Williams has been known to go sappy in these situations, but here he's in relative control as he helps Will accept his gifts and open himself to friendships and love. Affleck is fine as Will's pal (he and Damon wrote the film), Driver is an appealing love interest, and it helps to have the unsentimental Van Sant in control of film that maintains steady momentum.

GOSFORD PARK

Michael Gambon, Maggie Smith, Kristin Scott Thomas, Emily Watson, Bob Balaban, Ryan Phillippe, Helen Mirren, Jeremy Northam, Charles Dance, Stephen Fry

Directed by Robert Altman
2001. 137 minutes. R.

Altman renders a brilliant ensemble piece to rival his *Nashville* and *Short Cuts* in its masterly interweaving of characters and subplots.

In November 1932, more than a dozen aristocrats and their servants gather for a shooting party on the grand country estate of Sir William McCordle (Gambon), a randy old monster who richly deserves to be murdered and eventually is.

A houseful of suspects, and those associated with the suspects, present themselves. Constance, the Countess of Trentham (Smith), is adept at dispensing barbs of condescension, but they would hardly kill anyone. Sir William's icy wife, Lady Sylvia (Thomas), has enough reason, but she's primarily scornful of her husband and a discreet philanderer herself.

Others are too numerous to mention, but they include a raft of direct relatives and in-laws jockeying to make business deals or gain outright largess from Sir William, who made his fortune on the backs of virtual slave labor. And in the servants' quarters a maid named Elsie (Watson) has a relationship with McCordle.

For entertainment, the aristocracy has invited some commoners for the weekend, notably a gay American movie producer (Balaban), his bisexual boyfriend (Phillippe) and the real-life English matinee idol Ivor Novello (Northam).

It's all right not to keep up with the plot twists. With its shark tank of money grubbing, social climbing and scurrilous gossip, the film is far more satisfying as social satire than as mystery. At its best, the movie suggests a British *Rules of the Game.*

THE GRANDFATHER

Fernando Fernán Gómez, Rafael Alonso, Cayetana Guillén Cuervo, Agustin González, Cristina Cruz, Alicia Rozas, Fernando Guillén

Directed by José Luis Garci
1998. 151 minutes. Spanish with English subtitles. No rating.

It's an intriguing idea for a movie: A long-absent grandfather, Rodrigo, Count of Albrit (Fernán Gómez), returns to his family in northwest Spain intent on determining which of his two lovely, bubbling young granddaughters is legitimate and therefore his rightful heir—not that there's much more in it than the honor. The grand, kindly old fellow is broke.

That must mean the other granddaughter is illegitimate, and how did that happen? The answer lies with the alluring Lucrecia (Guillén Cuervo), the widow of Don Rodrigo's son. She was unfaithful to the boy, as Don Rodrigo realizes and she admits. Life is complicated, she says, and so are relations between men and women.

These days Lucrecia's liaison with a government minister enhances her own property in the village. Seeing Don Rodrigo as a threat, she uses her influence to try to have him confined to a monastery.

For his part, Garci uses all this to create a mystery and to study love, the influence of wealth and the true riches of life.

GRATEFUL DAWG

A documentary by Gillian Grisman
2000. 81 minutes. PG-13.

Grisman's film pays tribute to the long friendship and musical collaboration between Jerry Garcia, lead guitarist of the Grateful Dead, and her father, the banjo and mandolin player David Grisman. Any such enterprise conducts its interviews and hauls out its share of old photos and memorabilia. This one, fortunately, also has the music.

Garcia and Grisman, whom Garcia called Dawg, favored bluegrass, but their creativity and spontaneity took them into jazz, Cuban, reggae and other forms. Gillian Grisman bases her film on a dozen songs performed in their entirety (as examples, the banjo duet "Sweet Sunny South," the folk song "Off to the Sea Once More" and the sophisticated 17-minute "Arabia"). Deadheads are steeped in all this, of course; for others it's a chance to become better acquainted.

GREAT EXPECTATIONS

Ethan Hawke, Gwyneth Paltrow, Anne Bancroft, Robert De Niro, Hank Azaria, Kim Dickens, Josh Mostel

Directed by Alfonso Cuarón
1998. 111 minutes. R.

Employing his signature visual exoticism, Cuarón sends Charles Dickens's tale of a poor young man's rise to gentility looping off into modern precincts. Now we're in Florida, and Miss Havisham is Nora Dinsmore (Bancroft), the richest lady on the Gulf Coast and, jilted though she remains, definitely ready to party.

Dickensians may run for cover, but Cuarón gives the story an entertaining twist while adding touches of voluptuous visual style and mystical realism. Dinsmore hangs out at a great old impressionistic pile called Paradiso Perduto. Gone is Mr. Pip, replaced by Finnegan Bell (Hawke), who rises to recognition as a painter in New York.

As a boy, though, he still takes an emotional drubbing from Estella, who was reared to break men's hearts by the vengeful Dinsmore. And there's Lustig (De Niro), the escaped prisoner Dickens called Magwitch and had rearing out of a graveyard to scare the bejabbers out of young Pip. Here, Lustig materializes in the Gulf to do the same to Finnegan and more or less perform his Dickensian function in New York.

Paltrow, as the grown-up Estella, is glorious to look at and listen to (as usual). Estella is hard to figure in an underwritten script, but here she's a character more suited to a fairy tale.

GROSSE POINTE BLANK

John Cusack, Minnie Driver, Alan Arkin, Dan Aykroyd, Joan Cusack, Hank Azaria

Directed by George Armitage
1997. 106 minutes. R.

John Cusack doesn't seem a natural to play a hit man, which is a good part of the fun of *Grosse Pointe Blank*. When we first view Martin Q. Blank in the opening credits, he is taking aim at an assigned victim to the tune of "I Can See Clearly Now." Actually, Martin is developing blurred vision about his line of work in this dark comedy.

Appealing diffidence is Cusack's strong suit, and his wary style works well here. His secretary (Joan Cusack) thinks he should attend his 10th high school reunion in the high-end Detroit suburb of Grosse Pointe. He thinks not, but a busy schedule of assassinations takes him to the area, so why not?

There he reconnects with his old sweetheart (Driver) and starts to entertain serious doubts about his work, which is booming. His psychiatrist (Arkin) seems unsure how to give the best advice without getting shot. (A hit man with issues, Martin predates that other famous killer-in-therapy, Tony Soprano.) Then there is a competitor to deal with, an assassin named Grocer (Aykroyd), who suggests that all the professional killers generated by the cold war be unionized.

Much action occurs, with a major shootout, but it's the film's quirkiness and its sensitive antihero that make it stand out.

GROUNDHOG DAY

Bill Murray, Andie McDowell, Chris Elliott,
Stephen Tobolowsky

Directed by Harold Ramis
1993. 101 minutes. PG.

Ramis uses the hilarious and nasty sides of Bill Murray, adds the same kind of time-bending trickery employed to such good effect in *Back to the Future,* and comes up with something of an overlooked classic.

Assigned every year to report on the animal's shadow in Punxsutawney, Pennsylvania, the arrogant Pittsburgh weatherman Phil Connors (Murray) finds himself in a time trap. As recompense for his rude treatment of his broadcasting associates and disdain for the event and everybody and everything connected to it, some great unknown force in the sky decrees that time will stop and leave Phil stuck in a Groundhog Day that endlessly repeats itself.

That means Phil can act as badly as he likes without consequence, since the slate is always clean the next day, the same day. No amount of destructive behavior matters, not even smoking or jumping off a tall building. He can even rob an armored truck just for the heck of it. No one will remember.

But gradually he starts thinking about himself and his relations with others. He's always been mean to his attractive producer (McDowell), but now he'd like to impress her, and one way is to "do unto others," as they say.

What's undertaken with cynicism finally becomes heartfelt—inadvertently providing Phil with his only way out of the place—and Murray makes him as believable and appealing at these moments as he is when flinging insults.

GUN CRAZY

Peggy Cummins, John Dall

Directed by Joseph H. Lewis
1949. 87 minutes.

A forerunner of Terrence Malick's *Badlands*, Jean-Luc Godard's *Breathless*, Oliver Stone's *Natural Born Killers* and others of its ilk, Lewis's film is a true sleeper. The critic Pauline Kael called it a tawdry version of the Bonnie and Clyde story. "In its B-picture way, it has a fascinating crumminess," she wrote.

A paranoid gun freak named Bart Tare (Dall) hooks up with an unbalanced carnival crack shot, Annie Laurie Starr (Cummins), with deleterious effect to those they encounter on a robbery and killing spree that goes across the country before ending up with the pair laid out in a swamp.

Bart does much of the shooting, but Annie does the instigating, which led to the film's other title in the International Movie Database, *Deadly Is the Female*. Russ Tamblyn is among those who play Bart as he grows up more than a little twisted and gets caught stealing a pearl-handled pistol. The rest is preordained.

GUN SHY

Liam Neeson, Oliver Platt, José Zúñiga, Sandra Bullock, Michael DeLorenzo, Mary McCormack

Directed by Eric Blakeney
2000. 102 minutes. R.

In the hallowed tradition of *Analyze This* and *The Sopranos*, Blakeney's film sends a tough guy to a psychiatrist. This time, though, the patient, reduced to twitching doubt and ineptitude, is working for the law. An agent for the Drug Enforcement Agency, Charlie (Neeson) becomes dysfunctional after a dealer he was chasing trusses him up like a turkey and throws him facedown in a pile of watermelons. And it got worse, or would have if Charlie hadn't been rescued.

On top of the jitters he has gastroenterological problems. Group therapy is recommended for the former; for the latter he submits to the ministrations of a nurse named Judy (Bullock). His work proceeds apace, however, which places him in the middle of a very dicey deal involving an explosively murderous (and hilarious) mafioso type, Fulvio Nesstra (Platt), and Vaillar (Zúñiga), the yuppified son of a Colombian drug lord.

No one survives these guys, let alone a jumpy D.E.A. man with the trots. But with the help of Judy and the therapy group, Charlie somehow keeps the peace between the mafia and the Colombians. Neeson shows adroit comic reflexes, Platt is wonderful, and Bullock drops her perkiness in favor of open naturalness. But Blakeney, who wrote the film, does himself the biggest favor with a script that gives the actors a lot to work with.

HAMLET

Ethan Hawke, Kyle MacLachlan, Diane Venora, Liev Schreiber, Bill Murray, Julia Stiles

Directed by Michael Almereyda
2000. 112 minutes. R.

Set in contemporary Manhattan, with Shakespeare's language intact, this is a daring, stylish *Hamlet*.

New York gives the film a huge jolt of energy, as the story takes on a corporate spin—Claudius is an odious businessman—in an ultramodern city bristling with video cameras and listening devices. Here the "To be or not to be" soliloquy is delivered in a Blockbuster outlet with the word "Action" on the shelves to fit the style and mood of the picture.

MacLachlan, better known for *Twin Peaks* than for Shakespeare, is a standout as the too-smooth Claudius. Murray gives Polonius a ravaged dignity. Venora's Gertrude is finely distraught and brittle. Schreiber gives Laertes a resonant Old World elegance.

If Hawke seems never quite at ease with the language, he makes up for it with his intense portrayal of a Hamlet ready to jump out of his skin. Using corrupted wealth as a surrogate for depraved royalty, Almereyda's stunning film brings the play into the present while honoring its essence.

HAPPINESS

Jane Adams, Elizabeth Ashley, Dylan Baker, Lara Flynn Boyle, Philip Seymour Hoffman, Jared Harris, Cynthia Stevenson, Rufus Read

Directed by Todd Solondz
1998. 135 minutes. No rating.

A murderous comedy of manners establishes Solondz (*Welcome to the Dollhouse*) as a lacerating, funny and distinctive voice. Suburbia may be the setting, but taking the usual potshots at kitschy Americana isn't his aim here. Solondz wants to know why there are people out there who are more upset when a child's Tamagotchi dies than when a clean-cut family man turns out to be a serial pederast.

The film revolves around the dysfunctional love lives of three sisters. Helen (Boyle), a poet, is supposedly the torrid one constantly in demand on Saturday night. "You have no idea," she says. Her sister Joy (Adams) is as insecure as Helen is assertive. The third sister, Trish (Stevenson), as chirpy as her name indicates, loves to pity Joy's single status. "Just because you've hit 30 doesn't mean you can't be fresh anymore," she says.

It comes as a moderate surprise that the film's second-ranking deviate, a maker of obscene phone calls named Allen (Hoffman), finds an ardent listener in Helen.

Trish's problem, as she will discover, is the movie's chief deviate, her husband, Dr. Bill Maplewood (Baker). Bill, a child psychiatrist, sexually abuses his son's friends. All told, though, he's a nice guy and an honest one who frankly and completely discusses his transgressions with his young son, Billy (Read).

But if Solondz loads his film with enough misery to make a joke of its title, he also fills it with enough true, unexpected tenderness to warrant his view of the world.

HAPPY ACCIDENTS

Vincent D'Onofrio, Marisa Tomei, Nadia Dajani, Holland Taylor

Directed by Brad Anderson
2000. 110 minutes. R.

Anderson mixes science fiction and romantic comedy, of all the unlikely combinations, and by dint of clever plotting and a nice performance by D'Onofrio actually makes a lively, whimsical merger of two strange bedfellows.

Regard this as time travel meets *Sex and the City.* Sam Deed (D'Onofrio) and Ruby Weaver (Tomei) meet on a Manhattan park bench as he sits sketching. That appeals to Ruby, who has a low opinion of the city's supply of men, and the two almost immediately start living together.

Sam, though, has idiosyncrasies. He is inordinately terrified of little dogs and has a tendency toward glassy-eyed spells. At these times things run backward—with, for example, coffee going back into the pot as it's poured.

Sam is from Dubuque, Iowa, he says, and that's true, but the Dubuque of the year 2439. At that time, we learn, Dubuque is on the ocean, thanks to global warming. Ruby plays along, thinking it's a game. Her psychiatrist (Taylor) thinks Sam suffers from temporal-lobe epilepsy.

Anderson, who wrote the film, may get a little too involved in scientific explanation, and Ruby turns a little too stridently antimale, but the film has heart to accompany a moderate amount of flair.

HAPPY, TEXAS

Jeremy Northam, Steve Zahn, William H. Macy, Ally Walker, Illeana Douglas

Directed by Mark Illsley
1999. 98 minutes. PG-13.

A catchy story line and lively performances add up to an engaging satire in a part of the country where you might not expect to find a gay community. The escaped convicts Harry (Northam) and Wayne (Zahn) begin to get the picture when the Winnebago they have just stolen is pulled over by Sheriff Chappy Dent (Macy). The vehicle belongs to a gay couple who travel around the country presenting children's beauty pageants, and Chappy, who is gay himself, assumes he has stopped two experts who will whip Happy's Little Miss Squeezed Pageant into good enough shape to make the regional finals.

Under the circumstances, Harry and Wayne have little choice but to go along with the illusion and, in the process, plan to rob the bank. Harry, the suave and courtly type, attracts both Chappy, who takes him dancing at a cowboy gay bar, and the beautiful local banker (Walker). The rough-hewn Wayne does his best as a choreographer for pretty five-year-olds and learns to stitch shiny baubles onto costumes.

Critics argue whether the climax should have gone in the direction of a hilarious beauty pageant rather than the usual holdup and chase, but everybody agrees the film has such warmhearted fun getting to that point, it really doesn't matter.

HARD EIGHT

John C. Reilly, Philip Baker Hall, Samuel L. Jackson, Gwyneth Paltrow, F. William Parker

Directed by Paul Thomas Anderson
1996. 101 minutes. R.

Anderson's beautifully controlled first film, about a pair of gamblers, is full of surprising revelations that make perfect sense when you stop to think about them. At first, though, you have to wonder what a well-dressed, grimly formal older fellow wants with the surly young drifter he approaches at a desert diner near Las Vegas.

It appears that Sydney (Hall) is looking for a protégé on the casino circuit. After showing John (Reilly) how to bet $150 in such a way that prompts a gambling establishment to give him a free hotel room, Sydney has his man.

Two years later, Sydney and John, who idolizes the older man, are a team working their way around the Nevada casino circuit. But John has made certain associations that bear watching. Sydney dislikes a friend of John's, a cocky security guard (Jackson). John has fallen for a cocktail waitress (Paltrow) who's a hooker on the side.

Then, one night, Sydney is called on to deal with a badly injured man in John's motel room. Ever the calm problem-solver, Sydney handles the situation. To reveal where Anderson's screenplay heads from here would spoil the suspense in a nicely crafted mood piece steeped in sleazy cool.

HEAVEN

Cate Blanchett, Giovanni Ribisi, Stefano Santospago

Directed by Tom Tykwer
2002. 96 minutes. R.

Fate's role in life permeates Tykwer's engrossing film, written in part by Krzysztof Kieslowski, known for his own dreamy speculations about the vagaries of chance. He died in 1996, before he could finish the project.

Nothing makes sense to Philippa (Blanchett), a recently widowed English teacher living in Turin, Italy. In an act of vengeance, she plants a bomb intended to eliminate the high-level drug dealer (Santospago) responsible for her husband's death. Instead, the device kills innocent people in an elevator.

Since Philippa had written many letters to the police about the dealer and his threat to society, she is apprehended and collapses in horror when she learns of her mistake. But a rookie officer named Filippo (Ribisi) falls in love with her and offers to help her escape. She accepts, but not before finishing the original deadly mission she set out to accomplish.

She and the devoted Filippo fashion a long and almost idyllic escape into the Tuscan countryside, not a bad setting to work out her feeling that life makes no sense and to lay the groundwork for a spiritual transcendence.

HEDWIG AND THE ANGRY INCH

John Cameron Mitchell, Andrea Martin, Michael Pitt,
Alberta Watson, Stephen Trask, Rob Campbell, Theodore
Liscinski, Michael Aronov, Miriam Shor, Maurice Dean Wint

Directed by John Cameron Mitchell
2001. 95 minutes. R.

Calling itself "a post-punk neo-glam rock musical," a clever, funny, wildly innovative film tricked out with surreal pop embellishments bears an uncomfortably subversive message about the fluidity of sexual roles, disguise and self-invention in rock music.

Hedwig starts life as a bemused little boy in East Berlin, undergoes a botched sex-change operation (leaving him with the shortened appendage of the title) and ends up on a military base in Kansas with nowhere to go but on tour of grubby restaurants and clubs across the land.

So she forms a rock band and falls in love with a dumb Army brat and Jesus freak named Tommy (Pitt) with rockstar dreams. Then he takes off with her songs and makes himself famous.

Hedwig takes her emotional spills but goes on to entertain splendidly in a series of outrageously funny monologues, sight gags and hip musical jokes that constitute a wickedly knowing critique of recent pop history. As she relates the story with campy tongue-in-cheek grandeur, it builds into an ironic celebration of the pop impulse itself.

HEIST

Gene Hackman, Sam Rockwell, Rebecca Pidgeon, Ricky Jay,
Danny DeVito, Delroy Lindo, Patti LuPone

Directed by David Mamet
2001. 109 minutes. R.

A weary subgenre—the last-big-score picture—gets a fresh infusion from Hackman as an old jewel thief on his, swear to God, absolutely final job, and Mamet's tight, snug film moves surely across familiar ground to become an appreciation of the pleasures of collaborative work.

Joe Moore (Hackman) functions supremely well with Bobby Blaine (Lindo), forming a hand-in-glove partnership that will stand them in good stead in their dealings with a treacherous and terminally talkative fence named Bergman (DeVito) and Bergman's nephew, a double-crossing young hood named Jimmy Silk (Rockwell).

Joe builds sailboats as a cover for his thievery, which suffers a setback when he inadvertently gets in front of a video camera during a job. The old boy may be slipping, but Bergman needs him for a hugely complicated caper involving a planeload of Swiss gold.

As if the job isn't tricky enough, Bergman insists that Joe take Silk along as Bergman's eyes and ears, so to speak. To say that Silk shows no respect for the master is an understatement, and on top of this he has an eye for Joe's young wife, Fran (Pidgeon).

Since Mamet wrote all this, the dialogue is plentiful, swift and telling. Just when it seems Hackman couldn't get any sharper in his characterizations over a brilliant career, he does so in a film that covers no new ground but really doesn't need to.

HENRY FOOL

Thomas Jay Ryan, James Urbaniak, Parker Posey, Maria Porter, James Saito, Kevin Corrigan

Directed by Hal Hartley
1997. 138 minutes. R.

A work of brilliance and epic vision itself, Hartley's film uncovers a streak of genius in a squalid New York basement. "Get up off your knees," Henry Fool tells Simon Grim (Urbaniak), a downtrodden garbage man. After moving in with Simon, his medicated mother (Porter) and promiscuous sister (Posey), Henry urges the withdrawn Simon to start writing down his thoughts.

The expansive, expressive Henry is a writer himself and has reams of an unpublished novel—more "a philosophy," he calls it—to show for it. Simon keeps his first tentative efforts to himself, but gradually they emerge in the form of a long poem, which gains circulation in the neighborhood.

Viewers never get to sample actual passages (a wise move on Hartley's part), but the neighborhood is absolutely floored by what it reads. A mute girl sings. Another girl, who always bullied Simon, now becomes a fan in a beret. Simon's sister says she had her period a week and a half early after she read the poem. The ultimate encomium comes from the board of education, which decries the work as scatological. An artist has arrived.

And there could be some money in it. Hartley shifts gears from genius to celebrity by introducing slick young publishing executives who think far beyond books. Politics could be involved. Henry fans his dreams, but Simon stays rooted in his utterly genuine seriousness, and that generates tension, especially after it turns out that Henry hasn't been that forthright about his own writing efforts.

It's Hartley who's most eloquent in an absorbing meditation on art, loyalty and trust.

HIGH ART

Ally Sheedy, Radha Mitchell, Patricia Clarkson, Gabriel Mann, Anh Duong

Directed by Lisa Cholodenko
1998. 101 minutes. R.

Sheedy gives a fierce, finely shaded performance as Lucy Berliner, a celebrated fashion photographer gone to druggy ruin who is given a chance to return to past glories.

Undone by fame, Lucy has retreated to her apartment, which has become a mecca for her lesbian friends. Then a plumbing emergency introduces Syd (Mitchell), a young assistant at a desperately chic photography magazine called *Frame*. Dazzled by Lucy's work and bohemian world, Syd determines to draw Lucy out and put her in touch with *Frame*'s editors.

An intense wreck, Lucy is intrigued by the opportunity to shake the heroin and begin anew. She's also enamored of Syd, but that is complicated by her longtime relationship with Greta (Clarkson), a washed-up German actress who talks about herself and Fassbinder every chance she gets.

The possibility of a comeback establishes some drama, as does the budding relationship between the jaded artist and the pretty young thing. Sometimes, though, the spare naturalism of *High Art* can be a little too slick for its own good. Fortunately, Sheedy reinvents herself as a tough, fascinating presence.

HIGH FIDELITY

John Cusack, Iben Hjejle, Todd Louiso, Jack Black, Lisa Bonet, Shannon Stillo, Joelle Carter, Catherine Zeta-Jones, Tim Robbins, Lili Taylor

Directed by Stephen Frears
2000. 107 minutes. R.

Frears's witty, exquisitely fine-tuned adaptation of Nick Hornby's 1995 novel re-creates a hothouse world that has all but disappeared.

At Championship Vinyl, a Chicago record store specializing in hard-to-find albums, the manager, Rob Gordon (Cusack), and his clerks are so immersed in pop culture that they give the most important events of their lives hit-parade rankings. In Rob's case, that means grading his many breakups with the long string of women who have passed through his life. On that scale, he says, his most recently departed girlfriend, Laura (Hjejle), doesn't make the top five, who begin with his junior high school sweetheart (Stillo) and include Penny (Carter), Charlie (Zeta-Jones) and Sarah (Taylor). After reflection, he does rank Laura number 5.

Each gets her own vignette and flashback, and in the main it's a formidable group of young women, charming, smart and sexy, who showed Rob the door. Frears's film recognizes that Rob's pop fanaticism had led to arrested emotional development.

A master at projecting easygoing camaraderie, Cusack makes Rob so charming that even when he misbehaves, our reaction is to rationalize and forgive. If vinyl junkies like him are already prehistoric, Frears's film gives them the most heartfelt valediction they could hope for.

HILARY AND JACKIE

Emily Watson, Rachel Griffiths, David Morrissey, James Frain, Charles Dance, Celia Imrie

Directed by Anand Tucker
1998. 121 minutes. R.

Tucker's fact-based film is a rich and subtle tale of sibling rivalry, great musical talent, and tragedy. Watson plays the renowned cellist Jacqueline du Pré, dead of multiple sclerosis at 42 in 1987. Griffiths is wonderful as her less gifted sister, Hilary, overshadowed by Jackie's talents and personality.

In childhood Jackie was the immensely talented one—Hilary, a fine flutist, never made it to the concert stage—and the apple of her elitist family's eye. The two girls are close until Jackie departs on tour and marries the pianist and conductor Daniel Barenboim (Frain) and becomes part of a celebrity couple. But nothing has prepared the sheltered Jackie for the pressures of marriage, fame or illness.

Back home, Hilary marries a musician and gentleman farmer, Kiffer Finzi (Morrissey). One day Jackie, already feeling the coldness in her hands that signals the onset of her illness, appears on their doorstep. "I want to sleep with Kiffer," she whispers in Hilary's ear. The ever-accommodating Hilary, who doesn't dare upset the obviously fragile Jackie, stands by while her sister becomes her husband's lover

Jackie's selfishness could have made her seem monstrous, but thanks to Frank Cottrell Boyce's screenplay and Watson's blazing performance, she emerges the unluckier of the two sisters, a desperately needy child gone before she had a chance to grow up.

A HISTORY OF BRITAIN

A BBC production in association with the
History Channel.
Written and narrated by Simon Schama
2000–02. 900 minutes.

Schama introduces us to the "Protestant Taliban" in his colorful, riveting chronicle of the English experience from the Neolithic settlement of Skara Brae to the two Winstons (the other one referring to George Orwell).

Oliver Cromwell raises a sharp sense of theatricality in the snide, witty Schama, the historian, art critic and Columbia University professor. This is how he describes Cromwell's defense of his butchering of unarmed royalist soldiers at Drogheda: "It's not the confession of a genocidal lunatic, but it is the confession of a narrow-minded, pigheaded Protestant bigot and English imperialist, and surely that is bad enough."

Schama remains an inexhaustible, unfailingly fascinating storyteller, particularly when he relates the exploits of kings and queens in modern terms that embrace espionage, terrorism and public relations.

HOFFA

Jack Nicholson, Danny DeVito, Armand Assante, J. T. Walsh, John C. Reilly, Kevin Anderson

Directed by Danny DeVito
1992. 140 minutes. R.

David Mamet's script inflates the little labor leader, presumably done in by the mob in 1975, into a figure fit for a riveting film done in a flashy style best described as Las Vegas Empire.

In real life, Robert F. Kennedy, Hoffa's nemesis in the

hearing room, was struck by his diminutiveness; on screen, Nicholson's gigantic performance blows away Kennedy (Anderson), whom the actual Hoffa always regarded as a Harvard rich kid hungry for publicity.

Mamet and DeVito start at the end of the story and retrace the career of the man who made the International Brotherhood of Teamsters into the country's most powerful labor organization but always left one foot mired in corruption as he rose from organizer to big-time labor racketeer and master shakedown artist and influence peddler.

Nicholson is superlative, and DeVito is fine as Hoffa's jittery right-hand man. The film doesn't pass judgment on Hoffa but, by maintaining a discreet distance, appears to sanction a complicated and dubious, if colorful, character. Some might object to that, but this is a remarkable effort, an original and vivid cinematic work.

HOLLYWOOD HOMICIDE

Harrison Ford, Josh Hartnett, Lena Olin, Bruce Greenwood, Lolita Davidovich

Directed by Ron Shelton
2003. 116 minutes. PG-13.

Ford revives his harried, set-upon Indiana Jones persona and puts it to fine comedic use in the role of a beleaguered Hollywood police detective, Joe Gavilan, who careens around Los Angeles always one millisecond from personal and professional disaster.

Like many people in L.A., Joe basically wants to be someone else—in his case someone with a lot more money—so he pursues a sideline in real estate. While investigating the murder of four rappers at a club, he tries to sell the club owner a house.

His partner, K. C. Calden (Hartnett), moonlights as a yoga instructor and wants to be an actor, another misguided ambition. Together the old dog and the kid scramble around town on the rapper investigation, with Gavilan becoming ever more distracted by an internal-affairs officer (Greenwood) who wants his job, his money problems, his real estate entanglements and the various mangled personal relations that come to haunt him.

Shelton is especially good at depicting older men stretched thin by past failings, and Ford gives Gavilan just the right amount of desperation. And a fine complement of slapstick gags includes chases, dueling television-news helicopters and Robert Wagner being splattered with concrete as he is about to christen his star outside Grauman's Chinese Theater.

HOOP DREAMS

Steve James, William Gates, Arthur Agee, Emma Gates, Sheila Agee, Gene Pingatore

Directed by Steve James
1994. 171 minutes. PG-13.

James's fascinating documentary depicts an American saga as two 14-year-old basketball prospects from the Chicago projects, William Gates and Arthur Agee, are recruited by St. Joseph, the mainly white Roman Catholic school that once recruited the future N.B.A. star Isaiah Thomas. But at St. Joseph, the dream collides with the reality that in a sports-crazed society youngsters like William and Arthur are bodies fed into the maw.

Spike Lee visits a Nike basketball camp where coaches look over high school players. "The only reason you are here," he tells the kids, "is because you can make their schools win and they can make a lot of money." Of course, it's also true that the infinitesimal number of kids who make it to the pros will make a lot of money, too. For the rest, wealth and fame are carrots dangled by a cynical system uninterested in other aspects of their development.

Hoop Dreams affirms the role of the documentary as a medium for exploring social issues. Though it doesn't find the complex people behind the stereotypes, its achievement lies in revealing how William and Arthur are treated as social clichés.

HOUSEHOLD SAINTS

Tracey Ullman, Vincent D'Onofrio, Lili Taylor, Judith Malina, Michael Rispoli, Victor Argo, Michael Imperioli

Directed by Nancy Savoca
1993. 124 minutes. R.

Savoca's provocative film, based on Francine Prose's novel, is full of mysteries and possible miracles as it spans three generations of a family in Little Italy.

On a hot summer night, a sly young butcher named Joseph Santangelo (D'Onofrio) wins the hand of Catherine Falconetti (Ullman) in a pinochle game. A blast of cold air from a meat locker seems to cast a spell on the union. Joseph's witch of a mother (Malina) communes with her dead husband and makes life miserable for Catherine. It's no coincidence that the name Falconetti suggests Maria Falconetti, the star of Carl Dreyer's 1928 film *The Passion of Joan of Arc*. Catherine's daughter, Teresa (Taylor), wants nothing more than to become a saint. To her, quirky details—the sudden resuscitation of a house plant, the importance of sausage—take on great importance.

Teresa has a vision of Jesus while ironing her boyfriend's shirt, and Savoca treats such matters as everyday events, suggesting neither that Teresa is imagining them nor that they are truly miracles. The film's delicacy keeps it realistic and engaging.

HOUSE OF SAND AND FOG

Ben Kingsley, Jennifer Connelly, Ron Eldard,
Shohreh Aghdashloo

Directed by Vadim Perelman
2003. 126 minutes. R.

Perelman's accomplished first film, adapted from the novel by Andre Dubus III, skillfully builds a classical tragedy from the stresses and strains of contemporary life. What befalls these people never should happen, but somehow it does.

At the center is a clash over ownership of a house between an exiled Iranian Army colonel, Massoud Behrani (Kingsley), and a troubled young woman named Kathy (Connelly). Left to Kathy by her family, the house is mistakenly taken from her by the authorities for nonpayment of taxes and sold to the colonel.

Both are in utter desperate need of this modest piece of property. For Behrani, a proud man who works at menial jobs but changes into a suit and tie to drive home in a Mercedes, the house represents a first step back on the road to restoration of his life and position in old Tehran during the days of the shah. For Kathy, recovering from alcohol and drug addiction, the family homestead is simply what's left of her life.

In a confrontation that steadily grows more bitter, she demands that the colonel leave and he refuses. They aren't bad people, just intractable, for reasons we can sympathize with. No good end is coming, and we watch transfixed.

THE HUDSUCKER PROXY

Tim Robbins, Jennifer Jason Leigh, Paul Newman,
Charles Durning, Peter Gallagher

Directed by Joel Coen
1994. 111 minutes. PG.

Coen brothers' films (Ethan Coen wrote the film with Joel and Sam Raimi) revisit old movie genres, and though this story is set in 1958, its spirit lies in the 30's and 40's of Frank Capra, Preston Sturges and Howard Hawks.

Picture a lush, romantic New York that never was—a visually splendid crush of skyscrapers. Out there in the big town, Norville Barnes (Robbins), an innocent from Muncie, Indiana, lands a job in the mailroom of the huge Hudsucker Industries. Dozens of floors above, Waring Hudsucker (Durning), the company's president, shocks a board meeting by jumping up on a conference-room table, running its full length and diving through a window to his death.

There's nothing horrifying about this; the man goes with panache and a smile on his face. (And remember, we're in a satire.) Nevertheless there is regrouping to manage, which involves stock-price manipulation and introduces the crass and ruthless Sidney Mussburger (Newman), who takes the helm.

Mussburger decides that the company needs an imbecile in the president's chair, the better to scare investors and drive down stock prices to a level insiders can afford. Norville fills the bill.

"He's the bunk," the brassy, motor-mouthed reporter Amy Archer (Leigh) tells her editor. "I'll stake my Pulitzer on it." It's all a fairy tale, of course, fast, fun and great to look at.

HUMAN RESOURCES

Jalil Lespert, Jean-Claude Vallod, Chantal Barré,
Véronique de Pandelaère, Michel Begnez, Lucien
Longueville, Danielle Mélador

Directed by Laurent Cantet
1999. 100 minutes. French with English subtitles. No
rating.

Cantet's smart, wrenching film about a young man fresh from business school who takes a white-collar position far removed from his family's laboring origins never loses its poignant human dimension.

At first Franck (Lespert) is the pride of his blue-collar family, but then corporate politics put him and his father (Vallod) on opposite sides of a battle between management and labor. Problems begin when Franck proposes a 35-hour work week, an offer regarded skeptically by the tough labor leader (Mélador). When layoffs occur, Franck's father loses his job, which leads the son to bad choices made wildly and impulsively.

The film is so beautifully acted that the cast, especially the nonprofessionals who play factory workers, seem plucked from a provincial French town. Franck finds himself resented and feared by the workers, but he nevertheless remains pathetically beholden to his corporate bosses. Soon he learns that he can't be on both sides of a labor war.

The film doesn't strongly favor one side over the other, but it tilts toward labor. Franck and his father fight bitterly, perhaps irredeemably. The crowning irony is that the son has alienated the man who sacrificed to make his rise possible.

L'HUMANITÉ

Emmanuel Schotté, Séverine Caneele, Philippe Tullier, Ghislain Ghesquière, Ginette Allegre

Directed by Bruno Dumont
1999. 148 minutes. French with English subtitles. No rating.

By creating the raw sensory effect that the world is more intense than everyday life, Dumont's flawed masterpiece gives the sense that civilization is really a fragile membrane that barely separates us from our most brutal instincts.

Sights and sounds approach the psychedelic, with the exquisitely detailed soundtrack picking up fluctuations of the wind, the barking of dogs and the sounds of birds. Other sounds are disturbing, like the heavy breathing of the police detective Pharaon De Winter (Schotté) as he pedals his bike uphill.

It's the same heavy breathing heard at the start of the film when the body of an 11-year-old girl is discovered. The girl has been raped and murdered. As the camera surveys the body, an unidentified male figure who may or may not have committed the crime is seen running across a bluff.

The runner, we learn, is Pharaon. A repressed, clumsy little man who lives with his stern mother in a drab brick house, he must face the possibility that he committed the crime he is investigating. One narrative strand follows the case, which proceeds haphazardly, while another follows Pharaon's edgy relationship with Domino (Caneele), a spirited young factory worker whose affair with Pharaon's friend Joseph (Tullier) produces some of the most explicit sex scenes ever filmed for a nonpornographic movie.

As Pharaon tags along after her and Joseph, we feel intimations of violence everywhere in a film whose characters seem to be cunning, instinctual beasts peering out from their skins.

THE HURRICANE

Denzel Washington, John Hannah, Deborah Kara Unger,
Liev Schreiber, Vicellous Reon Shannon, David Paymer, Dan
Hedaya, Harris Yulin, Rod Steiger

Directed by Norman Jewison
1999. 125 minutes. R.

Some critics thought Jewison's film about the vindication of the boxer Rubin "Hurricane" Carter (Washington), convicted of murder, distorts some facts and blatantly manipulates the emotions on its way to a predictable glorious conclusion. There's some truth to that, but the strength of the movie lies in Washington's performance, probably the best of his career.

Despite the embellishments, the story is basically true. On screen, Carter's autobiography, *The 16th Round*, written from his cell, catches the attention of a teenage boy named Lesra Martin (Shannon) and three Canadians (Schreiber, Hannah and Unger), who move to the United States to help him reopen the case and win his freedom.

Behind bars Carter has become a kind of dual personality who wrestles with violent, destructive instincts while hanging on to his determination and self-discipline. Deeply affected by what he learns about the man, Lesra timidly starts to visit him and becomes his one real friend. As a mentor to the boy, Carter rekindles his hope in the future.

Everyone is either an angel or a monster in this film. In the latter category is a corrupt cop (Hedaya) whose sole purpose in life seems to be the destruction of a man he knows is innocent. Such one-sidedness doesn't serve the movie, but, again, Washington's Carter holds us with his fierce intelligence.

HUSBANDS AND WIVES

Woody Allen, Mia Farrow, Judy Davis, Sydney Pollack,
Juliette Lewis, Liam Neeson

Directed by Woody Allen
1992. 107 minutes. R.

Allen's very fine, sometimes-brutal comedy comes close to home as the novelist Gabe Roth (Allen) and his wife, Judy (Farrow, from whom Allen had recently and stormily parted company), try to absorb the news that their best friends, Sally (Davis) and Jack (Pollack), are separating.

Judy is furious, perhaps sensing that marital discord could spread to her and Gabe. But these are all well-to-do Manhattanites of a breed that seems to muddle along, especially in an Allen film, with help from a coterie of new lovers and potential mates.

Very successful at business, Jack is a personal bumbler who finds himself with a young aerobics instructor who isn't exactly the best fit with his older friends. Sally, meanwhile, is presented to an intensely sincere young doctor and proceeds to make him miserable.

Like any Allen character, Gabe has a girlfriend or two, and the younger the better. Rain (Lewis), an aspiring writer, is a student of Gabe's. At her 21st-birthday party at her parents' penthouse, she asks him to kiss her on the mouth. "Why is it," he says, "that I'm hearing $50,000 worth of psychotherapy dialing 911?"

Like the entire Allen oeuvre, this is a kind of personal cinema for which there is no precedent in modern American movies.

THE ICE STORM

Kevin Kline, Sigourney Weaver, Joan Allen, Christina Ricci,
Jamey Sheridan, Elijah Wood, Tobey Maguire

Directed by Ang Lee
1997. 112 minutes. R.

Lee's extraordinarily observant film captures unraveling
suburban life in the 70's. Things are a mess in New
Canaan, Connecticut. Watergate and marijuana smoke
are in the air. People anesthetize with drugs and liquor
and go to bed with one another's spouses. A lost generation of teenagers floats rudderless in the spiritual void
left by their elders.

In step with their soullessness, Lee hides these characters and their emotions. As a microcosm there are the
Carvers and the Hoods. Benjamin Hood (Kline), an oblivi-
ous sort, is having an affair with the chilly Janey Carver
(Weaver), the very model of someone not cut out to be a
suburban wife and mother.

While these two prepare for a tryst upstairs (Janey sud-
denly gets up and leaves), Benjamin's daughter, Wendy
(Ricci), insists that Janey's son, Mikey (Wood), put on a
Richard Nixon mask before they have sex in the basement.
Like Benjamin, Mikey's father (Sheridan) is too distracted to
know or care what's going on in his son's life.

Lee is sensitive to the dislocation. A boozy mate-
swapping party leads to tragedy in a substratum of society that lets go of roots and tradition in an elegant and
deeply troubling drama.

IDENTITY

John Cusack, Ray Liotta, Amanda Peet, John Hawkes,
Alfred Molina, Clea DuVall, John C. McGinley, William Lee
Scott, Jake Busey, Rebecca DeMornay

Directed by James Mangold
2003. 90 minutes. R.

A wild little hoot of a thriller trots out everybody but
Agatha Christie for some bloody shenanigans at a
sleazebag motel that is in the middle of nowhere to begin
with and is now cut off by a driving rainstorm that has
closed all the roads.

It's the dead of night, we should add, with the phone
lines down and the lights flickering. A semihysterical has-
been actress (DeMornay) has the one cell phone, but
that's kaput, though she covers herself with a shower cur-
tain and stumbles around in the downpour looking for
better reception.

She's the first one to have her throat cut, and others
soon follow in 10-little-Indians fashion according to their
room numbers. The prime suspect is a serial killer who is
being transported between houses of correction, but
even he seems not quite up to this level of bloodshed.
Maybe it's spirits from a neighboring burial ground.

Cusack portrays an ex-cop and Liotta is the prisoner's
chauffeur, which at least gives the rest of the group, including shrieking women, two people who know one end
of a gun from the other. But they provide little protection.

The cast list finds a lot of talent in a low-rent area, so
to speak, but there's a twisty climax ahead.

IGBY GOES DOWN

Kieran Culkin, Claire Danes, Jeff Goldblum, Jared Harris, Amanda Peet, Ryan Phillippe, Bill Pullman, Susan Sarandon

Directed by Burr Steers
2002. 98 minutes. R.

A runaway from military school, Igby (Culkin) rattles around Manhattan's East Village and points west in Burr's nastily funny portrait of postyuppie American affluence and its disappointments. Taking its cue from *The Catcher in the Rye*, the film gives us a teenage rebel with a brain to match his attitude.

A dark sense of humor is at work. At the start Igby and his older brother, Oliver (Phillippe), are seen doing away with their snoring, heavily sedated mother, Mimi (Sarandon), by fitting a plastic bag over her head. Or are they? They'd like to, but whether or not it's a fantasy isn't revealed until the end.

Earlier, Mimi had shipped Igby off to military school, supposedly as a remedy for his flunking out of many prep schools up and down the East Coast. But Igby soon bolts and turns up at an East Village loft that doubles as a dance studio occupied by Rachel (Peet), the trophy girlfriend of Igby's godfather and benefactor, D. H. Banes (Goldblum).

There he is taken in hand by Rachel's friend Russel (Harris), a strident performance artist, and given a tour of downtown bohemia. In need of money, Igby serves as a drug courier among Russel's circle of friends.

But the soul of the film involves his ambivalent relationship with his family. His father (Pullman) is in a mental hospital after a schizophrenic meltdown. A condescending smoothie, Oliver walks off with Igby's soulful romantic interest, Sookie Sapperstein (Danes), a Bennington dropout.

Igby needs to get out from under this bunch in a film

that drifts uneasily between satire and realism but maintains a ruthless emotional honesty.

I'LL SLEEP WHEN I'M DEAD

Clive Owen, Jonathan Rhys-Meyers, Malcolm McDowell, Charlotte Rampling, Jamie Foreman, Ken Stott

Directed by Mike Hodges
2003. 103 minutes. R.

Hodges's *Get Carter* (1971) set the tone of chilly elegance, poker-faced torment and moral chaos that still defines the British gangster film. Here his tricky, dazzling technique is deployed with almost casual professionalism, though you may have to work a little to follow what he's doing and to discern the structure underlying his riffs and inventions.

The film tells parallel stories. Owen is Will Graham, a former crime boss who long ago retreated from the scene, took up manual labor and grew shaggy. In London, his slick cad of a younger brother, Davey (Rhys-Meyers), is a drug courier who is invited to all the right parties, where he steals things and otherwise acts the rotten little stinker until one night he is grabbed by a couple of men and raped by their boss, a white-haired man named Boad (McDowell). The next day Davey commits suicide.

Will returns to avenge his brother. It's as basic as that, but with Hodges things aren't simple. The narrative plays out predictably, but what sticks are the creepy things around the edges of the story: the feeling of London at night, the fog of melancholy and menace in every scene, and Owen's haunted eyes as he moves toward the kill.

IN THE BEDROOM

Tom Wilkinson, Sissy Spacek, Nick Stahl, Marisa Tomei, William Mapother

Directed by Todd Field
2001. 130 minutes. R.

Sissy Spacek and Tom Wilkinson have had first-rate careers, but they have never been better than they are here as Matt and Ruth Fowler, grieving over the murder of their son, Frank (Stahl), and outraged at the fate of the man who killed him, Richard (Mapother).

When Frank was shot to death, he was a young architecture student figuring out what he wanted to do in life and meanwhile having an affair with Natalie (Tomei), a slightly older woman and the mother of two small children, who was separated from Richard but not divorced. Jealous of Frank, the unstable Richard kills him in cold blood. Because of a legal technicality, he is charged only with manslaughter; out on bail, he goes on with his life in plain sight of Frank's parents.

Field has said that his film is not about revenge but about the stress the situation puts on a long-term relationship. Nevertheless, revenge finds a way in this film, and it's about as nicely handled as any piece of reprisal to come along on screen in some time. Matt finds the need to act, which he does most effectively. But in carrying this out, he only deepens his own questions about his life, the woman he married long ago and whatever future they have left.

Adapted from a story by Andre Dubus, the film was nominated for an Oscar as best picture, with Spacek, Wilkinson and Tomei getting nominations as well.

I LOVE YOU TO DEATH

Kevin Kline, Tracey Ullman, Joan Plowright, River Phoenix, William Hurt, Keanu Reeves

Directed by Lawrence Kasdan
1990. 96 minutes. R.

Kline is hilarious and touching as Joey Boca, the wildly self-indulgent owner of a pizza parlor in Tacoma, Washington. A serial womanizer, he is forever ducking off to perform handyman chores for attractive young women who live in his building. That doesn't mean Joey doesn't love his wife, Rosalie (Ullman), and their two children. He even provides room and board to his hostile mother-in-law, Nadja (Plowright).

Joey is simply an exuberant louse; he can't help himself. Kline perfects a broad Italian-American accent and a persona that alternates between manic and laid-back. A waiter in his restaurant is in love with Rosalie and warns her that when Kline disappears for extended periods with other women, it's not to fix their plumbing.

At first Rosalie will hear none of this. Joey is Italian, and Italian men flirt. But then she talks the situation over with Nadja and decides to kill Joey. "If you don't kill him, kill yourself," says the practical Nadja.

At this point, Kasdan's film, based on a true story, gets caught in something of a no-man's-land between Joey's antics and the serious business of doing away with him. Fortunately, first-rate performances maintain the gusto to sustain a farce.

IL POSTINO (THE POSTMAN)

Massimo Troisi, Philippe Noiret, Maria Grazia Cucinotta, Linda Moretti, Renato Scarpa

Directed by Michael Radford
1995. 113 minutes. Italian with English subtitles. No rating.

A gentle, lonely man on a ruggedly beautiful Italian island finds liberation and fulfillment in his friendship with the celebrated poet Pablo Neruda (Noiret), who has come for a temporary peaceful respite after been exiled from his native Chile for political reasons.

Before Neruda's arrival, Mario (Troisi) had little to do but watch his ancient father slurp his soup. He knows little of poetry, but just the idea of having a famous practitioner among them is energizing, and when Neruda needs someone to deliver his mail, Mario leaps at the chance.

Every day he pedals his bicycle up to the hilltop abode Neruda shares with a woman he calls Amor. The poet is cordial. Mario's initial shyness gives way to inquisitiveness. What's it like to be a poet? Perhaps Mario will attempt some poetry himself.

Neruda is quietly obliging and helps Mario craft some verse that helps the mailman woo Beatrice (Cucinotta), a local beauty. But Mario imagines a closer relationship with Neruda and is sobered when, at the end of the poet's stay on the island, he tells a newspaper interviewer, "I lived in complete solitude with the most simple people in the world."

Mario wants to have mattered more but comes to see that he mattered enough in appropriate measure. And there is Beatrice.

IN THE LINE OF FIRE

Clint Eastwood, John Malkovich, Rene Russo, Dylan McDermott

Directed by Wolfgang Petersen
1993. 128 minutes. R.

***

Eastwood is in his charcoal-mellow groove as Frank Horrigan, aging Secret Service agent (somewhere over 50, or is it 60?) who gives the distinct impression that he could go down with a coronary as he trots beside a presidential motorcade. Frank has been guarding presidents for a lot of years. Some say he was remiss in his duties on the day Kennedy was shot in Dallas.

That memory still haunts Frank as he plays some piano and drinks too much in his favorite haunts around the capital. Guarding presidents is all he wants to do in life, a passion that has cost him his wife and family.

The Kennedy assassination hangs heavily over Frank, especially when an anonymous caller later identified as Mitch Leary (Malkovich) starts taunting him about dereliction of duty and telling Frank that he will kill the current president. Frank spreads the alarm among fellow agents, touching off a movie-long duel.

Peterson's thriller gets Frank and the climactic action just right. Frank's mix of competence and vulnerability interests Mitch, played to a malicious, slithery fare-thee-well by Malkovich. Mitch starts calling Frank at all hours to discuss the Kennedy lapse and wonder about Frank's ability to meet the challenge this time around.

IN THE MOOD FOR LOVE

Lai Chen, Maggie Cheung, Tony Leung, Chiu Wai, Rebecca Pan, Siu Ping-lam, Chin Tsi-ang

Directed by Wong Kar-wai
2000. 97 minutes. Cantonese and Shanghainese with English subtitles. No rating.

Wong thinks through the lens, which seems appropriate for a film that, like its protagonists, looks but doesn't touch. In an affair with a difference, Siu Li-zhen (Cheung) and Chow Mo-wan (Leung) are married to other people who, as it happens, are having an affair with each other.

It's 1962 in a very crowded Hong Kong. Chow and Su meet after renting rooms in adjoining apartments. They would like to consummate their desire but resist because "for us to do the same thing would mean that we are no better than they are." Instead, they contemplate their situation while the movie generates heat and mood around them with lush cinematography and pearly Nat King Cole songs throughout.

While they have stated their principles, abstinence is difficult to reconcile and it rankles both of them. Wong eroticizes their longing with his camera. He is said to have shot a sex scene but then rejected it, which was a good decision. This is a love story that derives its charge from the fact that the skin stays covered most of the time.

The camera perches like a voyeur as they struggle with their double lives. Most films about adultery are about the philanderers, but in this one we meet the cheating couple only indirectly when Chow and Su play-act a confrontation their real-life spouses might have with each other. Otherwise Wong's camera floats along while his heart spills out onto the screen.

THE INSIDER

Russell Crowe, Al Pacino, Christopher Plummer, Michael Gambon, Diane Venora, Bruce McGill, Philip Baker Hall, Lindsay Crouse, Gina Gershon

Directed by Michael Mann
1999. 157 minutes. R.

As the whistle-blower Jeffrey Wigand, Crowe steals Mann's engrossing film, which never loses taut momentum over its considerable length.

Wigand is a complicated, absorbing character. As a chemist employed by the Brown & Williamson Tobacco Corporation, he accepts a large salary essentially to look the other way when the company covers up evidence verifying that cigarette smoking is addictive. But Wigand is an activist at heart, and for all his reticence at coming forward to bite the hand that feeds him, he offers just enough of an opening for the television producer Lowell Bergman (Pacino) to latch on to a major story for the CBS show *60 Minutes* and its most renowned correspondent, Mike Wallace (Plummer).

Dark, sleek cinematography heightens a sense of danger and personal threat. Crowe's introverted, highly intelligent character plays off the voluble Bergman, played by Pacino in accustomed scenery-chewing form. Wigand, like Bergman a supremely intense man and a stickler for high standards, will throw away a lucrative job, and possibly endanger himself and his family, provided that he can trust CBS to handle the story the way Bergman assures him it will.

CBS, of course, doesn't, with the network caving in to corporate pressure and Wallace going along with the decision to hold the show. Eventually, Wigand, a brooding, embattled plodder, will be vindicated in a film that allows Bergman and Wallace their histrionics but never loses sight of its man, Jeffrey Wigand.

INSOMNIA

Al Pacino, Robin Williams, Hilary Swank, Martin Donovan,
Maura Tierney, Nicky Katt, Paul Dooley

Directed by Christopher Nolan
2002. 118 minutes. R.

A nicely handled noirish thriller packs a hounded Los
Angeles detective named Will Dormer (Pacino) off to
Alaska to help a former colleague solve a murder. Nolan's
tale is based on Erik Skjoldbjaerg's film of the same name
(also highly recommended), set in arctic Norway. There
the look was primarily white. Here it is green.

Never has a harried L.A. detective, under investigation
by his department's internal-affairs division, been deposited in such a sea of towering green trees and blinding
sunlight. Dormer, a sagging, dead-faced figure in a droopy
leather coat, can only blink and look dazed. At this time of
year the sun shines 22 hours a day, and no amount of cov-
ering taped across his hotel windows keeps out the light
entirely.

Will can't sleep anyway. A young woman has been
killed. An eager Alaskan detective named Ellie Burr
(Swank) is impressed by Dormer's quick take on the situation, but Will knows he has a tough case on his hands.
Then Hap Eckhart, an assistant Will has brought from L.A.,
is shot dead in a heavy fog. Eckhart figures in Will's
internal-affairs troubles back home. So, Ellie comes to
wonder, did Will shoot him?

Williams is good and creepy as Walter Finch, writer of
bad crime novels and murder suspect. Will chases him
around the landscape and across floating logs. In the end
they are two characters with no place to hide.

INTERNAL AFFAIRS

Richard Gere, Andy Garcia, Nancy Travis, Laurie Metcalf,
Annabella Sciorra, William Baldwin

Directed by Mike Figgis
1990. 115 minutes. R.

Steeped in brown Los Angeles murk, Figgis's film turns a sleek predator loose on the L.A.P.D. When Dennis Peck (Gere) isn't manipulating his fellow cops in some scheme or other, he's bedding their short-skirted, tousle-haired wives. Dennis has had four wives himself and nine kids, which adds up to an establishment with some large grocery bills. Despite that, he lives very large for a cop's salary.

The internal affairs division wonders why and assigns Sgt. Raymond Avila (Garcia) to head an investigation. It doesn't take Avila long to realize he has one rotten cop on his hands. Cornering the shrewd, slippery Peck may be more than he can handle.

In one of his better roles, Gere gives his man a smiling, lethal edge. Peck is supremely confident in his power over people, whether blowing someone away on a dark street or sliding his hand up a woman's thigh with her husband sitting across the table. Avila should fold fast, Peck figures, and there's his scrumptious wife (Travis) to put into play.

Being more or less a police procedural, Figgis's film is more conventional than his *Stormy Monday* (page 383). This one runs on pure menace and eroticism.

INTOLERABLE CRUELTY

George Clooney, Catherine Zeta-Jones, Edward Herrmann, Billy Bob Thornton, Geoffrey Rush, Cedric the Entertainer

Directed by Joel Coen
2003. 100 minutes. PG-13.

Always looking for fresh genres, Joel and Ethan Coen (Joel usually gets the directing credit, although the brothers collaborate on writing and directing) manage what hasn't been seen on screen for a long time: an intelligent, modern screwball comedy.

Clooney is in fine Cary Grant form as Miles Massey, a determinedly single matrimonial lawyer and creator of the ironclad Massey pre-nup, which has never been broken. He has never lost a case in divorce court, either, but that streak is now in jeopardy. With the motel frolics of his wealthy client, Rex Rexroth (Herrmann), on videotape for all to see, Massey produces a surprise witness who claims that Rexroth's wife, Marilyn (Zeta-Jones), set out to trap him into marriage and quickly strip him of all but his boxer shorts in a ruinous settlement. Marilyn is a specialist in this kind of thing, the witness states, but then who isn't in the L.A. divorce wars?

Clooney is perfectly charming while giving the film a slight wink and a nod to the past that updates the genre. Zeta-Jones shows an unexpected flair for comedy. And Thornton is the Texas oilman she leads to the altar like a bull on a nose ring. Massey finds this irresistible.

THE ITALIAN JOB

Mark Wahlberg, Charlize Theron, Edward Norton, Seth Green, Jason Statham, Mos Def, Franky G, Donald Sutherland

Directed by F. Gary Gray
2003. 110 minutes. PG-13.

As movie capers go, this is stock issue, but very nicely handled stock issue. You know the drill: put together a dream team of techno specialists for the big heist. There's the young mastermind (Wahlberg) to orchestrate it all and an old safecracker (Sutherland) to feel the tumblers click through a foot of steel. They'll need a computer nerd (Green), a getaway driver (Statham) who doubles as a womanizer, and a demolition man (Mos Def).

For a setting there is Venice. For swag there is $35 million in gold bullion in a safe so heavy it crashes through several floors on its way to a speedboat that races off through the waterways. Then you need a rat of a double-crosser (Norton) to turn on his colleagues, kill a couple of them and take the haul off to sunny Southern California.

Add a dazzling blonde (Theron), also a safecracker and breaker of security systems, who wants revenge. All that's left is a nifty chase in heavy Los Angeles traffic.

IT ALL STARTS TODAY

Philippe Torreton, Maria Pitarresi, Nadia Kaci, Véronique Ataly, Nathalie Bécue, Emmanuelle Bercot, Françoise Bette, Lambert Marchal

Directed by Bertrand Tavernier
1999. 117 minutes. French with English subtitles. No rating.

Shot with unassuming realism and beautiful to look at despite its lack of stylishness, Tavernier's film both celebrates the resilience of children and decries conditions that menace them.

Daniel (Torreton) is the director of a preschool in a depressed coal-mining region torn by chronic unemployment and its attendant miseries: alcoholism, domestic abuse, pervasive despair. School is about the only refuge for kids in this region, and Daniel and his colleagues sing songs, tell stories and supervise art projects and playground games.

Outside the classroom he copes with drunken parents, uncooperative child-welfare officials and elected politicians, ignorant inspectors, teenage vandals who trash the school. And he also tries to find time for his girlfriend (Pitarresi) and to help his aging parents.

Tavernier could have wandered into politically explicit drama, but the film can't be described as markedly leftist. French labor survives here as a demoralized underclass rather than the standard-bearer of radical tradition. Instead of confecting an ideological soap opera, Tavernier pulls off an emotionally rich and remarkably restrained piece of storytelling.

IT RUNS IN THE FAMILY

Michael Douglas, Kirk Douglas, Cameron Douglas, Diana Douglas, Rory Culkin, Bernadette Peters

Directed by Fred Schepisi
2003. 109 minutes. PG-13.

With Michael, Kirk, Cameron (Michael's son) and Diana (Kirk's ex-wife) together on screen, you might expect a feel-good domestic comedy. Instead, Schepisi's film offers a complex and subtle portrait of the Grombergs, a prickly, quarreling clan of New York achievers.

In his 80's, the cantankerous Mitchell Gromberg (Kirk Douglas) still chugs through his daily lap around the Central Park reservoir. Mitchell founded the law firm now run by his son, Alex (Michael Douglas), who is basically not a bad guy but has inherited bullying tendencies from his father.

The two Douglases chafed each other in real life, and here Alex, who is distressed with his life, and Mitchell abrade in the manner of driven competitors who can't help taking each other on within the family. Alex is happily married to Rebecca (Peters), but it wouldn't be Michael Douglas without an obsessive other woman throwing herself at him.

Alex and Rebecca's son (Cameron Douglas) is an arrogant part-time D.J. with a macho attitude and a drug problem. That leaves Diana Douglas, who plays Mitchell's devoted wife. And why does the old coot deserve such a woman?

In interlocking personal dramas, the Gromberg males confront one another nose-to-nose. Before the movie is over, two major characters are dead. Working with a complicated narrative and scenarios that could have turned histrionic, Jesse Wigutow's screenplay is a marvel of economy and restraint. No one asks you to like these people, but you have to admire Mitchell, who envisions ending it all atop a Viking-style funeral pyre.

JESUS'S SON

*Billy Crudup, Samantha Morton, Denis Leary, Jack Black,
Will Patton, Greg Germann, Holly Hunter, Dennis Hopper*

Directed by Alison Maclean
1999. 107 minutes. R.

Maclean's scruffy, likable film, adapted from a book of linked short stories by Denis Johnson, finds a loose, improvisatory rhythm that matches Johnson's discursive neo-beatnik riffing and gives her scenes a keen edge of surprise.

Crudup is transcendentally goofy as a druggie who maintains a curious innocence as he hitchhikes across the Midwest in filthy hand-me-down jeans. Whatever cohesion there is occurs in the first two sections, set in the brown Iowa winter of 1971, as the hero develops an on-again, off-again obsession with a gloomily passionate young woman named Michelle (Morton).

Characters encountered include Wayne (Leary), who drinks spilled booze out of a cocktail napkin, and Georgie (Black), a hospital orderly who's either a gifted healer or a dangerous psychopath.

As the film follows Crudup's character into recovery, it loses some momentum, but it hangs on to a surrealist, deadpan humor, visual and verbal. It may remind you of *Drugstore Cowboy* (page 118), which also imagined the early 1970's as the golden age of American junkiedom.

THE KID STAYS IN THE PICTURE

Robert Evans

Directed by Nanette Burstein and Brett Morgen
2002. 93 minutes. R.

As an actor, says the impossibly pretty Robert Evans, he was on his way to being the next Troy Donahue. What Evans really wanted was to be the next Darryl F. Zanuck.

Call him a lesser version of Zanuck, which is meant as no slight. In Burstein and Morgen's entertaining documentary, the producer tells it his way about making films in the 1970's. As the head of Paramount, he supervised the making of *The Godfather, Barefoot in the Park, Rosemary's Baby* and *The Odd Couple*. As an independent producer he helped make *Chinatown* and *Marathon Man*.

Evans was the man Ali McGraw dumped for Steve McQueen. In the 80's he succumbed to "the world of white," but he recovered and made the disastrous *Cotton Club*. Evans tells all this in good humor, and since he photographed every step of his career, the film has much to show that both bears out his generous self-assessment and occasionally reins him in a bit.

It's an evocative look at a certain era in Hollywood, full of sleek women on Evans's arm and studio execs with killer grins and shifting fortunes. As for the title, back in Evans's acting days, Ernest Hemingway told Zanuck that he wanted the dark, slicked-back actor out of an adaptation of his novel *The Sun Also Rises*. Zanuck disagreed and the kid stayed.

THE KING OF COMEDY

Robert De Niro, Jerry Lewis, Sandra Bernhard

Directed by Martin Scorsese
1983. 108 minutes. R.

In one his most flamboyant, complex performances, De Niro is Rupert Pupkin, a spectacularly self-delusional hanger-on circulating around the fringes of the stand-up-comedy scene. To say that Rupert, virtually talentless, is obsessive about his prospects as a comic is to say that the man has merely a moderate amount of ambition. Rupert is crazed, a true psychotic.

With De Niro we never know if or when he will get dangerous. Fortunately, Rupert is a likable psychotic, not the *Cape Fear* variety. He has decided his path to the top lies through a hilariously stately big-time comedian named Jerry Langford (Lewis), host of a late-night talk show. Rupert would kill (well, maybe not) for a 10-minute spot on the Langford show, and he spends a lot of time hounding people and waiting for an opening.

To help him he enlists another even more rabid Langford groupie. Marsha (Bernhard in her breakthrough role) has an East Side townhouse and enough brass to galvanize Rupert after he and his demo tape get the brush-off from Langford and the show.

Langford's mistake is to give Rupert the slightest of openings in the belief that it will help him get rid of Marsha, his principal pest. Major craziness lies ahead in a ruthless satire of fame, and the stalkers and wannabes it inspires, that was ahead of its time.

KISSING JESSICA STEIN

Jennifer Westfeldt, Heather Juergensen, Scott Cohen,
Tovah Feldshuh

Directed by Charles Herman-Wurmfeld
2001. 96 minutes. R.

If you can get by its obeisance to Woody Allen, this small comedy is diverting fun. A copy editor at a New York magazine, Jessica (Westfeldt) is forever correcting grammar and showing off her verbal dexterity. On the romantic front, she has struck out any number of times but still scours the personal ads for the right kind of partner. An ad with a Rilke quote appeals and leads her to Helen (Juergensen), an appealing downtown art dealer who knows nothing of Rilke but is after sex, a good time and about anything that's new.

A fluttery copy editor certainly falls into the new category for Helen, who is amazed that she finds herself attracted to someone like the flighty, skittish Jessica, who is still somewhat beholden to her hand-wringing mother.

The movie is at its best when the two are apart and Helen gets to be more of a character on her own. A slinky sexual beast of prey, Helen stays cool and amused when she can't coax Jessica into the earliest stages of foreplay. Now we have a sitcom. Will Jessica's boss and ex-boyfriend learn about her new partner? Will Helen ever kiss Jessica Stein?

KISS ME DEADLY

Ralph Meeker, Cloris Leachman, Paul Stewart, Gaby Rodgers, Maxine Cooper, Albert Dekker

Directed by Robert Aldrich
1955. 106 minutes.

Aldrich's noir classic not only gave us the best Mike Hammer ever (Meeker) but was banned in certain areas of the country. It riled a congressional subcommittee and wound up with its own little nuclear detonation, an upsetting way to conclude matters at the height of the cold war.

The movie had its problems from the start. Everybody is a rat in this film, which gave audiences little to grab on to in the way of a hero or even someone to like. Hammer, Mickey Spillane's detective, is as brutal and venal as the characters who knock him out and push him and his car off a cliff to get the case under way.

Bouncing right back, Hammer gets to the gangster responsible but quickly realizes that there are powers behind the scenes. Then his favorite mechanic has a car dropped on him, and his secretary (Cooper) is kidnapped. Hammer pounds on a lot of people. A key in the body of a dead woman (Leachman) leads to a house at the beach and a box that glows green with radioactive material.

The idea of greedy, gouging lowlifes (and none lower than Hammer) brawling over stuff that could destroy civilization upset people, as did the film's violence and cynicism. Senator Estes Kefauver, head of a subcommittee investigating juvenile delinquency, declared that the movie could corrupt youth.

KITCHEN STORIES

Tomas Norström, Joachim Calmeyer, Reine Brynolfsson

Directed by Brent Hamer
2004. 92 minutes. Swedish and Norwegian with
English subtitles. No rating.

Hamer deserves plaudits first for coming up with a charmingly original idea and then for taking the highly constricted world the story requires and infusing it with entrancing visual flair and a keen feel for the drily comical craziness that can pop up in an atmosphere of austere control.

In the 1950's, Folke (Norström), an expert from Sweden's Home Research Institute, stations himself in the home of a bizarre Norwegian codger named Isak (Calmeyer). The institute has taken upon itself to study the habits of bachelors like Isak in the hope of designing better kitchens. So, Folke sets up a chair on tall legs (not unlike perches used by tennis umpires) in Isak's kitchen and starts to observe.

Isak volunteered for this but quickly feels prevailed upon as the researcher, who is as bizarre as he is, stares down in clinical detachment. At one point Isak notes that the Swedes also just sat and observed during World War II. At other times he crawls into his attic and peeps down to observe the observer.

Eventually relations between the two thaw enough to let in a bit of Chaplinesque pathos. Folke buys Isak a birthday cake, and Isak lets Folke listen to radio signals coming through silver fillings in his teeth. The stoic freakishness is involving because the film is so fastidious, with Hamer's skill and discipline seeming to grow out of a hilariously demented brand of obsessive-compulsive disorder.

L.A. CONFIDENTIAL

Russell Crowe, Kim Basinger, Kevin Spacey, Guy Pearce,
James Cromwell, Danny DeVito

Directed by Curtis Hanson
1997. 138 minutes. R.

In the tradition of *Chinatown* and other great L.A. film
noir, Hanson creates a superb adaptation of James Ell-
roy's atmospheric, noirish mystery novel. Treachery skulks
among the palms in 1950's Los Angeles, glamorous,
corrupt and brutal. In his tabloid rag, *Hush-Hush,* the
columnist Sid Hudgens (DeVito) gathers every scrap of
"sinnuendo" and lays a lurid trail of mobsters, drugs and
whores made up to look like movie stars. The cops are as
brutal as the thugs in this milieu, and that goes for Bud
White (Crowe), who thinks nothing of beating up a wife
abuser and calling it justice.

Bud shows his tender side when he falls for the call girl,
Lynn Bracken (Basinger, who won an Oscar for the role), a
blond vision in white satin dressed and made up to let
clients fantasize that they are with Veronica Lake. Bud's viciously ambitious partner and rival, Ed Exley (Pearce), plays
by the book. And Jack Vincennes (Spacey), L.A.'s detective of
detectives at the moment, basks in his celebrity as a consultant to a *Dragnet*-style TV show.

Eventually, the films gets down to a case: a massacre
at a coffee shop called the Nite Owl. But it's the movie's
breathtaking atmospherics and stylishness, and its acting
strength, that bring fresh life to the genre.

LANTANA

Anthony LaPaglia, Geoffrey Rush, Barbara Hershey, Kerry Armstrong, Rachael Blake, Peter Phelps

Directed by Ray Lawrence
2001. 120 minutes. R.

Named for a delicate-looking Australian plant with a spiky interior, Ray Lawrence's film takes up prickly matters involving marriage, chance acquaintanceship and the difficult bond between therapist and patient.

At first we are confronted with what looks like a murder mystery. Though violence is never far from the surface, the real questions involve the hurt and puzzlement of everyday life. At the center is the bulky, dour Leon (LaPaglia), a Sydney police detective who has had much of the life drained out of him by middle age.

Beset by alternating rages and bouts of self-pity, Leon tries to jump-start some feelings through a fling with Jane (Blake). To ease her own dissatisfactions, his wife, Sonja (Armstrong), is in therapy with Valerie (Hershey). Valerie's own troubles center on her conviction that her husband (Rush), a law professor, is having an affair with a young gay man (Phelps). For his part, the professor is unable to emerge from the trauma caused by the death of their child.

If all this suggests soap opera, be assured that nothing is glib, easy or formulaic in Lawrence's astonishingly well-acted film. In pretending to be something like a detective story (one of the women appears to have been murdered) but refusing the logical conventions of the genre, *Lantana* keeps complexity and coherence in balance as it delves into the paradoxes of contemporary marriage.

LAST NIGHT

Don McKellar, Sandra Oh, Callum Keith Rennie, Sarah Polley, David Cronenberg

Directed by Don McKellar
1998. 95 minutes. R.

In McKellar's first film, set in Toronto, it is indeed the end of the world. At the stroke of midnight (it also happens to be New Year's Eve), everybody on the planet will cease to be. But don't expect Bruce Willis striding on for an apocalyptic comeuppance. It's not that people don't care; they just seem to take it in remarkably good stride.

We never learn the nature of the impending threat, which doesn't matter. Aside from some rioting in the streets, people are in a generally sanguine mood as they concentrate on the things that matter at such a time. Most are trying to be together with loved ones as the film turns its focus on two people who will fail in that quest and are left with each other at the end.

Rita (Oh) is desperately trying to contact her husband (Cronenberg). Young Patrick (McKellar), despondent over the recent death of a woman he loved, doesn't want to spend his last moments with his parents, so he spends the time helping Rita try to find a ride home.

As they wander, they come together in achingly intense fashion, at one point spilling their secrets to each other. The amazing thing about this understated, beautifully handled situation is that we become ardently involved.

LAST ORDERS

Michael Caine, Tom Courtenay, David Hemmings, Bob Hoskins, Helen Mirren, Ray Winstone

Directed by Fred Schepisi
2001. 109 minutes. R.

Schepisi relies on his elegant, unassuming visual sense and his instinctive feel for actors in his adaptation of Graham Swift's novel, a Booker Prize winner, which refracts history, place and social class through the smoky filters of dialect, consciousness and memory.

Narrative is subordinate to character and atmosphere as four working-class Englishmen escort the ashes of their friend, an East London butcher named Jack (Caine), to the seaside resort where he wants them scattered.

Twinkling with mischief even on his deathbed, Jack bears the brunt of choices made in life, as evidenced on this occasion by the fact that his wife, Amy (Mirren), chooses to be elsewhere. Accompanying the urn are a greengrocer, an undertaker and a racetrack tout, as well as Jack's grown son, Vince (Winstone), a car dealer who has supplied the Mercedes-Benz.

Courtenay, Hemmings and Hoskins are splendidly natural as the urn bearers. Through flashbacks we gradually become acquainted with rituals of work and family. A few secrets are uncovered, and some old grudges resurface as a deft portrait of a small, vital world slowly comes into focus.

THE LAST SEDUCTION

*Linda Fiorentino, Peter Berg, Bill Pullman, J. T. Walsh,
Bill Nunn*

Directed by John Dahl
1994. 110 minutes. R.

As a predator, Bridget Gregory (Fiorentino) has it all: hot, slinky looks and manner that say sex, rough and now; an exterior like armor plate (interior, too); a vicious streak of commendable depth; total disregard for any human other than herself; pure willingness to destroy anybody in her path.

On emerging from the shower, her husband, Clay (Pullman), discovers that she has walked off with all $700,000 from a drug deal he engineered. Clay isn't the nicest person either, but does he deserve to be left standing there with a towel around his middle?

To lie low for a bit and avoid the investigator (Nunn) she knows Clay will send after her, Bridget slides into little Beston, New York, near Buffalo. There she snares a man in seconds. In addition to having Bridget against a chain link fence, Mike Swale (Berg) makes the mistake of falling in love.

Mike becomes a pawn in Bridget's little murder scheme. We know she'll be the last man standing, and leave in the limo, too.

LATE MARRIAGE

*Lior Louie Ashkenazi, Ronit Elkabetz, Moni Moshonov, Lili
Koshashvili, Sapir Kugman*

Directed by Dover Koshashvili
2001. 102 minutes. Georgian and Hebrew with English
subtitles. No rating.

When it comes to being pushed around by your
mother, 31-year-old Zaza (Ashkenazi) has it as hard
as anyone else in Koshashvili's harshly funny comedy. A
handsome bachelor and graduate student in Tel Aviv,
Zaza belongs to a tradition-bound family of immigrants
who have moved to Israel from Soviet Georgia. As is made
clear by his mama, Lily (Lili Koshashvili, the director's
mother), anyone who hasn't married and started producing children by age 30 is a disgrace to his family.

Furthermore, tradition dictates that any wife he
chooses be younger and a virgin, and that until the right
bride emerges, the family has a perfect right to intrude in
Zaza's affairs. As much as that distresses him, he knows
this and accepts it.

So who's the lucky girl? Zaza's mother and father (who
at one point spits in Zaza's face for not fulfilling his duties
as a man) choose an eligible and arrogant 17-year-old
who's as much to his disliking as all the other prospects
he has rejected.

Yes, Zaza does have the right to reject, and when he
does (and for a very good reason), nothing is left for the
family but to yell insults and even death threats. It may
not be a pretty sight, but it's expectable behavior in a
powerful and very bitter comedy.

L'AUBERGE ESPAGNOLE

*Romain Duris, Judith Godrèche, Audrey Tautou,
Cécile De France, Kelly Reilly*

Directed by Cédric Klapisch
2002. 122 minutes. French with English subtitles. No
rating.

Klapisch's shaggy, likable film throws together an assortment of young Europeans into a sort of continental tossed salad.

When Xavier (Duris), a not altogether likable Parisian, hears that a mastery of Spanish economic policy will earn him a good job, he enrolls in an exchange program in Barcelona, where he takes up with an extended household of similar souls in a kind of *Real World Catalonia*.

Both their apartment and the film become cheery metaphors for the new transnational European identity. Xavier becomes involved with the wife (Godrèche) of a young French neurologist, and there is a Danish guy, his Spanish girlfriend and an Italian stoner. An Englishwoman (Reilly) is a bit standoffish.

Xavier is their natural leader. A Belgian lesbian named Isabelle (De France) teaches him how to seduce the neurologist's wife, but Xavier hankers more after Isabelle. "I wish you were a woman," she says to him.

Boyfriends and girlfriends from back home continually drop in on the group, among them Xavier's not very likable girlfriend, Martine (Tautou). In the end, Xavier gets his job with the European Union, but bureaucracy seems tame indeed compared to the pleasantly chaotic freedom he experienced in Barcelona.

LAUREL CANYON

Frances McDormand, Christian Bale, Kate Beckinsale,
Natascha McElhone, Alessandro Nivola

Directed by Lisa Cholodenko
2002. 103 minutes. R.

holodenko's film shows a good eye for upscale bohemian subcultures by giving us the kind of woman
we don't encounter much. The record producer Jane Bentley (McDormand) is a pot-smoking, free-loving throwback
to the 70's who hangs out at her big house and splashes
around the pool with Ian (Nivola), the lead singer of a
British band, who is a decade and half younger than
she is.

A together roustabout of a woman, Jane makes no
apologies for threesomes and other sexual romps organized by Ian. Smart, talented and rich, she can also be arrogant and insensitive. Such a person hasn't been the best
mother, and when her grown son, Sam (Bale), comes to
stay, old wounds are about to open.

Sam arrives with his fiancée, Alex (Beckinsale). Gradu-
ates of Harvard Medical School, they need a place for the
summer and expected Jane to have vacated the house.
But Jane's plans have changed, as they often do, and now
they find themselves tossed in with her and the band in
one roiling household.

Mother and son clash and feel each other out. The
straitlaced Alex looks askance at the frolicking but later is
seduced enough by the loose life to come very close to
jumping in. But where she and Sam are concerned, it's
now the square younger generation that disapproves of
their cavorting elders.

THE LAWLESS HEART

Bill Nighy, Douglas Henshall, Tom Hollander, Clémentine Célarié, Sukie Smith, Josephine Butler

Directed by Tom Hunsinger and Neil Hunter
2001. 86 minutes. R.

Hunsinger and Hunter use scrambled, nonlinear chronology to tell three stories that play off one another to capture some of the essential strangeness of life.

It begins at a funeral of someone we never learn much about, a restaurant owner named Stuart who drowned in a boating accident off the Isle of Man. Then three sections of the film pick up with three main characters: Stuart's morose brother-in-law (Nighy); Stuart's lover, a transplanted Londoner (Hollander); and Stuart's long-lost buddy (Henshall).

Who knows what, if anything, their ties to Stuart have to do with it, but all three now find themselves subjected to unpredictable and unsettling desires involving new relationships and the challenges they present.

The film intricately braids connections among these people, leaving you with the impression that it could go on and on picking up loose threads and exploring stray implications. And you wish it would. By the grace and intelligence of the actors and unassuming cleverness of the filmmakers, these absolutely ordinary people turn out to be infinitely interesting.

LEAVING LAS VEGAS

Nicolas Cage, Elisabeth Shue, Valeria Golino, Julian Sands

Directed by Mike Figgis
1995. 112 minutes. R.

Figgis's searing little film watches transfixed as an engaging alcoholic named Ben Sanderson (Cage) proceeds through the final stages of drinking himself to death.

Ben has come to Vegas after burning his bridges in Los Angeles with boozily destructive behavior. He spends $29 for a hotel room (a towel is complimentary) and cheerily goes marketing for liquor. He also purchases the services of an improbably gorgeous hooker named Sera (Shue).

Back at the motel, two lonely, despairing souls plumb deep needs in each other, accompanied by Figgis's own haunting jazz score. At one point the film veers off into Sera's story, but it's best when riveted on Ben. Cage never delivers a bad performance, but he's never been better at capturing the riotous energy of a character driven by inner demons who is headed for destruction and knows it. It would all be a little too sordid without his irrepressible good humor.

THE LEGEND OF RITA

Bibiana Beglau, Martin Wuttke, Nadja Uhl, Harald Schrott, Alexander Beyer, Jenny Schily

Directed by Volker Schlöndorff
2000. 103 minutes. German with English subtitles. No rating.

The "legend" refers to the names Rita Vogt (Beglau) makes for herself during different stages in her life. In the 1970's, when she helped rob banks with a group modeled after the left-wing Red Army faction in West Germany, she was the embodiment of revolutionary glamour. But after she kills a Paris police officer, her group takes refuge in East Germany.

Most of the group moves on to Beirut, but Rita stays, takes a factory job and develops an enthusiasm for harsh East German life. No one really believes her story that she fled the west after the deaths of her parents. (Who would come to a place like this?) But Beglau is so intuitive and charismatic as an actress and has such a genuine capacity for fraternity that it is entirely believable when Rita embraces a new life and wins a certificate for "exemplary socialist labor."

After the Berlin Wall comes down, she still champions the cause and berates her acquaintances for giving up so easily on a noble experiment.

Schlöndorff, best known for *The Tin Drum*, is less interested in scoring moral points than in exploring the feeling and logic of intense political commitment. Here he returns to the ethically complex and clear-sighted filmmaking of his strongest work.

LIBERTY HEIGHTS

Adrien Brody, Ben Foster, Bebe Neuwirth, Joe Mantegna, Orlando Jones, Carolyn Murphy, Rebekah Johnson

Directed by Barry Levinson
1999. 127 minutes. R.

Diner is Levinson's most famous Baltimore film, but in one of the two others listed in this book (see *Tin Men*, page 414), Levinson tells what it was like to grow up Jewish there in the 1950's, when teenage pop culture was about to engulf the country.

Ben (Foster), a high school student, and his slightly older brother, Van (Brody), are breaking out of their tight Jewish enclave and starting to circulate in Gentile precincts, where a sign at a country club still reads NO JEWS, DOGS OR COLOREDS.

Brash and lively, Ben leads his pals into hostile territory, so to speak, at a party swarming with bully boys eager to bang around Jewish kids. At the same affair, the smoother Van falls for a cool blond dream girl (Murphy), the girlfriend of a boy from the richest family in the city.

Ben's rebellious explorations go further. At Halloween he dresses up like Hitler just to see the horrified reaction. His mother (Neuwirth) is a lovingly strict conservative, his father (Mantegna) a wise model parent who runs a burlesque hall and a numbers operation on the side.

In 50's Baltimore, blacks had a harder time than Jews. Ben falls into a gentle relationship with a black classmate (Johnson) and discovers soul music at a James Brown concert.

And in a film of leisurely paced vignettes and nice comic touches, Van is puzzled by an elegant WASP manor. Couldn't they afford Formica tables and wall-to-wall carpeting?

L.I.E.

Brian Cox, Paul Dano, Billy Kay, Bruce Altman

Directed by Michael Cuesta
2001. 97 minutes. NC-17.

Cuesta's film is named for the Long Island Expressway, famously referred to as the world's longest parking lot but in this case as the road that took the lives of the singer-songwriter Harry Chapin, the filmmaker Alan J. Pakula and the mother of the movie's troubled teenager, Howie Blitzer (Dano).

Howie, a denizen of the town of Dix Hills, in Suffolk County, is on his own after his father (Altman) is convicted in a shady construction scheme and lands in jail. Howie aspires to be a writer, and a guileless curiosity could serve him in that pursuit. Meanwhile, he and his pal Gary (Kay) dream of going to California, and, for kicks, they break into houses.

That leads to trouble with an ex-Marine and pederast called Big John (Cox), who tracks Howie down and catches him with pistols stolen from his basement. Big John isn't one for frontal assaults. He's more inclined to silky approaches, reinforced by the unmistakable impression that things could quickly turn ugly in the event of frustration. He offers Howie a choice between arrest and friendship.

Howie decides on the latter, but he is unsure of what friendship means. After his father is arrested, Howie moves in with Big John. He presumes that sex is part of the bargain, but Big John assures him he is wrong. We aren't so sure.

While we never forget that Big John is devoted to preying on little boys, his depravity does have a curdled tenderness. Cox has mastered every facet of the man, while Cuesta explores the queasy ambiguities of the relationship with an impressively delicate touch.

LIFT

Kerry Washington, Lonette McKee, Eugene Byrd, Todd Williams, Sticky Fingaz

Directed by DeMane Davis and Khari Streeter
2001. 85 minutes. No rating.

A young woman with brains and taste, Niecy (Washington) does a high-wire act between her Boston inner-city neighborhood and Kennedy's, the high-end department store where she works. Niecy favors the high-style look, which can't always be accommodated by her employee discount. So she employs the five-fingered price drop.

Kelly steals a lot of clothes and stuff, and what she doesn't keep she sells. Davis and Streeter's film loads itself with many subplots involving shootings, robberies and a pregnancy, but at bottom the directors have taken on a tricky subject: the scourge of black youth's fashion obsession.

The film teems with life, with the cinematographer David Phillips shifting from a run-and-gun style for the foot-chase scenes to a slower pace that allows more care with Niecy and the other characters.

Niecy is trying to cope with her self-involved mother (McKee) and keep a relationship going with a boyfriend (Byrd) who has few prospects. But her vision never leaves the neighborhood. What makes the film seem so real is its focus on the small-mindedness of young African-Americans who believe that the world begins and ends within a few square blocks.

LIKE WATER FOR CHOCOLATE

Lumi Cavazos, Marco Leonardi, Regina Torné, Mario Iván Martínez, Yareli Arizmendi

Directed by Alfonso Arau
1992. 123 minutes. R.

When Tita (Cavazos) pricks her fingers on thorns and turns a meal of quails cooked in rose-petal sauce into something "voluptuously, ardently fragrant and utterly sensual," Arau's delightful film about three Mexican daughters and their willful mother turns food into the physical embodiment of desire. One sister rushes to a shower to cool off.

The youngest of the three, Tita gave Mama Elena (Torné) such a hard time during birth that the severe and sometimes histrionic Elena sentences the girl to serve her forever. That means Tita can never marry, which becomes a problem when she falls in love with Pedro (Leonardi). Or, to put this in food terms: When Tita felt his gaze, "she understood exactly how raw dough must feel when it comes into contact with burning oil."

A sly, reticent young woman who nominally does what's expected of her, Tita subversively insinuates her magical touch with food to loosen repressive attitudes. The film's title refers to a method of boiling and reboiling water with cocoa until it becomes a sticky sweet chocolate, and that describes Tita's feelings when she's around Pedro.

So that they can remain near each other, he agrees to marry another of the sisters. But "you can't just exchange tacos for enchiladas!" a servant exclaims.

LILLIE

Francesca Annis, Anton Rodgers, Denis Lill, Peter Egan, Jennie Linden, Patrick Holt, Peggy Ann Wood

Directed by John Gorrie, Christopher Hodson and Tony Wharmby
1978. Thirteen 52-minute episodes. No rating.

Before there were supermodels, there were Professional Beauties, and Lillie Langtry was the dominant P.B. of the Edwardian era. This classic BBC mini-series tells the story of Lillie (Annis), the country girl who escaped Jersey, in the Channel Islands, in the 1870's to go to London. Married to a dullard of a husband, she became the lover of the Prince of Wales (only one of many, many beaus) and a dear friend of Oscar Wilde and James McNeill Whistler, all of whom have large roles in the series.

Her rise in society was not easy, but she was inventive. Too poor to compete with the rich fashion plates around her, at first she wore the same black dress to every ball, making it her signature. And her star power and ambition never deserted her. In her middle age, her days as a respected favorite of the prince behind her, she even toured the Old West with a traveling show. Annis is sympathetic and convincing at every stage as the series follows her from Lillie's teenage years to her uncomplaining old age.

With its period details and a plot that turns history into a delicious soap opera, *Lillie* feels like the template for so many later *Masterpiece Theater*–style confections, and it remains one of the best.

LIMBO

Mary Elizabeth Mastrantonio, David Strathairn, Vanessa Martinez, Kris Kristofferson, Casey Siemaszko

Directed by John Sayles
1999. 126 minutes. R.

Four Sayles films are listed in this book, and his entire oeuvre, or most of it, could easily have been included. Here the scene is Alaska, where, as in other Sayles films, rampant development tears up the landscape while beleaguered individuals cling to lives in turmoil.

In this Alaska, entire islands are stripped of timber except for fringes of trees kept to appear like virgin forest to passing tourist boats. In Juneau, the well-seasoned folksinger Donna De Angelo (Mastrantonio) works the lounges, recovers from yet another disaster of a relationship and works at being a mother to a resentful teenager named Noelle (Martinez), a budding writer of considerable talent.

Donna's new boyfriend is Joe Gastineau (Strathairn), and she may have picked right this time. A former fisherman, Joe combines quiet intelligence with gentle but tough masculinity. Of course, he has his albatross: many years earlier he was responsible for two deaths in a freak sailing accident.

These are a couple of aging, hard-bitten romantics looking for the natural life, and they find more than they bargained for when they and Noelle become stranded for weeks on a deserted island. Overcoming initial panic, they find an abandoned cabin and scrounge what food they can. It doesn't help that Joe's wayward brother, Bobby, has involved them with murderous drug dealers who now prowl the wilderness looking for them. In the cabin Noelle finds a diary written by a girl her age long ago. She and her family apparently went mad. What's in store for these three?

THE LIMEY

Terence Stamp, Peter Fonda, Luis Guzmán, Lesley Ann Warren, Barry Newman, Nicky Katt

Directed by Steven Soderbergh
1999. 89 minutes. R.

Soderbergh's bravura direction and Stamp's coolly lethal performance make this a standout thriller and tale of revenge. A tough Cockney fresh out of prison, the man known only as Wilson (Stamp) journeys to L.A. to investigate the death of his daughter, once the girlfriend of a record producer named Valentine (Fonda).

Valentine's pricey chief security man (Newman) and other operatives from the Los Angeles demimonde who colluded with Valentine in some drug dealings learn the hard way that Wilson means business. He is the kind of man you can stomp to within an inch of his life one minute, only to have him get up and blow you away the next.

With the help of a Mexican-American (Guzmán) who took acting classes with his daughter, Wilson determines that she was probably done away with after raising objections to Valentine's drug deals. His infiltration of Hollywood's lush upper reaches takes on panache when he tosses a security man off the lofty deck of Valentine's cliff-hugging showcase of a house, right in the middle of a party.

Later, Wilson survives a couple of hit men in a parking

garage. Realizing that there's a dangerous man on their trail, Valentine, Valentine's current girlfriend (Warren), his security chief and a retinue of heavily armed body guards in sport utility vehicles retreat warily up the Pacific Coast Highway toward Valentine's seaside retreat at the Big Sur.

The film has no heavy-duty point to make, but it is loaded with mood and texture.

LITTLE ODESSA

Tim Roth, Edward Furlong, Vanessa Redgrave, Maximilian Schell, Moira Kelly

Directed by James Gray
1994. 98 minutes. R.

A deeply touching and tragic film, not about a crime family but about a family and crime. Roth is utterly convincing as Joshua Shapira, a hit man with the Russian mafia, whose assignment takes him back to the Russian Jewish community of Brighton Beach, in Brooklyn.

His father, Arkady (Schell), banished him from the neighborhood years before. Now, when Joshua tries to visit his terminally ill mother (Redgrave), Arkady calls him a murderer and throws him out of the house.

When Joshua first arrives, he checks in to a hotel and puts himself in plain view. He encounters an old girlfriend (Kelly) and they go to the movies. At Nathan's he meets his younger brother, Reuben (Furlong), and they resume a bond they both know is temporary.

Later, when he manages to see his mother, she holds out hope. "I know you can change," she says. "You don't believe it, but I know you can." That's not too likely, but there's no question that a need for emotional contact has brought Joshua back to Little Odessa.

Joshua himself becomes the hunted, a target of killers. "Where you gonna go?" Reuben asks. "We're the Jews, we wander," Joshua answers.

This is Gray's first film, made when he was 25. (His second, *The Yards,* page 469, also deals with a family pulled apart.) Its strengths come from its straightforward tone and a powerful, subdued performance by Roth.

LITTLE WOMEN

Winona Ryder, Trini Alvarado, Claire Danes, Kirsten Dunst, Susan Sarandon, Christian Bale, Eric Stoltz

Directed by Gillian Armstrong
1994. 115 minutes. PG.

A potent film virtually erupts with vitality as the March daughters come of age in Concord, Massachusetts, during the Civil War. In that era people created their own diversions, and if the Marches, headed by the noble matriarch called Marmee (Sarandon), weren't the most affluent in town, they must have been among the richest in their invention of amusements.

In those days they read and wrote—"Your spelling is atrocious; your Latin is absurd," says Jo March (Ryder) to her youngest sister, Amy (Dunst)—and staged amateur theatricals in the attic. The girls bicker and grow and suffer when one of them, Beth (Danes), dies of rheumatic fever. And, of course, they align themselves romantically, with the handsome, charming boy next door (Bale) and his bounding tutor (Stoltz) as possibilities.

On the DVD a talented cast of the 1990's talks about what the film is about: being a good person, following your heart, learning about yourself, doing the right thing. In the 1860's girls weren't allowed to be adolescents, but here they are.

LIVE FLESH

Liberto Rabal, Javier Bardem, Francesca Neri, Ángela Molina, José Sancho

Directed by Pedro Almodóvar
1997. 103 minutes. Spanish with English subtitles. R.

As a sign of things to come in his sensitive *All About My Mother* (page 5), Almodóvar shows an interest in motives and emotions in a stylish, sexy film noir alive with bold, sunny colors.

A quick sexual encounter with a wild Italian blonde, Elena (Neri), leaves the handsome, naïve young Victor (Rabal) yearning for more. But on their second meeting he finds her more interested in drugs than in a sexual neophyte like himself. An altercation between the two leads to police intervention and a shooting that leaves a detective named David (Bardem) gravely wounded.

Years later, while still in jail for the shooting, Victor sees David playing basketball on television as a wheelchair athlete. Cheering him on is his demure, brown-haired wife, Elena. Unjustly convicted, Victor seeks revenge, or at least to clarify what really happened that night, and he embarks on a regimen of reprisal that includes intensive sexual training with the wife (Molina) of David's former partner, Sancho (Sancho), who was also involved in the fracas that fateful night.

Victor's goal is still to make love to Elena, and Almodóvar, ever the master in matters of the flesh, doesn't deprive them of a long, languorous time together. But there is plenty of other deliciously intricate gamesmanship among characters depicted with sharp, lively precision.

LOLITA

Jeremy Irons, Dominique Swain, Melanie Griffith,
Frank Langella

Directed by Adrian Lyne
1997. 137 minutes. No rating.

———————————————————————————————

Because of money and fear of backlash over its ever-explosive subject, Lyne's entrancing adaptation of Vladimir Nabokov's novel never reached the big screen but went straight to the cable channel Showtime instead. Irons is Humbert Humbert, passionately in love with the 12-year-old nymphet Lolita (Swain).

"There are in his story depths of passion and suffering, patterns of tenderness and distress, that cannot be dismissed by his judges," Nabokov wrote in his own screenplay of the relatively wooden original 1962 film, and Lyne's film gives Humbert his own lyrical voice, from his own sad, tortured perspective. Swain makes a convincing Lolita, all saucy, teasing temptation, and Griffith is also convincing as her annoying widowed mother, Charlotte, from whom Humbert rents a room in 1947 and whom he eventually marries in order to remain close to the girl.

But this is Irons's film, and he gives a great, fearless performance, his face registering the complexity of Humbert's inner life and his voice-overs, taken from the novel, resonating with Nabokov's poetry and Humbert's stricken conscience. It is an enormously seductive performance, but one whose seductions are never on the surface.

Humbert calls himself "an artist, a madman." Lyne's film echoes Nabokov's transforming vision: it turns Humbert's madness into art.

LONE STAR

Chris Cooper, Matthew McConaughey, Kris Kristofferson,
Elizabeth Peña, Miriam Colon, Frances McDormand

Directed by John Sayles
1996. 135 minutes. R.

Sayles reaches epic scale in his biggest and, many would argue, best film. Nominally, a couple of generations of Texas lawmen, corrupt and racist as they come, are on view, but on a larger scale this is a wonderfully complex, beautifully integrated tale of cultural, racial, economic and familial tension.

Sayles likes poking around burial grounds (as we also see in *Sunshine State*, page 388). Outside the little town of Frontera, on the Rio Grande, the remains of a nasty former sheriff, Charley Wade (Kristofferson), are unearthed, and the current sheriff, Sam Deeds (Cooper), investigates the crime.

Sam's father, a brutal, dominating character named Buddy (McConaughey), was Charley Wade's deputy and is now the prime suspect in his murder. In a finely orchestrated to-ing and fro-ing among dozens of characters and various time periods, cultures and eras come alive. Sam's rekindled romance with a teenage sweetheart named Pilar (Peña), broken up back then by racial attitudes on both sides, serves as a link to ideas about crossing borders and challenging the past.

In a long, contemplative film, a town emerges from the shadows.

THE LONG GOODBYE

Elliott Gould, Sterling Hayden, Nina Van Pallandt, Mark Rydell, Jim Bouton

Directed by Robert Altman
1973. 112 minutes. R.

reely adapted from Raymond Chandler's novel, Altman's film was his best since *M*A*S*H* and *McCabe and Mrs. Miller*. This Philip Marlowe (Gould), Chandler's detective, is a solemn, conscientious guy, who sleeps with his clothes on, rarely shaves and tries to interest his cranky yellow cat in a plate of old cottage cheese.

This is a sensitive Marlowe. In spite of a lot of evidence to the contrary, he continues to believe that not all relationships need be opportunistic or squalid. Mind you, this is before he helps a hood and pretty boy (Bouton) escape to Mexico after the murder of his wife, is charged with being an accessory to murder himself, and is roughed up by the associates of a syndicate boss (Rydell) who suspects him of stealing $350,000.

And he is invited to find the drunken novelist husband (Hayden) of a tall, beautiful, self-assured blonde (Van Pallandt).

Altman makes eloquent reference to Chandler by packing the screen with bizarre visual and aural detail. Gould's Marlowe is a rather solemn nut who acts as if he's lucky to have survived the upheavals of the 1960's. The screenplay, by Leigh Brackett (who collaborated with William Faulkner on the script for *The Big Sleep*), creates an original character and almost original story in a funny but serious and unique work.

LOOKING FOR RICHARD

Al Pacino, Alec Baldwin, Kevin Spacey, Estelle Parsons, Winona Ryder; interviews with Kevin Kline, Kenneth Branagh, Derek Jacobi, James Earl Jones, John Gielgud, Vanessa Redgrave

Directed by Al Pacino
1996. 111 minutes. PG-13.

That's William Shakespeare's Richard III, or Richie, as Pacino might call him in his rollicking, crazily energetic attempt to make one of the Bard's more complicated works accessible to the contemporary unwashed.

"Sucks," says one street interviewee when asked what he thinks of Shakespeare on the whole. But never mind. Pacino plunges into *Richard III* from several angles with breezy interviews with the likes of Branagh and Jacobi and wonderfully fresh bits of performance from the play by himself (as Richard), Baldwin, Spacey, Ryder and others.

This is Richard light and fast. Pacino never lets up explaining, joshing, posturing and acting the genial tutor. "So Richard figured, let me get rid of Clarence and then I'll figure out how to get rid of the kids," he says. Well, Richie might put it that way.

LOST IN LA MANCHA

A documentary written and directed by Keith Fulton and Louis Pepe
2002. 89 minutes. R.

This chronicle of a misbegotten, never-made film is more fascinating than most dramas that make it to the screen. In 2000 the director Terry Gilliam went to Spain intent on filming *The Man Who Killed Don Quixote*, a version of Cervantes's novel starring Johnny Depp as a contemporary man who lands in the past as Quixote's servant. Also in Madrid were the documentary makers Keith Fulton and Louis Pepe, whom Gilliam had invited to make a film about the making of the film.

To understate things drastically, the Gilliam movie didn't work out. A big chunk of production money fell through at the last minute. Torrential rains and fierce winds hit the desert locations during filming, turning the ground into mud and destroying equipment. The French comic actor Jean Rochefort, in the role of Quixote, had a chronic bad back and had to be lowered by harness onto his horse. Eventually unable even to sit on a horse—a real liability for a Quixote—he dropped out of the film altogether.

Even as his movie fell apart around him, Gilliam encouraged Fulton and Pepe to keep recording the debacle as it was happening, up to and including the point where the project was abandoned.

The documentary is both a study in movie-making and a vision of artistic ambition as it crashes into practical realities. As happened with other films, notably *The Adventures of Baron Munchausen*, Gilliam let his extravagant imagination run away with him, but he emerges as a magnetic filmmaker who meets the horrifying spectacle with grace and a certain amount of rueful gallows humor.

LOVELY & AMAZING

Catherine Keener, Brenda Blethyn, Emily Mortimer, Dermot Mulroney, Jake Gyllenhaal, Raven Goodwin, Clark Gregg, James Le Gros

Directed by Nicole Holofcener
2001. 91 minutes. R.

A divorced matriarch from hell (well, maybe that's an exaggeration), her two slightly bent grown daughters and her neurotic adopted daughter, age eight, are stirred into a sharp, smart comedy.

Afflicted by society's obsession with looks, these are people who go to great lengths to find fault with themselves. When the slender actress Elizabeth Marks (Mortimer), one of two sisters in their 30's, is rejected for a role, she has sex with the vain leading man (Mulroney), then poses nude and asks him for an assessment of her body. She's really worried about some flabbiness in her arms, and when he doesn't mention that particular flaw, she asks him. Right, arms too, he says.

The mother, Jane (Blethyn), is preparing to have liposuction ($10,000 and uninsured) to whittle 10 pounds of fat from her waist. When the procedure goes bad and Jane is stuck in the hospital, Elizabeth and her freaky sister Michelle (Keener) must take care of little Annie (Goodwin), whose biological mother was a crack addict but for the moment is the most stable of this crew.

Michelle designs cute handcrafts for gift shops, reacting explosively when her goods are rejected. Her husband, Bill (Gregg), becomes annoyed when she doesn't produce her share of income. Naturally the relationships of all these people aren't the healthiest, and gradually this begins to take its toll on Annie, who begins to act strangely in a film that goes nowhere but maintains a keen eye and ear for the nervous tics of contemporary society.

M

Peter Lorre, Otto Wernicke, Gustaf Gründgens, Theo Lingen

Directed by Fritz Lang
1931. 110 minutes.

Lang's first talkie was cautious with dialogue but bold in concept. Never emerging from dark shadows and gritty surroundings, it paved the way for one of the movies' favorite characters—the serial killer—and helped establish a much-called-upon format, the police procedural.

In Berlin, a child molester kills little girls while the police struggle to find him. Lorre is Hans Beckert, a killer who whistles a few bars from *Peer Gynt* before striking and begs the police to find him before he strikes again. His performance is often rated one of the best ever.

Wernicke is fine as Inspector Lohmann, who leads hamfisted law enforcement in response to a city frantic with fear. The tactic is to round up every prostitute, pimp and street denizen the cops can lay their hands on. That doesn't turn up Beckert, but it does rally criminal elements who figure they had better find Beckert themselves if they want to get back to business without the police on their backs.

After cornering him, they stage a trial, which ends up posing questions society should ask but probably won't. Is Beckert a candidate for execution or should he be given help?

MABOROSI

Makiko Esumi, Takashi Naitô, Tadanobu Asano, Gohki Kashiyama

Directed by Hirokazu Koreeda
1995. 110 minutes. Japanese with English subtitles. No rating.

Events transpire, of course, but essentially Koreeda's film is a pictorial tone poem of astonishing visual intensity and emotional depth.

Yumiko (Esumi) is living in Osaka with her husband, Ikuo (Naitô), a factory worker, and 3-month-old baby son when the police appear and tell her that Ikuo has been killed while riding his bicycle, apparently a suicide. Several years later she takes the train to Noto, a fishing village on the Sea of Japan, to marry a widower in an arranged marriage.

By the sea her emotional and spiritual state blends with the harsh weather and changing seasons. *Maborosi* conveys a different sense of reality from most films. Going beyond psychological explanations, it looks for a deeper design to Yumiko's life. Recurrent images acquire a poetic resonance that transcends story and characters to suggest the fateful patterns that many lives seem to take.

Made with only natural light, the film draws in viewers with one breathtaking shot after another as the camera draws back to contemplate Yumiko from afar. She is a detached, mournful figure, but the scenes seem to look through her eyes with a Zen-like quality that makes it feel as if you're actually standing in her shoes.

Maborosi (the title is the Japanese word for "mirage") ultimately implies that the longing for death is as unpredictable and sometimes as irresistible as the illusory light on the horizon drawing fishermen out to sea.

THE MADNESS OF KING GEORGE

Nigel Hawthorne, Helen Mirren, Ian Holm, Amanda Donohoe, Rupert Graves, Julian Wadham, Rupert Everett

Directed by Nicholas Hytner
1994. 107 minutes. No rating.

No one knew exactly what made King George III act the nutty way he did, but eventually it was thought to be a metabolic imbalance called porphyria. In any case, here we have a monarch, played absolutely over the top by Hawthorne, who has a chat with a pig and refuses to let pregnant women sit at court. "If everybody who's having a baby wants to sit down, next thing it'll everybody with gout," he says.

Alan Bennett adapted his play about a stormy reign in which the monarchy lost much of its authority to Parliament and England itself lost its American colonies ("the place we mustn't mention," as they're called in the film). By no means a stupid man, poor George struggles to hold on to sanity as those around him become increasingly alarmed at his strange behavior. Challenges arise from Prime Minister William Pitt (Wadham), members of Parliament and the king's own scheming son, the Prince of Wales, played by Everett with memorable flamboyance. Eventually it's left to George to get a grip, with the help of a physician (Holm), who effectively scares the king back to his senses.

Mirren makes a formidable queen who is patient with her husband's condition, even after he lunges at her lady-in-waiting. And Hytner, a prodigiously talented stage director, crafts a vigorous first film that mixes the ebullience of *Tom Jones* with the royal treachery of *The Lion in Winter* into a deft, beautifully acted historical drama.

THE MAGDALENE SISTERS

Anne-Marie Duff, Dorothy Duffy, Nora-Jane Noone, Eileen Walsh, Geraldine McEwan

Directed by Peter Mullan
2002. 119 minutes. R.

A grim, powerful feature film goes behind the scenes, as it were, of an infamous real-life labor camp run by the Sisters of the Magdalene. As expressed by its chief ogre, Sister Bridget (McEwan), the call went out across the impoverished, repressed Irish countryside: Bring us your unmarried young women who have engaged in premarital sex, or any other kind of unruly activity, for that matter.

Nothing like a few years of confinement to straighten out that kind of behavior. The labor was laundry, endless mountains of it to be washed by hand. Girls were ripped from their homes, 30,000 of them before the Magdalene camp and other laundries were closed in 1996.

In Mullan's film there are failed escapes, small rebellions, brutal punishments. Margaret (Duff) is imprisoned after being raped at a party and then accused of being the instigator. Rose (Duffy) has her newborn taken from her and is renamed Patricia. Another inmate was merely the object of adolescent male attention.

Sister Bridget, who weeps mawkishly over Ingrid Bergman's performance in *The Bells of St. Mary's*, is more religious fanatic than sadist in a film (winner of the top prize at the Venice Film Festival) that is both painful and fascinating.

MAGNOLIA

Tom Cruise, Jason Robards, Philip Seymour Hoffman, Philip Baker Hall, William H. Macy, Julianne Moore, John C. Reilly, Ricky Jay, Jeremy Blackman, Melora Walters

Directed by Paul Thomas Anderson
1999. 188 minutes. R.

Anderson's film tries to wrap up a half-dozen intersecting stories with an improbable conclusion of biblical proportions, but until that point he keeps all his narrative balls in the air with nimble dexterity.

Wild twists of fate entwine characters suffering from a kind of societal media poisoning that infects spirits and family connections. A powerful television mogul (Robards) lies dying of cancer, estranged from his son (Cruise), who is a powerful guru to disenfranchised men who can't figure what happened to their maleness. Another television figure (Hall), host of a popular kids' quiz show, is also dying of cancer and can't reconnect with a daughter (Walters) who hates him.

On the quiz show, a boy genius (Blackman) is waylaid by knowledge overload and his father's pressure, and a former quiz-show star (Macy) is frittering away the rest of his existence.

If all that sounds grim, Anderson is good at shaping little vignettes and intuitive storytelling. He also has great skill with actors. Cruise is especially good as a macho man headed for a fall, and there isn't a weak performance in the lot.

MANHUNTER

William Petersen, Brian Cox, Kim Greist, Joan Allen, Dennis Farina, Tom Noonan, Stephen Lang

Directed by Michael Mann
1986. 124 minutes. R.

Perhaps the best thing about Mann's vastly underrated predecessor to the Hannibal Lecter films, *The Silence of the Lambs* and *Hannibal,* is Noonan's performance, not as Lecter, who sits in a jail cell, but as the killer on the loose, the truly scary blond giant Francis Dollarhyde.

A shadow for all his size, Dollarhyde takes out entire families—mom, dad, kids, pets—hiding out in trees beforehand to spy on his victims. F.B.I. agent Will Graham (Petersen) thought he was through chasing serial killers when he collared Lecter (Cox), but he's brought back to hunt the new menace.

It drives Graham almost crazy to think so, but it's said that he's so effective with serial killers because he thinks like one himself. Lecter taunts him with that theory on Graham's visits to his cell, where he's sequestered like a rare animal. "You caught me because we're just alike," he tells Graham.

Graham asks Lecter (spelled Lektor in this film) for some help, but the old master is rooting for Dollarhyde and communicates with him by code. The F.B.I. suggests drugging Lecter to extract information, but Graham says they tried that before and all they got out of him was a recipe for potato chips.

THE MAN IN THE MOON

Sam Waterston, Tess Harper, Gail Strickland, Reese Witherspoon, Jason London, Emily Warfield

Directed by Robert Mulligan
1991. 99 minutes. PG-13.

Mulligan (*To Kill a Mockingbird; Summer of '42; The Other*) doesn't allow fake emotion into his films, and here he lets a story about two young sisters in a small town in the 1950's unfold with a restrained, quiet grace.

The coltish Dani Trant (Witherspoon) has turned 14, a good age to develop a heavy crush on Court Foster (London), 17, who has just moved to town with his mother. Court thinks Dani may be a little young for that sort of thing, but he goes along until he meets Dani's older sister, Maureen (Warfield).

The Trants are a family in various stages of development, from a toddler sister to a pregnant mother (Harper) and a stern, decent father (Waterston) who, like the rest of them, longs for a boy but keeps loving watch over his girls.

Mulligan and his screenwriter, Jenny Wingfield, also steer clear of the precocious sexual ingredient in most movies about teenagers. These kids really remain relative innocents in a film that lets itself get boxed in to an inappropriately wrenching climactic incident but otherwise stays on course as a solid story about real, substantial people.

THE MAN ON THE TRAIN

Jean Rochefort, Johnny Hallyday, Pascal Parmentier

Directed by Patrice Leconte
2002. 90 minutes. R.

A spare comic melodrama presents an intriguing odd couple: a loquacious retired schoolteacher of the old school named Manesquier (Rochefort) and a gruff, virtually silent bank robber named Milan (Hallyday, the former French rock star).

Arriving in a scruffy French town to rob the bank, the baleful Milan needs a place to stay. Subject to headaches, he also needs a glass of water to dissolve his aspirin. In the town square, he runs into Manesquier, who invites him into his large, declining house and later offers him a bed because the local hotel is closed for the winter.

At first Milan sits stonily silent among the books and papers and periodicals strewn and piled around the place while Manesquier prattles on about life and the disappointments of same. Eventually, though, Milan begins to open up a little, revealing a keen intelligence and a fair amount of sensitivity.

As Manesquier talks on and on, Milan takes it all in with a dry tolerance. The older man, who faces heart surgery, is acutely aware of having squandered his chances for adventure and new experiences. To him Milan represents the existential life he's never experienced.

Milan just needs to hook up with his accomplices and get the bank job done. Manesquier offers him money to back out of the robbery, but Milan refuses. By now the two have formed a bond, and Leconte moves his camera back and forth between them, confident that they can make space for each other.

THE MAN WITHOUT A PAST

Markku Peltola, Kati Outinen, Juhani Niemelä, Kaija Pakarinen, Sakari Kuosmanen

Directed by Aki Kaurismäki
2002. 97 minutes. Finnish with English subtitles. No rating.

Look on the bright side. A metalworker (Peltola) is brutally mugged and left for dead on a park bench. Staggering out of a hospital, he collapses and wakes up without his money and his shoes and with no recollection of his previous life.

But that can be liberating. Wearing a soulful, deadpan expression on a handsome face weathered by hardship, the man (he has no name) finds a new life on the margins of society. He lives in an abandoned shipping container, makes friends among the homeless and the destitute and finds love with a melancholy Salvation Army worker and rock 'n' roll fanatic (Outinen). Despite their forlorn impassivity, the characters reveal their quirks and passions.

Unlike his protagonist, Kaurismäki is much taken with the past, especially old music and even older movies. In the film, the man's taste in music has survived his injury, and he turns the Salvation Army band into a swinging combo. When he rescues an old jukebox from a junk pile, the first song it plays is "That Crawlin' Baby Blues," by Blind Lemon Jefferson.

Similarly, *The Man Without a Past* has a sly silliness that recalls Preston Sturges and a resilience in hard times that suggests Charlie Chaplin without the sentimentality. And like the great films of the 1930's and early 40's, this one is at once artful and unpretentious, sophisticated and completely accessible.

MARIA FULL OF GRACE

*Catalina Sandino Moreno, Yenny Paola Vega, Guilied
Lopez, Orlando Tobon, John Álex Toro, Jaime Osorio Gómez*

Directed by Joshua Marston
2004. 101 minutes. Spanish with English subtitles. R.

Marston's harrowing film follows 17-year-old Maria (Moreno) on a plunge from a dead-end job in a Colombian flower factory into her desperate turn as a "mule," or runner, for a drug cartel smuggling heroin into the United States.

A rural girl from a poverty-stricken village, Maria finds herself pregnant by her deadbeat boyfriend and obliged to turn her minuscule salary over to her mother, grandmother and sister.

A charming cartel recruiter on a motorcycle (Toro) gathers many Marias and turns them over to his ominously soothing boss (Gómez). In a much-publicized procedure, couriers swallow 62 pellets of heroin, to be voided at a New Jersey hotel, where Maria and two friends (Vega and Lopez) are dosed with laxatives and held prisoner. If the pellets break, they will die of an overdose. If they run, they will be killed.

Maria's flight from Bogotá is one of the tensest journeys ever filmed. There are some cruel surprises ahead in a film that sustains an astonishing documentarylike authenticity but indulges in no moralizing or cheap melodrama. For her part, Moreno's Maria fends for herself with a fierce determination and an ingenuity that helps her bend with the circumstances but never lose her sense of decency and morality.

MARRIED TO THE MOB

Michelle Pfeiffer, Alec Baldwin, Dean Stockwell, Matthew Modine, Mercedes Ruehl, Joan Cusack, Ellen Foley, O-Lan Jones, Anthony J. Nici

Directed by Jonathan Demme
1988. 103 minutes. R.

Angela DeMarco (Pfeiffer) has a rough time as a mob wife in Demme's highly entertaining screwball farce. Other mobsters' mates (Ruehl, Cusack, Jones, Foley) insist on being friends "whether she likes it or not." Her husband, Frank (Baldwin), a hit man, is a major philanderer; her son, Anthony (Nici), runs a three-card-monte game in the backyard; and everything she and Frank own, as she puts it, "fell off the back of a truck."

When Frank is caught sporting with a waitress who in turn is cavorting with Frank's boss and family don, Tony the Tiger (Stockwell), he is blown away. Class act that he is, Tony waits until Frank's funeral to start hitting on the lovely Angela while F.B.I. cameras click away.

Tony's attentions are wearing on Angela, and she moves to the Lower East Side of Manhattan and becomes a beautician at an establishment called Hello Gorgeous. Tony follows, and so does the F.B.I., which assumes that Angela is involved with the mobster. Modine is engaging as a bemused agent sent to enlist Angela's help, but he and Pfeiffer strike no romantic sparks.

Instead, Demme's fine eye for garish detail makes the film, as do Ruehl and the other mob wives and certainly Stockwell's Tony the Tiger.

MATCHSTICK MEN

Nicolas Cage, Sam Rockwell, Alison Lohman, Bruce Altman, Bruce McGill

Directed by Ridley Scott
2003. 116 minutes. PG-13.

Scott is known primarily for splendid-looking action sagas like *Gladiator* and *Blackhawk Down* (see also *The Duellists,* page 120), but here he has a good degree of success at a smaller, quieter hybrid of a film (no less good-looking, by the way) that might be called "grifter flummoxed by teenager."

At the core is Roy Waller (Cage), an obsessive-compulsive Los Angeles con man who is so uncompromisingly neat and clean that a tendril of lint on the carpet is cause for intense vacuuming. At home Roy cowers behind drawn blinds expecting dirt attacks and other disorderly eruptions, but on the job (he prefers to be called a con artist) he is all suave confidence as he bilks people out of thousands over the phone and occasionally in person as an immaculate businessman.

The shaggy Rockwell is Frankie, Roy's predictably sloppy partner and setup man, and if Frankie doesn't get on the nerves enough, Roy's new shrink (Altman) suggests that he meet his teenage daughter, Angela (Lohman), whom Roy has never seen.

Roy and an anarchic teenager aren't a good match on either the domestic or the emotional front, particularly as Roy and Frankie embark on a complicated hustle. But Angela is an engaging kid, and soon Roy is instructing her in the ways of the scam.

MATILDA

Danny DeVito, Rhea Perlman, Mara Wilson, Pam Ferris,
Embeth Davidtz, Paul Reubens

Directed by Danny DeVito
1996. 102 minutes. PG.

DeVito adapts Roald Dahl's story about a bright little girl born to a mother and father seemingly of another species. Matilda (Wilson) actually reads books, much to the distress of her crass, acquisitive parents, Harry and Zinnia Wormwood (DeVito and Perlman).

Harry, a crooked used-car dealer, doesn't even want Matilda to go to school. "Who'd be here to sign for packages?" he says. The elder Wormwoods don't like anything about their offspring, who refuses to park herself in front of the television.

Matilda's troubles multiply at school, where she falls under the tutelage of Agatha Trunchbull (Ferris), a harridan in Army boots. Trunchbull intimidates all the kids (a cute bunch), and Matilda becomes the object of a tug-of-war between her and Miss Honey (Davidtz), a teacher sweet of temperament.

The school scene isn't quite as evocative as the home front, where Matilda begins to strike back at her loutish parents with slick dirty tricks in a film with playful flamboyance and dark verve.

MEMENTO

Guy Pearce, Carrie-Anne Moss, Joe Pantoliano, Mark Boone, Jr., Stephen Tobolowsky, Jorja Fox, Harriet Harris

Directed by Christopher Nolan
2001. 113 minutes. R.

Nolan established his reputation in the forefront of daring new filmmakers with this movie that runs backward in time, yet somehow keeps the viewer with it (usually, at least). At the start we learn that Leonard Shelby (Pearce) is after the man who raped and murdered his wife. The twist is that Leonard is so traumatized by the crime that he has lost his short-term memory. He remembers everything before the crime, but instantly forgets everything that happens afterward. He has no idea how he came by the suit he's wearing. He forgets where he was 10 minutes earlier and the names and faces of the people he was talking to.

To keep things straight, Leonard takes Polaroids of everything he sees (including the seedy Southern California motel where he's staying) and makes notes, with names and phone numbers, of every encounter as it happens. Records of really important things he injects under his skin as crude tattoos, and soon his body becomes a walking register of his strange quest to find his wife's killer. One teasing possibility is that he may have killed her himself.

As Nolan jumps backward, each new scene ends where the previous one began. If Leonard is suddenly wearing a bruise, a subsequent scene will show how it got there.

More than a stunt, *Memento* is an absorbing contemporary film with a B-thrillerish look and feel.

MERCI POUR LE CHOCOLAT

Isabelle Huppert, Jacques Dutronc, Anna Mouglalis, Rudolphe Pauly

Directed by Claude Chabrol
2000. 99 minutes. French with English subtitles. No rating.

This might more accurately be called *Beware of the Chocolate*; Isabelle Huppert has poisoned it. As Mika Muller-Polonski, the proper mistress of a chateau, Huppert is deliciously devilish in a film that displays Chabrol's legendary finesse at creating witty mysteries.

Mika has at last landed the man of her dreams, the celebrated pianist André Polonski (Dutronc), and they have moved into a forbidding mansion in Lausanne, bought with profits from her family's chocolate business. Polonski and Mika have been married before, a brief union 18 years ago. In the meantime, his second marriage yielded a son, Guillaume (Pauly), who hangs about in a pained state of resignation.

Don't ask precisely how, but because of a mix-up of babies at the hospital, Jeanne (Mouglalis), a lovely young pianist, was once misinformed that she was Polonski's daughter. She now shows up in Lausanne wanting piano lessons. Polonski is delighted; Guillaume grows increasingly insecure at his displacement.

The impassive Mika goes on serving everybody chocolate. Is she trying to kill them? Whom is she after and why? Chabrol's family intrigue keeps us in delightful suspense to the end.

MERMAIDS

Cher, Winona Ryder, Christina Ricci, Bob Hoskins,
Michael Schoeffling

Directed by Richard Benjamin
1990. 110 minutes. PG-13.

While *Tumbleweeds* (page 429) has a neurotic 90's mother dragging her besieged young daughter around the country on her quest for the right man, Benjamin serves up a lighter, sweeter comedy about a 60's equivalent named Rachel Flax (Cher).

Rachel is driven by relentless vengeance. To her, men are nothing more than passing providers of sexual services as she restlessly moves from place to place. Certainly they aren't to be relied on for the support of her or her two daughters, 15-year-old Charlotte (Ryder) and young Kate (Ricci).

In the Flaxes' latest port of call, in Massachusetts, she strikes up a utilitarian friendship with a good-looking young handyman and school-bus driver named Joe (Schoeffling). Charlotte—wide-eyed, enormously naïve, hugely sensitive and at the worst possible age for moves (Rachel has made some 18 of them) and school changes— also takes a shine to Joe, which leads to more than a little awkwardness with her mother.

Ryder's performance as the often incredulous teenager helps carry the film, as does Hoskins in the role of Lou Landsky, a sturdy, forthright shoe-store owner who would provide some stability for the family.

METROPOLIS

Alfred Abel, Gustav Fröhlich, Brigitte Helm, Rudolf Klein-Rogge

Directed by Fritz Lang
1927. 123 minutes.

When first released, Lang's gigantic story of the struggle between subterranean laboring masses and their rulers in the highly expressionistic metropolis above proved so overwhelming that the studio, Ufa, pulled it from theaters and cut 7 of the original 12 reels. Much was restored in a new 35-millimeter print issued several years ago and transferred to DVD.

Audiences had trouble grasping a sprawling science-fiction allegory with excursions into filial revolt, romantic love, political symbolism and the dominance of technology in the machine age. On screen, humans hold their own somehow. Above ground, the mega-industrialist Joh Fredersen (Abel) rules an empire of soaring structures, but after meeting a woman from the underworld, Joh's son Freder (Fröhlich) develops sympathy for the workers below and helps lead them to eventual liberation.

Liberals thought the film fascistic; fascists thought it communistic. These days we can only relish a splendid spectacle of expressionist originality.

ME YOU THEM

Regina Casé, Lima Duarte, Stênio Garcia, Luiz Carlos
Vasconcelos, Nilda Spencer

Directed by Andrucha Waddington
2000. 104 minutes. Portuguese with English subtitles.
No rating.

Avoiding prurience and sentimentality, Waddington's seductive, sinuous film nicely weds the humor and magic of a folk tale with the dynamics of relations between men and women and men and men in a macho culture.

When the pregnant Darlene (Casé) leaves her home in northeastern Brazil, her mother tells her, "God prevent you have a daughter." Darlene, in fact, returns with a son and goes on to have three more sons, each with a different father.

A mélange of rural neorealism, soap opera and sexual comedy, Elena Soarez's script, based on a true story on Brazilian television, puts together an unlikely but surprisingly practical ménage á quatre dominated by the voluptuous Casé, whose likes haven't been seen on screen since love Italian style went out of fashion.

The men fall into step: a wizened old bachelor (Duarte) with a well-built house to hold them all; his cousin (Garcia), a gentle timid soul who takes hot lunches to Darlene as she labors in the fields and is responsible for one of her son's blue eyes; and a handsome fellow laborer (Vasconcelos), whom Darlene invites to hang his hammock.

It's a crowd, but a narrative of romantic complication unfolds gracefully and easily in a film made and acted with intelligence and a love that deserves to be requited.

MIAMI BLUES

Alec Baldwin, Fred Ward, Jennifer Jason Leigh, Charles Napier, Obba Babatundé, Nora Dunn

Directed by George Armitage
1990. 97 minutes. R.

Adapted from one of Charles Willeford's superlatively droll, seedy crime novels, Armitage's film sends Detective Hoke Moseley (Ward) to look into the activities of a brash sociopath named Junior Frenger (Baldwin).

Junior is the kind of guy who steals a bag at the airport and tries to sell the contents to Susie (Leigh), a prostitute he has just hired. He also forges signatures and breaks a Hare Krishna's finger, but he is nowhere near as interesting as the scrambling Hoke, who's broke and not above helping himself to a suspect's food and drink.

Willeford's crime series centers on the detective, whereas Armitage puts the focus on Junior. A funny and fascinating bad guy (see *The Cooler*, page 83), Baldwin keeps things lively by rasping and acting dangerous. Meanwhile, Leigh steals the film as an impossibly ingenuous hooker who falls for Junior and wants only a future with her man.

A MIDNIGHT CLEAR

Ethan Hawke, Gary Sinise, Frank Whaley, Peter Berg, Kevin Dillon

Directed by Keith Gordon
1992. 107 minutes. R.

Gordon's gripping adaptation of William Wharton's novel combines the harsh reality of war with an unmistakable antiwar message. In the snowy Ardennes forest in December 1944, a special platoon of troops led by the baby-faced Sgt. Will Knot (Hawke) faces some odd phenomena.

Picked for their intelligence, they are assigned to reconnoiter an elegant country house in the forest, occupy it for a week to scope out German activity in the area and possibly take a prisoner. The notable actors who make up the group include Sinise (in his first film) as Knot's pal Mother Wilkins. Before long, half of the squad's 12 men are dead.

The war is drawing to a close, which has everything to do with the strange events that follow. The squad encounters the bodies of an American and a German frozen together in the act of dancing. German voices are heard in the night, but there is no other presence. Then, on patrol, they sight a group of enemy soldiers, old men and boys, chopping wood and tending a small shack in a hollow. The Americans withdraw without shooting. And the next day, the Germans refuse to shoot when they have the squad in their sights.

Things can't end that simply or peaceably, of course. The war may be winding down, but it's not over yet, and the film follows the squad to its brutal last battle. Gordon, who also wrote the screenplay, is uncompromising in his approach, which may be why this tough but moving film isn't better known.

MIDNIGHT IN THE GARDEN OF GOOD AND EVIL

Kevin Spacey, John Cusack, Jack Thompson, Irma P. Hall, Jude Law, Alison Eastwood, Dorothy Loudon, The Lady Chablis

Directed by Clint Eastwood
1997. 155 minutes. R.

All the gossip, anecdote, layers of history and voices of expert Southern storytellers that came to life on the pages of John Berendt's best-selling book lose some of their magic on screen, but Eastwood's film makes entertaining viewing nevertheless.

When the *Town & Country* writer John Kelso (Cusack in a role concocted for the film) arrives in Savannah, Georgia, he goes on a double-decker-bus tour through verdant little parks and past handsome architecture like Mercer House, home to a fabulous Christmas party and scene of a notorious murder.

Kelso plans to enjoy the former and investigate the latter. The elegant gay antiques dealer Jim Williams (Spacey) serves as host and guide, but propriety goes flying with the arrival of Williams's lover, the hustler Billy Hanson (Law). After the party, there is another killing. Forget the article, Kelso figures; maybe there's a book here.

In Savannah we also meet a man who walks an imaginary dog, the sexy Mandy Nichols (Eastwood, the director's daughter), the de rigueur grand dame (Loudon) and others, though none of them means much to the narrative in a film that is fortunately rescued by its excursion into gray moral areas, first-rate performances (especially by Cusack and Spacey) and fine atmosphere.

MIDNIGHT RUN

Robert De Niro, Charles Grodin, Yaphet Kotto,
Dennis Farina

Directed by Martin Brest
1988. 126 minutes. R.

Reviewing the film in *The New York Times*, Vincent Canby wrote that it wastes more talent than most movies ever hope to see—the point being that there was more than enough left over to carry a first-rate comedic action adventure.

The performances are everything. Jack Walsh (De Niro), a former Chicago cop turned bounty hunter, is offered $100,000 to retrieve the mild-mannered accountant

Jonathan Mardukas (Grodin), who stole $15 million from his firm after he learned it was run by the mob.

After collaring his man, Walsh moves him across country by plane, train, bus and automobile. Hounded by adversaries, they are occasionally forced to walk and swim. Action interludes are called for, of course, but the strength of the film derives from two unlikely characters' gradually coming to know and trust each other.

De Niro has a chance to be blatantly funny as the embattled, resourceful scrambler always one step ahead of disaster. Grodin is superb as the straight man, a sensitive, slightly quizzical do-gooder who has given most of his haul to charity and now strives to figure out this fellow charged with bringing him in.

Both give the film an unusual humane dimension.

MIFUNE

Anders W. Berthelsen, Iben Hjejle, Jesper Asholt, Sofie Grabol, Emil Tarding, Anders Hove, Paprika Steen

Directed by Soren Kragh-Jacobsen
1999. 99 minutes. Danish with English subtitles. R.

The stripped-down Dogma 95 style—handheld cameras; no artificial light, props or genre conventions—works quite passably in Kragh-Jacobsen's film. His asceticism can seem ostentatious at times, but by any standard this would be a pretty good movie.

In keeping with the cinematic Lutheranism, we are served a homily on the idea that suffering may be the sinner's surest way to grace. The narrative rests in two worlds. A Copenhagen businessman, Kresten (Berthelsen), takes his cell phone, BMW and trophy wife (Grabol) as signs that God loves him. As a kid, though, he grew up in a Danish translation of a Tennessee Williams play.

Called home to a rotting farmouse, he finds his father's corpse, draped with weeds, stretched out on the kitchen table. Hiding under the table is his mentally disabled brother, Rud (Asholt), who does things according to crop circles, comic books and the legendary Japanese movie star Toshiro Mifune.

A ménage forms with the addition of a prostitute on the run, a psychopathic telephone stalker and a raffish refugee from boarding school. If that sounds unsavory— and rest assured that it is—Kragh-Jacobsen's suppression of style also allows a surprising sweetness to emerge, demonstrating perhaps that even a dogmatist can be romantic.

THE MIGHTY QUINN

Denzel Washington, James Fox, Robert Townsend,
Mimi Rogers, M. Emmett Walsh, Norman Beaton,
Esther Rolle, Sheryl Lee Ralph

Directed by Carl Schenkel
1989. 94 minutes. R.

Washington played a tropical lawman in *Out of Time* (page 305), but in Schenkel's breezily entertaining film we encounter him early in his career as the F.B.I–trained police chief of a small Caribbean island.

A rich American businessman is found decapitated and simmering in a Jacuzzi, tossing tourism and the government into turmoil. Quinn (Washington), referred to with affectionate sarcasm as "The Mighty Quinn" after the Bob Dylan song, investigates a case stacked heavily against the prime suspect, Quinn's funny, dreadlocked, ne'er-do-well boyhood pal Maubee (Townsend).

Investigating further, Quinn tangles with a stuffy, shady hotel owner (Fox), his bored and available wife (Rogers), the governor (Beaton) and a scruffy, mysterious American tourist (Walsh). Rolle plays a witch who keeps deadly snakes in her parlor, and Ralph portrays Quinn's wife, an aspiring lounge singer.

All perform with engaging ease in a film that manages to be touristy without surrendering its intelligence, ideally colorful without being fraudulent.

MILLENNIUM ACTRESS

The voices of Miyoko Shôji, Mami Koyama, Fumiko Orikasa, Shôzô Îizuka, Masaya Onosaka, Shouko Tsuda

Directed by Satoshi Kon
2001. 87 minutes. Japanese with English subtitles. No rating.

Kon's beautifully drawn mélange of fantasy and history pays tribute to both current anime and the grand tradition of post–World War II live-action Japanese cinema, from samurai epics to urban domestic dramas to *Godzilla*.

At the core is a legendary actress named Chiyoko Fujiwara, who as a young woman fell in love with a dissident artist being pursued by the police. Now, a worshipful director, Genya, wants to make a film about her life, so she uses his film to go back and forth through the past on a quest to find the artist and return a key he gave her.

En route we move in and out Chiyoko's factual life, with the tribulations of her career and private life, and the fantasy of the roles she has played. Genya and his cameraman trot along, ardently recording it all, with Genya casting himself as her savior in several films. In the process we are treated to a wonderfully eccentric and deeply affecting expression of movie love.

MISSISSIPPI MASALA

Denzel Washington, Sarita Choudhury, Roshan Seth,
Sharmila Tagore, Charles S. Dutton

Directed by Mira Nair
1991. 118 minutes. R.

At the start of Nair's witty, moving film, a fender-bender near Greenwood, Mississippi introduces Demetrius (Washington) to Mina (Choudhury), a spirited young Indian immigrant who has come to the United States with her family after their harrowing expulsion from Uganda (shown in a preamble) in the era of Idi Amin.

Thus, two elements of the so-called New South are joined, one black, the other brown. Demetrius works hard at his rug-cleaning business. Mina belongs to an immigrant group that owns most of the area's motels. Despite social pressures and a mutual sense of cultural dislocation, they begin a relationship.

An engagingly idiosyncratic film examines the gulf between them without trying to tidy up differences and conflicts. Mina's father (Seth), a successful journalist in Uganda, never accepts being a motel clerk. Demetrius's family survives mainly by being polite to white society.

A huge cast conveys the sense of community in Indian life, as well as its roiling dissatisfactions, not the least of which is their misgivings about Mina and Demetrius. As for the couple, Washington's screen heft lends the film its dramatic point, and the warmly voluptuous Choudhury, in her first film, matches his wit and good humor.

MRS. DALLOWAY

Vanessa Redgrave, Natascha McElhone, Rupert Graves,
Michael Kitchen, Alan Cox, Lena Headey, John Standing,
Amelia Bullmore

Directed by Marleen Gorris
1997. 97 minutes. PG-13.

Virginia Woolf's interior novels are notoriously hard to translate to the screen, but Gorris's graceful adaptation captures what Woolf did: the inner life of Clarissa Dalloway as she prepares for a party. All the events take place on a single day in 1923, but as she moves about doing ordinary errands, Clarissa thinks back to her youth and how she became Mrs. Dalloway.

The film wisely creates two Clarissas: Redgrave is the elegant woman in her 50's and McElhone the vibrant young woman whose life could have gone in another and perhaps more adventurous direction.

As the older Clarissa prepares for the party, her thoughts drift back to the man she might have married, the dashing Peter Walsh (Cox) and a flirtation with the spirited Sally Seton (Headey). By 1923, Clarissa is married to the gentlemanly Richard Dalloway (Standing) but longs for the emotional excitement of her youth. The depth of her discontent is suggested by her identification with Septimus Warren Smith (Graves), an anguished, shell-shocked war veteran.

Woolf's *Mrs. Dalloway* may now be better known as the book that loosely inspired Michael Cunningham's novel *The Hours* and the subsequent film, but Gorris's film is a truer evocation of Woolf's lyrical immersion in the richness of an ordinary woman's thoughts.

MONA LISA

Bob Hoskins, Cathy Tyson, Michael Caine, Robbie Coltrane, Clarke Peters, Kate Hardie, Zoë Nathenson, Sammi Davis

Directed by Neil Jordan
1986. 104 minutes. R.

Named for the Nat King Cole song, Jordan's film is full of classy kitsch and high style, making it the kind of movie, Vincent Canby wrote in *The Times,* you don't have to hate yourself for liking.

In London a bullet-shaped, nasty-tempered hood named George (Hoskins) and his friend Thomas (Coltrane) peddle bizarre stolen goods and tell each other mystery stories to pass the time. In a kind of shaggy-dog fable, George develops a passion for a tall, reedy black hooker named Simone (Tyson), whom he chauffeurs about at the behest of his mob boss. This becomes George's story, as judged by Thomas.

That device denies events their immediate emotional importance, but the film survives on the strength of its performances. Hoskins is superb, and Tyson has a magical screen personality as a character who is beautiful and hard as nails. Caine adds class as the coolly vicious chief of a gang of pimps and blackmailers.

MONKEYBONE

Brendan Fraser, Bridget Fonda, Chris Kattan, John Turturro, Giancarlo Esposito, Rose McGowan, Dave Foley, Megan Mullally, Bob Odenkirk, Whoopi Goldberg

Directed by Henry Selick
2001. 92 minutes. PG-13.

Selick's somewhat jumbled but vastly underrated film, based on the comic book *Dark Town,* by Kaja Blackley, manages to double as comic delight and Freudian excursion into sublimation, neurosis and bad dreams.

A cartoonist named Stu (Fraser) is haunted by nightmares that threaten to turn his comic-book creations into a Boschian world of chaos. Fortunately, his girlfriend (Fonda) is a sleep doctor who can ease those inclinations, and what comes off Stu's board is a shifty but marketable little primate called Monkeybone.

Together in Stu's dream, monkey and cartoonist are in a car crash and descend into a brawling, creepy netherworld called Downtown. Double-crossing his creator, the treacherous Monkeybone returns to the surface, leaving Stu to engineer a wild escape that at one point involves commandeering a cadaver (Kattan) with a life of its own.

Selick (*James and the Giant Peach* and *The Nightmare Before Christmas*) takes us from the sunny world above, where the freed monkey is into all kinds of riotous shenanigans, back to Downtown and into sumptuous black-and-white dream sequences that pulsate with Stu's dim, primal fears. By definition the unconscious is a disorderly place for a film to visit, let alone with such mischievous insight.

MON ONCLE

Jacques Tati, Jean-Pierre Zola, Adrienne Servantie, Alain Bécourt, Lucien Fregis

Directed by Jacques Tati
1958. 110 minutes. French with English subtitles.

No one is better off left undisturbed to be his own man than Monsieur Hulot (Tati). Who but Hulot would notice that sunshine reflected on a windowpane makes the canary sing? Always distinctive in his fedora (often tipped to others in gentlemanly recognition), raincoat and pants that are too short, the pipe-smoking Hulot is not a fellow to be made over according to garish 1950's materialism.

Not that his sister, Madame Arpel (Servantie), doesn't

try. Proud possessors of a monstrosity of a house packed with gadgets to automate virtually every move, she and her husband (Zola) are positioned to do the habitually unemployed Hulot some good in the labor market.

At the Arpels' place, garage doors automatically close when they should open and the bizarre fountain can spout to impress the right people at the flick of a switch. Invited to dinner with Monsieur Arpel's boss, Hulot tangles with the household electronics and has a better time horsing around with his young nephew (Bécourt).

Nevertheless, the boss gives Hulot a job in his plastic-hose factory, where Hulot's hose comes out like a string of sausages. And so back to the canary he goes. As for Tati, he made only six films over 30 years, but this one won an Oscar.

MONSIEUR IBRAHIM

Omar Sharif, Pierre Boulanger, Gilbert Melki, Isabelle Renauld, Isabelle Adjani

Directed by François Dupeyron
2003. 95 minutes. French with English subtitles. R.

A charming, sentimental film with a New Wave feel looks back nostalgically on Paris in the mid-1960's, with loving reference to French movies of the period.

Bardot herself (Adjani) shoots a few scenes on the Rue Bleue. On one side of the street, a bright, spirited Jewish teenager named Momo (Boulanger) lives in a state of standoff with his depressed father (Melki). Across the way is the grocery store owned by old Ibrahim, a Turkish Muslim and neighborhood sage who seemingly knows everybody and everything about them.

A close relationship develops between boy and elder, with the old Muslim taking on a young Jewish protégé. In his 70's, Sharif has lost none of his charisma, and Boulanger shows winning self-assurance.

MOONLIGHT MILE

Susan Sarandon, Jake Gyllenhaal, Dustin Hoffman, Ellen Pompeo, Holly Hunter

Directed by Brad Silberling
2002. 117 minutes. PG-13.

Set in 1973 during the Vietnam War, Silberling's film about parental loss of a child casts an insightful eye on the strategies people adopt to absorb and process such a traumatic event.

After their daughter is murdered, the edgy JoJo Floss (Sarandon) is impatient with the rote expressions of sympathy spouted by her friends, while her lumpish, people-pleasing husband, Ben (Hoffman), greets every bromide with slavish obsequiousness. Caught in the middle is Joe Nast (Gyllenhaal), who was engaged to the departed.

Having no family of his own, Joe is taken in by the Flosses, who, like him, are clinging to some vestige of their daughter. A passive type with no real direction, Joe allows himself to become a surrogate child. The kindly Ben brings him into his commercial real estate business and even hangs out a shingle reading FLOSS AND SON.

This can't last, of course. The chance to break his dependence on the Flosses comes after the trial of their daughter's killer. This makes a candidly honest man of Joe in a film that could have succumbed to bathos but keeps people headed in directions they need to go.

MORVERN CALLAR

Samantha Morton, Kathleen McDermott

Directed by Lynne Ramsay
2002. 97 minutes. No rating.

Cutting up her boyfriend's body for disposal in the Highlands, a young Glasgow woman named Morvern (Morton) so craves musical distraction that she straps a Walkman to her arm. Based on a novel by Alan Warner, Ramsay's wonderfully lush film takes a more minimalist approach to its heroine's malaise but still comes close to making a rich experience out of nothing more than this kind of extreme neediness.

Having committed suicide on the kitchen floor, the boyfriend comes in handy as a release from Morvern's deep torpor. (No one plays near-catatonia like Morton.) Leaving the corpse where it lies (the dismemberment comes later), she goes off to a raucous Christmas party, where she meets her fun-obsessed best friend, Lanna (McDermott). Later the two take off with the dead man's credit cards for a rave vacation in Spain.

From this point the film becomes a nihilist road movie. The boyfriend was a writer with a novel in the computer, and he has willed the work to Morvern. So she removes his byline and inserts her own, and darned if the thing isn't worth some money.

And so it goes to no rosy conclusion, but there's a hardscrabble bravery in Morton's performance as Morvern puts distance between her old life and new pursuits.

MOSTLY MARTHA

Martina Gedeck, Sergio Castellitto, Maxime Foerste

Directed by Sandra Nettelbeck
2001. 109 minutes. German with English subtitles. PG.

Put Martha (Gedeck) on her shrink's couch and the disclosures become an ode to foodstuffs. Martha, who thinks and talks of little else, rates herself the second-best chef in Hamburg, and she gets no argument from her boss, a restaurant owner who puts up with her moodiness for no other reason.

In another foodie flick (see also *Big Night* and *Eat Drink Man Woman*, pages 35 and 122), Martha is consumed by her profession, pushing aside all social relationships. When overseeing every detail in a highly regimented kitchen becomes a little too much, Martha, a severe young woman in her early 30's, retreats into a walk-in freezer to brood and perhaps scream in frustration.

Surpassing competence doesn't add up to much of a life, however, and she finds herself totally unprepared to care for her 8-year-old niece, Lina (Foerst), who comes to live with her after her mother, Martha's sister, is killed in a car crash. Sullen and rebellious, Lina not only skips school but doesn't like Martha's cooking.

With the help of a likable sous-chef named Mario (Castellitto), Lina warms up quite a bit, and eventually so does Martha, in a film that penetrates the permafrost with a bit of love and humor. But don't look for sentimentality or cliché. Nothing outside the kitchen happens that easily with Martha.

THE MOTORCYCLE DIARIES

Gael García Bernal, Rodrigo De la Serna, Mía Maestro

Directed by Walter Salles
2004. 128 minutes. Spanish with English subtitles. No
rating.

In 1952, a 23-year-old medical student the world would
know as Che Guevara jumped on a sputtering motorcycle behind his rollicking friend Alberto (De la Serna)
and took off on a 5,000-mile journey of discovery that began in Argentina and ran virtually the length of South
America.

In those days Ernesto (Bernal) was devoted to literary
endeavor. Years later his passion would turn political, but
pounding along through rain and mud and snow the two
adventurers are essentially on a lark as they seek out
sights, experiences and cultural connections, not to mention any attractive young women they come across.

In Chile an angry crowd chases them out of town after
a failed romantic encounter. In Peru they work in a leper
colony for an extended period, and we see the beginnings
of Ernesto's susceptibility to egalitarian principles and
radical commitment that would later turn political in
Mexico and, of course, in Cuba at the side of Fidel Castro.

Here, though, we are primarily on an extended road
trip with an exuberant pair in a film convinced that travel
can enlarge the soul.

MOULIN ROUGE

Nicole Kidman, Ewan McGregor, John Leguizamo, Jim Broadbent, Richard Roxburgh, Garry McDonald

Directed by Baz Luhrmann
2001. 127 minutes. PG-13.

Luhrmann's extravagant circus of a musical is both a true original and a homage to an earlier era: MTV meets turn-of-the-century Paris. The film is set in Paris in 1899, the "summer of love," according to Christian (McGregor), an aspiring writer enamored of Satine (Kidman), a doomed performer at the great old dance hall in Montmartre, and the larger-than-life romantic presence who will ultimately dash Christian's hopes and break his heart.

The love story seems secondary, though, because this film can't wait to burst into explosive song and color. It never lets up even as Toulouse-Lautrec (Leguizamo) and his fellow performers crash through the ceiling and into Christian's flat while rehearsing a "spectacular spectacular."

Satine, who is suffering from a fatal disease, has also caught the fancy of the Duke of Worcester (Richard Roxburgh), who has the means to save the Moulin Rouge but threatens to shut it down unless he has his way with her.

McGregor and Kidman make a convincing and surprisingly cheerful pair of doomed musical lovers. And as always, Broadbent practically runs away with the film. Here he is Harold Zidler, a master of ceremonies and manager who has seen just about everything, and who knows what has to be done to save the Moulin Rouge.

MULHOLLAND DR.

Laura Harring, Naomi Watts, Justin Theroux, Ann Miller,
Robert Forster, Dan Hedaya

Directed by David Lynch
2001. 146 minutes. R.

Don't expect all the pieces of the puzzle to fit together
at the end of this dazzling neo-noir about Hollywood.
David Lynch, the master of brilliant weirdness, is interested not in neat answers but in leading us through unsettling shifts of time and identity until the characters
themselves hardly know who they are.

Just when a sultry, nameless brunette (Harring) is
about to be executed by a sinister pair who have driven
her to a remote spot in a limousine, drag racers slam into
the vehicle and it explodes. The brunette, the sole survivor, crawls off and finds refuge in a plush empty apartment.

There she is discovered in the shower by Betty (Watts),
a completely opposite type—an optimistic blonde and aspiring actress new to Los Angeles who is borrowing the
apartment from her aunt. The brunette's only injury appears to be amnesia. Unable to remember her name, she
spots an old movie poster on the wall and calls herself
Rita, as in Hayworth.

The women become friends and lovers. So far, matters
are intelligible, but then the film splinters into many
strands that seem impossible to connect. A hot young director named Adam (Theroux) takes orders from a waxen,
abusive relic called the Cowboy. Rita and Betty assume
new identities, and the film turns into feverish, deliberately disconnected images like those in a dream.

Soon we have an ever-deepening reflection on the allure of Hollywood and its power to make people disappear into other people's fantasies.

MUMFORD

Loren Dean, Hope Davis, Jason Lee, Alfre Woodard, Mary McDonnell, Pruitt Taylor Vince, Zooey Deschanel, Martin Short, David Paymer, Ted Danson

Directed by Lawrence Kasdan
1999. 112 minutes. R.

Hollywood's quaking reverence for psychotherapy takes a big hit in Kasdan's semiscrewball comedy. Renaming himself after the town he has just moved to, Mumford (Dean) hangs out his shingle as a shrink, though he has no credentials for the post. Mumford operates on intuition and common sense. In the age of Oprah, why not?

Patients are plentiful. Skip Skipperton (Lee), the town's version of Bill Gates, is on the couch. Skip's company makes 23 percent of the world's modems, but he remains an adolescent manchild zooming around on a skateboard.

Most of Mumford's patients have sexual and romantic problems. One of his clients lives in a steamy pulp-fiction fantasy, which the film dips into now and then just for the fun of it. Other caricatures include the repressed wife (McDonnell) of a despicable investment banker (Danson), a troubled teenager (Deschanel) and a depressed young woman (Davis) with chronic fatigue syndrome.

Mumford dispenses therapy with casual efficiency. In previous lives, we learn, he's been a ruthless I.R.S. investigator and a cocaine addict who virtually destroyed himself. But here he is at the center of a heartening Frank Capraesque social fable in which therapy frees people from their social isolation and brings them together.

THE MUSE

Albert Brooks, Sharon Stone, Andie MacDowell, Jeff Bridges, Mark Feuerstein, with cameos by Cybill Shepherd, Rob Reiner, Wolfgang Puck, Martin Scorsese, James Cameron

Directed by Albert Brooks
1999. 97 minutes. PG-13.

In one of Brooks's hilariously anguished cries about life, a blocked screenwriter wrestles with the disappearance of his abilities, the crassness of show-business ethics and the never-ending war of nerves brought on by ambition.

After the writer Steven Phillips (Brooks) wins a humanitarian award, his daughter asks him what a humanitarian is. "Someone who's never won the Oscar," he replies. Steven hasn't been producing up to his usual standards lately. "Go! Take some time off!" an arrogant young studio executive (Feuerstein) tells him.

Another writer, Jack (Bridges), cooking on all cylinders and reigning supreme in his walled mansion with tennis court, advises Steven to do what he does: consult an ethereal Olympian-looking woman named Sarah (Stone).

Sarah, it turns out, has direct links to the nine Greek sister goddesses who inspired art. As a muse, she can lift Steven from his creative miasma. But Sarah is extremely high-maintenance, demanding a $1,700-a-day suite and around-the-clock attention.

Scorsese is using Sarah and reports that he's making progress on a remake of *Raging Bull*, this time using a thin guy. She's effective, all right, but soon she takes up residence in Steven's guesthouse and treats him like an errand boy. Too high a price, perhaps.

MY ARCHITECT: A SON'S JOURNEY

A documentary written and directed by Nathaniel Kahn
2003. 116 minutes. No rating.

Another documentary about a son trying to find his roots? It sounds utterly trite, but Kahn's quest to understand his father becomes a triumphant piece of filmmaking, capturing both changing social standards over the last half century and his father's artistic achievements. Kahn is the illegitimate son of the great architect Louis I. Kahn, who led a compartmentalized and furtive life. Working obsessively and ever on the move, Kahn spread himself among three families, each aware of the others. There was the wife to whom he remained married until the end, as well as the women who gave birth to two of his children. One of them was Nathaniel's mother, Harriet Pattison, a landscape architect.

A small man whose face was disfigured by a fire in his youth, Kahn was charming, charismatic and a loving father—that is, when he appeared, all but unannounced, for fleeting, occasional visits in the night. Nathaniel Kahn is smart enough not to make himself the center of attention here. The film gathers Louis's two other children to share memories and try to sort out what their father was thinking; they'll never really know.

And in some of the toughest scenes Kahn quizzes his father's mistresses, including his own mother, about why they put up with such treatment. The man was a genius, his women say, and they allowed him to play by different rules because they so wanted him to be part of their lives.

The film also reconstructs Louis Kahn's career. His buildings include an addition to the Yale University Art Gallery, the Salk Institute in La Jolla, California, the Kimbell Art Museum in Fort Worth and, most notably, the National Assembly in Dacca, the capital of Bangladesh. Then there are the reams of drawings of unrealized projects that fell victim to Louis's nomadic ways and lack of attention to business matters.

In the end he was found dead of a heart attack in a washroom at Pennsylvania Station in New York, a solitary enigma beautifully captured in this loving but dispassionate film.

MY BEAUTIFUL LAUNDRETTE

Saeed Jaffrey, Roshan Seth, Daniel Day-Lewis, Gordon Warnecke, Derrick Branch, Shirley Anne Field, Charu Bala Choksi, Rita Wolf

Directed by Stephen Frears
1985. 97 minutes. R.

Frears's work moves around, as is evident in the range of his films: *Dangerous Liaisons, High Fidelity, Dirty Pretty Things*. Here we have a wise, rude social comedy about the son of Pakistani immigrants who goes into business with a Cockney former schoolmate in London.

Omar (Warnecke) and Johnny (Day-Lewis) plan to revitalize Churchill's, a failing Laundromat. To this point, Johnny, who affects a punk haircut and attitude, has been bashing Pakistanis with his pals, but now he figures it's time to get ahead in the world. At heart, Johnny is a patient, decent man, and Day-Lewis gives him plenty of emotional substance. Furthermore, Johnny is in love with Omar, which is all right with the Pakistani.

With these two as his base, Frears moves on to Omar's family, headed by a father (Seth), a successful journalist in Pakistan who in England spends his days in bed nipping vodka and carrying on against the system. "Oh, dear," he says in his fussy upper-class accent, "the working class is a great disappointment to me."

Uncle Nasser (Jaffrey) has a good-hearted English mistress (Field) who genuinely loves him. That outrages

Nasser's furiously jealous Pakistani wife (Choksi), who finally resorts to witchcraft.

Nasser's pretty daughter (Wolf) feels neither Pakistani nor English, the kind of in-between position adopted by the London-born screenwriter, Hanif Kureishi, whose father was Pakistani and mother was English. As merciless as Kureishi is to his Pakistani characters, he doesn't characterize them as good or bad in this fascinating, eccentric and very personal film.

MY DARLING CLEMENTINE

Henry Fonda, Victor Mature, Linda Darnell, Alan Mowbray, Walter Brennan, Tim Holt, Ward Bond, John Ireland, Cathy Downs, Don Garner

Directed by John Ford
1946. 97 minutes.

If you want to feel what it's like to lay out your bedroll in a cold driving rain under a poncho strung across a couple of sticks in the ground, this is your western.

Ford has his atmospherics just right as Wyatt Earp (Fonda), trying to be a good cattleman after years of gunslinging, and his brothers drive their herd near Tombstone, Arizona. Ford's sure touch with the darkness of night, the blinding light of day and all shades in between (as with rays of sun stabbing through black clouds) creates a brooding, nostalgic feel.

Everything heads for the famous showdown at the OK Corral. Out on the range, the Clanton boys rustle the Earps' cattle and kill the youngest brother. Wyatt was in Tombstone that night trying to get a shave. With no cows left, he again puts on a badge.

Mature is fine as Doc Holliday, the learned gunfighter and reluctant medical man who is racked with consumption and fleeing his past. The saloon madam, Chihuahua (Darnell), loves him, and so does Clementine (Downs), a slender schoolteacher who has tracked Doc all the way from Boston.

Ford shot the film in 45 days and moved on. Darryl F. Zanuck, the head of Fox and a Ford fan, decided that the film was too long and cut it by 30 minutes. The shorter version can be compared with the longer on the DVD. Ford had it right the first time.

MY DINNER WITH ANDRE

Wallace Shawn, Andre Gregory

Directed by Louis Malle
1981. 110 minutes. No rating.

Anyone who can't imagine sitting for almost two hours listening to someone else's dinner conversation should give Malle's very funny, extremely special film a try. Gregory is likely to have you as spellbound as he has Shawn with his entertainingly mesmerizing rattlings-on about a life spent wandering the world in search of himself.

The quest has taken him from the forests of Poland to the sands of the Sahara to the mountains of India and even to the estate of Richard Avedon on Long Island. Gregory, of course, is the former theater director and Shawn is the writer and actor. Drawing on hundreds of hours of conversation the two had in real life, they play fictitious characters modeled after themselves.

At first Andre seems an impossibly self-centered kook, but as dinner progresses at a posh Manhattan restaurant, he becomes a most winning character. Andre is dedicated to breaking free of life's restraints, getting in touch with original feelings. People, he says, are robots, on automatic pilot.

The older of the two, and originally the more practical, Andre has become crazily and wonderfully self-indulgent. Wally, on the other hand, reserves his own considerable wonderment and curiosity for more mundane matters. As Andre regales, he asks questions and registers his amazement with "wows," "goshes" and "Gods." But very much his own man, he is candid enough to say at one point, "I really don't know what you're talking about."

MY FIRST MISTER

Leelee Sobieski, Albert Brooks, Carol Kane

Directed by Christine Lahti
2001. 109 minutes. R.

The odd-couple subgenre has no more winning pairing than the black-clad 17-year-old Jennifer (Sobieski) and the buttoned-down 49-year-old Randall (Brooks). She's all zippers, tattoos, body piercings, acid tongue and spiky attitude. He runs a Brooks Brothers–style clothing store in a large Los Angeles shopping mall and is as bland as his occupation. Nevertheless, they will become the best of friends.

When Jennifer goes to the mall looking for a job, she taps Randall on the shoulder with the fingers of a mannequin while he's dressing a store window. Randall shoos her off at first, but when she hangs out by the store he figures she's scaring off customers and offers her a position in the stockroom if she will come back looking more presentable.

At opposite poles in every way imaginable, Jennifer and Randall have a lot in common. They profit by each other's company. By the end she will have dropped her animosity, changed her look, rented her own apartment and bought a battered Volkswagen Beetle. He will wear the funky shirt she bought him and join her in the cemetery to lie on graves and feel the energy of souls.

Then comes a development that will reshape their future.

MY LIFE AS A DOG

Anton Glanzelius, Anki Lidén, Tomas von Brömssen,
Melinda Kinnaman

Directed by Lasse Halström
1985. 101 minutes. Swedish with English subtitles. No
rating.

In the late 1950's life is complicated for a rambunctious
11-year-old named Ingemar (Glanzelius). His mother
(Lidén), always a hearty, demonstrative woman, has tu-
berculosis, and as she nears death it's apparent that Ingemar needs to be in another place. So he is sent to live with
his uncle Gunnar (von Brömmsen) in a small country village.

At times Hallström's film presents an idealized, sentimental view of kids; at others it treats Ingemar's situation
with the seriousness and sense of reality that it warrants.
Life in the country has its crazy side but is otherwise toler-
able. Uncle Gunnar is an all right fellow, if a bit cracked. A
skinny schoolmate has green hair. There is a girlfriend
with whom to share sexual awakening and an older,
buxom blond friend who works at the glass factory and
models nude for the local sculptor.

Ingemar doesn't smile a lot, but Glanzelius has good
chemistry with the others. In some ways Ingemar has
more space to figure out life, but he still suffers from loss,
dislocation and his own rush of development. At times he
feels kicked around like a dog, and, being a whimsical kid,
even gets down on all fours and barks like one.

Say this for Ingemar: at the conclusion, his namesake,
the fighter Ingemar Johanssen, scores an upset knockout
over the heavyweight champion Floyd Patterson.

MY WIFE IS AN ACTRESS

Yvan Attal, Charlotte Gainsbourg, Terence Stamp

Directed by Yvan Attal
2001. 95 minutes. French with English subtitles. No rating.

Matters strike close to home in Attal's noisily enjoyable film, which stars himself as the jealous husband, also named Yvan, of a gorgeous actress (Gainsbourg, who is Attal's wife in real life) starring in a film with a quietly devastating older leading man (Stamp).

You know your wife is attractive to other men when a police officer pulls the two of you over and asks for her license even though you're driving. In the manner of Preston Sturges's screwball comedy *Unfaithfully Yours* (and with a dash of Woody Allenish self-loathing), the neurotic Yvan convinces himself that his wife must be having an affair with her suave leading man.

Yvan denies this to others. "My wife doesn't sleep around," he tells a friend. "But it's her job," is the reply, exacerbating Yvan's fears. Stamp emits a relaxed joie de vivre, and he and Gainsbourg are good together in a film that deftly separates movie glamour from the real world. Yvan might just as well relax. "My wife's a cult," he says.

THE NAKED KISS

Constance Towers, Anthony Eisley, Michael Dante, Virginia Grey

Directed by Samuel Fuller
1964. 90 minutes.

Fuller's tale may offer his bleakest view of the nation's underbelly, but it does salute a brave former prostitute named Kelly (Towers), who slaps down some local hypocrisy along with a creepy leading citizen, whom she beats to death with a telephone.

Earlier, Kelly belabors her pimp with a spike-heeled pump and flees to a small town, where she has sex with the sheriff (Eisley). He suggests she join a brothel, but Kelly is looking for reform and starts nursing crippled children. That earns her favorable attention from the town's philanthropic millionaire (Dante).

Kelly falls in love and the two marry. She has made no secret of her past, and now she discovers something none too favorable about her new husband: the man is a child molester. After she kills him with the phone, she is branded a murderer. When she clears her name by revealing his true nature, she becomes a heroine.

That's not for Kelly, who moves on in a film that could have taken the misogynistic route of most noirish films, but instead goes in the unlikely direction, for 1964, of women's rights. Given Fuller's starkly effective way with a story, you could have worse advocates.

NAKED LUNCH

Peter Weller, Judy Davis, Ian Holm, Julian Sands, Roy Scheider, Monique Mercure, Nicholas Campbell

Directed by David Cronenberg
1991. 115 minutes. R.

Cronenberg's film strays from William Burroughs's novel in ingenious ways while matching the author's flair for the grotesque. If you don't mind a few outsize insects or worry whether what you're watching is real or hallucination, there is total fascination.

The going gets icky in a film that is clearly not for everyone. An exterminator and aspiring writer, Bill Lee (Weller), and his wife, Joan (Davis), are addicted to a narcotic bug powder that leads them to their "William Tell act," in which Bill shoots and kills Joan in a druggy haze (much as Burroughs shot his own wife one drunken evening in 1951).

The scene shifts to Interzone, a Tangier-like place where Bill takes up the life of a tortured literary exile struggling to write. But a typewriter in the form of an insect has a mind of its own, and the Mugwump, a hallucinatory man-size monster, introduces sexual ambivalence and other distractions. Later the narcotic of choice is the black meat of a giant Brazilian centipede.

Bill has friends in Interzone. (Davis doubles as the wife of another writer he meets there.) "Stay until you finish your book, but then come back to us," one tells him. But with all the slyly rendered terrors ricocheting around Bill's brain, what could be created?

NELLY AND MONSIEUR ARNAUD

Emmanuelle Béart, Michel Serrault, Jean-Hugues Anglade, Françoise Brion, Claire Nadeau

Directed by Claude Sautet
1995. 106 minutes. French with English subtitles. No rating.

An insightful tale told in a calm conversational manner scrutinizes the relationship between a beautiful young woman, Nelly (Béart), and a highly accomplished elderly man, Monsieur Arnaud (Serrault).

Arnaud has cultivated other such lovely creatures. One describes him as delicate and civilized. He has encountered Nelly in the past, and when reintroduced by a friend, he knows the right question to ask: "Are you still married?" Nelly is, but unhappily. When he offers to pay her debts and employ her as a secretarial assistant, she sees a chance to change her life.

Arnaud, who has always sidestepped true intimacy, realizes it may be too late to change his ways, but Nelly makes him want to try. She is determined to keep him at arm's length, which isn't difficult with a man whose reserve is so pronounced that he can only observe her as she types his memoirs.

Nelly is remote herself, and together they politely and coolly avoid genuine closeness. A triangle forms when she attracts the attentions of Arnaud's young publisher (Anglade). The appearance of Arnaud's long-departed wife (Brion) is just one beautifully handled defining gesture in a film that may be a little dry but is written with a particularly knowing sophistication.

THE NIGHT OF THE HUNTER

Robert Mitchum, Shelley Winters, Peter Graves, Lillian Gish, Billy Chapin, Sally Jane Bruce

Directed by Charles Laughton
1955. 93 minutes.

O f all the really bad guys on screen, one we haven't forgotten is the man with the words *love* and *fear* on his knuckles. An unofficial backcountry Bible thumper, Harry Powell (Mitchum) calls himself "preacher." In prison for stealing a car, he shares a cell with a bank robber (Graves) who has hidden his $10,000 take in his daughter's doll.

With the thief on his way to the chair for murder, Powell has no luck trying to find out what he did with the money. Out of jail, he heads for the robber's house and his wife, Willa (Winters), and two kids, John (Chapin) and Pearl (Bruce).

It's not healthy to frustrate the preacher man, and it must be said that Mitchum's performance still stands up as one of the screen's most menacing. The annoying Willa acts the sacrificial lamb as the preacher's blade descends, but the two kids lead him a not-so-merry chase that starts in the cellar and heads downriver and then out of state.

They run as if in a dream. Everywhere they turn, Harry is sure to be close behind, roaring biblical quotations as he wheedles and threatens. Finally they encounter a crusty old spinster (Gish) who stands up to Powell with a shotgun. Laughton never directed another film, but thanks to Mitchum his first one packs a scare a half century later.

NINE QUEENS

Ricardo Darin, Gastón Pauls, Leticia Brédice

Directed by Fabián Bielinsky
2000. 115 minutes. Spanish with English subtitles. No rating.

Bielinsky's caper movie combines a Hitchcockian paranoia with David Mamet's obsession with the finer points of gamesmanship and con artistry. It may be absurd, but you won't mind.

The title refers not to a fantasy poker hand but to some priceless stamps that are sought after as avidly as if they were the Maltese Falcon. Two swindlers serve as middlemen. Juan (Pauls) and Marcos (Darin) meet in a delicatessen after a bill-changing scheme goes bad and later decide to join forces to get the stamps and sell them.

Negotiations involve the sexual efforts of Marcos's beautiful sister, Valeria (Brédice), who works at the posh hotel where the prospective buyers are staying. They're slippery characters, all pursuing their own schemes. As for the two swindlers, Marcos plays swaggering tutor to Juan, who has the right animal instincts but seems naïve. We said *seems*.

NOBODY'S FOOL

Paul Newman, Jessica Tandy, Bruce Willis, Melanie Griffith, Dylan Walsh, Elizabeth Wilson

Directed by Robert Benton
1994. 110 minutes. R.

In one of his finest performances, Newman is Sully Sullivan, who is 60 and facing something of a last stand in life. Always his own man, perhaps a little too stubbornly at times, Sully finds himself both on slippery ground and needed by people to whom he hasn't paid too much attention over the years.

Benton's richly textured film, adapted from Richard Russo's novel, operates without cheap sentiment. Sully is no Butch Cassidy or Cool Hand Luke, but he faces life down in much the same way, which means with a good deal of humor.

Each day he razzes his starchy landlady (Tandy), who's as irascible as he is, and works construction now and then off the books for Carl Roebuck (Willis). Sully has no current woman (Russo's book has him involved in a long on-and-off-again affair), but he has a May–December flirtation going with Carl's wife, Toby (Griffith), a slowly fading beauty who knows her husband is cheating with his secretary.

That attraction will ultimately go nowhere, but Sully's major issues are with his son, Peter (Walsh), who has been fired and comes home with his wife and sons to spend Thanksgiving with Sully's fastidious ex-wife (Wilson).

Peter resents his father for walking out on the family when he was a baby and uses the reunion to take out his anger. Sully gets the message, and though he's not the best at earning redemption, he makes a good try.

NO MAN'S LAND

Branko Djuric, Rene Bitorajac, Filip Sovagovic, Simon Callow, Katrin Cartlidge

Directed by Danis Tanovic
2001. 97 minutes. Bosnian with English subtitles. R.

Caught in a trench together during heavy fighting, the Bosnian Ciki (Djuric) forces the Serb Nino (Bitorajac) to admit that the Serbs started the war in what was once Yugoslavia. Later the tables turn, and Nino forces Ciki to admit that the Bosnians were the instigators. If that sounds comic, be assured that Tanovic's engrossing film makes some harsh observations about the absurdities of war.

The film uncoils like an elaborate moral riddle as it widens beyond the trench. But in the trench there is another problem. The body of a man thought to be dead lies on a mine. Suddenly he comes to life; if he moves, the mine will explode. Wanting to help him, Nino and Ciki emerge waving white flags.

That attracts the United Nations humanitarian force and a global television network looking for a story. Nino and Ciki become the pawns of bureaucrats and media companies promoting their own agendas of spin and exploitation.

Callow is effective as a supercilious U.N. official who cares only about the organization's image, and Cartlidge is convincing as a snippy, coldhearted journalist whose ambition to get the story at any cost reflects a typical sense of entitlement exuded by many in her line of work.

The whole nasty exercise takes place in a countryside of surpassing beauty. It's an odd place for a fine film that presents a view of war that is so grimly, insistently realistic.

NORA

Ewan McGregor, Susan Lynch, Peter McDonald,
Roberto Citran

Directed by Pat Murphy
2000. 106 minutes. No rating.

The Irish director Pat Murphy has made an intriguing film, based on Brenda Maddox's biography of Nora Barnacle, the chambermaid who married one of the great literary geniuses of the 20th century, James Joyce.

Susan Lynch's Nora is a spirited, darkly beautiful country girl from Galway. She and Joyce are swept up in each other. Aware of the class differences between her and the scholarly writer, she doesn't let them interfere in the least. She shares his contempt for the conventions that get Joyce into trouble with the Irish mainstream and has the guts to flee their oppressive homeland with him, setting off for Trieste in 1904.

At the start of their 27-year relationship, both were barely in their 20's. Joyce was having trouble getting his work published and was given to fits of extreme jealousy. There were money problems, best handled by Joyce's brother, Stanislaus (McDonald), who recognizes a developing if insufferable genius when he sees one. In their tempestuous relationship, Nora takes on the role of Joyce's muse (most famously, she was the model for Molly Bloom in *Ulysses*) as well as that of his lover and the mother of his children.

McGregor's Joyce plays the tyrant given to stealing material from Nora's life for stories she only half understands. Following Maddox's interpretation, Nora is the partner undervalued by history, a lapse that this work tries to correct. Their relationship is impossible to fathom completely, yet the film makes their attraction and devotion to each other irrefutable.

NORTHFORK

*Peter Coyote, Anthony Edwards, Nick Nolte, Duel Farnes,
Daryl Hannah, James Woods, Ben Foster*

Directed by Michael Polish
2003. 103 minutes. PG-13.

A stunningly atmospheric film tells the tale of a wondrous visitation on the high plains of Montana. The time is the 1950's as a squad of government officials in dark suits and black Fords arrives to evacuate a town about to be inundated by a new hydroelectric dam. If that sounds clear-cut enough, Polish and his brother, Mark Polish, who collaborated on the script, deal in their own evocative if not immediately fathomable imagery and vision.

In a dreamy, elliptical piece of storytelling, angels roam the high grasses of a blanched, silvery landscape. A priest (Nolte) tends a dying boy named Irwin (Farnes), who was abandoned by his adoptive parents and given back to the church when he turned out to be "defective." Irwin sees "gypsies," or visiting angels from another time, in his feverish dreams and aspires to leave this place with them.

All the locals have angels on their minds, and the government men (Woods, Coyote, Mark Polish) offer them wings as incentive to leave the area. To prove to the angels that he is one of them, Irwin shows them scars on his back, presumably where the wings were removed. It would be hard to deny such a plea for departure.

Refusing to mark the boundary between dream and reality, a subtle handmade puzzle of a film treats the American past with a wonder-cabinet mysticism.

NOWHERE IN AFRICA

*Juliane Köhler, Merab Ninidze, Matthias Habich, Sidede
Onyulo, Karoline Eckertz, Lea Kurka*

Directed by Caroline Link
2001. 141 minutes. No rating.

Caroline Link mines a little-known piece of history in depicting the flight of Jewish refugees to Kenya in the 1930's, and creates a family story that is endlessly absorbing.

When Walter Redlich (Ninidze) senses what's coming in Germany, he departs for Kenya, where he becomes a farmer and prepares for the eventual arrival of his pretty, elegant wife, Jettel (Köhler), and their daughter, Regina (Kurka as a young child and Eckertz as an adolescent). When they arrive, Jettel is appalled by their ramshackle red-dirt abode. She tells their hired man Owuor (Onyulo) to leave the good china in the crates. They can't possibly stay here.

But they do. And Regina, the film's center, is ready and willing to grasp the new life, becomes fast friends with Owuor and reaches out to children from the villages.

When war breaks out, the British incarcerate the Redliches and all other Germans in Kenya. Walter is separated from Jettel, who is sent with Regina to a most comfortable resort. The Redliches' freedom was curtailed, but their lives were never threatened; whether the marriage will survive the forced separation is a different matter. If their story may be too picturesque at times, it is absorbing and moving.

THE NUTTY PROFESSOR

Jerry Lewis, Stella Stevens, Del Moore, Kathleen Freeman

Directed by Jerry Lewis
1963. 107 minutes.

A couple of Jerry Lewises emerge in the story of Julius F. Kelp, a supernerd of a college chemistry professor who falls for a very hot student, Stella Purdy (Stevens). Since a shy bumbler with beaverish teeth isn't likely to impress a girl who hangs out at a club called the Purple Pit, a makeover is in order.

As a chemistry professor, Kelp turns to ingredients on his workbench and whips up a potion that turns him into a strutting, obnoxious singer named Buddy Love. Stella and the crowd at the Purple Pit love Buddy, but the one problem with the potion is that it wears off at the wrong time.

Suddenly Buddy is Julius F. Kelp again. After it happens in midperformance at a dance, Kelp is left to explain to the kids why it's important to be yourself.

At his best, which is often the case in this film, Lewis is a master comic. Buddy Love is said to represent the other real Lewis, the pompous, overbearing figure who occasionally shows up in interviews and on television with an artistic chip on his shoulder. Here, like Lewis himself, part goof and part cynical show-business pro, the two make an entertaining pair.

THE OFFICE

Ricky Gervais, Martin Freeman, Mackenzie Crook,
Lucy Davis

Directed by Ricky Gervais and Stephen Merchant
2001–2004. Innumerable minutes.

Gervais's almost impossibly funny BBC series begins in the dreary suburb of Slough, where a BBC documentary is being made about all that goes on in the offices of Wernham Hogg, a paper supply company.

Which is pretty much nothing, but don't stress that point with David Brent (Gervais), the deluded egotist who has convinced himself that he runs the place, though no one pays him much attention. Brent grows steadily more deliciously creepy as he struggles to control his colleagues, all with their own inventories of foibles, and steer the BBC film in a favorable direction.

By the time the show returns to Wernham Hogg in a two-hour special (broadcast in October 2004), Brent has been fired and is now a traveling cleaning-supplies salesman. He is also trying to leverage his BBC image as a "boss from hell" into a career in show biz.

"There is no laugh track on television's funniest show," Alessandra Stanley wrote in *The Times* at the start of the second season. "There are no punch lines, no droll musical cues or snappy comebacks. Not even the tiniest pratfall relieves the deadpan brilliance."

OF MICE AND MEN

John Malkovich, Gary Sinise, Ray Walston, Casey
Siemaszko, Sherilyn Fenn

Directed by Gary Sinise
1992. 115 minutes. PG-13.

This quiet, powerfully moving film breathes new life into John Steinbeck's classic novel, too often remembered as a book we were force-fed in high school. Horton Foote's beautifully astute screenplay and Sinise's sensitive direction allow us to see the itinerant Depression-era friends, George and Lennie, as if for the first time.

As the slow-witted Lennie, who has the mentality of an 8-year-old, Malkovich uses his size to suggest the terrible irony of a child's mind in a large man's body. As George, Sinise is the patient caretaker, who turns out to be a bit naïve himself in thinking he can manage Lennie and treat him as a partner.

Their dream is to own a piece of land, and for a while that looks possible. The one-handed Candy (Walston) is ready to take the $400 he has saved and join the deal. But then there is trouble with Curly (Siemaszko), the ranch owner's nasty son, and Curly's wife (Fenn), who is attracted to Lennie after he has beaten Curly in a fight. But the child-like Lennie isn't equipped to deal with her mentally, however ready he may be physically.

The aftermath of their encounter sends George and Lennie fleeing, and the film heading to its heartbreaking end. As concise and powerful as the novel itself, this film is a classic in its own right.

OLD SCHOOL

Luke Wilson, Will Ferrell, Vince Vaughn, Jeremy Piven, Ellen Pompeo, Juliette Lewis

Directed by Todd Phillips
2003. 91 minutes. R.

All right, Phillips's farce earned heated opprobrium from the critics, but let's lighten up. It is pretty funny, howlingly so in parts. So what if it's stupid and derivative? Some films you just don't judge by the usual standards. Should this be one of them? Probably not, but with Ferrell and Vaughn in high gear (for Vaughn that would be low-down high gear), and Wilson lending some nice support, it more than passes for entertainment. (And it was a winner at the box office, remember.)

Call this one "late *Animal House*." When nice-guy Mitch (Wilson) finds that his girlfriend prefers group sex, he retreats to a rented house near Harrison University, his alma mater. His buddy Beanie (Vaughn), a home-electronics mogul, persuades him to give a party, which gets out of hand. Another pal, Frank (Ferrell), newly married and newly sober, falls off the wagon and, buck naked, into the bushes.

A near riot by partying hordes angers a prissy university dean (Piven), who declares the house college property and tries to evict Mitch. With the nimbleness he's honed as an entrepreneur, Beanie retaliates by declaring the place a fraternity house. Never mind that many of the members, "a nonexclusive community brotherhood," as Beanie calls it, are approaching 30 (or are well past that) and have nothing to do with the college. Let the good times recommence.

Anyway, Ferrell has never been funnier, nor Vaughn crasser. Which is good.

ONCE UPON A TIME IN THE WEST

Henry Fonda, Charles Bronson, Jason Robards, Claudia Cardinale, Keenan Wynn, Woody Strode, Frank Wolff, Gabriele Ferzetti, Jack Elam

Directed by Sergio Leone
1968. 165 minutes. PG.

Gunfighters are titans in Leone's western, and they are given the grandest of visual stages. The movie is glorious to look at, from its desert vistas to the raw planking of sets thrown together to let the outdoors inside and give the half-finished look of a country building so fast it can hardly keep up with itself.

By contrast, the film is languidly paced, as befitting men in a profession that requires prolonged sizing-up before making lightning moves. Eyes are everything. Bronson's are reptilian as he plays the mysterious stranger called Harmonica, who blows away three gunmen waiting to dispatch him at a railhead in the film's drawn-out and unforgettable first scenes.

As Frank, a sadistic viper and child killer, Fonda feared that his famous blue eyes were indelibly Mr. Nice Guy, so he had brown contact lenses made up and grew a mustache. Leone dispensed with that; he saw something cold and distant in Fonda just as he was.

The primary quarrel is between the inscrutable Harmonica, obviously a man on a mission, and Frank, the hired gun of a crippled railroad baron (Ferzetti). As Jill McBain, a prostitute from New Orleans, Cardinale (the first woman to star in a Leone western) runs a burgeoning establishment left to her after her husband was gunned down by Frank. Robards is very fine as a craggy old gunfighter named Cheyenne.

ONE FALSE MOVE

Michael Beach, Billy Bob Thornton, Cynda Williams,
Bill Paxton

Directed by Carl Franklin
1992. 105 minutes. R.

In one of those instances when a director's first film may still be his best, Franklin comes up with a down-and-dirty little road-saga gem that puts his subsequent big-budget productions to shame. (Well, maybe not *Devil in a Blue Dress,* page 99).

Despair, terrible irony and a sudden chance for redemption mark a fine piece of film noir that begins in what seems exploitive fashion with the vicious wipeout of an entire family by three drug dealers on the run.

But they are an unusual trio. Fantasia (Williams) is more sensitive than might be expected. Ray (Thornton, who wrote the screenplay) is the recognizable mad dog of the unit, but it's the phlegmatic Pluto (Beach) who's the most treacherous: placid office-accountant type one minute, deadly savage the next.

Together they head cross-country from Los Angeles to Star City, Arkansas, trailed by a team of L.A. detectives. In Arkansas they come up against a tightly wound sheriff, Dale "Hurricane" Dixon (Paxton), who yearns to be a big-city cop like the boys from L.A. but will need all his down-home smarts and guts to handle what's headed his way in a film with a head-on collision and new beginnings.

ONLY ANGELS HAVE WINGS

Cary Grant, Jean Arthur, Richard Barthelmess, Thomas Mitchell, Rita Hayworth

Directed by Howard Hawks
1939. 121 minutes.

Hawks's tale mixes comedy, adventure, romance and tragedy in South America, where chances that a piece of airmail will get to its destination depend on whether a little band of pilots can coax their overtaxed bangers of aircraft over the very high Andes.

Characters are stirred to order. The hardboiled Geoff Carter (Grant) runs the mail-delivery company. Bonnie Lee (Arthur) would like his attention, but he's all business. There's a discredited pilot (Barthelmess) who would like a second chance and gets one from Carter. The pilot's wanton wife (Hayworth) has a history with Carter and wouldn't mind writing a new chapter.

Mitchell had what might be called a career year in 1939, working in *Gone with the Wind*; *Mr. Smith Goes to Washington*; *The Hunchback of Notre Dame*; and *Stagecoach*. In Hawks's picture he's an old pilot with failing eyesight, a surrogate father to Carter and an ideal candidate to go down in a crash.

Though much of the action never leaves a saloon, the film is fast-moving and entertaining. As in other films of the era (Frank Capra's *Lost Horizon,* for one), limited special effects work wonderfully well, allowing a respite of sorts from all the digitizing and in no way detracting from the hairier takeoffs and landings.

ONLY THE STRONG SURVIVE

Rufus Thomas, Carla Thomas, Isaac Hayes, Wilson Pickett,
Mary Wilson, Sam Moore, the Chi-Lites, Ann Peebles,
Jerry Butler

Directed by Chris Hegedus and D. A. Pennebaker
2002. 95 minutes. PG-13.

Part concert film, part where-are-they-now documentary, Hegedus and Pennebaker's film concentrates on the classic soul that emanated from the Memphis music scene in the 1960's and 70's.

Stax/Volt Records' red-hot house band defined the genre's raw, supercharged sound, and in Memphis the film finds the 82-year-old soul music pioneer Rufus Thomas working as a D.J. on the radio station WDIA with his partner, Jay Michael Davis.

The journalist and soul aficionado Roger Friedman provides sporadic narration to a film that hops from Memphis to New York, where most of the more recent performance takes place. The film also goes to Motown for a visit with Mary Wilson, the former Supreme, who sings "Love Child," and to Chicago, home of the Chi-Lites and Jerry Butler, where the soul was sweeter and more cosmopolitan.

Peebles offers a smoldering performance of "(I Feel Like) Breaking Up Someone's Home," and Pickett is as strong as ever with his hits "In the Midnight Hour" and "Land Of 1,000 Dances." With all the strutting, growling and crying going on, the film is so pumped with adrenaline that young viewers might just long for the days before pop turned digital.

THE OPPOSITE OF SEX

Christina Ricci, Martin Donovan, Lisa Kudrow, Lyle Lovett,
Johnny Galecki, Ivan Sergei, William Lee Scott

Directed by Don Roos
1998. 105 minutes. R.

---

on Roos's acerbic comedy is honed to a nice nasty edge by its manipulative antiheroine, 16-year-old Dede Truitt (Ricci).

Seeing no future back home in Louisiana, Dede heads north and crashes the life of her gay half-brother, Bill (Donovan), a high school teacher. The person who lets Dede get a foot in the door is Bill's hunky live-in lover, Matt (Sergei). But Matt doesn't seem totally gay to Dede, who quickly gets him to bed.

Already pregnant, Dede could use a guy, so she clears out most of Bill's bank account and takes off with Matt, who figures he must be at least bisexual. Bill is an endlessly patient, long-suffering type who, upon finding a kid scrawling a defamatory message about him on a school restroom wall, merely corrects the boy's grammar. But he's stirred to action by the spirited and very funny Lucia (Kudrow), the sister of Bill's former lover, who has died of AIDS.

Bill and Lucia track the "human tabloid," as Lucia calls Dede, to a motel where she is found sexually embroiled not with Matt but with a fellow teenager from home. This is a dark film that, refreshingly, doesn't insist on concluding that everyone is good and kind.

ORANGE COUNTY

Colin Hanks, Schuyler Fisk, Catherine O'Hara, George Murdock, Jack Black, Lillian Hurst, John Lithgow, Lily Tomlin, Kevin Kline

Directed by Jake Kasdan
2002. 83 minutes. PG-13.

Orange County is not just another teen movie (and is no relation to the Fox television hit *The O.C.*, which arrived later). It is a social comedy that happens to be about getting into college, written by the always shrewd observer Mike White (see *The Good Girl,* page 155).

When a large wave wipes out a surfer friend, Shaun (Colin Hanks, son of Tom) finds a book on the beach by the novelist Marcus Skinner (Kline). Shaun wants to be a writer, so he sends a story of his to Skinner and an application to Stanford, where Skinner teaches.

But a spacey school counselor (Tomlin) sends the wrong transcript, one that means Shaun will never get to Stanford. He seems destined to stay in Orange County with his sweet, sensible girlfriend (Fisk, daughter of Sissy Spacek), and his boozy, codependent mother (O'Hara), who can't bear the thought of losing her boy. His usually stoned brother, Lance (Black), wants him around to supply clean urine samples for Lance's parole officer.

Shaun's father, Brad (Lithgow), a snaky lawyer who has moved on to another wife and family, could buy Shaun's way into Stanford but won't. But then Lance, of all people, takes charge and drives everybody off to the dean's house for a last-second plea in this comedy about family ties and desperate escapes.

OSAMA

Marina Golbahari, Arif Herati, Zubaida Sahar, Khwaja Nader, Hamida Refah

Directed by Siddiq Barmak
2003. 82 minutes. Dari Farsi with English subtitles. No rating.

Barmak's film, the first made in Afghanistan after the Taliban lost power, is a harrowing story about the Taliban's brutal suppression of women, seen through a young girl's eyes.

Golbahari, a nonprofessional actor like all the others in the film, plays a girl who masquerades as a boy. With starvation a real prospect, Mother (Sahar) and Grandmother (Refah) shave her head and send her out as a boy to work for a sympathetic shopkeeper. A local boy recognizes her and calls her Osama. Sent to a training camp that indoctrinates boys, Osama is finally revealed by her reluctance to take part in a cleansing ritual played out by an old mullah. Even before that, she has witnessed the Taliban's repression of women, driven into their hovels, forbidden to emerge even to work.

While there isn't much actual violence in the film, the constant dread of the Taliban infuses every moment. The slightest transgression earns the harshest punishment, often death.

In commentary on the DVD, Barmak says he cast Afghan children who were still afraid of the Taliban. That fear is reflected in their faces.

THE OTHERS

*Nicole Kidman, Fionnula Flanagan, Christopher Eccleston,
Elaine Cassidy, Eric Sykes, Alakina Mann, James Bentley,
Renée Asherson*

Directed by Alejandro Amenábar
2001. 104 minutes. PG-13.

Amenábar confines Kidman to a haunted house in the Channel Islands, adds an elaborate conceit and delivers exposition with the efficiency of a word problem in a math textbook. Later on, his film may not make perfect sense, but it does provide its share of sensations.

When Grace (Kidman), a strict, high-strung mother of two, takes an isolated house on the island of Jersey, she briefs the three servants, all in funereal black. The children are fatally allergic to sunlight. Windows must be covered with heavy curtains; no door can be opened unless the one before is closed.

The house appears to be haunted. One of the children reports seeing a little boy and an old woman. Locked doors spring open. A piano plays itself. But is this really going on? Or are the children playing tricks on their hysterical mother? Could any ghost be scarier than Grace herself, whose temperament compounds religious dogmatism, vengeful discipline and desperate need?

Amenábar knows how to scare us, and Kidman is something to behold as she barrels through murky hallways in a confused, determined rage, brandishing a shotgun.

As the tale moves away from its elegant minimalism, it becomes a bit too cluttered and intricate, but it is refreshing to see a young filmmaker embrace old-fashioned conceits with care. It's an even deeper pleasure watching Kidman's Grace transcend the ghostly mumbo-jumbo threatening to envelop her.

OT: OUR TOWN

Catherine Borek, Karen Greene, Ebony Starr Norwood-Brown, Archie Posada, Armia Robinson, Jackie Oliver, Christopher Patterson, José Pérez

Directed by Scott Hamilton Kennedy
2002. 76 minutes. No rating.

In Kennedy's modest, moving documentary, students from Dominguez High School in the tough town of Compton in Southern California prepare to perform that stage staple of American secondary education, Thornton Wilder's *Our Town*.

A play drenched in nostalgia for a long-vanished New England might not make much sense for young Mexican- and African-Americans from a place more associated with Crips, Bloods and gangster rap. Two English teachers, Catherine Borek and Karen Greene, had the idea, and by way of introduction students are shown the 1977 television version of the play with Hal Holbrook as the avuncular Stage Manager.

At first the students resist efforts to bring the play closer to their own lives, fearing they will present stereotypes of themselves. Later they bring a lot of themselves to Wilder's text. An outspoken girl named Ebony, who plays the Stage Manager, and a moody boy named José, who plays the town drunk, share life stories of abandonment, suicide and parental waywardness.

Kennedy quietly observes and lets the students explain themselves with candor, heart and humor. In the end, Wilder's play reveals itself to them through a vibrant new program they create about their own world. "*Our Town* is *Ghetto!*" one of them exults.

OUR LADY OF THE ASSASSINS

Germán Jaramillo, Anderson Ballesteros, Juan David Restrepo

Directed by Barbet Schroeder
2000. 98 minutes. Spanish with English subtitles. No rating.

Schroeder was in Newport, Rhode Island, for his *Reversal of Fortune* (page 337), and here he is in Medellín, Colombia, the cocaine capital, where he made the movie at considerable physical risk to the participants.

After 30 years abroad, a homosexual writer in his 50's named Fernando (Jaramillo) has returned home to die, only to find himself left standing after a protracted bloodbath in a town torn by gang wars and drive-by slaughter. A somewhat grandiose man, Fernando at first imagines his surroundings as a nihilistic comfort zone immune to tragedy. That view will change with the death of his lover, an avid, boyish street thug named Alexis (Ballesteros).

Alexis thinks nothing of gunning down a hippie neighbor whose incessant drumming has annoyed Fernando and a cabdriver who refused to turn his radio down. Fernando looks on aghast. The boy regards the killings as simply good deeds.

After assassins do the same to Alexis, Fernando, now awakened to tragic loss, visits the city's churches in a kind of personal Passion play, lighting candles and gazing at statues who look back at him in perfect indifference.

Schroeder shot the movie in high-definition video, giving it a paradoxically hallucinatory and realistic feel, in keeping with a man who, like the movie, faces deadly reality and steeps himself in impassioned Roman Catholic mysticism.

OUR SONG

Kerry Washington, Anna Simpson, Melissa Martinez, the Jackie Robinson Steppers Marching Band

Directed by Jim McKay
2000. 96 minutes. R.

Washington plays a light-fingered character in *Lift* (page 221), and in this earlier film she is one of three teenagers who shoplift now and again as they grow up in Brooklyn.

Lanisha (Washington), Jocelyn (Simpson) and Maria (Martinez) live in Crown Heights, where they spend an anxious summer dreaming about their futures and navigating the treacherous tides of sexuality, social ambition and loyalty to one another.

But *Our Song* is so unlike most Hollywood coming-of-age stories as to seem downright revolutionary. It is hard to imagine a film less self-indulgent, or one more completely absorbed in the complex humanity of its subjects.

Each of the three undergoes decisive change and faces a life-defining choice. One of them gravitates toward a more worldly group; another unexpectedly becomes pregnant; the third tries to stay true to her friends while steering her own course.

All of this is presented with passionate sympathy and quiet good humor, and almost entirely without melodrama. Watching Simpson, Martinez and Washington, you forget they are acting, which means they are acting very well indeed.

OUT OF THE PAST

Robert Mitchum, Jane Greer, Kirk Douglas, Rhonda Fleming, Virginia Huston, Richard Webb, Steve Brodie, Ken Niles, Paul Valentine

Directed by Jacques Tourneur
1947. 97 minutes.

Tourneur crams a lot of plot into what many regard as one of the best noir films ever. After some very rough knocks as a private eye, shown in a 40-minute flashback, Jeff Bailey (the droopy-eyed Mitchum) is running a gas station in northern California when he's summoned by a big-time gambler named Whit Sterling (Douglas). In the old days Sterling hired Bailey to track down a murderous girlfriend (Greer) who had stolen $40,000 from him. Suffice it to say, there were complications, with Bailey falling for the girlfriend and his partner (Brodie) getting killed in the process.

Now Sterling wants Bailey to find some incriminating tax records in San Francisco. The girlfriend is back, and as treacherous as ever. There's also a slippery lawyer (Niles), his voluptuous assistant (Fleming) and a hit man (Valentine). All of it may be a little hard to follow, but with Tourneur's tight direction and Daniel Mainwaring's punchy screenplay peppered with one-liners, it really doesn't matter.

OUTSIDE PROVIDENCE

Shawn Hatosy, Alec Baldwin, Jon Abrahams, Jack Ferver, Amy Smart, George Wendt, George Martin, Timothy Crowe

Directed by Michael Corrente
1999. 95 minutes. R.

You may not have known that Peter Farrelly of the Farrelly brothers was a novelist, but here he and his brother, Bobby, Providence boys to the core, helped Corrente write his film based on Peter's raffishly funny book about a kid at risk called Dunph and his blustery father, Old Man Dunphy. It doesn't get more Providence than this.

Or more accurately Pawtucket, where young Dunph (Hatosy) is hanging around drugging with his pals when he rams his car into a police cruiser, which is a good way to call attention to yourself. Roused from his perpetual card game with his bigoted cronies, the elder Dunphy (Baldwin) doesn't take kindly to the news.

Especially adept at playing gruff and, when the occasion warrants, extremely nasty people (see *Glengarry Glen Ross* and *The Cooler*, pages 152 and 83), Baldwin gives the old man (somewhere in his late 40's) enough bite to curl wallpaper, but with an ember of feeling for the boy somewhere beneath the bluster.

Young Dunph, old Dunph declares, needs straightening out at prep school. "Prep. Prepare to not get your neck broken by me," he tells the boy. But who's supposed to pay for this? A friend puts up the money.

Prep school, as in those stately brick establishments in leafiest Connecticut. Dunph arrives with his belongings in a trash bag and no idea what is going on. Here the film does a very nice thing by not making him the crucified outsider. Cornwall Academy is snooty enough, but Dunph knows who he is and sticks to his plain Pawtucket values.

That appeals to the other kids, who give him space and a measure of respect. But Dunph's druggy connections hound him, and there's trouble on campus. Old Dunph doesn't put much stock in the prep experience, even though it was his idea in the first place, but he sticks with his boy in what he would never admit is an eminently likable film.

OUTSKIRTS

Aleksandr Chistyakov, Sergei Komarov, Yelena Kuzmina, Nikolai Bogolyubov

Directed by Boris Barnet
1933. 98 minutes. Russian with English subtitles.

Whereas the Russians tend toward the grand and momentous on screen, Barnet's classic first sound film takes a more playful absurdist approach that seems all the more unique and adventurous given the circumstances.

Set in a small town during World War I, *Outskirts* merges comedy and drama in a distinctive and disruptive manner, shifting tones with a freedom that suggests all human experience is hopelessly mixed. A horrifying sequence of trench warfare is suddenly shot through with joy when a Russian soldier discovers that a German soldier he believes he has killed isn't dead after all; a violently repressed strike becomes the occasion for a young slacker to pick up a pretty girl (and to wink at the audience when he succeeds).

Barnet uses the primitive sound of the time to add to the playfulness. A naturalist and a humanist at a time when formalism was in favor, he created films filled with humor, warmth and tenderness, all the while balancing various elements to keep censors at bay. *Outskirts,* also called *Okraina,* may be his best.

OUT OF TIME

Denzel Washington, Eva Mendes, Sanaa Lathan, Dean Cain

Directed by Carl Franklin
2003. 106 minutes. PG-13.

In a diverting thriller, performances and atmospherics override somewhat clumsy plotting. In the steamy little South Florida town of Banyan Key, the police chief, Matt Whitlock (Washington), stays one step and several seconds ahead of a disastrous situation he has brought on himself.

Matt's a decent guy and a reasonably bright one, but he miscalculates royally when he "borrows" $400,000 in confiscated drug money he's been holding in his office safe and gives it to his lover (Lathan) to have a cancer operation. When she and her abusive husband (Cain) die in a fire, the funds go up in smoke with them. Or do they?

About now, federal drug agents demand delivery of the money supposedly in Matt's safe. And fresh down from Miami, bristling with efficiency, is Detective Alex Diaz Whitlock (Mendes), Matt's soon-to-be former wife, who's been assigned to the case.

Between parrying Alex and tracing the money, Matt is kept jumping, with Washington bringing a nice of mix urgency, sangfroid and humor to the challenge. Critics always expect the best from Franklin (*One False Move* and *Devil in a Blue Dress,* pages 292 and 99); here they get brisk direction and some high-swamp style.

PAID IN FULL

Wood Harris, Mekhi Phifer, Cam'ron, Chi McBride, Esai Morales

Directed by Charles Stone III
2002. 97 minutes. R.

Stone's film is loosely based on the true adventures of AZ Alpo, a Harlem drug dealer who made $50,000 a day at the height of the 1980's crack epidemic. Ace (Harris) acts as narrator as he takes over the coke business of his cocky best friend, Mitch (Phifer), after Mitch goes to jail.

The movie certainly doesn't blame Ace, who can't resist the lure of riches and the chance to become a neighborhood celebrity. When Mitch is released, he and Ace join forces with the hotheaded Rico (Cam'ron). Ace is the level-headed one, relatively speaking, but his sense of caution doesn't save him from being shot and nearly beaten to death.

Without getting flashy or preachy, the film goes into the streets, where a gold-rush atmosphere corrodes souls and wrecks the closest friendships. As the field becomes crowded and dealing competitive, paranoia leads to betrayal, kidnapping and murder. The performances are as plain-stated, with distinctive characters who are as vulnerable as they are full of bravado.

PANIC

William H. Macy, Donald Sutherland, Neve Campbell,
Tracey Ullman, David Dorfman, John Ritter

Directed by Henry Bromell
2000. 88 minutes. R.

Alex (Macy) has a few balls in the air. Ask him what he does for a living, and he'd probably say he runs a small mail-order business selling lawn ornaments, kitchen gadgets, sexual aids—things like that. But he has another professional calling: professional killer. In this career he works for his father (Sutherland), a crass old hit man who never honored the fact that Alex didn't like to shoot squirrels as a kid.

Until now he has managed to juggle a bourgeois life with his unsuspecting wife (Ullman) and young son (Dorfman) with his other duties, but lately the pressures of a double existence have brought about an uncharacteristic loss of control. So he repairs to a therapist (Ritter) for an assessment of the situation.

Alex is a good killer, but he hates the work. His defense has always been a calm veneer and pleasant manner, which attracts another of his therapist's clients, a vibrantly sexy, complicated young woman named Sarah (Campbell). Alex would make a fine estate planner for his victims, but beneath the composure is a panicky desperation that has taken hold of other Macy characters, notably in *Fargo*.

Bromell's narrative beautifully balances the comic possibilities of Alex's situation with its ironies. Sarah thinks a fling with her might do him some good, but she's no real answer. Talking to the therapist, he details his own life as meticulously as if he's preparing for a hit. As the pressure grows, Bromell pulls together these various elements, skillfully adding the layers.

THE PAPER

Michael Keaton, Robert Duvall, Glenn Close, Marisa Tomei, Jason Robards, Jason Alexander, Randy Quaid

Directed by Ron Howard
1994. 112 minutes. R.

Without ever capturing the essence of authentic, ink-stained, fedora-tilted-to-the-back-of-the-head newspapering (see *His Girl Friday*), Howard's bighearted, boisterous film stays plenty busy inside and outside the offices of *The New York Sun* (no relation to the actual paper of that name), a lively rag that lies somewhat above the seediest tabloids but never would want to be mistaken for the snooty sheet uptown that reads a lot like *The New York Times*.

Reporters, columnists and editors spout jargon and constantly interrupt one another in energetic pursuit of stories and personal agendas. The metropolitan editor, Henry Hackett (Keaton), has a pregnant wife (Tomei) and a job offer from the stuffier publication. *The Sun*'s top editor (Duvall) has a serious health problem. The paper's devious managing editor (Close) ratchets herself up the city's power ladder while approving stories she knows to be bogus.

Quaid, as a dissolute columnist; Alexander, as someone the columnist has maligned; and Robards (who's been at a better publication than this with Woodward and Bernstein), as *The Sun*'s publisher, all add dimension and create the feeling that there are real people behind an entertaining but fairly superficial screenplay.

PEEPING TOM

Carl Boehm, Anna Massey, Moira Shearer, Maxine Audley

Directed by Michael Powell
1960. 109 minutes.

Powell's notorious thriller is intriguing on a couple of fronts: not only is it a brilliantly innovative piece of filmmaking, but the controversy it created also brought down the career of a major director responsible for *The Red Shoes*, *Stairway to Heaven* and *Black Narcissus*.

Sitting in the dark watching other people do things, movie audiences are voyeuristic by definition. But here they are asked to join another voyeur, and he's not a pleasant fellow. A photographer of women, Mark Lewis (Boehm) kills them with the sharpened leg of a tripod while photographing the act and the police as they arrive to investigate.

It takes Helen (Massey), a young boarder in Mark's house, to get at the root cause of such behavior: his father brutalized him as a child. Mark is fond of Helen, leaves his camera at home when they go out and mightily resists his impulses when he is around her. It may be a losing battle.

Audiences are accustomed to a movie's looking through the viewfinder, but here Powell sets up Mark's camera so that we have to look through it, too. Being forced to look rather than just see disturbed a lot of people, and in response the studio quickly recut the film, virtually destroying it. A restored version was released in 1979.

A PERFECT MURDER

Michael Douglas, Gwyneth Paltrow, Viggo Mortensen

Directed by Andrew Davis
1998. 107 minutes. R.

In a sleek Manhattan of the late 90's, a sleeker couple circle each other like sharks looking for an opening. Davis's film is based on Frederick Knott's play *Dial M for Murder*, which seems like a nursery rhyme in comparison. Steven Taylor (Douglas, looking like a "wattled, riled-up rooster," Stephen Holden wrote in *The Times*) is a Wall Street bond salesman who has made millions but is about to go bust along with one of his Asian schemes. On top of this, he's learned that his wife, the glossy Emily Bradford Taylor (Paltrow), is having an affair with a Brooklyn artist named David Shaw (Mortensen).

These are not nice people. David is a con man and gigolo who's done prison time. Emily, a translator at the United Nations, is as independently wealthy as her name implies and heretofore has sailed comfortably over life's vicissitudes. Soon, though, we'll see that she's as tough as she has to be.

As the other half of a chilly, childless relationship, Steven appreciates a trophy wife but obviously not her waywardness. Being Steven, he concocts a deal. Since David is so fond of money, Steven offers him $500,000 to do away with Emily and make it look like the work of an intruder.

Where all this is headed shouldn't be divulged, of course, but it's creepy fun and holds some surprises. As eye candy, there is the Taylors' endless apartment, fit for the Sun King.

PERSONAL VELOCITY

Kyra Sedgwick, Nicole Murphy, Parker Posey, Tim Guinee,
Ron Liebman, Fairuza Balk, Seth Gilliam

Directed by Rebecca Miller
2002. 86 minutes. R.

Miller uses digital video to full advantage, which is to say she goes smaller in stories, adapted from her book, of three very different women at crisis points and how they choose to address their problems.

Basically, all three are trying to fix what's wrong in their lives. The loose, rollicking Delia (Sedgwick) escapes a violently abusive husband and takes to the road with her children, though that's not necessarily the answer. In the second section, a cookbook editor named Greta (Posey) flies along in her career and feels safe on the home front with a husband she knows will never leave her. But finally she realizes that she will leave him.

In the third part, Paula (Balk), like Delia, runs away from a tumultuous relationship and is pulled into another one with a young hitchhiker, which makes her come to grips with her future. Not many actresses can communicate fear so economically, and Balk's large, dark eyes take in all the details of the horrors of her own life and of those around her.

All three performances are superb. As for the "personal velocity," the film implies that we all go at our own pace. Miller's is unhurried, allowing her to develop her dramas in a free-floating manner.

PERSUASION

Amanda Root, Ciarán Hinds, Susan Fleetwood, Phoebe Nicholls, Fiona Shaw, John Woodvine, Corin Redgrave

Directed by Roger Michell
1995. 107 minutes. PG.

A BBC production does a smart, unglamorized job with Jane Austen's tale. As the intelligent, down-to-earth Anne Elliot, unmarried at 27 and given another chance to secure a love she spurned at 19, Root heads a cast in perfect sync with Austen's warm but piercing style. Hinds is appealing and substantial as the now wealthy Captain Wentworth, rejected by the Elliot family years earlier when he was a penniless naval officer.

Of course, Anne has always loved Wentworth, who can be excused for feeling resentful and guarded. As in all Austen, a crowd of relatives and friends with their own agendas swirls around a couple gradually working their way together through all the societal interference.

The Elliot family includes the vain Sir Walter (Redgrave), who is beset with money problems and must rent Kellynch Hall to the kindly Admiral Croft (Woodvine) and decamp to fashionable but less expensive Bath. Various daughters and in-laws make fine chatterboxes and snippy naysayers in a glorious-looking, profoundly truthful film, with drawing rooms opening on fields reaching to the sea and nurturing Austen's sense of emotional longing.

THE PIANO TEACHER

Isabelle Huppert, Benoît Magimel, Annie Girardot, Anna Sigalevitch, Susanne Lothar, Udo Samel

Directed by Michael Haneke
2001. 130 minutes. French with English subtitles. No rating.

An icon of Gallic severity and self-containment, Huppert gives one of her greatest screen performances as Erika Kohut, a haughty, sexually repressed priestess of high culture in Haneke's powerfully disturbing film, based on the novel by the 2004 Nobel Prize winner Elfriede Jelinek.

Portraying an imperious music instructor at a Viennese conservatory, Huppert plunges into dangerous territory. Erika mixes extreme sexual kinkiness with her forbidding persona at work. A compulsive voyeur, she frequents pornographic bookstores and spies on couples having sex in cars. At home she is in an embattled, suffocating relationship with her bossy, meddlesome mother (Girardot) that is incestuous in all but deed.

Then she unexpectedly finds herself pursued by a handsome and adoring student, Walter Klemmer (Magimel), who imagines himself to be in love. But Erika refuses him sex and instead leads him on an erotic journey according to her own perfectionist standards based on the strictures of her art.

Erika approaches sex the way she teaches Schubert, whose dynamics, she says, range from "scream to whisper, not loud to soft." Erika is like that herself. Unable to give herself to Walter in any conventional sense, she insists that he engage in an elaborate ritual of bondage, pain and humiliation.

Though infuriated and disgusted, he is infatuated, and perhaps curious, enough to play along in an almost-great film whose saddest message may be that art and life aren't the same and shouldn't be confused.

PICKUP ON SOUTH STREET

Richard Widmark, Jean Peters, Thelma Ritter, Richard Kiley,
Murvyn Vye

Directed by Samuel Fuller
1953. 80 minutes.

___

Fuller goes mainstream (sort of) in a B-flick set among a crowd of bottom-feeders in New York.

Skip McCoy (Widmark) may be the only pickpocket in town who dresses immaculately in suit and tie and sleeps in a hammock strung up in a picturesque waterfront shack that would command the high six figures in today's real estate market. One day he picks a wallet belonging to a nurse named Candy (Peters). Inside is top-secret microfilm she is unwittingly transporting for her rat of a boyfriend, Joey (Kiley), who she thinks is a lawyer but is really a commie agent.

Ritter received an Oscar nomination for her performance as an old ex-pickpocket who has the thankless task of fending off all those who now want to get their hands on Skip McCoy. These include Joey, who reacts badly when she won't give him McCoy's address. That irritates Skip and triggers violence and a couple of surprises.

PICNIC AT HANGING ROCK

Rachel Roberts, Vivean Gray, Helen Morse, Kirsty Child,
Karen Robson

Directed by Peter Weir
1975. 115 minutes. PG.

___

Disappearance is to be neither dead nor alive, so I thought it was an interesting area to take a film," Weir said in an interview when the DVD edition was released in 1998. Based on Joan Lindsay's novel, itself supposedly based on a true case, his movie about disappearance is maddeningly effective for the questions it leaves unanswered, just hanging there with the buzzing insects in the blazing Australian heat.

In some situations there just is no answer, a disturbing prospect in a world that demands conclusions and reasons for everything. That would be the world outside central Australia, where, during a picnic on St. Valentine's Day 1900, a group of schoolgirls is hypnotically compelled by an unknown force to climb the craggy, overgrown, bug-infested dome called Hanging Rock. Three of them and a chaperone who went to find them disappear without a trace.

Search parties scour every cranny. Theories grow: Did they fall into a crevice? Were they raped and buried by two teenage boys on the rock that day? Were they carried off and perhaps killed by some unseen party afoot up there? Or is the so-called unnatural at work—unnatural, that is, to those who need to assign corporal blame?

Records reveal no such incident in real life. Lindsay was "a very playful woman," Karen Robson said in an interview. Looking up at the rock, ever silent, anything seems perfectly possible.

PIECES OF APRIL

Katie Holmes, Derek Luke, Patricia Clarkson, Oliver Platt, Alison Pill, John Gallagher Jr., Alice Drummond, Sean Hayes

Directed by Peter Hedges
2003. 81 minutes. PG-13.

A smart, touching comedy stirs in just enough pathos without overpowering the flavor. Such balance doesn't describe the culinary efforts under way in the apartment on the Lower East Side of Manhattan where April Burns (Holmes) is preparing, if that's the word, her first Thanksgiving meal for her family, which is fast descending from suburban New Jersey.

A surly young woman with a temperament as spiky as her hair, April walked out on the other Burnses after an impasse with her mother, Joy (Clarkson). April and the feisty Joy Burns, probably cut too much from the same cloth, had come to the breaking point, but now that her mother has cancer April has extended an olive branch, so to speak, in the form of an invitation to share her first turkey.

If it ever gets cooked, that is. When her stove quits, she goes around the apartment building asking to borrow other people's ovens. In New Jersey, the Burnses aren't exactly looking forward to the trip to Manhattan, but they're doing it for Joy, who is critically ill and determined to make the effort.

April's relaxed boyfriend, Bobby (Luke), is supportive of the effort but disappears on his bike for a while, adding a layer of tension she doesn't need at this point. A neighbor (Hayes) lends her his oven but then bars her from the bird after she offends his delicate sense of feeling appreciated.

It's somehow fitting that all the Burnses will convene, finally, in the apartment of an elderly Asian couple who barely know Thanksgiving, only its spirit.

THE POSITIVELY TRUE ADVENTURES OF THE ALLEGED TEXAS CHEERLEADER-MURDERING MOM

Holly Hunter, Swoosie Kurtz, Beau Bridges, Frankie Ingrassia, Elizabeth Ruscio

Directed by Michael Ritchie
1993. 99 minutes. No rating.

A funny, whackily astute HBO film gets right down to the nitty-gritty of a true story, a sensation in the tabloids and on the tube at the time, about a Texas housewife who set out to help her eighth-grade daughter's prospects as a cheerleader by plotting to murder the mother of a rival classmate.

It's not as if Wanda Holloway (Hunter) is Jeffrey Dahmer or something. "It's not even funny, O.K.?" she drawls on a sleazy TV show after her conviction for attempted murder was declared a mistrial on a technicality. Wanda never actually killed anybody. She just tried to get Terry Harper (Bridges), a much-married slob and petty bad guy, to eradicate the woman, Verna Heath (Ruscio).

On TV, Wanda gets to tell her story in a voice that would boil grits. The daughter of strict Baptists, she never was a cheerleader, and she is still the pianist at church. It's just that Verna's daughter is more talented at cheerleading than Wanda's daughter, Shanna, and getting rid of Verna might undermine her kid in some way.

Kurtz is fine as Terry's wife, Marla, who sees furry things on the wall and tries using Drano to remove the hair on her legs. At the trial she doesn't make a credible witness.

Now and then some serious elements emerge, like the repercussions of an explosion at an oil refinery that shakes already fragile lives. In its last stages, the film turns to the publicity circus around Wanda. The case makes it onto Carson. A battle for rights breaks out, and everybody collects clippings. The real Verna objected to casting Hunter as Wanda. She would have preferred Susan Lucci.

POSTCARDS FROM THE EDGE

Meryl Streep, Shirley MacLaine, Dennis Quaid, Gene Hackman, Richard Dreyfuss

Directed by Mike Nichols
1990. 101 minutes. R.

How would you like to have Joan Crawford as a mother?" screams Doris Mann (MacLaine), a musical comedy star of the 1950's and 60's, at her daughter,

Suzanne (Streep), who is about to leave a rehabilitation center.

Doris has gotten hers in terms of success, and now she wants it known that all she wishes for Suzanne, in addition to a good man and a competent business manager, is that she, too, do well. Having kicked, or so she believes, cocaine, acid and Percodan, Suzanne wants nothing more than some breathing room to get on with her own acting career.

Streep is magnificent as a smart woman with a pragmatic wit who doesn't minimize her predicament but can't help standing a little outside it. Suzanne's first postclinic affair is with a glib movie producer (Quaid), and an acting role as a uniformed cop requires that she spend a day tied to a cactus.

MacLaine is very fine as the no-nonsense Doris, who doesn't have her daughter's problems in differentiating reality from make-believe.

In writing the screenplay adapted from her novel, Carrie Fisher, daughter of Debbie Reynolds and Eddie Fisher, has not so much gone by her book as been inspired by it. Her collaboration with Nichols is a perfect one, an oddball tale of woe that fits Nichols's particular ability to discover the humane within the absurd.

PRAISE

Peter Fenton, Sacha Horler, Marta Dusseldorp, Joel Edgerton, Yvette Duncan, Ray Bull, Gregory Perkins, Loene Carmen

Directed by John Curran
1998. 98 minutes. No rating.

Curran's "love story" doesn't involve the most attractive people in the world. Gordon (Fenton) may look poetic, but he's a chain-smoking asthmatic, a slender slacker and heroin addict whose passivity is a part of his charm. And

Cynthia (Horler)? Imagine a nymphomaniac with severe eczema who snaps up Gordon and overwhelms him with the sheer intensity of her needs.

Unusual and challenging, *Praise* made good festival material, the kind of film that had audiences talking afterward. Take it on its own terms, and it will work that way at home, too. Curran shoots some humor into the scene, which takes place in a big, empty room littered with beer bottles where Cynthia falls all over Gordon.

Horler gives a frank performance as a woman whose appetites will far outstrip Gordon's inclinations and capacity. Cynthia realizes he's no match for her, but she determines to get what she can from him anyway. The story has the aimless feel of a bad love affair, and that floating quality, as the relationship moves from one bad incident to another, is precisely what Curran is after.

Explicit detail spells out the compulsiveness of the characters, which keeps them together. Horler gives a frank and compelling performance in a kind of story that could either repel you or draw you into every seamy, often hilarious turn.

PRIMARY COLORS

John Travolta, Emma Thompson, Billy Bob Thornton, Kathy Bates, Rob Reiner, Adrian Lester

Directed by Mike Nichols
1998. 143 minutes. R.

Nichols's adaptation of Joe Klein's novel, a fictional version of the Clinton ascendancy, is a shrewd, entertaining and cynical political satire.

With his drawl and molasses charm, Travolta captures all the charisma of a certain former Southern governor who juggled noble zeal with wayward behavior on his way up the political ladder. His Jack Stanton mixes ruthlessness, empathy with the people and idealistic passion.

He's also a master of concealment. No one seems able to pin Jack down entirely, including his wife, Susan (Thompson), who contends with his uphill political battle and his philandering. Thompson's is the most compelling character of all; Susan is as ambitious and driven as her husband, as deeply compromised, and underneath it all terribly wounded by his betrayals.

Bates is splendid as the Stantons' tortured adviser, Libby Holden, profoundly disillusioned with her old friends, who were once so idealistic. And Thornton is hilarious as a facsimile of James Carville.

LA PROMESSE

Jérémie Rénier, Olivier Gourmet, Assita Ouedraogo, Rasmane Ouedraogo

Directed by Jean-Pierre and Luc Dardenne
1996. 93 minutes. French with English subtitles. No rating.

A wrenching moral quandary faces Igor (Rénier), a skinny 15-year-old who works for his father, Roger (Gourmet), in a Belgian construction business that employs and exploits illegal immigrants.

When a worker from Burkina Faso falls from a scaffold, Igor quickly drags him out of sight of inspectors visiting the plant that day. The dying man makes him promise to look after his wife and baby, who have come from Africa with him. Eager to hide the body, Roger forces his son to help him bury it in cement.

From that moment the boy is torn between his father, who is loving if sometimes brutal to him, and his pledge to help the wife, Assita (Assita Ouedraogo), and the child. The father-son confrontation is one of scariest ever filmed.

Overall, a casually devastating movie casts a critical eye on European multiculturalism and hostility toward immigrants, who aren't passive victims but tough, angry workers. The racist xenophobia is disturbingly matter-of-fact, and at the end nothing is left neat and tidy.

PUMPING IRON

Arnold Schwarzenegger, Lou Ferrigno, Bud Cort, Franco Columbu

Directed by George Butler and Robert Fiore
1977. 85 minutes. No rating.

***

Will Arnold Schwarzenegger inspire the constitutional amendment needed to allow foreign-born citizens to run for the presidency? At the Republican National Convention in 2004, the California governor exuded alarming intimations of such a possibility, and here Butler's film about Schwarzenegger's days as a championship body builder suggests where such ambitions might have originated.

It's hard to totally dislike the young Arnold, all vaguely lethal charm and cheery condescension as he closes in on his sixth Mr. Olympia title in South Africa. Other contestants are praised as colleagues and treated like children being led to the physical and psychological slaughter under the gaze of judges who, Schwarzenegger realizes full well, will succumb to his aura.

It's inevitable. Sheer presence does it, as Arnold knows. Ferrigno, who will become the Incredible Hulk, is a big guy, but he's clumsy. Franco Columbu, Arnold's congenial training mate, can pick up a car, but he's a small man (meaning less than 200 pounds) who can be overwhelmed out there under the glaring lights. No one can stop Arnold.

Schwarzenegger skips his father's funeral to keep on training, which he says he finds as enjoyable as sex. In a documentary on the DVD about the making of *Pumping Iron*, he contends that the Butler film was fictionalized in places to make him appear more ruthless and add dramatic interest. Often that's not the real Schwarzenegger, he says with a smile.

PUNCH-DRUNK LOVE

Adam Sandler, Emily Watson, Philip Seymour Hoffman, Luis Guzmán, Mary Lynn Rajskub, Ashley Clark, Julie Hermelin

Directed by Paul Thomas Anderson
2002. 95 minutes. R.

Sandler's character vaults all the way from typical Sandleresque schlub with anger problems to the New York Film Festival, where the film played in 2002. Anderson's exuberantly expressive way with a tale has a lot to do with that, but in a deft, nuanced performance Sandler steps up to a whole new level of social maladroit.

A wholesale bathroom-supply salesman, Barry Egan (Sandler) veers between frightening bursts of anger and a demeanor of stricken, lobotomized self-control when the shy, whispery Lena (Watson) decides, for some reason, to fall in love with him. From that point the film is about the sudden, unnerving eruption of grace, love and self-knowledge into his sad, chaotic life.

Anderson delights in choreographing distress. Part of Barry's comes from his seven sisters, who constantly hector and humiliate him and can't understand how they contribute to his tears and raging, mumbling weirdness. Then there are the four blond brothers who have been dispatched to extort money from him by a phone-sex entrepreneur (Hoffman).

With Barry, discretion is the better part of valor, which adds to his frustrations. Lena takes his behavior with unflappable equanimity, even after he trashes a restroom in a rage. Watson's smart, quiet oddness plays beautifully off Sandler's wildly veering bipolarity. As for Sandler, because Barry's cowardice is so excruciating and the injustices and annoyances he suffers so excruciating, his fury comes close to poetry.

QUEEN MARGOT

Isabelle Adjani, Daniel Auteuil, Jean-Hugues Anglade, Vincent Perez, Pascal Greggory, Virna Lisi, Julien Rassam

Directed by Patrice Chéreau
1994. 143 minutes. French with English subtitles. No rating.

Ah, 1570's French religion and politics. At their wedding in sweltering Paris, the Catholic Marguerite de Valois (Adjani), called Margot, mentions their mothers to her new husband, the Protestant Henri de Navarre (Auteuil). "Yours hated mine," she says. "Yours *killed* mine," he replies.

Catholics are about to massacre thousands of Protestants in Chéreau's feverish, wildly flamboyant film, but it's the machinations and outsize personalities that drive the tale and make it great, if bloody, fun. The principal troublemaker is Catherine de Médicis (Lisi looking startlingly chalky and gaunt in white makeup), who backs the hysterical Charles IX (Anglade) and her diabolical, sadistic son, the Duc d'Anjou (Greggory).

The madly sensual Margot (requiring a virtual tag team of lovers, or so it seems) and the much set-upon, puckishly bright Henri (who would go on to become one of France's ablest kings, but that's years from now) don't cotton to each other, but they realize that they had better make a deal if they want to keep their heads on their shoulders.

Both are subject to the murderous impulses of d'Anjou (Margot's brother) and the lunatic Charles, by turns weeping, raging and simpering. Henri manages to survive by converting to Catholicism for the time being and ducking assassination attempts in back rooms. Margot, who's a problem for d'Anjou and Catherine, is kept a prisoner in the Louvre.

How they bleed, these people, and all over everything, from ball gowns to the bed linens. Margot is forever mopping up her primary lover, La Môle (Perez), who is much sliced and shot while trying to arrange her escape to Navarre. And when poisoned by arsenic, Charles bleeds through his pores.

THE QUICK AND THE DEAD

Sharon Stone, Gene Hackman, Leonardo DiCaprio, Pat Hingle, Russell Crowe, Woody Strode

Directed by Sam Raimi
1995. 107 minutes. R.

Between his campy *Evil Dead* series and his *Spider-Man* blockbusters, Raimi directed this engaging postmodern western. As usual, he embraces a genre even as he sends it up.

The first twist is that Sharon Stone is the stranger who rides into town, as a gunslinger named Ellen.

The local strongman who runs the town of Redemption, a psychotic despot named Herod (Gene Hackman), stages an annual shooting competition. Last person standing takes the pot. This year the contest gets its first woman, and maybe its youngest competitor ever in the person of the Kid (a very kiddish-looking Leonardo DiCaprio), who says he is Herod's son. And Russell Crowe is the former gunman turned pacifist who once again must pick up a weapon.

Herod usually swaggers through the gunfights, but this year he is distracted. He denies that he is the Kid's father. And he is smitten with Ellen; he thinks she looks very fine in leather pants and even better in an evening dress with a décolletage down to there.

Raimi keeps the action going and the suspense building until the final showdown, when all personal mysteries are cleared up and secrets revealed.

THE QUIET AMERICAN

Michael Caine, Do Thi Hai Yen, Brendan Fraser

Directed by Phillip Noyce
2002. 101 minutes. R.

Caine has one of the richest roles of his career in this alluring film, based on Graham Greene's novel about British and American interlopers in 1950's Vietnam. Thomas Fowler (Caine), a British journalist and man of the world, is in Vietnam ostensibly to report on the fight for independence from the French, but to him the political turmoil is of little concern. He is besotted with the steamy mystique of Saigon, and not coincidentally with a beautiful young former taxi dancer named Phuong (Do Thi Hai Yen).

For all his sophistication, Fowler possesses a streak of fatalism. Though he'd like to take Phuong back to England, his wife won't give him a divorce; their relationship will last only as long as he remains in Saigon.

Of course, Fowler isn't the right age or the perfect prospect for Phuong, a fact noted by her family. A more favorable match might be with Alden Pyle (Fraser), a young American economic-aid officer who is really a government agent. Fowler and Pyle compete for Phuong yet remain wary friends, even after Pyle and Phuong start living together.

The men are caught in actual danger: shootings and explosions that remind us that the foreign presence in Vietnam is no game. But Noyce is more interested in characters than in action, and through Fowler's jaded, wistful gaze this becomes one of the finest of Greene adaptations.

QUIZ SHOW

Ralph Fiennes, John Turturro, Hank Azaria, Rob Morrow,
Paul Scofield, David Paymer, Christopher McDonald

Directed by Robert Redford
1994. 133 minutes. PG-13.

Revivals of megabuck quiz shows leave us with few illusions about the form, but Redford's elegant, thoughtful parable, based on the book by Richard N. Goodwin, tells of an earlier America awakening from a shining, innocent dream and finding itself in a world of cynicism, slipping standards, lies and a sensation-seeking public that preferred falsehoods to the truth.

In the story of Charles Van Doren (Fiennes), the learned fellow who dropped in from the intelligentsia to win a string of rigged victories on the 1950's game show *Twenty-One*, Redford takes his own lifetime of experience as an American icon and uses it as a mirror of the culture that chose to lionize him.

Van Doren is no Redford, but his refined air and academic credentials convince the show's producers they should jettison the current winning contestant, a voluble character and man of the people named Herbert Stempel (Turturro), and install Van Doren.

"Why would a guy like that want to be on a quiz show?" asks Jack Barry (McDonald), the show's suave host.

The answer lies in Charles's feelings of inadequacy in the shadow of an eminent father, the historian Mark Van Doren (Scofield). Redford presents Van Doren the elder presiding over a bravura garden party attended by Edmund Wilson, Thomas Merton and the like. Even their ears prick up at the size of Charlie's winnings on the show.

For a while he enjoys his new family supremacy, but then, of course, he's caught accepting answers and scandal erupts. Charlie is left with the golden boy's special sense of failure in a rich, handsome, articulate film marked by knowing, meticulous performances.

RABBIT-PROOF FENCE

Kenneth Branagh, Everlyn Sampi, Tianna Sansbury, Laura Monaghan, David Gulpilil, Ningali Lawford

Directed by Phillip Noyce
2002. 95 minutes. PG.

Noyce's eye-opening film is based on the true story of several Aboriginal girls who took a three-month walk home.

From 1905 to 1971 the Australian government practiced ethnic cleansing by kidnapping children of mixed race from Aboriginal communities and shipping them to settlement camps hundreds of miles away. A. O. Neville (Branagh) is the film's villain, the designated chief protector of the Aborigines and enforcer of a law that forbids children of mixed marriages to marry full-blooded Aborigines. In three generations, he boasts, all Aboriginal characteristics will have disappeared in the offspring of an interracial marriage.

Hearing of three young girls running wild in the desert depot of Jigalog, Neville has them wrested from their mothers' arms. Molly (Sampi), 14, her sister, Daisy (Sansbury), 8, and their cousin, Gracie (Monaghan), 10, are mixed-raced children fathered by itinerant white fence workers. The girls are shipped to a settlement 1,200 miles away.

After being told that they have no longer have mothers, the girls escape and begin a three-month trek home using a fence that runs the length of the country to guide them. Molly is the leader, an indomitable, resilient force and the stuff of legend in a film that could have become a brutal hunt but instead upholds the decency of the many people who helped the fugitives answer the powerful call of home.

RAIN

Alicia Fulford-Wierzbicki, Sarah Peirse, Marton Csokas,
Alistair Browning, Aaron Murphy

Directed by Christine Jeffs
2002. 92 minutes. No rating.

Jeffs's film about adolescent confusion and family collapse handles its volatile material with devastating
calm.

It's summer at the shore as 13-year-old Janey (Fulford-
Wierzbicki) and her younger brother, Jim (Murphy), swim,
play and get into mischief. Meanwhile, their parents, the
passive, kindly Ed (Browning) and the sorrowful Kate
(Peirse), drink and, in the evening, have their friends over to
drink some more and frolic naked in the surf.

Kate has a hankering for a rugged photographer who
lives on a fishing boat in the bay, and one day she paddles
off drunkenly to have sex with him. Ed seems too foggy to
react, but this is a marriage that doesn't seem to make
much sense to begin with, especially to Janey, who is developing a growing awareness of the grown-up world.

Janey sees and understands what is happening between her mother and the photographer long before her
father does, and she also understands her mother's boozy
disaffection. Then there is her own nascent sexual power,
which leads to some experiments with a local boy.

But Janey and Jim are left to cope with self-absorbed
adults who expose them to moral and physical peril. For
Janey, that is leading to a hurried, unsentimental abandonment of childhood.

We can see trouble coming here, but for the most part
Jeffs sidesteps melodrama. Her gorgeous, fluid compositions are charged with metaphor but aren't obvious or
easy. The visual beauty of the film, rather than distract
from the disturbing story, makes it more disturbing still.

RAIN MAN

Tom Cruise, Dustin Hoffman, Valeria Golino

Directed by Barry Levinson
1988. 130 minutes. R.

Hoffman's famous turn as the autistic savant Raymond Babbitt dominates Levinson's wonderfully quirky road movie, but the film's true central character is Raymond's confused brother, Charlie, beautifully played by Cruise even when he has to be straight man to his co-star.

A cocky California importer of high-end sports cars, Charlie finds himself strapped and, inexplicably and outrageously to his way of thinking, cut out of his father's $3 million estate save for one notable item: a stunning 1949 Buick Roadmaster convertible. All the rest has been left to Raymond, who, despite a cracked brilliance with numbers, is unable to care for himself and lives in a home in Cincinnati.

Jumping into the Buick, Charlie blasts east with the idea of springing his brother and having himself named guardian. Their trip west is a classic, with Raymond refusing to travel in rain and Charlie scrambling to keep up with all his other idiosyncrasies. By the time they reach Las Vegas, Charlie fully understands his brother's acuity with numbers and puts it to work at the gaming tables.

From the moment Raymond comes on screen, a small figure who avoids eye contact and speaks in tight little sentences that match his mincing steps, Hoffman demands that attention be paid to his intelligence and invention as an actor.

All the while, though, Cruise's Charlie is reconsidering his past behavior and coming to terms with his growing feelings for his brother. It may be no accident that both Charlie and Cruise survive as well as they do. Charlie is a lot like the edgy, self-deluding characters who have turned up in other Levinson films, most notably by Richard Dreyfuss in *Tin Men* (page 414).

RAISING VICTOR VARGAS

Victor Rasuk, Judy Marte, Melonie Diaz,
Altagracia Guzman

Directed by Peter Sollett
2002. 88 minutes. R.

Sollett's altogether satisfying romantic comedy dives into a small, packed household on the Lower East Side of Manhattan where, in a tiny space chockablock with his brother and sister, the frisky 16-year-old Victor (Rasuk) chafes under the rule of his prickly grandmother (Guzman).

Victor is really a nice kid; it's just that right now he's bursting with machismo and teenage assertion. Project number one is losing his virginity, and he zeroes in on "Juicy Judy" (Marte), the neighborhood's unobtainable beauty.

Other romances flourish in a film refreshingly free of drugs and violence. Grandma, a strict Catholic of the very oldest school, looks on in narrow-eyed suspicion at Victor's frolics. The devil lurks everywhere in Grandma's view, but she, too, is a loving person, and with rebellion brewing she finally begins to take her grandson for who he is in a true find of a film with a vital daffiness all its own.

RAMBLING ROSE

Laura Dern, Robert Duvall, Diane Ladd, Lukas Haas, John
Heard, Kevin Conway

Directed by Martha Coolidge
1991. 112 minutes. R.

Despite a little molasses at the outset and a bit of goo at the close (excusable enough in a tale of Southern derivation), Coolidge's film is as honest and engaging as its perky, disreputable heroine.

A middle-aged Willcox Hillyer (Heard) recalls the dusty

old days when he was a 13-year-old called Buddy (Haas) and had a life-shaping crush on a wild young woman named Rose (Dern). After being pursued by too many men at home, Rose is sent to work for the Hillyers, and as she appears in their yard she manages to appear innocent, gawky and provocative all at once.

The Hillyer household is full of types, with Ladd as the smart but slightly loony mother and Duvall as the crusty, gentlemanly husband. When Rose becomes as drastically infatuated with him as Buddy is with her, she flings herself into the elder Hillyer's lap and demands to be kissed. To him it's an astonishing role reversal. "A man is supposed to be a fool about this," he yells, but not a woman. "What are you, a nincompoop?"

Looking for some innocent comfort from Buddy, the distraught Rose finds that he wants only sex. Later she marches off to town to find a man, and soon "scoundrels," as Mr. Hillyer calls them, are fighting over her in the front yard. "Girls don't want sex; they want love," Rose says a bit too tritely in an otherwise uncommon coming-of-age story in which a whole family questions the mysteries of sex, loyalty and love.

READ MY LIPS

Emmanuelle Devos, Vincent Cassel, Olivier Gourmet

Directed by Jacques Audiard
2001. 115 minutes. French with English subtitles. No rating.

With a typically French eye for the gritty details of small lives, Audiard's swift, deft film presents the adventures of Carla Bhem (Devos), office worker. Carla is hearing-impaired to the extent that she reads lips. A mousy soul, she's the kind of person who exists to be exploited for free babysitting or lending her apartment for adulterous trysts.

But beneath the submission is a fury that is gratifyingly given a chance to break loose. When her boss allows her to take an assistant, she chooses a mopey ex-convict named Paul (Cassel), who proves nonthreatening and useful to Carla in extracurricular ways that stray far from the office.

Paul assumes that her interest in him is sexual, which it is to a point, but Carla also uses his criminal skills to take revenge on a piggish co-worker. With her organizational abilities and lipreading, Carla actually is pretty good at crime, and she and Paul turn a workplace comedy into a violent caper film when they get involved with a coarse nightclub owner (Gourmet).

With a big bag of money to be heisted and nasty characters to contend with, Carla proves that she can also read eyes and body language.

REAL WOMEN HAVE CURVES

America Ferrera, Lupe Ontiveros, Jorge Cervera Jr., Ingrid Oliu

Directed by Patricia Cardoso
2002. 90 minutes. No rating.

Cardoso's rousingly effervescent and satisfying crowd-pleaser (her first film) had audiences up and cheering at the 2002 Sundance Film Festival.

Flying in the face of a domineering mother, Ana (Ferrera) assumes her own identity. It's not that Carmen (Ontiveros) is mean or wishes ill of her hefty daughter. She just feels that Ana's zaftig figure could use some trimming down to make headway in the quest to find a husband.

To the fiery Carmen, weight loss is Ana's one route out of the Los Angeles sweatshop where Carmen and Ana's older sister (Oliu) toil in accepting subservience. Ana envisions going to college, which only agitates Carmen, who won't hear of such a thing.

Carmen is a diva, whirling about and making pronouncements that keep everybody flustered, including her mellow husband (Cervera). In Ana she meets her match, partly because the daughter is so like the mother. In a way, the two are in a competition—a good place for Ferrera, who is edgy and self-confident and has a blush that turns radioactive when Ana is provoked.

RECKLESS

Robson Green, Francesca Annis, Michael Kitchen, David Bradley

Directed by David Richards and Sarah Harding
1997. 480 minutes. No rating.

In this hugely entertaining tale of passion and civilized revenge, *Masterpiece Theater* let its hair down with an up-to-date mini-series about a 30ish surgeon and the wife of his boss at the hospital.

Dropping a prestigious post in London, Owen Springer (the appealing Green) returns to his working-class roots in Manchester, where he takes a job at the local hospital and falls for an enticing woman in her 40's. As it happens, Anna (Annis) is married to the hospital's arrogant chief of surgery, Richard Crane (Kitchen).

It takes Owen 45 minutes of the first episode to learn that Anna is married and to whom. By then, he is in love.

Despite class differences between herself and Owen, Anna gives in to the affair after she learns that Richard has been involved with another woman. Though they claim to be emotionally tortured, all three actually have a splendid time lying and cheating.

Green's Owen is full of brash intensity. Kitchen brings a sputtering comic sense to the egotistical Richard. Anna, both distraught at her husband's infidelity and exultant at her own, is the formidable one in this triangle, and Annis's understated performance holds *Reckless* together.

After the two men finally get into a fistfight at the hospital and land in jail, she wonders what she's doing with either of them.

RED ROCK WEST

Nicolas Cage, Dennis Hopper, Lara Flynn Boyle, J. T. Walsh, Dwight Yoakam

Directed by John Dahl
1992. 98 minutes. R.

---

ahl's second feature, a deliciously crazy thriller set in Wyoming, is one of the better films to appear on video without benefit of a theater run. (Technically speaking, *Red Rock West* made its debut on HBO and began playing in a small number of theaters at about the same time it was released on cassette in 1994.)

Trivia aside, the movie still jumps out from the pack. Prospects are bleak for an honest oil worker named Michael (Cage), who loses a job on a rig after confessing to a bad knee and, down to his last five dollars, winds up in the little town of Red Rock.

In a smoky bar owned by the forbidding Wayne Brown (Walsh), Michael is mistaken for a man named Lyle—or "Lyle from Texas"—who Michael assumes is the new bartender but is actually a killer hired to blow away Wayne's young wife, Suzanne (Boyle).

The naïve Michael catches on to the situation none too quickly, but even he figures out that Suzanne is having an affair with a handsome young gent who lives in a trailer. When Suzanne learns about Wayne's intent, she tries to hire Michael to finish her husband.

Cage is all anxiety as a well-meaning fellow who wants only to clear out. But then the real Lyle (Hopper in affably deadly nut-case mode) appears and insists on taking him back to the bar for a drink. Will Michael ever get out of Red Rock?

THE REF

Judy Davis, Kevin Spacey, Denis Leary, Robert J. Steinmiller Jr., Glynis Johns, Christine Baranski

Directed by Ted Demme
1994. 92 minutes. R.

This edgy marital comedy should warm the hearts and touch the nerves of dysfunctional families everywhere.

As if it's not hard enough defeating alarm systems, a jewel thief named Gus (Leary) suddenly finds himself playing peacekeeper for the couple whose house he has invaded. Forced to take them hostage after a botched job, Gus has the misfortune to choose the warring Caroline (Davis) and Lloyd (Spacey), who happen to be heading back to their luxurious Connecticut home after another unproductive session with their marriage counselor.

Back in the house, Caroline and Lloyd go right on battling as if Gus and his gun don't exist. Caroline has been having an affair out of sheer boredom; Lloyd is a whiner. And their son, Jesse (Steinmiller), is back from military school, where he has been blackmailing a teacher.

Since this is Christmas, other relatives are descending in a stream from Boston. It's obvious that Gus is exasperated but no killer, so Caroline and Lloyd agree to let him pose as their marriage counselor. With everybody gathered, Caroline edgily settles into preparing a grand Christmas dinner with a Scandinavian theme.

This is a smart cast in a film with a wonderfully pitched tone, which is relentlessly dark yet never becomes mean-spirited—if only because these people deserve each other.

RESTAURANT

Adrien Brody, Elise Neal, David Moscow, Simon Baker,
Catherine Kellner

Directed by Eric Bross
1998. 107 minutes. R.

Bross's film has a lot to say about friendship, race, class and ambition as the occasion arises among a group of workers at a swank Hoboken bar called J.T. McClure's. It's a haphazard community thick with complications and maybe a few too many story lines, but then so is life.

At the core is Chris (Brody), bartender, recovering alcoholic and aspiring playwright who finds that the actor who slept with his girlfriend has been cast as the lead in his play. That's enough to throw any 12-stepper off stride right there.

A newly hired waitress wants to be a singer; a hostess is about to be married; a bartender is looking for a roommate. For its first third, *Restaurant* shapes up as a well-made romantic comedy or young-adult drama. But then it heads off to examine slowly emerging racial themes in a world where race is said not to matter but actually matters a lot.

The performances, Bross's smooth camerawork and Tom Cudworth's understated script stand up well—right up to the very end, that is, when the filmmakers lose touch with their better storytelling instincts and the actors must prevent the movie from swerving into melodrama.

RETURN TO PARADISE

Vince Vaughn, Joaquin Phoenix, David Conrad, Vera Farmiga, Anne Heche

Directed by Joseph Ruben
1998. 111 minutes. R.

In Ruben's intelligent, brooding drama about loyalty and moral responsibility, three friends on a post-college frolic face the consequences of a mistake that threatens the life of one of them.

In Malaysia, an American named Sheriff (Vaughn) wrecks a rented bike, and when that accident brings the police, he tosses a brick of hashish into a trash bin. He and Tony (Conrad) leave the country, but Lewis (Phoenix) stays to work on a project with orangutans. The police find the hash and arrest Lewis. He is sentenced to death.

Two years later, Sheriff and Tony learn that their friend has eight days to live. Unless they come forward, he will hang. Luckily, Lewis has a fiercely dedicated lawyer (Heche), but she has to sway the others. As Sheriff, Vaughn projects chilly skepticism in a film with a fine cast, a cool, sober texture and a cerebral take on the ethical issues.

REVERSAL OF FORTUNE

Jeremy Irons, Ron Silver, Glenn Close, Annabella Sciorra, Uta Hagen, Fisher Stevens, Christine Baranski

Directed by Barbet Schroeder
1990. 110 minutes. R.

Jeremy Irons comes close to being too good to be true in an affected, edgy performance as Claus von Bulow, the socialite eventually acquitted of attempting to murder his heiress wife (Close) in the celebrated case and media circus during the early 1980's.

Schroeder based his lively, provocative film on a book about the case by Alan M. Dershowitz, the lawyer and Harvard law professor. In 1982, after being convicted of two counts of assault with the intent to kill his wife, Martha, called Sunny, von Bulow hired Dershowitz to handle his appeal and win a new trial.

Irons's performance nails his character's intriguing, affected elusiveness. On screen, von Bulow greets the lawyer (Silver) as royalty would a minor functionary: "Mr. Dershowitz, hello, hello, hello. How good of you to come." As it seemed in life, and as reported by Dershowitz in his book, there is no end to von Bulow's slippery charm.

If Irons's performance gives the film its satiric edge, Silver infuses Dershowitz with a singularly tough, unsentimental conscience. The movie, like the book, follows the lawyer as he puts together a large team of assistants, including some of his students, to tear apart every facet of the case. Though little of the film takes place in court, Dershowitz's intense perusal of his client has the confrontational air of a trial before a judge and jury.

So Sunny von Bulow was immensely rich and Claus von Bulow wasn't. Did he try to kill her? On screen, her disembodied voice describes her condition as she lies comatose in a hospital room attached to machines that feed and cleanse her system. "Brain dead and body better than ever," she says.

RICHARD III

Ian McKellen, Annette Bening, Jim Broadbent, Robert Downey Jr., Nigel Hawthorne, Kristin Scott Thomas, Maggie Smith, John Wood

Directed by Richard Loncraine
1995. 105 minutes. R.

Upper-class English life in the 1930's provides the milieu for Loncraine's transplanted *Richard,* based on

Richard Eyre's stage production of Shakespeare's play. Blasé aristocrats dressed to the nines in gilded halls are just the sort who would tolerate a fascistic takeover by Richard (McKellen). This usurpation drips money, power, glamour, drugs and kinky sex.

An elegant film full of fabulous tableaux, each more fabulous than the last, gives this action thriller a *Masterpiece Theater* look. As Shakespeare's most monstrous monarch, McKellen imagines him as a Rex Harrison type, a Machiavellian with the soul of Hitler. He's also the devil in Rolling Stones parlance, a man of wealth and taste, and in a film with a sense of humor he decides that he is literally the devil in his final moments.

Bening's Queen Elizabeth spits her denunciations of Richard with fiery venom, and as the king's mother, Smith curses the day he was born. A Nuremberg-style rally without swastikas or goose-stepping avoids Nazi symbols but conveys the same quasi-religious fervor. Murders are arty, with the blood of Richard's trusting brother Clarence (Hawthorne) swirling prettily after his throat is slit while he is submerged in a bathtub.

Shakespeare's dialogue has been pared to the famous speeches, the better to make room for pageantry and gore in a film acted to the hilt by an all-star cast.

RIDE WITH THE DEVIL

Tobey McGuire, Skeet Ulrich, Jeffrey Wright, Jewel, James Caviezel, Jonathan Rhys-Meyers, Simon Baker

Directed by Ang Lee
1999. 138 minutes. R.

Set in Kansas during the Civil War, Lee's chilly epic presents a colorful, rather curious look at the struggle within a struggle fought far from formal battlefields.

Out in the dust and mud and untamed woods, bushwhackers of Southern allegiance fought Jayhawkers of

Northern persuasion in a wild, free-form donnybrook. Goaded by each other's atrocities, combatants gun one another down in cold blood and torch everything in their path, but at least for the bushwhackers there's a bit of gallantry involved, not to mention chivalry extended to the womenfolk sobbing over their freshly slaughtered husbands.

These are fighters on fast horses who wear feathers in their caps and at times resemble high school kids on a rampage. Among the standouts is Jake Roedel (McGuire), a runty fellow with more sensibility than most for the meanings of things and what's acceptable under the circumstances and where the savagery crosses the line.

In Quantrill's Raid on Lawrence, Kansas, an abolitionist stronghold, Roedel refuses to take part in a massacre that leaves 150 dead. That angers some bushwhackers, but it salvages Roedel's humanity and his hide for marriage to Sue Lee (the pop star Jewel), who has been widowed about as fast as she could get hitched.

Ang Lee was after a searching meditation on a critical point in the country's history, and his devotion to the details of time and place sometimes creates the detached feel of an anthropological study. But these boys sure can ride and shoot.

RIDING IN CARS WITH BOYS

Drew Barrymore, Steve Zahn, Brittany Murphy, Adam Garcia, Cody Arens, James Woods

Directed by Penny Marshall
2001. 132 minutes. PG-13.

In a complex performance that requires her to age from 15 to 35, young Barrymore stays on her feet beautifully through the multiple disasters of Beverly Donofrio, a hard-luck gal from Wallingford, Connecticut, who may not be the most graceful or adept person in the world but eventually triumphs (if that word applies to a Beverly Donofrio).

It's in a car with a boy named Ray (Zahn in a brilliantly nuanced performance) that the teenage Beverly makes trouble for herself by becoming pregnant. Her father (Woods) is a stony cop, but a ragtag wedding is arranged. Poor Ray means well, but parental responsibility is beyond him and his life gradually disintegrates.

Beverly is left to raise their boy, Jason (Arens as a child and Garcia as an adult), by her own devices, and all told it's a demeaning experience. Having a child probably costs her the college scholarship she wants so desperately. Reared by a severely taxed but protective, demanding mother, the grown Jason (Garcia is two years older than Barrymore) wrestles with their relationship.

Eventually, Beverly ends up in New York as a tough working journalist writing a book about her life. Marshall's film, adapted from the real Beverly Donofrio's book, jumps back and forth in time, skillfully interweaving humor and drama. Barrymore never once loses her way.

RIO BRAVO

John Wayne, Dean Martin, Angie Dickinson, Ward Bond, John Russell, Claude Akins, Ricky Nelson, Walter Brennan

Directed by Howard Hawks
1959. 141 minutes.

Hawks was annoyed by *High Noon*, in which a beleaguered marshal asks the townsfolk for help against four killers. He and Wayne agreed that no self-respecting lawman would enlist untested citizens, so they set out to make a movie along similar lines, but with a marshal who handles things himself.

That pits the lone John T. Chance (Wayne) against a cattle baron (Russell) and a virtual army of bad guys who descend after Chance jails the cattleman's loco brother (Akins). Chance's deputy (Martin) was a good man, but he has succumbed to drink and is of little use. An old coot named Stumpy (Brennan) stands at the cell door with a shotgun, for all the good he'll do.

Chance refuses help from an old pal (Bond), who is shot in the back anyway. But there is one civilian Chance keeps his eye on, a kid with a quick gun hand named Colorado (Nelson). But the lad is reluctant to join other people's quarrels. Chance likes that.

In *High Noon*, a gunman tips his location by breaking a window, a fatal mistake. In *Rio Bravo*, a gorgeous saloon girl (Dickinson) throws a flowerpot and sets off a gun battle.

Hawks's western may not be the greatest ever, but it is hugely entertaining. Martin was fine once he stopped trying to be a fancy dude and started being a drunk. Nelson, son of Ozzie and Harriet, was a leading pop singer and brought over the teenagers, a boost at the box office. On screen, Hawks keeps him on a leash.

RIPLEY'S GAME

John Malkovich, Dougray Scott, Ray Winstone, Lena Headey, Uwe Mansshardt

Directed by Liliana Cavani
2002. 110 minutes. No rating.

If you're wondering why you never encountered Liliana Cavini's constantly entertaining thriller in movie theaters, it's because marketing disagreements blocked the film's release and sent it straight to cable and DVD.

Using all his creepy appeal, Malkovich makes a fine, middle-aged Tom Ripley, a much-ripened version of the Patricia Highsmith character last met on screen as Matt Damon in Anthony Minghella's *The Talented Mr. Ripley* (1999). In that film, Tom's talent for slipping in and out of the evil he creates seems positively fuzzy-cheeked next to this Ripley's icily urbane machinations.

The beautiful Tuscan countryside is the setting for Ripley's latest close call. These days Ripley peddles high-end art of dubious provenance and dispatches a bodyguard with a fire poker when necessary. When a shady club owner name d Reeves (Winstone) asks Ripley to assassinate his Russian competitor in Berlin, Ripley refuses. He doesn't do that kind of work, but he has a diabolical suggestion. Earlier he has been insulted by a picture framer named Trevanny (Scott), who called him a "bloody philistine American." Trevanny has terminal leukemia, and Ripley drily suggests that he might be lured into committing the crime for enough money to ease his family's financial burden.

Thus, Ripley is able to torture Trevanny and his family while he gains his sinister revenge and remains irresistibly fascinating and vile in this small gem of a thriller.

ROAD TO PERDITION

Tom Hanks, Paul Newman, Jennifer Jason Leigh, Ciaran Hinds, Stanley Tucci, Daniel Craig, Tyler Hoechlin

Directed by Sam Mendes
2002. 119 minutes. R.

There's mythic grandeur in a film about the downfall of mob characters in the winter of 1931, but Mendes's film is most memorable for its atmospherics. Nothing better evokes the chill of a dark winter's day than men standing in soppy woolen overcoats in a driving rain, or better conveys the horror of a massacre than flame but no sound coming from submachine guns that never seem to stop.

As personal hit man for the crusty Irish mob boss John Rooney (Newman), Michael Sullivan (Hanks) witnesses the impulse killing of one of Rooney's men by Rooney's unbalanced son, Connor (Craig). Also looking on, unnoticed through a window in the rain, is Sullivan's young son Michael Jr. (Hoechlin), who hid himself in the rumble seat of his dad's car and went along to see what the old man does for a living.

The senior Sullivan presents a dichotomy that few would handle better than Hanks: the decent man as ruthless character. An efficient killer and highly respected in his trade, Sullivan is undone by Connor's act. After catastrophic repercussions for his family, Sullivan and his son flee to Chicago, where he tries to go to work for the mobster Frank Nitti (Tucci) but finds his way blocked by the Rooneys.

Michael has always been treated like a son by the elder Rooney, a sentimental, treacherous old coot who realizes full well that in Connor he has an incompetent psychopath for an heir. But family blood is family blood, to Michael's disadvantage. The one mission now is to save young Michael in a film that has the feel and moral fiber of a classic western.

ROGER DODGER

Campbell Scott, Jesse Eisenberg, Isabella Rossellini,
Elizabeth Berkley, Jennifer Beals, Mina Badie,
Ben Shenkman

Directed by Dylan Kidd
2002. 105 minutes. R.

Kidd's small, pungent film has many noteworthy performances, particularly Scott's as Roger Swanson, a crass 40ish New York advertising copywriter with the mind of a high school lothario.

In the opening scene Roger is regaling a crowded New York bar with his theories about male sexual obsolescence. According to him, evolving technology will render men superfluous to human reproduction. Uneasily amused at all this, his girlfriend, Joyce (Rossellini), who is also his boss, grows steadily more put off as he tries to crash her apartment and becomes increasingly abusive and stalkerlike.

Years of Machiavellian sexual ploys have left him with no fresh gambits to try with the women he now accosts. Given the juiciest of roles as a misogynous screen baddie in the Neil LaBute tradition, Scott brilliantly sheds the skin of the earnest, sincere characters he usually plays and lets his usual empathetic sensitivity curdle into something smarmy and ferretlike.

When his 16-year-old nephew, Nick (Eisenberg), comes to town eager for his first sexual experience, Roger the self-styled mentor takes the boy in hand and teaches him all he knows about picking up women.

Soon thereafter the film reaches a critical juncture where it can refute Roger's cynicism. As the uncle and nephew tour the bars, Eisenberg's Nick takes over the film with a lovely balance of crude adolescent avidity and a winning inner sweetness that contradicts everything Roger stands for.

ROMY AND MICHELE'S HIGH SCHOOL REUNION

Mira Sorvino, Lisa Kudrow, Janeane Garofalo, Alan Cumming

Directed by David Mirkin
1997. 91 minutes. R.

Sorvino and Kudrow are leggy, shrewd perfection as a sweetly birdbrained duo who, as the bimbo Bill and Ted, travel back in time to their 10th high-school reunion. So what have Romy (Sorvino) and Michele (Kudrow) been up to in the interim?

Forced to face high school classmates who remember

them basically as Material Girl wannabes, they stoke plenty of self-doubt about how to present themselves. It's not as if that they haven't achieved anything during their lives as roommates in Venice Beach, California. "All we really need are better jobs and boyfriends, right?" says Romy, the smarter of the pair, who is a cashier at a Jaguar dealership.

So they borrow a car and don little black dresses. Now all they need is an achievement, which, they decide, will be the invention of the Post-it. "We could say that you were, like, the designer," Romy tells Michele. "Like, I thought of them but you thought of making them yellow."

Skepticism awaits at the reunion. (Can you imagine being these two in the presence of Janeane Garofalo, who plays a stubbier former classmate?) But as a comedy team, Sorvino and Kudrow take bubbleheadedness to a delightful new level.

RONIN

Robert De Niro, Jean Reno, Natascha McElhone, Stellan Skarsgard, Sean Bean, Skipp Sudduth, Michael Lonsdale, Jonathan Pryce

Directed by John Frankenheimer
1998. 121 minutes. R.

In Frankenheimer's dark, expert thriller, two carloads of mercenaries barrel over a divider and scream off at speeds approaching 100 miles per hour. Having landed on the wrong side of the highway, they are going against traffic.

"There are 300 stunt drivers coming at us," Frankenheimer says in a commentary on the DVD. "You can see with the suspensions working on these cars, nothing's fake." At the wheel of the pursuing car is Robert De Niro, looking distinctly as if he wishes he were elsewhere.

(Actually the wheel is a dummy; the real steering wheel, on the other side of the car, is in the hands of a French Grand Prix driver.)

De Niro is Sam, a former C.I.A. man who is the glue that binds a crack team of hardened operatives hired to obtain a mysterious case containing lord knows what that is coveted by both the Russians and the Irish Republican Army. Reno plays the burly French strongman of the crew; Bean is the weapons expert; Skarsgaard portrays an ex-K.G.B. computer wiz; Sudduth does the driving.

McElhone is Deirdre, the icy Irishwoman who hires them. Deirdre and Sam will warm to each other, but not for long in a game of double-cross and disappearance. They're all tough customers, but they've got nothing on Frankenheimer, who directs a tightly knit plot like a world-weary Hitchcock.

British commandos advised on the gun battles. On the DVD, Frankenheimer talks about quick, clean transitions in dramatic scenes. No dissolves, and no slow motion in the action sequences. "Violence happens fast," he says.

THE ROOKIE

Dennis Quaid, Rachel Griffiths, Jay Hernandez, Beth Grant, Brian Cox

Directed by John Lee Hancock
2002. 127 minutes. G.

A collision of tired formulas—the triumph of the trampled high school underdogs and the comeback of the old-timer—rises above its parts in a surprisingly fine film about baseball and the hearts of those who don't quit. There are several reasons for this success, but the credit belongs primarily to Quaid.

Hancock's film begins with a bit of mysticism on the dusty West Texas plains in the 1920's, when some nuns gouge out a ball field for the oil workers. Decades later, not much grass has grown on the spot, now used for the local high school team, the league doormat. Football is the sport in these parts, and if these kids played that game, one of them remarks, their field would look like Tiger Woods's backyard.

As it is, the deer chomp what little grass there is on the field in Big Springs, home of the hapless team coached by Jim Morris (Quaid), who also teaches at the school. Quaid once owned a major league fast ball, but he didn't get past the Milwaukee Brewers farm system after his arm gave out. A native of West Texas, he's been home ever since.

How can he give his kids a lift? One day he suddenly discovers that he can throw over 90 miles per hour again. He and the team, a game, hardheaded group, make a bargain. If they can win the regionals, he'll try again to make the majors.

The film gets baseball right, and Quaid takes over a story (a true one) about an aging, care-worn man with a family to support and no grand illusions. Certainly there's sentimentality along the comeback road, but as he did in *Any Given Sunday*, Quaid turns striving for glory into good hard honest work.

THE ROYAL TENENBAUMS

Alec Baldwin (Narrator), Gene Hackman, Anjelica Huston, Bill Murray, Ben Stiller, Luke Wilson, Gwyneth Paltrow, Danny Glover, Owen Wilson

Directed by Wes Anderson
2001. 109 minutes. R.

Wes Anderson's whimsical family history makes messed-up psyches extremely amusing.

In a richly colored, cartoonish New York, Chas, Margot and Richie Tenenbaum (Stiller, Paltrow and Luke Wilson) were reared to be prodigies and became, respectively, a financial wizard, a prize-winning playwright and a tennis champion. Already this doesn't add up. Their father, Royal Tenenbaum (Hackman), abandoned the family to go off and live a separate life, mostly on credit, leaving their upbringing to their mother, Etheline (Huston). Now Royal is back, a disbarred lawyer trying to reconcile himself with the family by pretending to be terminally ill.

Hackman's portrayal is a wonder of many shifting moods, tenderness to belligerence, and shameless ploys.

Paltrow is deadpan as Margot, who is in an unlikely marriage to a neurologist (Murray) and has a lover who seems more her type, a stoner novelist (Owen Wilson). Etheline is courted by her bridge partner and accountant (Glover).

Anderson doesn't try to make sense of the Tenenbaums; one of his points is that families never make sense, and this one descends into farcical chaos instead of neat reconciliation. He may be unconcerned with narrative pull, but he's a master of quirky, enjoyable characters.

RUNAWAY JURY

Gene Hackman, John Cusack, Dustin Hoffman, Rachel Weisz, Bruce Davison

Directed by Gary Fleder
2003. 127 minutes. PG-13.

A courtroom thriller based on a John Grisham novel and featuring Hackman, Cusack and Hoffman in a game of cat and mouse (or is it cobra and mongoose?) is bound to have promise. And this one introduces a slick, if creepy, game called "let's weed out the jury."

In a clandestine C.I.A.-like basement full of computers and technicians, the legal consultant Rankin Fitch (Hackman) calls up detailed information on each and every soul being screened to serve on a jury in a civil suit against a gun manufacturer. Fitch, a very nasty piece of work, is working for the gun makers and against Wendell Rohr (Hoffman), the lawyer for the plaintiff, a woman whose husband was gunned down in an office massacre.

As Fitch accepts or rejects each jury candidate, his decision is radioed to the defense lawyer (Davison) in the courtroom. It's probably impossible to dredge up the goods on a large group of people on immediate notice and fling it all up there on screen just like that, with video to boot, but it's fun to watch. "I hate Baptists as much as I hate Democrats," Fitch snarls as he passes over a prospective juror.

Poor Rohr is the tortoise to the hare in this league, but you have the suspicion that genteel and honorable will count for much. Fitch may be sharp at shaping just the right panel, but despite his suspicions a sleeper named Nick Easter (Cusack) gets past him and onto the jury.

That's Fitch's mistake in a stylized courtroom potboiler that is over the top in some respects but works best when setting up the case.

RUN LOLA RUN

Franka Potente, Moritz Bleibtreu, Herbert Knaup, Armin Rohde, Joachim Król, Nina Petri

Directed by Tom Tykwer
1998. 81 minutes. R.

Tykwer's thriller is considered more of a stylistic exercise than a film, but the result is fascinating—as is Potente in the title role. Like *Memento* (page 247) and numerous other films, it throws out bits of narrative and then doubles back to modify and get itself out of seeming impasses.

We begin at a dead run down apartment-house stairs with Lola, as appealing a loper as you'll come across, responding to an emergency call from her inept boyfriend, Manni (Bleibtreu). A drug deal has gone bad; if she doesn't get him $100,000 in 20 minutes, he's dead.

Lola's long, muscular stride takes her flying across the city. First she has to get the money. A quick strike into the offices of her estranged father puts the finishing touches on a nonexistent father-daughter relationship and gets her tossed out of the building. But where there's a will, there has to be a way. If she can only get to Manni in time.

She doesn't. But wait. Tykwer stops and does it again and again with some alterations and a different result.

RUSHMORE

Jason Schwartzman, Bill Murray, Olivia Williams, Brian Cox, Seymour Cassel

Directed by Wes Anderson
1998. 93 minutes. R.

Anderson's offbeat film about a precocious teenager catches the imagination. A pillar of Rushmore Academy on the extracurricular front—chess, astronomy, debating, beekeeping, fencing, double-team dodge ball and drama being a few of the activities he heads with mercurial aplomb—15-year-old Max Fischer (Schwartzman) is cutting corners in his classes, all of which he is flunking. Elevate those grades, he is told, or adios. "Couldn't we just let me float by?" Max asks.

Max is at Rushmore solely for the entrepreneurial charge he gets from running everything on campus. Those inclinations amuse and attract an eccentric local steel baron named Blume (Murray), Rushmore's primary benefactor. A dispirited figure, the middle-aged Blume has an undefined longing to try doing things differently, which makes him a natural soulmate for the unorthodox Max, despite their age difference.

Soon they both fall in love with Miss Cross (Williams), a first-grade teacher, and become rivals as if they were contemporaries. After one of Max's schemes finally gets him tossed out of Rushmore, he sets up shop at Grover

Cleveland High School. But life doesn't come together for anybody until a spectacular production of Max's explosive (literally) new play, set on a Vietnam battlefield.

THE SAFETY OF OBJECTS

Glenn Close, Dermot Mulroney, Jessica Campbell, Patricia Clarkson, Joshua Jackson, Moira Kelly, Timothy Olyphant

Directed by Rose Troche
2001. 120 minutes. R.

Out in suburban fields of dysfunction, guilt, frustration and sexual perversity (what are the suburbs for anyway?), Troche's film animates the harsh, deadpan prose of A. M. Homes's book of stories. But though Troche emphasizes Homes's stringent fatalism, she paces the movie with enough artfulness to avoid overwrought soap opera.

The cast treads lightly through even the swampiest emotional terrain. Close, with wounded, chilly grace, plays Esther Gold, a middle-aged woman whose life is devoted to attending to a beloved and gifted teenage son who lies comatose after a car accident. (Dad won't even look at the kid, regarding the boy's mishap as some kind of betrayal.) Upstairs, her daughter, Julie (Campbell), drifts through days in erotic reverie.

Jim Train (Mulroney) is an ambitious lawyer who cracks up, albeit in a somewhat amusing and not altogether fruitless manner, after being passed over for a partnership. Meanwhile, his young son is having a passionate affair with one of his sister's dolls, while one his playmates is abducted by a troubled young landscaper (Olyphant).

There are other subplots, but to enumerate them might trivialize a film that casts an unnerving spell. At times Troche shows the strain of editing together so many disparate elements, but with the help of a nearly flawless ensemble, she assembles the damaged elements of Homes's world with patience and precision.

SALAAM BOMBAY!

Shafiq Syed, Sarfuddin Quarassi, Raju Barnad

Directed by Mira Nair
1988. 113 minutes. Hindi with English subtitles. No
rating.

In a remarkably fine first feature film, Nair cast 11-year-old Shafiq Syed, a street kid himself, as a country boy named Krishna who is kicked out of his house by his mother and drifts to the nearest big city, Bombay.

There we might expect him to disappear into a sea of thieves, prostitutes and drug dealers, but while there's no shortage of these types and worse, Krishna quickly learns how to survive. Being Indian-born herself, Nair understands that what appears to tourists as hopeless degradation and despair is not necessarily the entire reality. Actually, some of these people are quite respectable.

A bright lad and an operator, Krishna finds his way effortlessly and exuberantly in the city's ancient demimonde. Nair gets exceptionally good performances from her actors, most of them amateurs. Action is character and dialogue is spare in a film that accepts squalor as the natural order of things and gets on with life.

SALVADOR

James Woods, James Belushi, Michael Murphy, John Savage, Elpidia Carrillo

Directed by Oliver Stone
1986. 122 minutes. R.

Stone is in early conspiratorial mode in a fast, gritty film set in El Salvador during the guerrilla war in the early 1980's. Right-wing death squads terrorized the land. Among the thousands murdered were Archbishop Oscar

Anulfo Romero and four United States churchwomen.

The scene exerts a strong pull on an American gonzo-style journalist and freeloading boozer named Rick Boyle (Woods). Gathering up his friend, a whacked-out disc jockey (Belushi), he drives down from Mexico and jumps in wherever the action is, from military headquarters to right-wing hangouts to guerrilla camps to the United States Embassy.

Woods puts lots of nervous energy and self-mocking wit into the character, who is part scrounger, part scoop-seeker, part friend of the common man and part sharp political analyst. (The real Richard Boyle collaborated with Stone on the screenplay.) *Salvador* has plenty of speed, grit and grime, but the movie also has a larger political point to convey.

Taking his cue from Constantin Costa-Gavras, Stone lays blame for the chaos on conservative forces in the United States, a contention he never nails down but fans effectively in the flood of events on screen. One look at the youthful, idealistic guerrillas and you know where Stone's heart lies.

SALVATORE GIULIANO

Frank Wolff, Pietro Cammarata, Salvo Randone, Frederico Zardi

Directed by Francesco Rosi
1962. 125 minutes. Italian with English subtitles. No rating.

Rosi's docudrama about a renowned Sicilian bandit is more involving for what it doesn't reveal than for the facts of the matter. We begin with Giuliano (Cammarata) laid out dead in a sunny courtyard, with the corpse being contemplated by blasé townsfolk as if it were a trophy fish.

Two guns are by its side. In life as on screen, Giuliano was a charismatic leader devoted to robbing and killing.

As a 22-year-old already practiced in the ways of violence, he served the Sicilian separatist movement. After World War II, the story grows foggier as he all but disappears into the hills around his hometown of Montelpre.

His most infamous act occurred in 1947, when he and his band massacred Communist Party members at a May Day celebration. Why he did it, and at whose bidding, is one of the unanswered mysteries in a film that masterfully hints at the connections and machinations among police and military and other centers of power in a fascinatingly shrouded society.

History never clarified these matters, and Rossi doesn't try. This is a film to be relished for its slow rhythm, simple eloquence and especially its appreciation of the impenetrability of it all.

THE SCARLET EMPRESS

Marlene Dietrich, John Lodge, Sam Jaffe, Louise Dresser

Directed by Josef von Sternberg
1934. 104 minutes.

In the sixth of her seven collaborations with von Sternberg, Dietrich is a Catherine the Great to contend with, but primarily she serves as a focal point for what he called an excursion into the grand style.

As a child in a royal German household, Sophia Frederica (played by Dietrich's daughter, Maria Riva) is stripped of all things German, including contact with her parents, and trained for marriage to the deranged and crippled Grand Duke Peter (Jaffe), who is to be crowned emperor of Russia.

History tells us how unlikely Catherine was to tolerate a foppish madman (though she was married to him for 18 years). An affair with a count (Lodge) and another with a captain of the guard help her up the political ladder and provide her with a royal newborn, respectively.

Dietrich is forceful, but whatever story and characterizations here are in the service of von Sternberg's opulent motifs and decor in a phantasmagorical world.

SECRETS & LIES

Brenda Blethyn, Marianne Jean-Baptiste, Claire Rushbrook, Timothy Spall, Phyllis Logan

Directed by Mike Leigh
1996. 142 minutes. R.

___

Noted for instilling his methods in virtually his own repertory company of actors, Leigh decided to keep his cast in the dark about the racial identity of one of the characters. Not all the white performers who play relatives of Cynthia Rose Purley (Blethyn), the bighearted cockney at the center of the film, realized that her long-lost daughter, Hortense (Jean-Baptiste), would be black.

Hortense's arrival at a party comes as a shock, touching off a crisis that actually has relatively little to do with race as these two characters collide and adjust. Blethyn's warmly heartrending performance gives emotional life to the film. A wistfully lost soul, Cynthia has made plenty of mistakes in life. Now she works at a box factory and worries over the daughter she did bring up, the surly Roxanne (Rushbrook). A brother (Spall) is married to a woman (Logan) who wants to keep Cynthia at arm's length.

Ending her search for her birth mother, Hortense is as surprised as anybody by the racial difference. The two work through the shock of their first encounter and proceed to a long get-together that lets them begin to see each other clearly. This is Blethyn's film, and she conveys every nuance of emotion as she moves from grief to comedy to compassion.

SECOND SIGHT

Clive Owen, Claire Skinner, Art Malik, Finbar Lynch

Directed by Charles Beeson
1999. 180 minutes. No rating.

Owen is unforgettable as the gaunt, hollow-cheeked Ross Tanner, a brilliant police detective who contracts a rare eye disease and is gradually going blind. Over time the condition becomes harder and harder to conceal from his colleagues and superiors. As his sight dims, he must rely on his other senses and eventually on a tough new female deputy, Catherine Tully (Skinner), who agrees to help him if he shares credit for his investigative successes. Eventually she becomes not only his eyes but his lover.

In one episode from the show's second season, broadcast on PBS's *Mystery!*, the whispering around the squad room centers on the pair's romantic troubles. The team reopens a two-year-old case involving the murder of a superstar violinist who was found dead in her apartment along with her traumatized 10-year-old son. The suspects now are the same as they were before: the boy's father (Lynch), who as his son's trustee can get his hands on the violinist's money, and a high-profile doctor (Malik), who was devastated by the end of their affair.

To compensate for his failing eyesight, Tanner has an exact replica of the victim's living room built so he can literally get the feel of the place. Tanner is full of such surprises in this ingenious suspense series.

SECRETARY

James Spader, Maggie Gyllenhaal, Jeremy Davies, Lesley
Ann Warren, Stephen McHattie, Patrick Bauchau

Directed by Steven Shainberg
2002. 104 minutes. R.

In a small, groundbreaking comedy, two lonely people
discover a miraculous if unorthodox erotic harmony.
The endearing heroine, Lee Holloway (Gyllenhaal), is a repressed, masochistically inclined young secretary who
blooms under the spanking hand of her boss, E. Edward
Grey (Spader), a grim, tight-lipped lawyer.

Lee, who has spent time at both a mental hospital and
a business school, has a history of cutting and burning
herself. When she misspells too many words in a business
letter, Edward administers corporal punishment by making her bend over while he gives her a spanking that
leaves her flesh reddened.

A large gulf opens between her self-abuse and the
spankings administered by Edward. At home she has an
overprotective mother (Warren) and a tentative romance
with a former high school classmate (Davies) whose inex-
perienced gropings leave her repulsed. At work, Edward's
dominance sets her aflame, and he becomes a kind of
cruel Pygmalion whose blunt instructions on how to
dress, eat and even answer the telephone give her life a
shape and direction.

Before long she craves his spankings so intensely that
she begins devising tricks to spark his ire. Spader, who has
always specialized in fish-eyed yuppies haunted by inner
demons, is ideally cast as a shy sadomasochist whose
spankings are delivered with an ardent choked-up tenderness.

In Gyllenhaal's Lee the film has a heroine who is
kinky, to be sure, but also plucky as she plots her sexual
emancipation. It's not too much of a stretch to regard the
movie as a wholesome self-help fable about magical

transformation of shame into pleasure and personal liberation.

THE SECRET LIVES OF DENTISTS

Campbell Scott, Hope Davis, Denis Leary, Robin Tunney,
Gianna Beleno, Lydia Jordan, Cassidy Hinkle

Directed by Alan Rudolph
2002. 104 minutes. R.

Rudolph's films often take us to the heart of families in flux, and here we find a couple of dentists, husband and wife, and their three daughters. Few movies have so perfectly captured the underground rivers of doubt and anxiety in a middle-class marriage.

David Hurst (Scott) is the protagonist. A bright, sympathetic character, he peevishly frets over his children, who are hard to control, and over the loyalty of his pretty blond wife and dental partner, Dana (Davis), whom he suspects is having an affair.

Dana says she wants to be closer to her husband, but David has trouble responding. As his suspicions about her and anxieties about his own life deepen, the atmosphere is further clouded by the arrival of Slater (Leary), David's cocky, loudmouth patient who also pops up continually in his imagination to plant additional fears and offer destructive advice.

David suspects that Dana is involved with a man she has met while performing in a local opera company. Is this true or a figment of his imagination? Slater tells him he'd better believe it's true and he'd better get out of the marriage.

For a long while the Hursts are left teetering while David wrestles with his demons, at one point storming out of the house and disappearing for a while. But for all his neuroses, Scott gives him warmth, intelligence and ultimate decency.

SEE THE SEA

Sasha Hails, Marina de Van, Paul Raoux

Directed by François Ozon
1997. 52 minutes. French with English subtitles. No rating.

In a little less than an hour Ozon sets up a creepily inter-esting situation that packs a feature-length wallop. A well-to-do Englishwoman named Sasha (Hails) is spend-ing her days in privileged isolation at the shore with her baby daughter. One day, a backpacker named Tatiana (de Van) appears at the door and asks if she can camp out in Sasha's backyard.

If that's not strange enough, Tatiana, a sullen, rude type, doesn't so much ask as demand. Stranger still, after some initial hesitation Sasha agrees to accommodate the guest, who clearly should raise a warning flag.

And so Tatiana pitches her tent. In expertly chilling fashion, Ozon establishes an uneasy rapport between the two. The withdrawn Tatiana makes no effort to pay back the hospitality, but the lonely Sasha clearly needs the company enough to let her guard down and tentatively try to make connections that take on a sexual connota-tion.

Eventually, as it must, all of this comes to a boil when she leaves the child in Tatiana's care, leaving Ozon to adeptly play on all the fears he has so exquisitely instilled.

SENSE AND SENSIBILITY

Emma Thompson, Alan Rickman, Kate Winslet, Hugh Grant, Gemma Jones, Greg Wise, Emilie François

Directed by Ang Lee
1995. 135 minutes. PG.

In the Jane Austen boom of the 1990's, Lee's film, adapted from Austen's first published novel, may not match the brilliant incisiveness of Roger Michell's *Persuasion* (page 312), but it certainly makes for a colorful, contemporary comedy of manners.

Lee and Thompson, who wrote the film as well as played its central figure, Elinor Dashwood, do away with Regency-era stuffiness and modify the Austen text to suit broader comic tastes.

When Mr. Dashwood, a country gentleman, dies, his widow (Jones) and three daughters, Elinor, Marianne (Winslet) and Margaret (François), must be disinherited in favor of his son by his first wife. Banished from the Dashwood estate, they set up housekeeping in a small cottage provided by a benefactor.

That settled, the next task is to find marriageable prospects for the two older daughters. Edward Ferrars (Grant) is a genteel heartthrob of immaculate amiability and financial credentials. The swashbuckler John Willoughby (Wise) never goes anywhere without a book of Shakespeare's sonnets, a combination that appeals to Marianne, who is the more passionate of the two sisters.

Older and more pained, Colonel Brandon (Rickman) proves that patience and decency have their value in the hunt for a Dashwood. Like other suitors parading to the countryside, the colonel pops off to London on the slightest pretense when affairs aren't proceeding to his liking.

Left to stew and ruminate, the Dashwoods mount an excursion to the big city for a final resolution of a movie that surpasses any other Austen screen adaptation for sheer fun.

SEXY BEAST

Ben Kingsley, Ray Winstone, Amanda Redman, Cavan Kendall, Julianne White, Ian McShane, Álvaro Monje, James Fox

Directed by Jonathan Glazer
2000. 89 minutes. R.

When freshly shaved, Kingsley's skull suggests a range of things. In the role of Gandhi, Kingsley and his head (remarkably like Gandhi's own head) helped symbolize peace and wisdom. In Glazer's film, the head brings to mind the business end of an artillery shell. As the London hood Don Logan, Kingsley portrays a human projectile.

Logan has been dispatched to the sunny Spanish coast to collect a safecracker named Gal (Winstone). Now an easygoing retiree, Gal lounges about his hillside villa overlooking the sea with his wife, Deedee (Redman), and schmoozes with his old London associate Aitch (Kendall) and his wife, Jackie (White).

One night at dinner, Aitch and Jackie have alarming news. Logan is on his way from London to pay Gal a visit. As mellowed out as they are these days, all these people know trouble, and Logan's imminent arrival sets off alarms. At Gal's house Logan struts about, perching here and there like a panther in a tree. Gal and the others realize full well what they're dealing with: a predator and psychopath who could explode at any second.

It's hard to tell what Logan's problem is exactly, beyond the obvious fact that he likes to prod and push people to the point of inevitable violence. Nominally he's down from London at the bidding of the kingpin Teddy Bass (McShane), who wants Gal to undertake one last job.

Gal resists, so we know where this is headed. What's special are the performances, especially Kingsley's and Winstone's as a bearish, quietly sexy middle-aged man who conveys tenderness and hurt at unexpected moments.

SHACKLETON

Kenneth Branagh, Phoebe Nicholls, Matt Day, Lorcan Cranitch, Mark McGann, Embeth Davidtz

Directed by Charles Sturridge
2002. 184 minutes. No rating.

The A&E mini-series about the great Antarctic explorer is part period soap opera, part rousing adventure tale, and thoroughly entertaining. Branagh commands attention as Shackleton, who intends to lead the first expedition to cross the Antarctic continent on foot.

On the home front he has a wife (Nicholls) and a mistress (Davidtz) to juggle. And in 1913, with World War I brewing, he must win supporters and open deep pockets in an upper-crust world that has more pressing matters on its mind. This is exploration as business and life's work, with promotional deals and contractual arrangements to be made with collaborators like Frank Hurley (Day), the photographer whose extraordinary images of the voyage are a primary reason why we remember and celebrate Shackleton today.

As their ship, the *Endurance,* is caught in a vise of deadly ice floes and begins to break up, Hurley repeatedly dives into the flooded hull to retrieve his photographs. Shackleton and crew are now alone on the shifting floes, aided by the noble dogs who would be their companions until the food ran out.

At the end of the ice, they face nothing but open sea. Behind them is nothing but death. In an incredible feat of seamanship, Shackleton and a few of his men sail a tiny lifeboat across 800 miles of wild ocean to bring help to the rest of the party. Through it all Branagh makes an indomitable leader, fiercely determined that not one of his party would perish—and, incredibly, not one of them did.

Sturridge (one of the directors of *Brideshead Revisited*, page 54) manages to combine the vastness and visual splendor of the adventure with the intense isolation of the men.

SHAKESPEARE IN LOVE

Gwyneth Paltrow, Joseph Fiennes, Geoffrey Rush, Colin Firth, Ben Affleck, Judi Dench, Rupert Everett, Simon Callow, Jim Carter

Directed by John Madden
1998. 122 minutes. R.

Not hamstrung by too much biographical information about Shakespeare, Madden's uproariously entertaining film, written by Tom Stoppard and Marc Norman, has plenty of room for invention.

In 1593, people behind on their debts got their boots burned (with their feet in them). With cash-flow problems at the Rose Theater, the heat is on for a marketable piece of work from a rakish and normally confident young man on the local drama scene named Will Shakespeare (Fiennes).

Trouble is, about the best Will can offer at the moment is something he calls *Romeo and Ethel, the Pirate's Daughter*. Frankly, it's not his best work. Will's gifts have dried up, in fact, and with them his sexual appetite. Life, he tells his therapist, is like "picking a lock with a wet herring."

A rival up-and-comer named Christopher Marlowe (Everett) half-mockingly offers some pretty good suggestions for turning around *Romeo,* but it isn't until Will sights the gorgeous, high-born Viola de Lesseps (Paltrow) that he jump-starts himself both creatively and sexually. Viola has dramatic aspirations herself, but since it is illegal for women to appear on stage, she dresses as a boy.

A wildly passionate relationship ignites. In bed, the two couple steamily. At the writing stand, Will strips feathers from his quill and scribbles madly, with the still-wet pages of the forming masterpiece rushed on stage to be rehearsed by his Juliet (Viola with a penciled mustache).

For her, theirs is a "love that overthrows life." Unfortunately, Viola has been promised to Lord Wessex (Firth), in a union approved by Queen Elizabeth herself (Dench). And Will, it evolves, has a wife up in Stratford-upon-Avon. It's a mess, but the play's the thing.

SHALLOW GRAVE

Kerry Fox, Ewan McGregor, Keith Allen, Christopher Eccleston, Ken Stott, Kerry Fox

Directed by Danny Boyle
1994. 92 minutes. R.

anny Boyle's first film is an uncompromising dark comedy about three Edinburgh roommates who turn into killers after having their heads turned by a pile of money. It also suggests the beginning of an unofficial Boyle repertory company, featuring McGregor, who would memorably team up with Boyle again in *Trainspotting,* and Eccleston, who pops up in Boyle's *28 Days Later* (page 430).

Three roommates—Juliet (Fox), a doctor; Alex (McGregor), an insolent wise-cracking journalist; and David (Eccleston), a suppressed accountant—are searching for a fourth person to share an expensive flat. They ridicule all manner of applicants until the quiet but mysterious Hugo (Allen) is accepted.

Soon the new roommate turns up naked and dead in his room, leaving behind a suitcase full of cash, which the other three decide they would like. What they don't need is any trace of Hugo.

Before long Alex is patrolling a hardware store for the right tools, and, having drawn the short straw, David is assigned the task of removing the head and hands, all of which could lead to identification. The next challenge materializes in the form of two thugs who descend looking for the money. There may be more shallow graves to dig.

David, traumatized by the dismemberment and overcome by paranoia, retreats to the attic, where he drills holes in the floor, the better to observe the blossoming romance between Juliet and Alex. (Or are they using each other to get a bigger share of the money?) There are further gleefully dark twists.

Although you might draw some lessons about the destructiveness of greed, at heart the film is Boyle's enormously confident and visually stylish calling card. It holds up wonderfully.

SHINE

Geoffrey Rush, Armin Mueller-Stahl, Noah Taylor, Alex Rafalowicz, Lynn Redgrave, John Gielgud, Googie Withers

Directed by Scott Hicks
1996. 105 minutes. PG-13.

Hicks beautifully captures one of the more harrowing father-son relationships ever filmed. YOUNG DAVID ON THE ROAD TO FAME, reads the headline of a newspaper story about David Helfgott (Taylor), a charming adolescent piano prodigy in Australia. Tragically, however, the boy is under the thumb of his psychotically possessive father, Peter (Mueller-Stahl).

Though David remains a passive victim (making his plight all the more poignant), this is parent-child warfare of an extreme order. Driven by memories of losing his family in the Holocaust, Peter combines his passionate love for music with a determination that his son will succeed at all costs.

With his life shut down, often brutally, by his controlling father, David begins to crack under the pressure. He plays beautifully, but as a symbol of things to come a piano he uses in a competition literally rolls away from him across the floor. Gradually he develops the tics and mannerisms that signal an impending emotional breakdown.

Fearing he will lose control, the father won't allow his son to go to America on a scholarship, but David escapes to London to study at the Royal College of Music. There he plays the infamously difficult Rachmaninof Piano Concerto No. 3 in D minor ("Rach 3" for short) well enough to win top prize, but the effort opens the floodgates to mental collapse.

But this is far from the end for David, played by Rush as a delightfully eccentric adult.

THE SHOP AROUND THE CORNER

James Stewart, Margaret Sullavan, Frank Morgan, Joseph Schildkraut

Directed by Ernst Lubitsch
1940. 99 minutes.

Imagine Stewart as a Hungarian shop clerk and without the drawl of later roles. In Lubitsch's delightful romantic comedy (considered one of the best ever made), he's in high natural gear as Alfred Kralik, the star employee of Matuschek & Company, a gift emporium in Budapest owned by the comically imperious Hugo Matuschek (Morgan).

If he keeps up the good work, Kralik is in line to become manager. He's also in love with a woman with whom he's been anonymously corresponding, and he resolves to meet her in the flesh. Nowadays, of course, people do this kind of thing online in films like *You've Got Mail,* based on Lubitsch's movie.

In Budapest, Kralik's little work world is disrupted by Klara Novak (Sullavan), who needs a job. At first Matuschek rudely dismisses her, but he changes his mind after she convinces a rotund woman that she can use a cigar box just as well for candy.

Kralik and Klara don't get along in the wonderfully delicious way two people actually attracted to each other don't get along, especially if they're as in sync as Stewart and Sullavan and under the direction of a hand as light and deft as Lubitsch's.

SHOT THROUGH THE HEART

Linus Roache, Vincent Perez, Lia Williams,
Karianne Henderson

Directed by David Attwood
1998. 112 minutes. No rating.

This taut HBO thriller re-energizes the cliché—true of every civil war—about best friends torn apart. In the former Yugoslavia, Vlado (Roache) and Slavko (Perez) were on the Olympic shooting team and later enjoy a cosmopolitan life in Sarajevo. Slavko, the slightly better shot, is a carefree bachelor and best friends with Vlado, who is married with a young daughter. But since Slavko is a Serb and Vlado a Croat married to a Muslim, they are torn in different directions when ethnic conflict erupts.

When the hostilities begin, Slavko is called to train Bosnian Serb army recruits. To Vlado's astonishment, Slavko says he will report for duty.

He also begs Vlado to take his family and flee the country, but Vlado refuses. Soon it is too late. Vlado watches Sarajevo degenerate into a war zone with Serbian snipers picking off people in the streets and in their homes. Taking up his rifle, he joins the city's defenders.

Told that one sniper is particularly adept at shooting people in the head from great distances, he knows who that must be and that he must stop him.

Attwood's film understates the violence in favor of affecting the viewer though steadily accumulating mundane losses. In a performance that suits that tone and style, Roache is remarkable as a self-satisfied, middle-class businessman turned guerrilla, who displays more regret than vengefulness even as he sets his sights on his best friend.

SILKWOOD

Meryl Streep, Kurt Russell, Cher, Craig T. Nelson, Diana Scarwid, Fred Ward, Ron Silver

Directed by Mike Nichols
1983. 131 minutes. R.

One intriguing thing about Karen Silkwood (Streep), the outspoken, freewheeling plutonium-recycling worker who blew the whistle on the Kerr-McGee Corporation, is that she drank and drugged on her own yet wouldn't tolerate threats of contamination at work.

Nichols's film is based on a true story of murky dimensions. Some say Silkwood was murdered, presumably by a Kerr-McGee hit man, when her car flew off the road one night near Crescent, Oklahoma; others say she was high on drugs and lost control.

At the plant Silkwood was known as a tough-talking, hard-living party gal, and Streep gets that just right. At home, a ramshackle place where she lives with her boyfriend (Russell) and her lesbian friend (Cher), the talk is about Kerr-McGee and disturbing signs of worker illness.

In life, Silkwood's fellow workers were torn between admiration for her willingness to speak out and resentment at raising issues that could force the plant to shut down. The film never tries to get at the truth of Silkwood the reformer and the circumstances surrounding her death. But it succeeds beautifully as a vehicle for first-rate performances and for creating a creepy sense of corporate indifference to both workers and the environment.

A SIMPLE PLAN

Bill Paxton, Billy Bob Thornton, Bridget Fonda, Brent Briscoe, Gary Cole

Directed by Sam Raimi
1998. 120 minutes. R.

Exactly how and why a chance event escalates to such intensity is at the heart of Raimi's devastating thriller, adapted by Scott B. Smith from his suspenseful and highly cinematic best-seller.

Hank Mitchell (Paxton), his childlike brother Jacob (Thornton) and Jacob's friend Lou (Briscoe) happen upon a small plane that has crashed while carrying $4 million in cargo. Hank is the only one of the three who shows any sign of taking charge in such a circumstance, and he decides that they will hide the money for a while to see who claims it. The decision will shape their fates forever.

Hank's wife, Sarah (Fonda), suggests that to ward off suspicions of looting, they replace $500,000, which takes them back to the plane and into an encounter with a nosy farmer. That's just the beginning of lethal complications in a film that becomes a well-honed morality tale rising to a near-biblical level of retribution for its characters' transgressions.

By behaving expediently, Hank undertakes a series of steps leading to a downfall captured in all its discreet horror. Thornton gives Jacob, the film's showier role, a haunting mix of menace and fragility, and Smith's screenplay refines his book to create wrenching conflict between the brothers. By their final encounter, the viewer has watched a supposedly small film turn into something that isn't simple at all.

SLING BLADE

Billy Bob Thornton, Natalie Canerday, Dwight Yoakam, J. T. Walsh, John Ritter

Directed by Billy Bob Thornton
1996. 135 minutes. R.

Thornton made his film back in the days when critics still needed to identify him in their reviews (a former country musician and screenwriter, most notably of *One False Move*, page 292).

Here he concocts a tale about a man on the road to making the same mistake twice. The terse, withdrawn Karl Childers (Thornton) has just emerged from 25 years of incarceration in what he calls the "nervous hospital." Mildly retarded and raised with a sense of biblical justice, Karl murdered his mother when he found her having sex with a menacing character.

Beginning a new life in a small Southern town, he befriends a boy whose mother, Linda (Canerday), offers him a place to live in her garage. Linda has a belligerent, beer-swilling boyfriend, Doyle (Yoakam), who's never short of loud, abusive opinions. He's especially boorish about the boy and Linda's boss (Ritter), a homosexual who appoints himself Linda's protector.

Karl basically stays out of other people's business, but it's hard to remain neutral when it comes to Doyle. A sling blade is the grass-cutting device Karl used on his mother.

SLUMS OF BEVERLY HILLS

*Alan Arkin, Natasha Lyonne, Marisa Tomei, Kevin Corrigan,
Carl Reiner, Rita Moreno, David Krumholtz, Jessica Walter*

Directed by Tamara Jenkins
1998. 91 minutes. R.

Jenkins's playfully autobiographical film follows a clan of what she calls "Jewish Joads" as they traverse not dust-bowl stretches but the wilds of Beverly Hills in search of an affordable place to lay their heads, however briefly, in one garishly named apartment complex or another.

Determined to keep his three kids in a good school district, a wonderfully idiosyncratic, tersely blasé divorced father, Murray Abramowitz (Arkin), constantly packs up the family vehicle and heads for new digs they can afford. Suffice it to say, Murray is not headed up the economic ladder, and the upheavals naturally add to the already considerable teenage angst suffered by his daughter, Vivian (Lyonne).

In the throes of sexual coming of age, Vivian experiments with the boy next door, a guy named Eliot (Corrigan) who sports Charles Manson T-shirts. To further educate her in the subject, her glamorous cousin Rita (Tomei), fresh from rehab, flounces around in the buff and introduces Vivian to the vibrator.

Somehow, Vivian remains a center of sanity in a gaggle of eccentrics in a film full of wit, confidence and small surprises.

SMALL TIME CROOKS

*Woody Allen, Tracey Ullman, Tony Darrow, Hugh Grant,
George Grizzard, Jon Lovitz, Elaine May, Michael
Rappaport, Elaine Stritch*

Directed by Woody Allen
2000. 95 minutes. PG.

Dropping all intimations of Bergman, Kafka and Chekhov, Allen gets back to being flat-out funny with a tale of two strivers who try robbing a bank as a route to their dreams. The nebbishy Ray Winkler (Allen) comes up with the idea: rent a vacant store next to the bank and tunnel into the vault. A normal bank caper calls for skilled specialists; all Ray and his accomplices succeed in cracking is a water main.

Meanwhile, Ray's wife, Frenchy (Ullman), a former New Jersey stripper, is making all the money they need and more by selling cookies in the store. Frenchy is really the one with social pretensions, and she envisions climbing the A-list in Manhattan. To this end she engages a smarmy art dealer (Grant) to teach her how to elevate her act. Need we add that the dealer puts some moves on Frenchy?

Having uproariously switched gears from heist to social farce, Allen veers back into crime with a scheme to swipe a fabulous necklace from the neck of Chi Chi Potter (Stritch), a wealthy art patron. At this point the proceedings are relying on sitcom plot twists, not to suggest they aren't funny.

THE SNAPPER

Tina Kellegher, Colm Meaney, Ruth McCabe, Colm O'Byrne, Pat Laffan

Directed by Stephen Frears
1993. 87 minutes. R.

As evidenced by his four other films in this book, Frears likes to genre-jump, and here he plumbs the essence of the small, mundane comedy.

Roddy Doyle adapted his novel set in Barrytown, in working-class North Dublin. An unmarried supermarket checkout clerk named Sharon Curley (Kellegher) is "up the pole," as pregnancy is referred to in these parts. Surprisingly, her parents don't regard this as any great disaster. (Sharon is 20, after all, and not getting any younger.) Her father, Dessie (Meaney), even invites her to join him for a pint at the pub.

But then it is suggested that she was impregnated by George Burgess (Laffan), a wimpish middle-aged family man and father of one of Sharon's best friends. Suddenly she is branded as a tart and a homewrecker.

Sharon insists that the father is a handsome, mysterious Spanish sailor just passing through, so to speak, and her mother (McCabe) prefers to believe that story. Frears stirs in much domestic tumult and barroom camaraderie, and he allows his characters a good degree of gallantry.

SOAPDISH

Sally Field, Kevin Kline, Whoopi Goldberg, Robert Downey Jr., Cathy Moriarty, Elisabeth Shue, Carrie Fisher, Garry Marshall

Directed by Michael Hoffman
1991. 97 minutes. PG-13.

It's frantic, certainly, but Hoffman's comedy is also funny enough to get away with a little too much mayhem.

Existing at the edges of his profession, the actor Jeffrey Anderson (Kline) escapes from dinner theater in Opa-Locka, Florida, to work on a soap opera, *The Sun Also Sets*, starring an old nemesis, Celeste Talbert (Field). Years earlier Anderson had been thrown off the show after offending Celeste, queen of the soaps, and the two reapproach each other warily.

On the set, done up in an infernolike red, the show's writers and creative team stoop to any contrived, dishonest trick and plot development to further their own interests.

"Two words I like," says the network honcho Edmund Edwards (Marshall). "I like the word 'peppy,' and I like the word 'cheap.'" Charged with displaying concern for common folk, the crazily perky Celeste dresses up to work in a soup kitchen and, after landing in prison in one episode, declares herself "guilty of love in the first degree!"

Away from the show, personal lives turn into amusing antic melodrama, but the film does best when it sticks to show-biz ambience.

SOUTH PARK: BIGGER, LONGER & UNCUT

The voices of Trey Parker, Matt Stone, Mary Kay Bergman

Directed by Trey Parker
1999. 81 minutes. R.

This is the *South Park* film for people who don't necessarily like *South Park* (and of course for those who do). Infinitely funnier than the series and just as clever, the ambitious film is both a social satire and a brilliant send-up of Hollywood musicals. It includes the Oscar-nominated song "Blame Canada," one of the few here whose lyrics could be sung on network television.

Tackling the issue of censorship head-on, the story begins with the South Park kids—Cartman, Kyle, Stan and Kenny—bribing a drunk with a bottle of vodka to escort them into a foul-mouthed R-rated movie made in Canada. The boys emerge two hours later speaking almost entirely in profanities.

That enrages Sheila Broslofski, a mother who starts a national crusade for censorship. A professor invents a V-chip that gives children an electrical shock every time they curse. Finally, Sheila blames Canada, war breaks out and Canada bombs the Baldwin brothers.

Kenny gets killed, as he does in all *South Park* adventures. Best of all, he goes to hell, where, in the film's funniest episode, Satan has fallen in love with Saddam Hussein in a movie ahead of its time.

THE SPANISH PRISONER

Campbell Scott, Steve Martin, Rebecca Pidgeon, Ben Gazzara, Ricky Jay

Directed by David Mamet
1997. 110 minutes. PG.

In *The Times*, Janet Maslin called this film Mamet's "craftiest and most satisfying cinematic puzzle." Joe Ross (Campbell), a smart, reasonably O.K. guy, has come up with a valuable scientific formula, known only as "the Process," which is tightly guarded by the company he works for. On a business trip in the Caribbean, he asks his boss (Gazzara) when he might expect to be financially rewarded for his efforts, and he is told not to worry about it.

Enter Jimmy Dell (Martin), a charming sharpster who steps off a seaplane. Jimmy is a Master of the Universe type who impresses Joe as he picks up his expensive car, entertains at his club and dangles the possibility that Joe might date his beautiful and very rich sister. To Joe that sounds like a distinct improvement over Susan Ricci (Pidgeon), the secretary who has been pursuing him with candid ardor.

Who but Jimmy could coax the Process out of the safe? You take it from there in a good cat-and-mouse game with a keen ear for language.

SPEED

Keanu Reeves, Sandra Bullock, Dennis Hopper

Directed by Jan De Bont
1994. 116 minutes. R.

Proving that action needn't be dumb, De Bont's furiously paced obstacle course of a film provided some original fun that still plays well a decade later.

Reeves is Jack Traven, an L.A. cop who specializes in spoiling the fun of psychopaths like Howard Payne (Hopper). Howard can't even blow up an elevator full of innocent hostages without Traven's swooping in to pull the fuse, so to speak. But Howard is a good man with tape, explosives and voltage meters, and in a bit of payback he dreams up an idea involving a Santa Monica bus: to attach a bomb that activates when the vehicle hits 50 and will detonate if the bus then falls below that speed.

Let's see Traven deal with that in L.A. traffic. The airport has some open pavement, but inevitably the bus, full of passengers, has to take to the freeways, with Traven scrambling all over and under it trying to find and disarm the device.

So who's at the wheel? Annie Porter (Bullock) has never driven a bus, but with sporadic encouragement from the very busy Traven, she proves adept at keeping the thing upright around tight turns, shooting it through narrow spaces and even flying it over a large gap in the highway. Hopper acts crazy, of course; Bullock stays terrified but perky; Reeves remains stalwart. Is there time for flirting?

SPELLBOUND

A documentary profile of eight contestants at the 1999 National Spelling Bee

Directed by Jeff Blitz
2002. 97 minutes. G.

Blitz's film jumps around the country visiting championship spellers, who are about 13, and their families. Preparations are under way for the national spelling bee in Washington, but first the eight have to survive the state contests. Most of them are old hands at this, having won perhaps several times at the regionals before moving on to try for the national crown.

Someone jokingly refers to the pressure as "a different form of child abuse," but spellers and their families don't reflect that at all. Kids are determined, and parents are supportive. In Ambler, Pennsylvania, April says she spells for eight or nine hours a day, and her father worries that she's not getting to the mall with her friends. In San Clemente, California, Neil drills with his father, who says they race through 7,000 words a day.

Spellers are from various backgrounds, but their families share a common devotion to their children. In Washington, they join 240 other contestants. Some advance, while others fall. One of the nicest things about this warm and exciting film, which remains a cliffhanger to the last syllable, is that spellers and their families find such hopeful and constructive things in defeat.

SPIRITED AWAY

The voices of Daveigh Chase, Suzanne Pleshette, Jason Marsden, Susan Egan, David Ogden Stiers, Lauren Holly, Michael Chiklis, John Ratzenberger

Directed by Hayao Miyazaki
2001. 125 minutes. PG.

Miyazaki's richly animated film has a wonderful way of putting a young girl in peril and then lifting her from her fears by the strength of her own self-discovery.

For Chihiro (Chase) the journey begins with dislocation and passes through a phantasmagoric dreamland where, as is the way in dreams, one never knows who is friend or foe. In an animated world the two can change shapes and roles at any moment.

On the way to a new home, she and her parents become lost in what looks like a huge, abandoned theme park. Succumbing to temptation, her mother and father partake of mysteriously unattended heaps of food and literally turn themselves into pigs. Chihiro is left on her own.

In the park, shadowy, oddly shaped creatures appear among formidable pagodas. In the interiors, armies of workers turn out vast quantities of food and other products. Chihiro quickly learns that humans are unwelcome. A boy with magical powers (Marsden) may or may not be her friend, and a witchy bathhouse proprietor named Yubaba (Pleshette) puts her to work in her steamy establishment.

Chihiro sees that the best way to survive is to do her best. The job has its indignities, but she saves the place from an odious pile of slime called the Stink God. Dangers are mainly inventions of the mind, but that doesn't make them any less scary on the road back to Mom and Dad.

STAKEOUT

Richard Dreyfuss, Emilio Estevez, Madeleine Stowe, Aidan Quinn

Directed by John Badham
1987. 115 minutes. R.

Badham's exciting, good-humored film remains a classic of sorts. No movie with or about cops posted to keeps tabs on people has ever done it better.

Dispatched to shadow Maria (Stowe), the girlfriend of an escaped killer (Quinn), Chris and Bill (Dreyfuss and Estevez) watch her house. Then Chris has occasion to meet the woman, and darned if they aren't attracted to each other. Soon Chris is regularly in the house, in effect becoming the subject of his own surveillance.

Much subterfuge is called for as Chris disguises himself and his voice to fool police cameras and microphones. That's Chris crawling under the bed and fleeing the premises in a pink beach hat. Bill can only stand by. "I'm in love," Chris tells his partner. "I have to face up to my heterosexuality. But don't worry, you'll be provided for."

The killer has to show up, of course, but, thanks to

Quinn, even he is likable in a film, reminiscent of 1930's knockabout comedies, that rises on its deft performances.

THE STATION AGENT

Peter Dinklage, Patricia Clarkson, Bobby Cannavale,
Michelle Williams, Raven Goodwin, Paul Benjamin

Directed by Tom McCarthy
2003. 88 minutes. R.

One of those little-movies-that-could, the low-budget, Sundance-award–winning *Station Agent* is the delicate, unexpectedly cheering story of three emotionally wounded misfits.

Fin McBride (in a great, tough performance by Dinklage) is 4 feet 5 inches tall and works in a model-train store. When the proprietor dies, he leaves Fin an abandoned railroad station in Newfoundland, New Jersey. Fin decides to live in the dilapidated station, where he settles into comfortable isolation.

Whether he wants it or not, Fin has company in an ebullient Cuban named Joe Oramas (Cannavale), who parks his coffee wagon on the largely untraveled road that passes the station, and Olivia (Clarkson), a neighbor in the throes of a divorce and mourning the death of a child. All loners, they gravitate to one another, if uneasily.

The film is sometimes painfully honest. Tired of being gawked at in town, Fin leaps up on a bar one night and tells everybody to go ahead and have a good look. But the pain is leavened by humor—the scatterbrained Olivia nearly runs over Fin with her car, not once but twice—so the film is not mawkish or depressing. Tom McCarthy's beautifully balanced story never treats its characters as eccentrics, which is one reason why the film seems so fully alive and humane.

STEALING BEAUTY

*Liv Tyler, Jeremy Irons, Sinéad Cusack, Jean Marais,
Miranda Fox, Donal McCann, Richard Reed, Stefania
Sandrelli, Rachel Weisz*

Directed by Bernardo Bertolucci
1996. 110 minutes. R.

Say what you will about a bunch of aesthetes and
dilettantes lolling around a gorgeous Siena hilltop and
ogling a dazzling 19-year-old American visitor, Lucy
Harmon (Tyler). There are worse uses of screen time, and
Bertolucci makes beautiful work of it.

There's a sculptor (McCann) and his wife (Cusack), a fey
writer in failing health (Irons), a jewelry designer (Fox), an
entertainment lawyer (Reed) and an advice columnist
(Sandrelli). All are in a state of drowsy torpor one hot day
when Lucy, asleep herself through most of her journey, arrives to break up the siesta.

Tyler, in her third film, makes a stunning presence. All
Lucy has to do is stand there, or perhaps romp and gam-
bol a bit, to get the hilltop jumping with middle-aged ad-
mirers dusting off old moves and assorted young rakes
piling in from the countryside to try their luck.

Not the sharpest arrow in the quiver, Lucy surveys it all
with vapid curiosity and amusement, deflecting passes
gracefully, though at one point she has to fight a boy off.
She's there ostensibly to learn the identity of her father.

Seduction is about all Bertolucci has in mind for this
film, and he keeps it as dreamy as a mirage, contemplated
from the wistful standpoint of adults yearning to re-
experience first love vicariously.

STOP MAKING SENSE

A performance film with Talking Heads, David Byrne

Directed by Jonathan Demme
1984. 88 minutes. No rating.

Demme's pioneering use of 24-track digital recording and his coolly iconoclastic visual style results in one of the greatest concert films ever. No screaming crowds or backstage scenes here—just thrilling performance through the eyes and ears of a major filmmaker. (The DVD has interviews with band members.)

A sexually and racially integrated nine-member group in playsuits and white sneakers, jogging in place as if doing aerobics, makes an arresting sight. Byrne is the focus, of course, as he wanders on stage to start the show with the stark and rousing "Psycho Killer." Classics include "Life During Wartime," "Heaven," "Once in a Lifetime" and "Burning Down the House."

STORMY MONDAY

Melanie Griffith, Tommy Lee Jones, Sting, Sean Bean

Directed by Mike Figgis
1988. 93 minutes. R.

Figgis creates a moody atmosphere and gathers a superb cast for this sultry romantic thriller.

A ruthless Texan, Cosmo (Jones at his most menacing), wants to take over a waterfront nightclub district of Newcastle, England. The club is owned by the cool Finney (Sting, who slips easily into the role). When Cosmo wants something, he likes to import the kittenish, breathy Kate (Griffith) to apply sexual pressure. This time, though, Kate is thrown off by her attraction to Brendan (Bean), who works in the club. The two of them are now caught between Cosmo and Finney, and while that business is worked out effectively if bloodily, we are just as caught up with saxophones in the night and the jazz-tinged score, composed by Figgis.

An assortment of thugs and functionaries lends background and texture. As if getting in step with Cosmo, Newcastle is in the middle of a hokey celebration of all things American, which includes a jarring rendition of "The Star-Spangled Banner." Otherwise this is a smoky scene, glistening with neon and wet pavement, made enticing by Figgis's stylish direction.

STORYTELLING

Selma Blair, Robert Wisdom, Leo Fitzpatrick, Paul Giamatti,
Mark Webber, Noah Fleiss, John Goodman, Julie Hagerty,
Jonathan Osser, Lupe Ontiveros

Directed by Todd Solondz
2001. 87 minutes. R.

Solondz's ear is preternaturally attuned to the self-deluding pieties and scrambled certainties that make up so much of the American idiom. His meticulous, deadpan sense of comedy shamelessly trawls for laughs and then turns laughter into shame.

Here he fashions two self-contained asymmetrical stories, "Fiction" and "Non-Fiction," that reflect how narrative tends to distort, exploit and wound. In "Fiction," a young woman (Blair) is humiliated by a creative-writing teacher (Wisdom) and badly treated in a sex scene so comic-dreadful that a red rectangle was placed over it for theater showings in this country. "Non-Fiction" travels to the suburbs for some satire in which the grotesquery of the characters is more a dimension of their humanity than a denial of it.

The focus here is on Scooby (Webber), who evolves from a caricature of teenage slackerdom into someone thoughtful and intuitive. For example, after his mother notes that since her family escaped the Nazis, she and her children should be called Holocaust survivors, Scooby counters that if it weren't for Hitler, none of them would have been born.

That gets him banished from the dinner table by his domineering father (Goodman), but it demonstrates how Solondz is drawn by the unspeakable and tries to dispel taboos that make us either hold our tongues or speak reassuring nonsense.

What finally makes *Storytelling* a genuinely valuable painful experience (rather than a chicly uncomfortable one) is that Solondz cares for his characters even as he doesn't entertain illusions about their goodness or innocence.

THE STRAIGHT STORY

Richard Farnsworth, Sissy Spacek, Harry Dean Stanton, Wiley Harker

Directed by David Lynch
1999. 112 minutes. G.

W hat the gol darn are you doing lying on the floor?" a friend asks the elderly Alvin Straight (Farnsworth), whom he finds unable to pull himself up from the kitchen linoleum one afternoon. Taken to the clinic by his mildly retarded daughter, Rosie (Spacek), Alvin learns what he knows already: his hips are gone, his eyes are going, diabetes threatens and he's in the early stages of emphysema.

Time to lay off the cigars and braunschweiger. But Alvin is a stubborn fellow. When he learns that his estranged brother, Lyle (Stanton), has had a stroke, he determines to go see him. Denied a driver's license because of his eyesight, he decides to drive anyway—on his John Deere lawn mower.

Along 300 miles of road, Lynch, of all people, presents the flip side of *Blue Velvet* (page 42) and turns it into a supremely improbable triumph.

Alvin lives in Iowa, Dean in Wisconsin. The mower, hauling a homemade trailer with a few belongings, goes three or four miles per hour. All day Alvin chugs along the shoulder of the two-lane road. At night he pulls off into the fields and sleeps under the stars. An open, gracious man, he charms everyone he meets with his gentle humanity, self-sufficiency and determination to finish the trip the way he started it.

As the journey proceeds, so does the story of Alvin Straight: his boyhood, his experiences as a sniper in World War II, his marriage and 14 children (seven of whom survived), his resilience, sagacity and love of family. The mower gives out on several occasions, but never Alvin.

STRANGE DAYS

Ralph Fiennes, Angela Bassett, Juliette Lewis, Tom Sizemore, Michael Wincott, Vincent D'Onofrio, Glenn Plummer

Directed by Kathryn Bigelow
1995. 145 minutes. R.

Bigelow unleashes a ferocious sci-fi whirlwind in which vicarious thrills can be had by clapping on a skullcap called a squid (superconductor quantum interference device) and living your favorite fantasy, sexual, homicidal, you name it. The experience seems totally real, but since it's virtual, nothing really happened (which is nice when you've just killed somebody).

Squids are illegal, but sleazy black marketers like Lenny Nero (Fiennes) peddle shots to the brain in the dark, seething streets of a Los Angeles that has gone crazy with violence and anarchy. Lenny has a tough, together cab-driver named Lornette (Bassett) for an ally, but plenty of troubles with bad people who cross a few wires in brain games that go to new extremes of savagery.

As usual the L.A.P.D. gets another black eye, but Bigelow's film, written by Jay Cocks and James Cameron, who was once married to Bigelow, boils down to a familiar set of film noir moves involving sexual treachery and betrayal. Ms. Bigelow sustains a credible look while inventing one surprising and sinister tableau after another.

But the particulars are dwarfed by the grandly decadent backdrop. *Strange Days* is visionary enough to invent a future world that appears to be on the brink of Armageddon yet looks awfully like the world we already have.

SUNSHINE

Ralph Fiennes, Jennifer Ehle, Rosemary Harris, James Frain, John Neville, William Hurt

Directed by István Szabó
1999. 180 minutes. R.

Fiennes brilliantly plays three generations of characters—grandfather, father and son—from a Hungarian Jewish family as it flourishes and falters from the start of the 20th century through the fall of communism.

"I predict this will be a century of love, justice and tolerance," says the grandfather, Ignatz Sonnenschein, a rising figure in the Austro-Hungarian legal system. We know how wrong he'll turn out to be, and Szabó's film depicts the gradual disillusionment of the Sonnenscheins as they discover the century's failings firsthand.

Ignatz's story, running from his 19th-century upbringing to 1930, is punctuated mainly by tumultuous family rows at the dinner table. In this phase he develops his passion for his adopted sister, Valerie (Ehle), whom he later marries, paving the way for the next generations.

By then Ignatz has changed the family name to Sors. His son Adam converts to Christianity, becomes a champion fencer but succumbs to snobbery and anti-Semitism. After World War II, Adam's son Ivan joins the Communist secret police out of his rage at fascism.

As the family history goes on, the film gains momentum and power, and a sense of quiet grace.

SUNSHINE STATE

Edie Falco, Jane Alexander, Ralph Waite, Angela Bassett, Bill Cobbs, James McDaniel, Mary Steenburgen, Timothy Hutton, Gordon Clapp, Mary Alice

Directed by John Sayles
2002. 141 minutes. PG-13.

Sayles throws a dozen indelible characters into a spacious multigenerational, multicultural epic about the proposed development of the fictional Florida town of Delrona Beach and by extension the greedy misuse of the country at large.

At the center of the community's soul-searching about whether to take the developers' money and move or stand their ground is the sardonic, quick-witted, worn-down, thoroughly attractive Marly Temple, smashingly played by Falco with an almost mesmerizing rightness of feel and tone. A former mermaid in an aqua show, Marly needs most of the film to come to the reluctant conclusion that it may be time to cash in the family business, the strategically located Sea-Vue Motel.

Sayles organizes his story around two families, one white (the Temples), the other black (the Stokeses). Marly's grandly histrionic mother, Delia (Alexander), known as the local Sarah Bernhardt, cares for her husband, Furman (Waite), the founder of the Sea-Vue and combative advocate of holding on to it.

As matron of the Stokes family, Eunice (Mary Alice) is the stiff-backed pillar of Lincoln Beach, a black-owned middle-class enclave ripe for the bulldozers. The return of

Eunice's beautiful daughter, Desiree (Bassett), driven away by her mother's unforgiving rectitude, opens old wounds.

Sunshine State isn't the first Sayles film to imply a larger social view, but it is the first to evoke it with the grandeur of a first-rate Robert Altman movie.

SWEET AND LOWDOWN

Sean Penn, Samantha Morton, Uma Thurman, Anthony LaPaglia, Gretchen Mol, John Waters

Directed by Woody Allen
1999. 95 minutes. PG-13.

In one of Allen's least typical films, Penn plays a brilliant jazz musician and Morton is the mute woman who adores him. As the title hints, this piece, set in the 1930's, is sweeter and slower than Allen's fast-talking, contemporary, cosmopolitan movies.

The fictional Emmet Ray, "the second-best jazz guitarist in the world," is modeled after Django Reinhardt, who ruled the Paris clubs from the 1930's to the 50's and might have been the best despite having lost some fingers in a childhood accident. Emmet is also a pimp and a kleptomaniac, but then no great artist is perfect.

Penn is terrific in the role, making Emmet likable even though we know he acts despicably. "I'm an artist," he says. "I like women, but they gotta have their place."

His girlfriend, Hattie, accepts this. Morton is most affecting as a laundress who acts like a silent-film star. At times she combines the baleful loneliness of Buster Keaton with a Harpo Marx sweetness. Hanging on to Emmet isn't easy for her, especially given the attentions of a socialite named Blanche (Thurman) who's attracted to artistic men.

Now and then the movie pauses for seductive standards like "Sweet Sue," "All of Me," "I'm Forever Blowing Bubbles" and "I'll See You in My Dreams." Stocked with

evocative characters—including LaPaglia as a gangster—
the film leaves plenty of room for the music.

THE SWEET HEREAFTER

Ian Holm, Sarah Polley, Bruce Greenwood, Tom McCamus,
Gabrielle Rose, Arsinée Khanjian, Alberta Watson

Directed by Atom Egoyan
1997. 112 minutes. R.

Like Russell Banks's novel, from which it is adapted,
Egoyan's film makes a many-faceted moral inquiry into
a calamity that has befallen a small Canadian town, and
the book's narrative strength carries over to help make
this Egoyan's most accessible film.

The pivotal event occurs midway through the film
when a school bus slides off an icy road and sinks into a
lake, drowning 14 of the town's children. Until then and
afterward, Egoyan uses a carefully fragmented approach
to explore the community's pain and anger.

First there is the inevitable ambulance chaser. "Let me
direct your rage," says Mitchell Stephens (Holm), who arrives burning with self-righteous indignation. But there is
much more than litigation to explore in a mosaic narrative that moves between time frames before and after
the crash.

Parents are seen sometimes sending their children off
to school and sometimes overcome by numbing grief.
Other matters intervene, like the eerily serene love between a teenager (Polley) and her father (McCamus), or
the affair between a widower (Greenwood) and an unhappily married woman (Watson). But the accident's
transforming effect is the common denominator in a film
that carries the exhilaration of crystal-clear artistic vision.

SWEET SIXTEEN

Martin Compston, William Ruane, Annmarie Fulton,
Michelle Abercromby, Michelle Coulter, Gary McCormack

Directed by Ken Loach
2002. 106 minutes. R.

Compston, a slim, gawky kid in his first film, takes to the camera with remarkable ease in Loach's involving look at the eroding effect of life on the underside in an impoverished part of Scotland near Glasgow.

When we first meet Liam (Compston), the boy is living with his sister while awaiting his mother's release from prison. His ambition at this point is to provide her with a decent home—he has his eye on a trailer—and he decides that the way to get it is to steal a stash of drugs from his nasty grandfather and his mother's rotten boyfriend.

On the street he learns how to defend himself, and he also attracts the attention of primary pushers in the area, who want to recruit him for their own operations. At first Liam's childish innocence and affection for his mother impart a kind of sweetness, but later he turns simultaneously likable and repellent as he sinks deeper into a life of crime.

Loach propels the picture with a documentary sureness, leaving no room for sentimentality in a film reminiscent of the socially conscious melodramas of the 1930's.

SWIMMING POOL

Charlotte Rampling, Ludivine Sagnier, Charles Dance, Marc Fayolle, Jean-Marie Lamour, Mireille Mossé

Directed by François Ozon
2003. 102 minutes. R.

Any film that turns Charlotte Rampling into a dowdy, repressed writer is definitely up to something original. As it moves from London to the South of France, an observant study of cross-generational sexual rivalry turns into an existential suspense thriller. At the center is Sarah Morton (Rampling), a successful if somewhat dried-out mystery writer of a certain age who needs to recharge and accepts her editor's offer of his country house in France.

A model of British starchiness, Sarah likes everything just so, and she establishes a rigid routine even on vacation. Then, totally unannounced, the editor's teenage daughter, Julie (Sagnier), turns up to stay in the house, too.

Julie brings a string of drunken men home from bars for noisy sex, exhibiting all the wayward qualities Sarah associates with the French. Intense animosity sets in, with the teenager every bit as wise to Sarah's problems as the older woman is disapproving of the girl's behavior.

Eventually there is a thaw between the two; Sarah even loosens up enough to have a romp with the gardener. As the relationship changes, the film does, too. Now it is a mystery about Julie's past, complete with a dead body in the pool that the women have to get rid of. The film is mischievous and enjoyable, even if the ambiguous ending doesn't satisfy quite as well as it should.

SWINGERS

Jon Favreau, Vince Vaughn, Ron Livingston, Patrick Van Horn, Alex Désert

Directed by Doug Liman
1996. 96 minutes. R.

A loser hero taking his lumps in L.A. might not tickle everybody's interest, but Liman's comedy scores with an inverted sense of style that turns square into counter-cool.

As for the square, a hilariously self-absorbed would-be stand-up comic named Mike (Favreau) heads west from Queens intent on making it on stage and with women. He has plenty of friends, but they're all male. With women, Mike flops spectacularly.

So his friend Trent (Vaughn) takes him to Las Vegas to show him how it's done. In Vegas and L.A., Liman's camera (the director is his own cinematographer) restlessly prowls settings so hopelessly retro and tacky that they have a reverse cachet.

Favreau wrote the movie himself, with his real friends in mind, and the cast's camaraderie is apparent. Mike and Trent are so outré that they are shunted to the bad tables even during off hours in empty places. Together they roam the bars looking for women who will reject them. Mike adds an intellectual flavor to his come-ons, but no one knows what he's talking about. "Hang on, Voltaire," a cocktail waitress tells him.

TADPOLE

Sigourney Weaver, Aaron Stanford, Bebe Neuwirth, Robert Iler, John Ritter

Directed by Gary Winick
2002. 78 minutes. PG-13.

Winick's film, a Sundance favorite shot in two weeks with a handheld camera, reverses the typical May-December romance. A precocious 15-year-old stumbles into an affair with his stepmother's best friend in this sophisticated farce about sex and coming of age.

Oscar (Stanford) is bright, a Francophile and an absolute fount of Voltaire quotes. Understandably, girls his age don't interest him.

Diane (Neuwirth) is an earthy, playfully seductive chiropractor and the best friend of Oscar's stepmother, Eve (Weaver), who is unhappily married to Oscar's father (Ritter).

One massage by Diane to help relieve Oscar's hangover is all it takes to set things in motion. Neuwirth gives the film its erotic snap. Weaver's unsuspecting Eve is a little uneasy at Diane's reminiscences about their wild rock 'n' roll times 25 years ago, so it's lucky she isn't at the table when Diane tells her girlfriends that for an adolescent Oscar is pretty adept at recreational sex.

Of course, the secret will have to come out in this mature film about one confused and lucky boy.

Winick did a lot less with a much bigger budget when he went Hollywood to direct the Jennifer Garner movie *13 Going on 30*.

THE TAILOR OF PANAMA

Pierce Brosnan, Geoffrey Rush, Jamie Lee Curtis, Leonor Varela, Brendan Gleeson

Directed by John Boorman
2001. 109 minutes. R.

It's always fun to see what work old spy masters dream up for themselves after the cold war (there must be plenty these days), and here Boorman and John Le Carré, who wrote the screenplay, based on his novel, with Boorman and Andrew Davies, take us to Panama for a post-Noriega scramble involving a couple of displaced operatives from the old school.

Short of work, a semidisgraced MI6 agent named Andy Osnard (Brosnan) arrives in Panama City badly in need of cloak-and-dagger atmospherics. Problem is, there are none, really, so he has imported his own bit of nasty business from London.

Casting Brosnan, the screen's most recent 007, is a clever touch. A sleazy character, Andy turns to boozing and tired womanizing. Fundamentally bored, he enjoys stirring in some B-movie melodrama, and so does Harry (Rush), a half-Jewish cockney ex-convict who has used Panama to establish himself and his tailor shop as elegant extensions of Savile Row.

Harry's unsavory past and present debt make him a target for Andy, who bullies and badgers information out of him about dissident groups Harry has gleaned from his wife (Curtis), who works for the government. Andy then forwards what he's learned to his bosses in London, thereby justifying his existence.

It's all a game, of course, and Boorman and Le Carré dispatch the conventions of the spy genre with a flourish of self-parody.

THE TALENTED MR. RIPLEY

Matt Damon, Jude Law, Gwyneth Paltrow, Cate Blanchett, Philip Seymour Hoffman

Directed by Anthony Minghella
1999. 139 minutes. R.

Identity theft being such a depressing electronic business these days, it's a pleasure to watch a natural talent at work in the flesh during the lush Italian summer of 1958. Tom Ripley (Damon) has been dispatched abroad to help persuade a Princeton classmate, Dickie Greenleaf (Law), to quit lolling in the sun and return home to get on with his life.

Tom never went to Princeton, of course. Coming from humble origins, he wants to assume Dickie's identity, not so much for the money, of which there is plenty, but because of his need to be someone else. "This is my face," he tells himself as he trains his binoculars on Dickie.

Greenleaf's breezy arrogance as a spectacularly charismatic dilettante helps set him up. Something about Tom bothers Dickie's girlfriend, Marge (Paltrow, as savvy a character actress as she is a leading lady), but Dickie accepts Tom into his circle. Eventually Tom becomes Dickie, but can he sustain the deception?

Minghella's film makes more of the sexual buzz between Tom and Dickie than the book did, and Damon's character is generally less loathsome and more conscience-stricken. But Ripley has plenty of sting in a reptilian murder story with the same complex allure as Minghella's *English Patient*.

TALK TO HER

Javier Cámara, Dario Grandinetti, Leonor Watling, Rosario Flores, Geraldine Chaplin, Mariola Fuentes, Lola Dueñas

Directed by Pedro Almodóvar.
2002. 112 minutes. Spanish with English subtitles. No rating.

One of Almodóvar's most touching, lyrical and resonant films achieves a stunning emotional depth with the story of two physically damaged women and two emotionally tortured men.

We meet Benigno (Cámara), a nurse, lovingly tending to the comatose Alicia (Watling). She was once a dancer, but after an accident she lies unconscious while Benigno strokes her gently and tells her soft things to encourage and sustain her. In the same situation, Marco (Grandinetti) ministers to his girlfriend (Flores), a bullfighter in a coma after being gored.

Then comes a surprise. We discover that the sympathetic Benigno has no real ties to Alicia and has obsessively "adopted" her inert form in the hospital and made it his to caress and nurture. In this movie about sympathy, loyalty and being trapped in various prisons, Almodóvar portrays Benigno and Marco's devotion to the women as both admirable in its selflessness and creepy in the men's twisting of their dedication to their own needs.

And as Benigno moves beyond the bounds of the imaginable, Almodóvar demands empathy for someone whose actions are appalling. No other filmmaker could have handled this material with the same delicacy and understanding. This is the film of a master at the top of his form.

THE TALL GUY

Jeff Goldblum, Emma Thompson, Rowan Atkinson, Emil Wolk, Geraldine James, Kim Thomson

Directed by Mel Smith
1989. 92 minutes. R.

A peculiar British blend of Monty Python's satirical sharpness and music-hall gags, Mel Smith's comedy is wickedly endearing thanks to the off-kilter characters.

Dexter King (Goldblum) is a gangly, hapless American actor in London whose stage career has ascended no further than *The Rubber-Faced Revue*, a raucous music-hall production in which he plays second banana to the laugh-hogging star (Atkinson). But the awkward, juvenile Dexter (who sleeps in Superman pajamas) never loses hope. "Some director's gonna come into the show and say, 'Hey! That guy in the skirt! That's our Macbeth,'" he exclaims.

Or our something. Dexter's destiny eventually lands him the lead role in an Andrew Lloyd Webber–style extravaganza called *Elephant!*, a musical version of *The Elephant Man*. Dexter's bad jobs account for some of the film's best scenes, and at the climax the elephant rises to his reward as the chorus sings, "Somewhere in heaven there's an angel with big ears."

Offstage, Dexter's life consists primarily of sneezing attacks and the wrong women. At an allergy clinic he meets a levelheaded nurse named Kate (Thompson, in a role that reminds us that she was once known for sketch comedy), whose sensible approach to romance is no barrier to hilarious, room-wrecking sex.

Goldblum is a charming innocent, a guy who pedals his bicycle through London wearing his elephant head in mad pursuit of his love.

TANGO

Miguel Ángel Solá, Cecilia Narova, Mía Maestro, Juan Carlos Copes, Carlos Rivarola, Julio Bocca

Directed by Carlos Saura
1998. 115 minutes. Spanish with English subtitles. No rating.

With all the heat and agility it has to work with, Saura's Oscar-nominated film about the dance hardly needs a plot. Planning his own movie, a director named Mario (Solá) imagines some steamy scenarios and turns on a wind machine. A dressing room full of beautiful women comes to life, two of them step into a tango of taunting suggestion, and we're off.

As each tango encounters something new, Saura uses screens, silhouettes and color filters to augment the choreography. There's a decorous tango at a dance party, a furiously angry tango between Mario and his ex-wife (Narova), a tango of bitter jealousy, another of first love.

A *West Side Story*–style gang tango involves two groups of men, and two male soloists dance a fiery duet. Locked in perfect unison, lovers and adventurers burn up the screen.

TASTE OF CHERRY

Homayon Ershadi, Abdolrahman Bagheri, Safar Ali Moradi

Directed by Abbas Kiarostami
1997. 95 minutes. Farsi with English subtitles. No rating.

This is a film about a man who drives around the Iranian countryside in a dusty white Range Rover looking for someone to bury him after he has committed suicide. If that sounds off-putting, be assured that Kiarostami will have you wondering about Mr. Baddi (Ershadi).

Once one settles in to the film's deliberate pace and thoughtful silences, the story becomes an involving mystery. Baddi drives along dusty, hilly roads looking for an accomplice. He plans to swallow all his sleeping pills and then lie down in a shallow grave he has dug for himself by the side of the road. For 200,000 tomans, the person he hires is to visit the site the next morning, make sure Baddi is dead and cover the body with 20 spadefuls of earth.

At no point do we learn why Baddi, a prosperous, good-looking man of about 50, wants to end his life. "There comes a time when a man can't go on," he tells a seminarian whom he tries to recruit. "He's exhausted and can't wait for God to act." The seminarian lectures him about the evils of suicide. "God entrusts a man's body to him," the seminarian says. "Man must not torment that body."

Another prospect tells Baddi to get away from him or he'll smash his face. Others are drawn by his intensity and natural air of authority. All of them refuse to do his bidding, save an elderly taxidermist who once tried to kill himself, then thought better of it. "Have you seen the moon?" he asks Baddi. "Do you see the stars?"

A TAXING WOMAN

Nobuko Miyamoto, Tsutomo Yamazaki, Masahiko Tsugawa, Hideo Murota

Directed by Juzo Itami
1987. 127 minutes. Japanese with English subtitles. No rating.

Itami's freewheeling sensibilities turn to Japan's staggering affluence and materialism in the late 1980's, cleverly alighting on tax collection as a way into the subject. Taxes are polarizing society. On one side are the people—from moms and pops to hoodlums—who are trying to hang on to their money. On the other are those selfless government functionaries making sure the government gets its piece of the pie.

In the latter camp is Ryoko Itakura (Miyamato), recently divorced and with a 5-year-old son to support, who finds her true calling with the Japanese equivalent of the I.R.S. To all appearances, she is mild-mannered and shy. Just don't cheat on your taxes.

After warming up on some moms and pops, Ryoko jumps into the books of a big-time mobster, Hideki Gondi (Yamazaki), who runs a string of what he calls "adult motels." Taxes aside, the two are attracted to each other, but business is business in a film thick with the inscrutably complex methods of tax evasion and the high-tech methods of the law. The film is more witty than laugh-out-loud funny, but Itami brings it to life with his sharp sense of the world and the passions of his obsessed characters.

TEA WITH MUSSOLINI

Maggie Smith, Judi Dench, Joan Plowright, Lily Tomlin, Charlie Lucas, Baird Wallace

Directed by Franco Zeffirelli
1999. 117 minutes. PG.

Zeffirelli draws on a chapter of his autobiography in a tale about a small colony of Englishwomen living comfortably and obliviously in Florence in the late 1930's. This is the kind of film, Stephen Holden wrote in *The Times*, in which "star turns, romance and melodrama are swirled together with pretty scenery and a dash of camp into a confection that used to be called a woman's picture." True enough, but it's fun.

As queen of the pack, referred to as Scorpioni by the locals, the long-necked Lady Hester Random (Smith) looks down on the rest of humankind with withering disdain. The others fall in line in no particular pecking order. Arabella Delancey (Dench) is a dithery art fancier with a cherished pooch called Billyboy. Mary Wallace (Plowright), a bit more hardheaded, is the caretaker of a young, artistically inclined Italian boy (Lucas) placed in her care by a businessman who wants his son to learn some English manners.

Satellites to the core group include a leathery archaeologist (Tomlin) and a wealthy, gadabout former Ziegfeld Girl (Cher), who drops in now and then to make high-end art purchases underwritten by her multiple marriages to very rich elderly men.

But not even Lady Hester can completely ignore the onset of war, though she tries with all the entitlement she can muster. Widow of a former ambassador, she visits Mussolini and obtains Il Duce's assurances that she and her friends will be well insulated from any unpleasantness.

Such isn't the case, of course, but all in all it's a soft landing.

THELMA AND LOUISE

Susan Sarandon, Geena Davis, Brad Pitt, Harvey Keitel, Michael Madsen

Directed by Ridley Scott
1991. 129 minutes. R.

One of the great road films always deserves revisiting. Louise (Sarandon), a coffee-shop waitress, and Thelma (Davis), a desperately bored housewife, have had it with their lives. We are in Arkansas. "Are you at work?" the sweet Thelma asks when Louise calls her from the restaurant. "No, I'm callin' from the Playboy Mansion," snaps Louise, who then suggests that the two drop everything and go fishing.

Louise provides her turquoise Thunderbird convertible; Thelma dresses in ruffles and denim and pearls and borrows her husband's gun. The weapon figures prominently as Louise rescues Thelma from an attempted rape. Now the ladies are on the run and, frankly, having themselves one hell of a good time.

A charming slickster named J.D. (Pitt) hitches a ride, thrills Thelma in bed and gives lessons in how to hold up a convenience store. It can't last forever, of course. A detective named Hal (Keitel) is on their tail, though he's sympathetic to their cause, which is nothing more or less than the liberation of two beautiful, interesting women.

His English roots notwithstanding, Scott reveals a feel for vibrant American imagery, caught in a sparkling screenplay by Callie Khouri and by Adrian Biddle's glorious cinematography, which lends a physical dimension to the notion that life can be richer than one thinks.

THIRTEEN

Evan Rachel Wood, Nikki Reed, Holly Hunter, Jeremy Sisto, Brady Corbet, Deborah Kara Unger

Directed by Catherine Hardwicke
2003. 100 minutes. R.

Hardwicke's harrowing portrait of a 13-year-old girl straying into sex, drugs and alienation in Los Angeles avoids the tired clichés strewn through most movies about willful teenagers. Tracy (Wood) and her friend Evie (Reed) are on a road to ruin, and Tracy's harried single mother, Melanie (Hunter), seems unable to stop them.

Evie is the instigator, the middle-school snake in the grass with all the cool vices and a coterie of shoplifting sidekicks. (Reed and Hardwicke wrote the film, based on Reed's own experiences.) Tracy is fascinated, all the more so when Evie taunts her as being a frilly little girl. To prove otherwise, Tracy lifts a wallet from a woman's purse and falls in step.

Soon the girls are drugging and carousing. In her private moments Tracy mutilates herself with scissors and a razor. Gradually more aware of what is happening, Melanie tries to reach her but doesn't know how, which adds to her own frustrations.

Without any kind of supervision herself, Evie moves in with Tracy, which pushes matters beyond the breaking point. Fortunately, there is Melanie, the one hope, and she grabs her daughter physically and emotionally and holds on tight.

13 CONVERSATIONS ABOUT ONE THING

Matthew McConaughey, John Turturro, Amy Irving, Clea DuVall, Alan Arkin, Barbara Sukowa, Tia Texada, Frankie Faison

Directed by Jill Sprecher
2001. 104 minutes. R.

Four separate but interwoven fables of urban dissatisfaction are brought together by elements that defy precise definition—chance, perhaps, or fate or order of the universe—but in human terms could be described as happiness, good fortune, the meaning of life. "Ask yourself if you're happy," says one of the titles interspersed throughout the film. At bottom, that's what the conversations are about.

A physics professor (Turturro) lectures students about the rules of the universe and leaves his wife (Irving) for reasons that are as cold and exact. A cocky young prosecutor (McConaughey) has a barroom debate with a sour older fellow (Arkin) about luck, guilt and happiness and then by pure fate gets into a hit-and-run auto accident that changes his life.

The older man, a midlevel insurance executive, is a seemingly insensitive fellow who can't reach a son caught up in drugs and is driven crazy at work by an underling who always has a smile on his face, no matter what the circumstances. Finally, a dreamy young house cleaner (DuVall) floats through days of menial work convinced that her life has a grander design.

In the nonsequential fashion of *Pulp Fiction, Memento* and other films, Sprecher's narratives don't proceed in a straight line, but fold back on themselves and one another, interconnecting at various points. But the feelings expressed and the quiet naturalism of the acting balance that artifice in a film that is thrillingly smart but not merely an excuse for its own cleverness.

THIRTEEN DAYS

Kevin Costner, Bruce Greenwood, Steven Culp, Dylan Baker, Michael Fairman, Kevin Conway, Tim Kelleher, Len Cariou

Directed by Roger Donaldson
2000. 145 minutes. PG-13.

You're not playing quahtaback for Hahvahd anymore, Kenny," John F. Kennedy (Greenwood) tells his aide Kenneth O'Donnell (Costner) in Donaldson's chewy, satisfying thriller about the Cuban missile crisis of 1962.

No, indeed. J.F.K. and his people, including his brother Bobby (Culp), are in a mess. Soviet intermediate-range ballistic missiles have been spotted in Cuba. A briefing officer tells it straight: once operational, in about 10 days, the missiles would need five minutes to reach Washington. Estimated dead: up to 80 million.

Greenwood is most convincing as the aggravated but icily calm president. Kennedy wants the missiles removed peacefully, while the generals want them taken out by air strike. A furious battle of wills ensues, with the Kennedys, O'Donnell and empathetic advisers like Secretary of Defense Robert McNamara (Baker) and Ted Sorenson (Kelleher) constantly retreating to private meeting rooms where they try to outmaneuver not only Khrushchev but Gen.

Curtis LeMay (Conway) and the rest of the Joint Chiefs of Staff.

Signals are sent and misconstrued. Khrushchev hints that he may want to deal, but then there's a reversal of that indication. O'Donnell may not be at Harvard anymore, but he does quarterback the president's response, coordinating the military in some tricky maneuvers that if botched could bring on war. Ultimately the biggest decisions fall to the Kennedys. "Jack and Bobby, they're smart guys," O'Donnell says.

THIS IS SPINAL TAP

Rob Reiner, Tony Hendra, Patrick MacNee, Michael McKean, Christopher Guest, June Chadwick, Kimberly Stringer, Chazz Dominguez, Shari Hall

Directed by Rob Reiner
1984. 82 minutes. R.

Reiner narrates his very funny deadpan satire about the sag, if not quite yet the collapse, of a rock group that has earned "a distinguished place in rock history as one of England's loudest bands."

Spinal Tap has already been through two stages: the imitation-Beatles days with floppy hair and sappy grins, and the psychedelic period with beatific expressions and accompanying go-go dancers. Now on an American tour, Spinal Tap seems to be in its final incarnation as a metal band. The songs are screamingly loud, and the members dress in skin-tight spandex. A giant horned skull serves as stage prop.

"The Boston gig has been canceled," says their manager, Ian Faith (Hendra), "but I wouldn't worry about it, though. It's not a big college town." Faith's duties are to handle the head of the group's record company, Sir Denis Eton-Hogg (MacNee), and quell backstage disturbances over, say, the right bread for the cold cuts.

At Elvis Presley's grave Spinal Tap tries to sing "Heart-break Hotel" but can't agree on the harmony. Reiner makes the rockers all look fairly idiotic without stooping to condescension.

THE THREE COLORS TRILOGY: BLUE, WHITE AND RED

Juliette Binoche, Zbigniew Zamachowski, Julie Delpy, Irène Jacob, Jean-Louis Trintignant, Jean-Pierre Lorit

Directed by Krzysztof Kieslowski
1993–94. French with English subtitles. No rating.

Kieslowski's three fascinating films have been characterized as all kinds of things, from solemn and perhaps a little pretentious to rich and lighthearted to seductive and magical. As far as the colors are concerned, they are those of the French flag and stand for, respectively, liberty, equality and fraternity.

In *Blue* (1993, 100 minutes), Julie (Binoche), the grieving widow of "one of the most important composers of our time," tries to move on with her life after her husband and daughter are killed in a car crash. She moves to Paris, takes a large, perfectly located apartment and settles down to making a new life. She swims. She befriends a prostitute. She finds out that her husband may not have been all that devoted.

In *White* (1994, 91 minutes, Polish and French with English subtitles), Karol (Zamachowski), a harassed but dead-game hairdresser in Paris, loses his business and his beautiful wife, Dominique (Delpy), and decides to return to Poland. Without funds, he accepts a fellow Pole's offer to send him home in a suitcase. When the bag is misdirected, he winds up in the hands of thugs, who beat him up. Still, he has reached his destination. "Home at last!" he cries.

Such resilience stands him in good stead as a shady

entrepreneur in a Euro-Poland where anything can be bought and sold, even a corpse. As a rich man, he can realize his dream of reclaiming Dominique, but this becomes a nightmare with bitter and tender results.

In *Red* (1994, 99 minutes), the richest and most complex of the films, Kieslowski explores the role of blind fate in life. On pure chance, a young model, Valentine (Jacob), crosses paths with a gruff, reclusive former judge (Trintignant) who spies on his neighbors.

The two become close. Concurrently but separately, we meet a young man named Auguste (Lorit), who is unknown to Valentine. Will they meet? Should they? Kieslowski is particularly expert at constructing overlapping patterns that affect lonely people. Together the three movies suggest a broader design to people's lives in which chance and coincidence assume a moral weight in the scheme of things.

THREE KINGS

George Clooney, Mark Wahlberg, Ice Cube, Spike Jonze, Nora Dunn

Directed by David O. Russell
1999. 114 minutes. R.

Russell's bizarre, evocative take on the Persian Gulf war of 1991 seems an intramural affair next to the complications of the present conflict, but the film's quick-strike pace and free-form craziness are still every bit as effective at getting the madness across.

Nothing makes the least bit of sense in the desert. "Are we shooting people or not?" an American soldier asks. Supposedly defeated Iraqi troops have turned their attention to terrorizing their own population, virtually ignoring their American invaders. Fleets of luxury automobiles and tons of consumer goods fill vast underground bunkers under the sands. Everything is for sale.

Appearances on CNN being of paramount importance, warring parties pause to gather around the media. Civilians are executed point-blank and willy-nilly, including a mother in front of her shrieking little girl.

Under the cover of chaos, Capt. Archie Gates (Clooney) figures he can make off with $23 million in gold bars, and he recruits a little band of troopers to help him. Sgt. Troy Barlow (Wahlberg) is a new father; Staff Sgt. Chief (Ice Cube) is a reservist on "a four-month paid vacation from Detroit." A slightly crazed Texan named Conrad (Jonze) is their little D'Artagnan.

There are some wild Humvee rides and hairy encounters with unpredictable Iraqis, some cooperative and others lethal. In the end there is a moral choice to be made. That Russell ultimately chooses the high road for Archie and crew doesn't spoil the fun.

3 WOMEN

Shelley Duvall, Sissy Spacek, Janice Rule, Robert Fortier, Ruth Nelson, John Cromwell

Directed by Robert Altman
1977. 124 minutes. PG.

In a DVD commentary, Altman says that Americans need everything to add up, but don't try too hard with this film. As a director, he says, you "vaguely do the impression, but you don't want to do the hard lines." Emotions are vital. "The audience has to feel but not understand."

The film unfolds as if in a dream. Millie (Duvall) works at a senior center in the California desert, lives in an apartment complex nearby and spiritually inhabits the pages of women's magazines that show her how to be pretty and popular. When Pinky (Spacek), a simpleminded young woman from the South, comes to work with the seniors, the kindhearted Millie takes her home to live with her.

The apartments are run by a boozy lecher (Fortier)

whose wife, Willie (Rule), the movie's primary mystery woman, remains apart in a lone reverie and paints fantastical figures on the bottom of the swimming pool.

Millie's efforts to make herself popular at work and at the apartments are met with scorn, but Pinky emulates her to the point that she actually takes over her identity. Other oddities occur, like the appearance of an elderly couple who may or may not be Pinky's parents. She says she doesn't know them.

Millie's desire to please may be pathetic, but at least she has the decency to stand by Pinky. As they confront their situation, Willie emerges as a unifying center of unspecified character and dimension in a film that is as intriguing as it is mystifying.

TIMECODE

Salma Hayek, Jeanne Tripplehorn, Julian Sands, Holly Hunter, Steven Weber, Richard Edson, Saffron Burrows, Stellan Skarsgard, Glenne Headly, Xander Berkeley

Directed by Mike Figgis
2000. 97 minutes. R.

In a nifty departure that proves there's always a new way to make a movie, Figgis set out with four digital cameras and a large, malleable ensemble of actors. The idea was to shoot four movies at once in real time, each lasting 90 minutes in one long take and each occupying one quadrant of screen.

Four movies going on at once, diverging and crisscrossing, may seem more distraction than anything else, but a nicely handled integration of story lines and increased volume for one or the other when called for help prevent a mishmash.

And what is going on that warrants such multiple treatment? As a subject befitting the method, Figgis gives us four tales of adultery in Hollywood, but, as in films like Robert Altman's *Player*, a statement of faith in the medium forgives movie folk their transgressions.

In one quadrant two women take a tense limousine ride, and next to that is another woman's therapy session, and beneath that a morning meeting at Red Mullet productions. The geometry may be complex, but it's certainly an adventurous demonstration of the possibilities of film.

TIME OUT

Aurélien Recoing, Karin Viard, Serge Livrozet, Jean-Pierre Mangeot, Monique Mangeot, Nicolas Kalsch, Marie Cantet, Félix Cantet

Directed by Laurent Cantet
2001. 134 minutes. French with English subtitles. No rating.

Cantet could be described as the chronicler of workers' woes at the management level. Employees aren't necessarily browbeaten, but they have their own set of troubles, as we see in Cantet's earlier film on the workplace, *Human Resources* (page 183). *Time Out* is really a metaphysical meditation on the abstractions of the modern corporate workplace and the anomie of pushing papers and crunching numbers.

Management types can be laid off as fast or faster as anybody else, of course, and so it happens with Vincent (Recoing), in his 40's, who loses his management job. But instead of setting out to find a new one, he drops out.

He lies to his wife, telling her that he has gone to Switzerland to take another position. While wandering about Geneva, he devises a scheme to persuade friends to invest in a nonexistent business. He travels aimlessly through stunning Swiss snowscapes. Sometimes he sleeps in his car, and there are extended night-driving sequences.

In a film permeated with abstracted sadness, Vincent finally takes a real job importing shoddy imitations of brand-name products. As it happens, that deception proves less dishonest than Vincent's old management job.

A TIME TO KILL

Matthew McConaughey, Samuel L. Jackson, Ashley Judd, Sandra Bullock, Kevin Spacey, Brenda Fricker, Oliver Platt, Charles S. Dutton, Chris Cooper, Donald Sutherland

Directed by Joel Schumacher
1996. 149 minutes. R.

If this film were a book—which it was, actually, a John Grisham page-turner—you'd take it to the beach. An outstanding cast, a gripping story and a tempestuous Southern backdrop help lift a picture that hit theaters exactly when McConaughey was at the height of his appeal.

When a rural black factory worker named Carl Lee (played scorchingly well by Jackson) kills two rednecks who raped and beat his 10-year-old daughter, he hires Jake Brigance (McConaughey), a small-town lawyer, to defend him. In racially polarized Clanton, Mississippi, Lee wants a white man to defend him because Brigance knows how white jurors think.

Brigance knows how Lee thinks, too. Before he killed the rapists in front of witnesses, Lee told Brigance that's what he would do.

They will plead insanity, though both know that the killings were premeditated. The town heats up with all kinds of colorful types, including a flashy, impertinent law student (Bullock, looking great in a role that's too young for her) who rolls into town in a black Porsche to help out the defense.

It helps that Brigance's gorgeous wife (Judd) conveniently leaves town halfway through the movie. About that time, too, the Ku Klux Klan arrives to heat things up perhaps somewhat more than needed. Spacey plays the natty prosecutor, Cooper is a cop and so is Dutton, playing a tough local sheriff.

TIN CUP

Kevin Costner, Rene Russo, Cheech Marin, Don Johnson

Directed by Ron Shelton
1996. 135 minutes. R.

Costner and Shelton teamed up to good effect in *Bull Durham*, but that was baseball and this is golf, of all the unlikely subjects for a surprisingly bright, alluring film.

Once again there is a beleaguered old-timer, and once more he's Costner, this time as the golf pro Roy McAvoy. Roy had possibilities on the tour once, but now he's relegated himself to Salome, Texas, where he runs a nicely broken-down driving range (kind of cactus chic), lives in a trailer and guzzles an ocean of beer and hard stuff with a gaggle of locals.

One day a leggy therapist, Dr. Molly Griswold (Russo), shows up looking for lessons. (Only in the movies.) When it comes to teaching the golf swing, the relaxed, matter-of-fact McAvoy waxes practically metaphysical. Give a nod to the gods, he advises, heed the "tuning fork in the loins," waggle it and "let the big dog eat" (smack the ball with the driver).

Molly finds that kind of attractive but backs away from Roy's attentions. Roy's brand of individuality, or however you want to put it, raises warnings flags, and besides, she has another pro on the hook, an arrogant, caramel-smooth top money-winner (Johnson).

Puzzled by her aversion, Roy offers himself up for therapy, which somehow seems wasted on such a one-of-a-kind, albeit a bit eccentric, who needs primarily to dry out. There's certainly nothing wrong with his sense of self-worth and how that translates on the golf course. When

Molly continues to resist him, he sets out to win the U.S. Open. Don't bet against him.

TIN MEN

Richard Dreyfuss, Danny DeVito, Barbara Hershey, John Mahoney, Seymour Cassel, Bruno Kirby, Michael Tucker

Directed by Barry Levinson
1987. 110 minutes. R.

Levinson's second Baltimore film, richly textured, pits a couple of aluminum-siding salesmen in a battle royal that escalates from hilariously cutting insults to the transfer of one man's wife to the other (a good thing, too, in the opinion of her husband).

The first Baltimore film, *Diner*, was set in 1959. Now it's 1963, and people are still talking about their favorite characters on *The Ed Sullivan Show*. Over at Gibraltar Aluminum Siding, B. B. Babowsky (Dreyfuss) has put one-sixteenth of a mile on his new blue Cadillac when it is rammed by the yellow Cadillac belonging to Ernest Tilley (DeVito).

Tilley, the cruder of the two, works for a rival siding outfit that is probably a bit more unscrupulous, if that's possible. While Tilley and B.B. like the same automobile, they differ greatly in style. The crumpled sheet metal is only the start of the aggravation between them. To rile Tilley, the avenging B.B. chases his wife (Hershey), who moves her cookie jar, shaped like a sheep's head, from Tilley's home to B.B.'s.

Levinson's first-rate screenplay fuels Dreyfuss's substantial performance, and there are fine contributions from Mahoney, Cassel, Kirby and Tucker as salesmen from the competing companies. But these people won't last forever. A film of rueful nostalgia imparts a wistful feeling of regret for a golden age nearing its end.

TINKER, TAILOR, SOLDIER, SPY

Alec Guinness, Michael Jayston, Anthony Bate, Ian Richardson, Bernard Hepton, Beryl Reid

Directed by Frances Alcock and John Irvin
1979. 290 minutes.

Once we had Guinness on board, we were able to empty the National Theater of its cast," John Le Carré said in an interview in *The New York Times*. As the British superagent George Smiley, Guinness anchored the BBC adaptations of Le Carré's novels *Tinker, Tailor* and *Smiley's People*, both as absolutely smashing on DVD as they were on television.

In *Tinker, Tailor* a double agent, or mole, working for Russia's K.G.B. has infiltrated the top levels of British intelligence, called the Circus. Smiley, a "disgusted patriot" earlier unhorsed by the Circus's intramural treacheries, is brought back to root him out.

Like the novels of Dickens, Le Carré's stories indulge in what he called "the loving, almost perverse, dwelling upon minor characters." Thanks to Guinness's participation, "there wasn't a character who wasn't a substantial actor himself," he said. "It could be argued that Alec, for all the luster he had, basically was a character actor, too."

This is an enthralling production (as is *Smiley's People*), but it requires some work on the part of the viewer. "Whereas in the movies you don't say anything if you can't show it, television is a talk medium," Le Carré said. "People expect to have to listen and to concentrate, which they can do in the privacy of their living room." Well, some people.

TO BE AND TO HAVE

A documentary by Nicolas Philibert
2002. 104 minutes. French with English subtitles. No
rating.

Philibert's film ventures on tiptoe into a small school in
the rural Auvergne, where it settles in to observe the
lives of a dozen children (ages 4 to 11) and their quiet, patient, tenacious teacher, Georges Lopez.

Six hundred hours of film have been edited into a slow,
subtle chronicle that follows the cycle of the seasons
and rarely moves beyond the school's gates. Lopez, a
distinguished-looking fellow, tells what brought him, the
son of a migrant laborer from Spain, to his profession.

Philibert makes only one visit to a student's home, and
we meet few parents. The film belongs to Lopez, whose
teaching methods are rooted in the French tradition of
strict attention to rules and reliance on drills and formal
exercises. This is a portrait of an artist, a man whose work
combines discipline and inspiration.

Only Lopez seems to understand all the daily dramas.
On the last day of the year, the impassive teacher fights
back tears when students leave his intimate garden of
learning, some for the last time.

TO DIE FOR

*Nicole Kidman, Matt Dillon, Joaquin Phoenix, Casey
Affleck, Illeana Douglas, Alison Folland*

Directed by Gus Van Sant
1995. 106 minutes. R.

There are times when we get exactly the satire we deserve, and this is one of them," Janet Maslin wrote in
The Times. That was 10 years ago, but in its send-up of

celebrity-crazed pop media and their worshippers, Van Sant's sharp, sly shots at the cheap and cheesy are still close to the mark.

No one lights up at the flash of paparazzi's flashbulbs like Suzanne Stone (Kidman), a small-town gal hell-bent on fame no matter whom she has to—well, kill. Suzanne has the Barbie Doll looks, vacuous manner and inane patter to land a spot as the weather girl on a New Hampshire station, the first stop, she's certain, to the media–show-biz fast lane. To her husband, Larry (Dillon), the son of a local mobster, she's the "girl of my dreams," as they say in tabloid speak. Still, he'd appreciate her staying around the house a little more.

No meteor on a trajectory to celebrity could abide such restrictions, so Suzanne seduces a teenage hunk (Phoenix) and persuades him and a couple of his friends to help her with her little Larry problem. It almost stands to reason that a culture that produces a Suzanne will let her get away with it.

TOKYO STORY

Chishu Ryu, Chieko Higashiyama, Sô Yamamura, Haruko Sugimura, Setsuko Hara, Kyôko Kagawa, Shirô Osaka

Directed by Yasujiro Ozu
1953. 136 minutes. Japanese with English subtitles.

F ew directors have captured the family dynamic as simply and poignantly as Ozu. An elderly couple living in the Japanese port city of Onomichi make their first trip to Tokyo to visit their children, a doctor and a beautician who love their parents but are so busy with their own lives that they can barely take time for the distraction. Only the couple's widowed daughter-in-law makes them feel welcome.

After politely going through the motions for a while, the old folks make the trip home, but on the train the mother falls ill and soon dies. Now there is cause for some reflection, which is undertaken with all sincerity but hastily, since lives must resume.

Set low to the ground, Ozu's camera takes everything in with quiet reflection. The film never spills over into sentimentality or emotion. It's a sad tale, most of all because deeper feelings that might better be explored by loved ones go unexpressed in the rush of mundane routine.

"Isn't life disappointing?" one daughter observes. "Yes, it is," replies the daughter-in-law. They smile, sharing a cheerful sense of misery. In Ozu's hands, such bittersweet moments are unforgettable.

TOM DOWD AND THE LANGUAGE OF MUSIC

Tom Dowd, Ray Charles, Eric Clapton, the Allman Brothers Band, Les Paul, Lynyrd Skynyrd, Aretha Franklin, Ahmet Ertegun

Directed by Mark Moormann
2003. 82 minutes. No rating.

In Moormann's documentary about Dowd, the producer and recording engineer who died in 2002, Clapton says that before they met he never realized what a critical contribution a sound technician could make to creative approach and output. Listening to Dowd describe his role in the evolution of studio recording, from monaural to stereo to multitracking to digital, one begins to understand how machines have shaped the changing sound of pop.

It takes an artistic hand to make the machinery effective, and Dowd was as much a musician as he was a wizard at the mixing board. In the 1950's he was the house producer for Atlantic Records and engineered recordings for the jazz greats Ornette Coleman, John Coltrane,

418

Thelonious Monk and others, as well as rhythm-and-blues classics by Ray Charles, Ruth Brown, Bobby Darin, and Sonny and Cher.

In the 60's he worked with Aretha Franklin and Clapton and Cream, then went on to produce seminal albums by the Allman Brothers Band and Lynyrd Skynyrd that helped define Southern rock. One artist after another thanks Dowd, a likable music enthusiast and problem solver nonpareil in the recording booth.

TOPSY-TURVY

Jim Broadbent, Allan Corduner, Ron Cook, Timothy Spall, Alison Steadman

Directed by Mike Leigh
1999. 160 minutes. R.

Leigh's jubilant film catches the curiously matched personalities of the librettist William Schwenk Gilbert (Broadbent) and the composer Arthur Sullivan (Corduner) at a time when they have to switch gears and reinvent themselves if they are to stay at the top of musical theater in the 1880's.

Famed for their operettas, the two are coming off a flop, *Princess Ida,* and must revive a partnership made none the easier by the fact that they really didn't get along too well. The newly knighted Sullivan has begun to turn his back on the kind of operetta that won him wealth and celebrity. The dour Gilbert can't abide this, but it takes the impresario Richard D'Oyly Carte (Cook) to convince him that there's a problem.

The pair needs a vehicle, and after Gilbert is dragged to an exhibition of Japanese culture, it materializes as *The Mikado.*

From this point on, Leigh's film describes everything about the preparation of the operetta for the stage. Gilbert has some priceless ideas about how to direct actors. And

419

they have their side of the story. Long known for the arduous preparation of his own actors, Leigh gets wonderful performances from players who are as at home in full *Mikado* regalia as they are behind the scenes.

TOUCHING EVIL

Robson Green, Nicola Walker, Shaun Dingwall, Charles Dale

Directed by Bill Eagles and Dave Moore
1999. No rating.

This noirish series, vastly different and dark, may be the best that PBS's *Mystery!* has to offer. Robson Green plays the intense homicide detective Dave Creegan, whose work necessitates that his wife and children be put in a protective custody so tight even he doesn't know where they are. That might prompt some men to switch jobs and live a little, but Creegan's obsession with tracking the worst of England's killers has reached the point where it challenges his sanity. Even his equally intense partner, the smart, blunt Susan Taylor (Walker), suggests that he "go home, go to bed and at least pretend to be a normal person."

But that wouldn't make much of a series. In this episode from the third season (one of several episodes from various seasons available on DVD) Creegan is back from a forced leave—necessitated by "nervous exhaustion," according to his superiors—looking none the better for the layoff.

Out there, someone has hung a mutilated woman's body over a river. Creegan and Taylor recognize the killing as the first of a string, carried out in following episodes, in which a woman's heart is cut out and put in garbage bags. The murders follow the modus operandi of a confessed killer who has just been released from prison.

As always, the series may be a bit slow to start, but it is impossible to leave.

TOUCH OF EVIL

Orson Welles, Charlton Heston, Janet Leigh, Joseph Calleia, Akim Tamiroff, Victor Millan

Directed by Orson Welles
1958. 108 minutes.

Welles's rich, wild noir set along the Mexican border tells a bizarre tale, but its impact lies in the shadows and angles and all the things Welles does like no other.

In a famously bravura opening, a car with a bomb about to detonate drives around for more than three minutes while the film introduces Mike Vargas (Heston), a Mexican lawman, and his wife, Susan (Leigh). After the explosion, which eliminates a local crime boss, in steps Sheriff Hank Quinlan (Welles).

A huge pile of a man, Quinlan has quirks and hatreds as bulky as his physique, which was padded for effect. (Welles was big, but not that big.) Quinlan knows how to set up a man, and soon a shoe box with dynamite in it is found in the possession of a young Mexican (Millan). That alerts Vargas, who volunteers his services in the investigation. Vargas could swear there was no dynamite in the shoe box when he looked at it earlier. The explosive was planted, or so it seems.

Meanwhile, Susan runs afoul of a drug lord (Tamiroff) who tells her that Vargas should stay out of the case. Later she is drugged and framed for murder herself.

Welles had his own troubles with the studio, in this case Universal. When the film was finished, he went off to South America to make another picture, only to discover on his return that *Touch of Evil* had been truncated into a 95-minute version. On the DVD that stands corrected.

TRAFFIK

Bill Paterson, Lindsay Duncan, Jamal Shah, Talat Hussain, Julia Ormond

Directed by Alastair Reid
1989. 315 minutes.

A British television production, broadcast on PBS's *Masterpiece Theater* in 1990 and repeated in 2001, makes far more interesting viewing than Steven Soderbergh's film *Traffic* (not that we don't recommend that, too), which tells the same story after moving it to Mexico and the United States.

Reid's epic, the blueprint for the Soderbergh film, is set in Pakistan, source of the heroin production that is both the sustenance and the scourge of its characters, Germany (the "k" in traffik is for the German role in the drug trade) and London. There, the British counterpart (Paterson) of the American drug enforcement czar (played by Michael Douglas in *Traffic*) battles his own quiet despair as well as the heroin flow. Like the Douglas character, he has an addicted daughter (Ormond in her first screen role).

In Germany, the wife (Duncan) of an executive caught smuggling drugs fights to salvage her life, and in Pakistan, a farmer named Fazal (Shah) is forced out of his poppy fields and into the drug business in an effort to save his family.

In almost six hours, Reid's film has opportunity to examine character in much greater depth than does Soderbergh's movie. Simon Moore, who wrote the mini-series, said he had tried to avoid traditional views of good and bad, a big departure from the American film. *Traffik* places the problems in a larger context of political and human relations, always taking into account the shadings of conduct that make an act not so much right or wrong, but just as a result of the way things work.

THE TRIGGER EFFECT

Kyle MacLachlan, Elisabeth Shue, Dermot Mulroney,
Richard T. Jones, Michael Rooker

Directed by David Koepp
1996. 93 minutes. R.

Koepp's engrossing film captures an urban dread that emanates from alarming omens. The fear starts with the jitters, as people behave rudely to one another at the movies, then escalates after an undefined occurrence causes a blackout that cripples the country.

As in a Spielberg film, this happens on the eeriest of nights. Matthew (MacLachlan) and Annie (Shue), who have been feeling some strain in their marriage, find themselves without power in a house torn up by renovations. The baby has an ear infection and needs medicine. There is no phone or computer or radio or cash, or any way to get a prescription.

Behavior starts to alter under these conditions, with both Matthew and Annie finding that they like to live dangerously. She flirts outrageously with a handsome friend (Mulroney) who is spending the night. Matthew strikes out to do what it takes to get the medicine, which means stealing it. At a gun shop, business is alarmingly brisk.

Mathew crosses paths with a volatile bully (Rooker) and a black man named Raymond (Jones), who heightens tensions. Eventually all end up on a scenic prairie dominated by a nuclear power plant, a crow and a dead tree. On cue and with characteristic acuity, Koepp then shows a stream of traffic headed in one direction: away from town. There is no explanation, but a quiet, controlled and ultimately strange film delivers with a cool elegance.

THE TRIPLETS OF BELLEVILLE

*The voices of Jean-Claude Donda, Michel Robin,
Monica Viegas, Béatrice Bonifassi, Michèle
Caucheteux, Charles Prévost Linton*

An animated film written and directed by
Sylvain Chomet
2003. 80 minutes. PG-13.

Rarely does a work of total originality come along, and practically never one as jaw-droppingly original as Chomet's first feature. With a perverse pen and a peculiar imagination, he has created a dense, wonderfully strange urban world bursting with insouciant whimsy.

The film sashays through highly stylized cityscapes, its odd characters adding to the spectacular eccentricity. In an indelibly French city of chain-smoking truck drivers and accordion-squeezing pop singers, a resourceful crone named Madame Souza raises her chubby orphaned grandson to become a freakishly muscled Tour de France racer. His pedaling prowess draws the attention of gangsters, who ship him off, pedaling all the while on a treadmill-style conveyor, to a teeming vertical city resembling Manhattan.

It's called Belleville. Following her grandson across the Atlantic in a tiny craft (a pedal boat at that), Madame Souza encounters the trio of the title, three stringy scat-singing sisters who entertain in clubs and throw out a rhythm you won't get out of your head for a week. They also hunt frogs with dynamite.

There are two lines of intelligible dialogue, but no talk is needed in a world so sweet and sinister, spicy and grotesque, invitingly funny and forbiddingly dark.

THE TRIUMPH OF LOVE

Mira Sorvino, Ben Kingsley, Jay Rodan, Fiona Shaw,
Ignazio Oliva, Rachael Stirling, Luis Molteni

Directed by Clare Peploe
2001. 112 minutes. PG-13.

If you had to transform from rake into princess and back
again, and fast, you could do no better than Sorvino
does here. As a bogus princess and a couple of other people in Peploe's adaptation of Marivaux's 270-year-old romantic comedy, Sorvino looks as fetching in breeches and
hose as she does in lacy décolletage.

A princess can wind up in a dungeon or worse for
pulling identity stunts, especially when, like this princess,
she has no legal right to her royal position. But she decides to take a risk after spotting a lithe young fellow
named Agis (Rodan) as he is skinny-dipping. Recognizing
him as the legitimate occupant of her position, as well as
someone she wouldn't mind getting to know in any
event, she decides to get at him where he lives, so to
speak.

That would be the castle of the austere philosopher
Hermocrates (Kingsley), famously hostile to love, and his
spinsterish sister, Leontine (Shaw). Assuming a dazzling
androgyny, the princess soon has them both in romantic
thrall as she focuses on her central mission.

Kingsley and Shaw throw off the burdens of being important actors and ham it up delightfully in a rich comedy
that succeeds in part because the objectively ridiculous,
overdrawn emotions of the characters seem real and immediate to them.

TROUBLE IN PARADISE

Kay Francis, Miriam Hopkins, Herbert Marshall, Charlie Ruggles, Edward Everett Horton

Directed by Ernst Lubitsch
1932. 83 minutes.

The Production Code of 1934 hadn't yet spoiled the fun, so Lubitsch's suave, luminous romantic comedy is free to be sexy to just the right degree, which is to say unmistakably yet understatedly.

Setting their sights on a merry widow (Francis), two jewel thieves, Gaston and Lily (Marshall and Hopkins), take jobs as her secretary and maid.

The writers Samson Raphaelson and Grover Jones create a perfect mix of tone and style. Francis is elegant, wry and sensual as a woman who might not mind being victimized if it helped her seduce Gaston. Hopkins, good with comedy and one of the most underrated actresses of the 30's, stays sly and feisty as she undertakes thievery while negotiating the romantic currents.

TRUE LOVE

Annabella Sciorra, Ron Eldard, Aida Turturro, Roger Rignack

Directed by Nancy Savoca
1989. 104 minutes. R.

Greeks or no Greeks, Savoca's film still stands as a benchmark among exuberant, raucous ethnic-wedding movies. In this case, a lot of those involved in the Italian-American nuptials of Donna (Sciorra) and Michael (Eldard) have their doubts about the union, including the bride and groom. But this Bronx extravaganza is ready to roll and there's no stopping the momentum.

A bustling cast drives a film that has a lot of affection for specific neighborhood touches. In her first feature, Savoca shows her knack for creating real-looking settings on a very low budget and finding unknown actors who manage to be natural and uproariously funny at the same time. Sciorra's gentle beauty and tough negotiating style make Donna a touching and fully drawn character. Eldard makes Michael a similar mix of contrasts, blustery yet sweet and decent.

One thing he will not stand for is sky-blue mashed potatoes, just one of the caterer's classy touches. And would it be all right if Michael went out for a bit with his buddies after the ceremony, just for an hour or so?

TRULY MADLY DEEPLY

Juliet Stevenson, Alan Rickman, Bill Paterson, Michael Maloney, Jenny Howe

Directed by Anthony Minghella
1991. 106 minutes. PG.

Before Minghella directed the lavish romance of *The English Patient,* he made this exquisite, fanciful love story about a woman who feels her dead lover is still with her. Stevenson and Rickman are at their most charming as Nina and Jamie, the lovers who seemed perfectly matched. They shared enthusiasms: classical music (he on the cello, she on the piano), sex, poetry, old movies. Then one day he gets a sore throat and that's that.

Nina takes a picturesque flat in London and tells her analyst that she hears Jamie's voice everywhere. Then, one evening as she is playing the piano, he materializes as if in the flesh.

Jamie says he is back because he didn't die properly. Once again they sing and dance and enjoy many of the things they shared together. Nina's friends can't understand why she is suddenly so happy again.

Momentum begins to build for her to cast her lot with the living, though. How long can she go on watching *Fitzcarraldo* on video with Jamie and his friends from the beyond?

Minghella warmly makes a case for honoring the past, while finding a way—however bizarre—to let go and move on.

THE TRUMAN SHOW

Jim Carrey, Laura Linney, Noah Emmerich, Ed Harris, Natascha McElhone, Holland Taylor, Brian Delate

Directed by Peter Weir
1998. 103 minutes. PG.

Truman Burbank (Carrey) first begins to suspect that something is out of whack when he spots his father (Delate), supposedly lost years ago at sea, walking around the pristine little enclave of Seahaven. From that moment it takes a while for Truman to realize that he has lived every minute of his 30 years as the central character, or central exhibit, in a wildly popular television show that beams his every move to a country addicted to his life down to its tiniest detail.

Manicured 1950's Seahaven is in fact a set, and all the neat 1950's people scurrying here and there are actors (including Truman's long-lost dad, who makes the mistake of wandering back onto the set).

The show's concept belongs to Christof (Harris), its grandiose producer. In the hermetic world of Seahaven the very sky belongs to Christof ("Cue the sun!") and his technicians.

At the heart of Weir's film is an inspired screenplay by Andrew Niccol, whose own film *Gattaca* had the same transfixing sci-fi intensity. The real star of *Truman* is its premise. What if our taste for trivia and voyeurism led to a life as a show-biz illusion? What if that life not only became the ultimate paranoid fantasy but achieved new heights of narcissism?

Weir, known for the thoughtfulness and idiosyncrasy of his films, handles the tricky job of gradually poking holes in the deception.

TUMBLEWEEDS

Janet McTeer, Kimberly J. Brown, Jay O. Sanders, Gavin O'Connor, Michael J. Pollard, Laurel Holloman, Lois Smith

Directed by Gavin O'Connor
1999. 102 minutes. PG-13.

McTeer dominates the film with an astoundingly vital performance as a sexy, free-spirited Southern lady with one foot perpetually out the door. Bailing out of her umpteenth violently abusive relationship, Mary Jo Walker shoos her 12-year-old daughter, Ava (Brown), into a battered car and heads off vaguely toward Arizona with a stop in Jefferson City, Missouri, where she plans to snare a man she knew in high school. "Now he finally can have me," she tells her daughter.

A sweet young girl, Ava is appalled, but, being deeply attached to her mother, she goes along as gamely as she can. When the Missouri man is less than remembered, Mary Jo heads for California.

A lusty, good-looking woman with a roving eye, she is fond of tossing clothing out the car window and yelling, "Yahoo!" Near San Diego, they go swimming and take up housekeeping with Jack (O'Connor), a conservative, bossy truck driver. Mary Jo enchants a school chum of Ava's. "I love your life and your four marriages, and I think it's so great," the girl exclaims.

The resilient Ava blossoms and wins the role of Romeo in a school play. Mary Jo drops Jack, and mother and daughter become closer. But Mary Jo is itching to head for Arizona, the primary reason being that she no longer has a boyfriend. Then Ava makes a stand.

(A largely similar and equally worthwhile film, *Anywhere but Here*, stars Susan Sarandon and Natalie Portman as, respectively, a more fragile and much more mature mother and daughter.)

28 DAYS LATER

Cillian Murphy, Naomie Harris, Christopher Eccleston, Megan Burns, Brendan Gleeson

Directed by Danny Boyle
2002. 113 minutes. R.

One of the smartest and most stylish of a new breed of horror films with special resonance for an age of biological warfare and other plagues, Boyle's film winks at old movies yet can still make you jump. At the start, animal rights advocates set free chimpanzees in a London laboratory, accidentally letting loose a virus that infects people with a murderous fury, turning them into angry, violent and highly contagious zombies.

In a hospital for unrelated reasons, a bike messenger named Jim (Murphy) awakens from a coma 28 days later and finds the city deserted. While he slept, the city, and pretty much the entire country, killed itself off.

With some finely inventive location shooting, Boyle manages to vacate London streets of all but blowing refuse, creating an eerie apocalyptic landscape. Jim encounters other isolated survivors, first a smart, tough young woman named Selena (Harris), who has figured how the virus works and how to stay out of the clutches of crazed victims (easier figured out than done). Together they find a benign cabdriver named Frank (Gleeson) with a flair for guns and gadgets, who is hiding out with his teenage daughter, Hannah.

As this band tries to escape, they are beset by zombies blocking the streets of London, but they make their way to the country, where they are taken in by a military unit that has taken over a mansion. Unfortunately, the unit's commanding officer (Eccleston) is a tyrant, in charge of a troop of sexual predators as dangerous as the infected attackers.

Be sure to check out the alternate ending, included on the DVD; it's tougher and truer to the film's trajectory than the original.

25TH HOUR

Edward Norton, Brian Cox, Barry Pepper, Philip Seymour Hoffman, Rosario Dawson

Directed by Spike Lee
2002. 135 minutes. R.

One of Lee's best, least-recognized films, this is a small-scale character study about fathers, sons and surviving in New York.

Norton is as good as he has even been as Monty Brogan, a midlevel drug dealer about to start a seven-year prison sentence. In the 24 hours before he goes to prison, he has some last-minute affairs to attend to. He has accounts to settle with Russian mobsters. He needs to say good-bye to his father (Cox), a retired firefighter who now tends bar on Staten Island, and to his friends, including a cocky lawyer (Pepper) and a bumbling high school teacher (Hoffman). Monty also needs to find a home for his dog, and to learn if it was his girlfriend (Dawson) who gave him up to the feds.

Monty is a lot of contradictions: a dutiful son and a tough guy, arrogant and scared. A scene in which he asks his friends to beat him as a preparation for prison is a brutal but accurate expression of his character. And although the explanations about why and how his life developed seem too pat, the film succeeds as a dazzling, wrenching succession of moods. Basing the work on a novel by David Benioff, Lee exercises his prodigious visual talents, yet keeps the film so controlled and measured that its bursts of wild invention are electrifying.

24-HOUR PARTY PEOPLE

Steve Coogan, Keith Allen, Rob Brydon, Enzo Cilenti, Ron Cook, Chris Coghill

Directed by Michael Winterbottom
2002. 117 minutes. R.

Winterbottom's career is nothing if not varied. (See *The Claim*, page 74, and *Welcome to Sarajevo*, page 455.) This is one of his most gleeful films. Although it sets out to be a fake documentary about the Manchester music scene from the late 1970's through the 90's, the film has such fresh energy that it will appeal even to people who know and care nothing about that era. Steve Coogan (well known as a comic in Britain) plays the megalomaniacal Tony Wilson, a co-founder of Factory Records and a journalist turned impresario.

Pop England is at its headiest and most volatile since the Beatles as Wilson skips across the scenes (sometimes justifying himself as he talks to the camera) with a skewed craziness that blends drug-fueled bravado with a corporate pose. He was right about the coming of punk and the Sex Pistols, whom he put on his Manchester TV show. He was always wrong about money. Factory Records worked as a concept but in the long run flopped financially. When he tries to sell the failing company, Wilson tells prospective buyers that it's not really a company at all but more "an experiment in human nature."

Fake bands portray real bands here, but the buoyant soundtrack is mostly background for the rise and fall of Wilson, messing up his life as well as his business empire.

21 GRAMS

Sean Penn, Naomi Watts, Benicio Del Toro, Charlotte Gainsbourg

Directed by Alejandro González Iñárritu
2003. 125 minutes. R.

The title refers not to drugs but to the weight a body loses when it dies—the weight of a soul. González Iñárritu's film sets up three separate story lines about characters in crisis. At first the segments lie about in pieces and don't cohere. They will, though, and in the meantime it's best to give yourself over to the wrenching performances by a first-rate cast.

Prof. Paul Rivers (Penn) needs a heart transplant or he will die. At the last moment the heart is there, but the transplant leaves Paul torn by guilt and determined to approach the donor's family in hopes of resolving his feelings of remorse and self-worth.

Cristina (Watts) is a former party girl, and a former lover of Paul's, who has lost her husband and children in an auto accident. She is so torn by anguish that she goes back to her old life.

And Jack (Del Toro) is a former convict who has found that Jesus is the best tool to stay off drugs. His relentless fundamentalism becomes his way of ruling his family, sometimes brutally.

This is González Iñárritu's second film since the acclaimed *Amores Perros* (page 11), and he lays out the pieces until, by the end, they fit together powerfully.

At heart, the strength of the film is not so much its odd structure as its intimacy. González Iñárritu reveals the characters so powerfully that their suffering becomes intriguing and unforgettable.

ULEE'S GOLD

Peter Fonda, Patricia Richardson, Christine Dunford, Tom Wood, Jessica Biel, Vanessa Zima, Steven Flynn

Directed by Victor Nunez
1997. 113 minutes. R.

Fonda gives probably his finest performance as a reclusive beekeeper who pulled away from life after his wife died six years earlier. Now, though, Ulee is being force-fed some human contact by his two granddaughters, the schoolgirl Penny (Zima) and the rebellious teenager Casey (Biel).

The girls have come to live with him because their wayward mother, Helen (Dunford), has wandered off with two criminal pals of Ulee's son, Tom (Wood), who might be expected to contribute some parenting if he weren't in jail.

At first Ulee is powerfully uncomfortable around the girls and treats them in standoffish fashion. Then he winds up with the drug-addicted Helen on his hands. As Ulee begins to rise to the challenges of getting out of himself and caring for these people, Nunez's film begins to gather dramatic momentum. But with Ulee's wariness and penchant for understatement setting the tone, the changes are gradual and intended to be savored.

UNDERGROUND

Miki Manojlovic, Lazar Ristovski, Mirjana Jokovic, Mirjana Karanovic, Slavko Stimac

Directed by Emir Kusturica
1995. 167 minutes. Serbo-Croatian with English subtitles. No rating.

One of DVDs' special niches—outstanding films seen by relatively few—profits greatly from Kusturica's riotous satire. Though it won the Palme d'Or at the 1995 Cannes International Film Festival, a wildly excessive, hugely long account of 50 years of Balkan history told in Serbo-Croatian can't expect too much of a run in American movie theaters.

Satire may be the best approach to the Balkans. Beginning during World War II, *Underground* erupts with mad fervor and surrealistic craziness, accompanied loudly and mockingly by a brass band that never lets up.

When the Germans bomb their town and take over their country, the madcap Marko (Manojlovic) and Blacky (Ristovski) rise up in alcohol-fueled fervor for the resistance led by Marshal Tito. Not that there isn't opportunity for personal gain. After the impetuous Blacky does great damage to himself with a hand grenade, Marko shepherds him and a crowd of partisans into a basement and tricks them into staying underground for many years while he profits from their labors as weapons makers and rises to prominence in Tito's bureaucracy.

Marko also makes off with Natalija (Jokovic), the country's leading movie star, who is so smoldering that she virtually makes love to herself while waiting to ravish and be ravished. Accounts are settled years later when Blacky emerges from the basement to become a crazed militia leader in Bosnia. And the band plays on during a comic but oddly uplifting ending that holds out a kind of sick hope for the Balkans.

It's all great, horrifying fun. But don't look for madcap

DVD extras. Interviewed briefly in his tuxedo at Cannes, Kusturica talked of pain and controversy. "Making a movie is an awful thing," he said.

UNDER THE SAND

Charlotte Rampling, Bruno Cremer, Jacques Nolot, Alexandra Stewart, Pierre Vernier, Andrée Tainsy

Directed by François Ozon
2000. 92 minutes. French with English subtitles. No rating.

As a middle-aged couple, Jean and Marie Drillon (Cremer and Rampling), set out from Paris for their country cottage by the sea, everything suggests a time-worn routine followed weekly by a long-married couple fondly if somewhat sadly attached to each other for what seems, and not that onerously, like an eternity. Then, at the beach for a swim, Jean inexplicably disappears. The authorities suspect he has drowned, but Marie, thunderstruck with shock, can't accept that conclusion, or any other, for that matter. To her, Jean simply hasn't gone away at all. Surely he will reappear.

What has begun as an observation of comfortable domestic routine now becomes a wrenching examination of loss. Back in Paris, Marie is still unable to accept Jean's death and continues to speak of him in the present tense. In her state of denial, she begins an affair with Vincent (Nolot), and since Jean is still on the scene in her mind, she feels like an adulteress.

As if in some sense of cooperation, Jean reappears. Is he a ghost, or a manifestation of his wife's unsettled emotional state? In any event, he seems to approve of her move in Vincent's direction and even joins the lovers, at least in Marie's perception. Still, she can't accept his absence, and the common experience of grief takes on an intoxicating, sometimes comic strangeness.

Ozon keeps us slightly off balance as his story moves into its heartbreaking final scenes at a leisurely, thoughtful pace. Never immersing us melodramatically into Marie's emotional condition, he observes with a cool sympathy.

UNFAITHFUL

Diane Lane, Olivier Martinez, Richard Gere

Directed by Adrian Lyne
2002. 124 minutes. R.

Hollywood usually serves sex in sparing portions of titillation, but Lyne's film crashes through the mold by acknowledging that sex, especially reckless, adulterous sex, can rock people's lives and have catastrophic consequences.

When Connie Summer (Lane), a beautiful, supremely assured wife and mother, heads to Manhattan from her higher-end suburban enclave, a sudden white-hot affair with a stranger isn't on her list of expectations.

Then she collides with Paul Martel (Martinez) on the sidewalk and skins her knees. Martel is a rare-book dealer with smoldering good looks, a splendid borrowed apartment and some Band-Aids. He is also one of those seize-the-moment types. Connie doesn't yield then and there, but Martel's adventurous philosophy appeals to a woman caught in the confining routine of marriage and parenthood.

So she engineers another visit, with predictable results. Connie and Martel make love everywhere with a ravenous intensity.

Back home, her husband, Edward (Gere), becomes suspicious. In a fine natural performance, Gere conveys the fierce watchfulness and grinding tension you might expect in a fairly high-powered if nondescript suburban businessman. When Edward has photographic evidence of his wife's infidelity, he visits her lover's loft for an encounter that turns violent.

But the most unsettling part of Lyne's film is the inability of Edward and Connie, for all their sophistication, to communicate on anything but the most superficial level. Having weathered the crisis, they can only cling to each other in fear and uncertainty. All she can say is, "I'm scared."

UNFORGIVEN

Clint Eastwood, Gene Hackman, Morgan Freeman, Jaimz Woolvett, Richard Harris

Directed by Clint Eastwood
1992. 131 minutes. R.

Looking more mysteriously possessed than he did in Sergio Leone's westerns, if that's possible, Eastwood becomes almost a force of nature in a riveting film about a reluctant gunfighter who goes back to bounty hunting one more time.

Just why Bill Munny (Eastwood) does that is unclear. A lot of bad things have happened. After his wife died, he turned to pig farming and raising his kids, and that's the way he wants it, or so he at first insists to a young rider who calls himself the Schofield Kid (Woolvett). The Kid wants Munny's help in collecting $1,000 offered by the prostitutes of Big Whiskey to anyone who will kill the man who disfigured one of them with a knife. Munny finally agrees. It may be the money, but one never knows.

His old pal Ned Logan (Freeman) also goes along. In Big Whiskey they encounter the sheriff, Little Bill Daggett (Hackman), who discourages bounty hunters and all but beats one to death. Suspecting Munny, Daggett nearly kills him, too.

The odd thing is that Munny just takes his beating without resistance or retaliation. Hackman's Daggett makes a pretty scary sadist, but Munny as victim is scary himself. Is he so caught up in his own defeat that all the fight goes out of him? We suspect different.

The man is a great shot, which helps him pick off the face slasher out in the open spaces. But will he overcome his soul sickness? And will he go head-to-head with Daggett in Big Whiskey? A great-looking film is full of broad skies and chilly landscapes and heavy with portent.

USED CARS

Kurt Russell, Jack Warden, Gerrit Graham, Frank McRae, Deborah Harmon, Al Lewis

Directed by Robert Zemeckis
1980. 113 minutes. R.

The summer of 1980 didn't lack for comedy. In his review in *The Times*, Vincent Canby ranked *Used Cars* behind *Airplane!* but ahead of *The Blues Brothers* and *Caddyshack*, all released that year.

Zemeckis says on a DVD of his *Back to the Future* that *Used Cars*, crass and smart and a little out of its mind, got attention but not enough to attract major financing for future projects. (For him, that would come after *Who Framed Roger Rabbit*, page 459.)

Used Cars makes sly use of ham-fisted exaggeration. Out there under the fluttering plastic pennants on a strip of desert highway, two car lots owned by feuding brothers (both played by Warden) offer a sea of banged-up, barely operative wrecks representing every type of boxy abomination on the road in the 1970's.

Rudy Russo (Russell), slick and motor-mouthed, will sell you anything, even if he has to keep the bumper on with a wad of bubble gum. Rudy has political ambitions. If he scares up 40 grand to contribute to the local party boss, Rudy will be anointed a candidate for state senate.

In the good-guy, bad-guy tradition, one brother has a weak ticker and a love for every oil-stained aspect of the business. Across the road, his evil, wheeler-dealer sibling would dispossess him to take advantage of a profitable land deal.

Someone is buried in an Edsel, and a high school student-driver class serves as the cavalry riding to the rescue in a film unafraid of a little picaresque crudity and loaded with brash skepticism of many concepts Americans hold dear.

VANILLA SKY

Tom Cruise, Cameron Diaz, Penélope Cruz, Kurt Russell, Jason Lee, Noah Taylor

Directed by Cameron Crowe
2001. 136 minutes. R.

Crowe, the most warmhearted of Hollywood mainstream directors, strays into chillier territory in a peculiarly entertaining tale of redemption, not to mention outright confusion, in the upper reaches of Manhattan yuppiedom.

Cruise is about perfect as the always grinning David Aames, smug king of the world, just turned 33, who has inherited a publishing empire, lives in an apartment the size of the Getty Museum, has any woman he wants and just has to grin and shrug in mock amazement, and not a little sarcasm, at how great it all is.

Aames grins most when there's nothing funny, as if to emphasize his incredulity at anything outside his range of expectation. Only nightmares, harrowing and having to do with abandonment and loss of identity, wipe the grin off his face.

While he keeps grinning, he's not amused by Julie Gianni (Diaz), a leggy blonde who feels that her sharing his bed obligates Aames to show some feeling for her. At a party Aames meets Sophia (Cruz), a young woman he does care for. But then he loses his face in a car crash that leaves him grotesquely disfigured. He also loses Sophia.

At this point he enters a world between reality and dreams. Identities keep changing. Sophia becomes Julie. His face appears to be miraculously restored until he looks in the mirror and finds it disfigured again. There's been a killing. He stands accused of murder. A psychiatrist (Russell) has a theory. Aames has had enough.

THE VANISHING

Gene Bervoets, Johanna ter Steege, Bernard-Pierre Donnadieu

Directed by George Sluizer
1988. 107 minutes. Dutch with English subtitles. No rating.

Sluizer's thriller manages the very rare feat of setting up a stunner of a mystery, then more or less lets us in on what happened. That would deflate almost any cliffhanger, but Sluizer's tale, adapted by Tim Krabbé from his book *The Golden Egg*, doesn't lose one iota of suspense.

On vacation in France, an attractive couple from Amsterdam, Rex (Bervoets) and Saskia (ter Steege), pull into a rest area. Saskia goes inside for cold drinks and never returns. She has completely disappeared.

Sluizer, directing with the spooky, matter-of-fact precision of nonfiction crime writing, builds a disturbing horror story that seems quite real. Leaving Rex at the point when he realizes that his wife's disappearance is serious, the film joins Raymond (Donnadieu), a placid-looking French chemistry professor who has become a hero after saving a drowning child but is given to peculiar pronouncements like, "Watch out for heroes; they're capable of excess."

Raymond keeps a bottle of chloroformlike anesthetic in his car, and he has devised a formula connecting "dosage" with "minutes unconscious" and "miles." At one point he is seen trying to lure women into the vehicle, and he even practices his technique on one of his children.

Right here the story might deflate, but, as Rex and Raymond cross paths, Sluizer maintains grim fascination right to the very end.

VELVET GOLDMINE

Ewan McGregor, Jonathan Rhys-Meyers, Toni Collette, Christian Bale, Eddie Izzard

Directed by Todd Haynes
1998. 124 minutes. No rating.

Haynes (who went on to make the acclaimed *Far from Heaven*) brilliantly recaptures and refashions the glam-rock 1970's into a brave new world of theatricality and sexuality. In its slender frame of a story, a young journalist in the 80's looks at the past era and the giant who created it.

At the center is the shimmering protean aura of David Bowie, here manifested in the form of the pretty, insolent Bowie stand-in Brian Slade (Rhys-Meyers, who requires 11 wigs and 17 makeup changes). Slade becomes a near-mythological presence before staging his own assassination at a concert and disappearing from public view. What better way to generate mystique and an enduring legend? He's the rock star who never ages.

Grabbing on to the Slade myth, a new young star named Curt Wild (McGregor) erupts in the glittery 70's pop utopia. McGregor is hilariously decadent as Wild, who eventually becomes such a huge star that he fascinates even his inspiration, the supposedly dead Slade.

Haynes is always interested in cultural imagery, and along the way the film actually goes back to Oscar Wilde, whom it imagines as a schoolboy who wants to be a pop star. Along with the enticing performances, the vibrant soundtrack evokes the glam era with fondness and fascination.

THE VERDICT

Paul Newman, Jack Warden, Charlotte Rampling, James Mason, Milo O'Shea, Ed Binns

Directed by Sidney Lumet
1982. 129 minutes. R.

It's always interesting when a major movie star gives himself over to a down-and-out character. Frank Galvin may be an alcoholic failure as a lawyer, but in a shrewd, substantial performance Newman believably rescues the man and lands him among the virtuous.

When we meet Frank, he's hanging around funeral homes pretending to be an acquaintance of the deceased and handing out business cards in case his services are needed. They never are, so he spends his time in bars and playing pinball. Frank, in fact, has lost whatever few cases he's had during his career and owed his job, lost long ago, to the fact that he married the boss's daughter, whom he also lost.

His one case now, if you can call it that, involves a malpractice suit against a Roman Catholic hospital in Boston. Frank is hired by the church's prestigious law firm to offer a woman a cash settlement and rake off some for himself.

That's stooping too low, even for Frank. In a burst of resolve, he takes the case to court, where he is opposed by the archdiocese's sleek mouthpiece, Ed Concannon (Mason). Frank has the shakes during his opening statement, but by the time he delivers his climactic summation, Newman the star has scored as Frank the formerly ignoble in a film that never loses plausibility.

THE VIRGIN SUICIDES

Kirsten Dunst, James Woods, Kathleen Turner, Hanna Hall, Chelse Swain, A. J. Cook, Leslie Hayman, Danny DeVito

Directed by Sofia Coppola
1999. 97 minutes. R.

Coppola's first film beautifully captures the dreamy mood of longing, sadness and loss in Jeffrey Eugenides's first novel, about five teenage sisters who mysteriously perish without ever escaping the confines of their suburban household.

In Eugenides's book and the script Coppola adapted from it, the five Lisbon girls, ages 13 to 17, exist only as objects of masculine desire, which turns into longing after they're gone. Most alluring to the teenage boys who surround the house and peer inside is Lux Lisbon (Dunst), a provocative mix of suburban innocence and Lolita-like eroticism.

Outside the house, presided over by spiritless parents (Woods and Turner), the boys climb trees with binoculars to catch a glimpse of girls who are more like creatures of fantasy or legend. With only their imaginations to carry them from there, the boys envision the Lisbon girls in golden meadows or rolling cloudscapes.

No one knows why they die. An inventive filmmaker, Coppola relieves the book's somber mood with some playful touches, though she is eager to confront the pain, frustration and grief that simmer beneath her tranquil suburban enchanted land.

WAG THE DOG

Robert De Niro, Dustin Hoffman, Anne Heche, Woody Harrelson, Denis Leary, Willie Nelson

Directed by Barry Levinson
1997. 97 minutes. R.

Made in the era of Bill Clinton and James Carville, this savagely funny satire works just as well for the time of George W. Bush and Karl Rove because the real target is not political ideology but political spin itself, a subset of show business. When the president is caught making a pass at an under-age Firefly Girl just 11 days before an election, he finds himself the butt of opposition commercials set to the tune of "Thank Heaven for Little Girls." White House damage control turns to Conrad Brean (De Niro), a public relations repairman who's never come up with a face-saver that underestimates the intelligence of the American public.

What's needed, of course, is a distraction. Brean suggests concocting another crisis in the Balkans. Start a war with Albania, he suggests. "Why Albania?" asks the president's motor-mouthed blond assistant, Winifred Ames (Heche). "Why not?" Brean replies.

Like much else in this society, war comes with show-business connections. To add dramatic arc to the conflict, Brean brings on the movie producer Stanley Motss (Hoffman), who is found ordering a veggie shake while emerging from the tanning machine at his palatial California house. Soon Stanley has brought in the troops, along with Willie Nelson to write an anthem and a fad king (Leary) to whip up some appropriately themed bric-a-brac. A bogus battle scene is filmed for the evening news.

David Mamet wrote the merciless screenplay with Hilary Henkin (based on the book *American Hero,* by Larry Beinhart). The title has already entered the language as a common phrase for a politically convenient, manufactured crisis, and here is where it began.

WAITING FOR GUFFMAN

Christopher Guest, Catherine O'Hara, Parker Posey, Eugene Levy, Bob Balaban, Fred Willard

Directed by Christopher Guest
1996. 84 minutes. R.

This may be the funniest of Christopher Guest's relentlessly clever satires (although a sizable faction would give that honor to *Best in Show,* page 32). Guest plays the artistic and sensitive Corky Sinclair in a spoof of the theater world that takes in everything from Beckett to television commercials.

The mock documentary follows Corky, who arrives in Blaine, Missouri, with plans to put together a musical extravaganza, *Red, White and Blaine,* in honor of the town's 150th anniversary. The town used to make footstools and earned some fame when much of the population was carried off by space aliens. Corky intends to put on a show that will rival *Oklahoma!* He doesn't have much to work with, though, and the town's lack of talent is one of the film's delicious treats: Willard and O'Hara, as married travel agents who never travel, audition with a medley of "Midnight at the Oasis" and the theme from a Taster's Choice commercial. Levy plays a tone-deaf dentist, Balaban an earnest music teacher and Posey a Dairy Queen waitress. The Guffman of the title is a major New York theater figure supposedly on his way to Blaine to look at the show and undoubtedly propel the town straight to Broadway.

Most of the cast consists of Guest regulars, who demonstrate once again that it takes a huge amount of talent to depict people so hilariously untalented.

WAKING THE DEAD

Billy Crudup, Jennifer Connelly, Molly Parker, Janet McTeer, Paul Hipp, Sandra Oh, Hal Holbrook

Directed by Keith Gordon
2000. 106 minutes. R.

Romance, politics and obsession intersect in a haunting, moody film directed by Gordon (see *A Midnight Clear,* page 252), based on Scott Spencer's novel.

In the 1970's, Fielding Pierce (Crudup), a working-class golden boy making his way in the tough world of Chicago politics, meets Sarah Williams (Connelly), a beautiful, headstrong idealist. Sarah, who believes he is selling out by working for reform within the establishment, goes to Chile to help feed the poor and organize resistance to the right-wing government. After her return to Minneapolis in 1974, she is killed by a car bomb.

Or is she? Fielding gets on with his life, becoming a candidate for Congress. He is engaged to be married, but Sarah is so strongly with him that he begins to see her on the street. Did she escape the bombing and go underground for self-protection? Eventually his fixation threatens his mental well-being, as well as his marriage and political career.

Connelly projects a burning presence, whether Sarah is dead or alive. And Crudup is especially captivating in one of his best roles, as a smart, ambitious, rational man so emotionally tortured that he loses his grip.

WAKING LIFE

Wiley Wiggins, Julie Delpy, Adam Goldberg, Timothy (Speed) Levitch, Ethan Hawke, Steven Soderbergh

Directed by Richard Linklater
2001. 99 minutes. R.

To throw out a bouquet of wildly fanciful theories about human consciousness, Linklater hit on the brilliant idea of transforming photographed reality into a sophisticated cartoon world by superimposing brightly hued digital animation on live-action digital video.

In an expressionist landscape, images are constantly rippling and heaving to suggest a universe in ceaseless flux. At the center of much frantic activity is an unidentified protagonist, played by Wiley Wiggins, who experiences a metaphysical identity crisis: he awakens in a dream in which he levitates, rides the highway in a boat and has other peculiar adventures.

Wiggins's laid-back character has the look and attitude of a perennial college student drifting through life accumulating information. As he randomly encounters teachers, students, street people and television personalities (some portrayed by Hawke, Delpy and Soderbergh), they all eagerly spout theories drawn from the likes of Jean-Paul Sartre, the film critic André Bazin and the science-fiction writer Philip K. Dick.

It's enough to leave one buoyed and a little awestruck at the crazy quilt of human experience. But this is no throwback to the millennial 60's trip movie. A technological coup, the film is so verbally dexterous and visually innovative that you can't absorb it without all your wits about you. Even then, you may want to see it again to enjoy its subtle humor and warm humanity.

WALKABOUT

Jenny Agutter, Lucien John, David Gulpilil

Directed by Nicolas Roeg
1971. 100 minutes. PG.

A collision between "civilization," if that's the word for modernity, and the spirits of a vast and timeless world is played out in the accidental wanderings of a pair of pampered private-school children in the Australian outback.

Roeg works in mysterious ways (as in *Don't Look Now,* page 113), and here a strange and beautiful allegory brings together children from irreconcilably different cultures for a brief magical period that gets to the essence of life.

Two children, 14 and 6, called Sister (Agutter) and Brother (Lucien John, Roeg's 6-year-old son), are taken for a picnic in the wild by their stressed-out father, a cipher of a man who works in the city as a geologist. After laying out the picnic things, the father opens fire on his children with a handgun, then blows himself up in the car.

Unhurt and barely ruffled, Sister and Brother, dressed in their school uniforms, set off on a long, hot walk into the burning expanse. Sister, a long-legged teenager, seems mildly inconvenienced, but she rallies her brother for the trek. Before long they encounter an Aborigine boy (Gulpilil) who is traveling the desert on walkabout, a six-month test of skills that signifies his passage into manhood.

Together the three explore a world of immense beauty and wonder. But their idyll passes as if in a dream, leading to a sad inevitability in a film that ends with a quote from A. E. Housman's *Shropshire Lad*: "Those happy highways where we went and cannot come again."

A WALK ON THE MOON

Diane Lane, Viggo Mortensen, Liev Schreiber, Anna Paquin, Tovah Feldshuh

Directed by Tony Goldwyn
1999. 105 minutes. R.

No one plays wives at risk like Lane (most recently in *Unfaithful*, page 437), and here she stands out as Pearl Kantrowitz, who is spending the summer at a Jewish camp in the Catskills with her children, among them her rebellious teenage daughter (Paquin), and her mother-in-law (Feldshuh), while her husband (Schreiber) works in New York City.

The year is 1969, and with Neil Armstrong about to walk on the moon and Woodstock about to explode just down the road, the atmosphere is full of seismic currents. Something is bound to happen to relieve the pleasant but dull routine, and it materializes in the form of the Blouse Man, otherwise known as Walker Jerome (Mortensen), a peddler who visits the camp selling his wares.

In his pre–*Lord of the Rings* era, Mortensen had a track record as silkily erotic catnip for attractive married women (see *A Perfect Murder*, page 310), and here his seductive presence leads to steamy romance, a family crisis and its inevitable fallout.

Schreiber is very fine as the Blouse Man's absolute opposite: Marty, the aggrieved husband, who makes a touching, insistent presence. Forget the preposterous ending. Even when it turns turbulent, the movie sustains a summer glow while making itself a moral conversation piece.

THE WAR OF THE ROSES

Kathleen Turner, Michael Douglas, Danny DeVito

Directed by Danny DeVito
1989. 116 minutes. R.

The Turner-Douglas team may be best known for the bland *Romancing the Stone* but is far more entertaining in Danny DeVito's fiercely funny divorce comedy. DeVito also plays Gavin D'Amato, the lawyer who narrates the story. "Divorce is survivable," he says, except when it comes to Oliver and Barbara Rose (Douglas and Turner).

They started out so well, young lovebirds who met at an auction while bidding on a cheap figurine. They were willing to scrape and save and work for the future. Then came two kids, two cars, a big house. Oliver, a lawyer, makes a lot of money; now the figurines are Staffordshire, and he keeps his shoes in a lighted, glassed-in closet.

Gradually the Roses come to hate each other. Oliver gets the message the day Barbara fails to show up at the hospital after she's been told that he's dying. Later she tells him how happy she was at the thought of getting rid of him. When Barbara makes a little money selling her legendary pâté, she wants a divorce, and the nasty battle for possessions and vengeance begins.

A very physical war breaks out. Oliver holes up in a bedroom, keeping his precious figurines from joining Barbara's arsenal. He tries to wreck one of her dinner parties; she barricades him in the sauna. A chandelier becomes a lethal weapon.

The Roses may be caricatures, but DeVito's gleeful, vicious comedy is wonderfully fresh.

WATER DROPS ON BURNING ROCKS

Bernard Giraudeau, Malik Zidi, Ludivine Sagnier, Anna Thomson

Directed by François Ozon
2000. 90 minutes. French with English subtitles. No rating.

Ozon's brilliant satire of emotional politics takes its material from an unproduced play by Rainier Werner Fassbinder. The setting is Berlin in the 1970's. An empty apartment awaits the entry of Léopold (Giraudeau), the suave 50-year-old who lives there, and Franz (Zidi), a 19-year-old he has just picked up. The conversation winds to a foregone conclusion: "Have you ever slept with a man?"

Six months later they have settled into the tedium and petty power struggles of a long-term relationship, but here Fassbinder's love of complication introduces some fresh faces in the persons of Franz's loyal, fresh-faced fiancée (Sagnier) and Leo's possibly transsexual old flame (Thomson). From this point the film slides seamlessly from soigné sex farce into orgy, musical tragedy and morality play.

Fans of Fassbinder, who died at 36 in 1982, will be enthralled, but this is Ozon's film. By taking a few liberties with the script, he presents a beguiling and disconcerting blend of anxiety and comedy, and he achieves an improbable marriage of Gallic levity and Teutonic gravity.

THE WEATHER UNDERGROUND

Lili Taylor and Pamela Z (narrators), and Bernadine Dohrn, Mark Rudd, Brian Flanagan, David Gilbert, Bill Ayers, Naomi Jaffe, Todd Gitlin, Laura Whitehorn, Don Strickland, Kathleen Cleaver

Directed by Sam Green and Bill Siegel
2002. 92 minutes. No rating.

In this engaging documentary, 1960's radicals look back on their youthful idealism as Green and Siegel unearth a great story forgotten by some and entirely unknown to a new generation.

"Like Bonnie and Clyde, many of them were attractive personally," says Gitlin, a former president of Students for a Democratic Society. "They were into youth, exuberance, sex, drugs. They wanted action." So people like Dohrn, Rudd and Ayers broke away from S.D.S. and created a splinter group known as the Weathermen. They were determined to overthrow the government of the United States, by violence if necessary, on grounds that the country was criminally waging war in Vietnam and persecuting minority groups like the Black Panthers.

The film conveys their passions and anger, slyly contrasting the group to the peace-and-love tenor of the larger protest community. "We felt that doing nothing in a period of repressive violence was itself a form of violence," says Jaffe, a former Weatherman. "That's the part I think is hardest for people to understand."

The film doesn't excuse the group that claimed responsibility for bombing two dozen public buildings. Flanagan compares what they did to the 1995 Oklahoma City bombing. But the documentary illuminates the tensions and arguments of the period, and it captures the Weathermen's contradictions of good intentions and self-absorption.

THE WEDDING BANQUET

Winston Chao, Mitchell Lichtenstein, May Chin, Sihung Lung, Ah Lei Gua, Tien Pien

Directed by Ang Lee
1993. 106 minutes. English and Chinese with English subtitles. No rating.

Food and sex are the stuff of Lee's *Eat Drink Man Woman* (page 122), and so it is here as a sumptuous wedding feast in New York escalates into a riotous celebration that leaves the bride, Wei Wei (Chin), and groom, Wai Tung (Chao), backed into a hotel room full of guests and huddled under the bedcovers without any clothes on.

But the wedding is a sham. Wai Tung, a gay real estate entrepreneur living with his lover, Simon (Lichtenstein), has staged the whole thing to appease his parents, a Taiwanese Army general (Lung) and his very proper wife (Gua), who want nothing more than to have a grandchild and who have flown from Taipei for the occasion.

The bride, one of Wai Tung's tenants, is marrying him because she needs a green card. She also finds him attractive, and wedding-night pranks played on the couple facilitate a pregnancy.

The general and his wife are staying for two weeks, necessitating much subterfuge on the part of Wai Tung and Simon, who is presented as Wai Tung's landlord and roommate in an apartment stripped of all telltale gay accoutrements.

Gradually a sophisticated light comedy darkens as the general runs into an old army compatriot who owns a New York restaurant and insists on giving the couple a banquet neither wants. Wei Wei begins to feel pressured. Fortunately, the pregnancy is handled in a way that leaves everybody wiser and more compassionate.

WELCOME TO SARAJEVO

Stephen Dillane, Woody Harrelson, Marisa Tomei, Emira Nusevic

Directed by Michael Winterbottom
1997. 103 minutes. R.

Winterbottom's harrowing take on the Balkan conflict is also a tough-minded comment on journalistic objectivity. The movie focuses on two journalists of different styles and temperaments. Flynn (Harrelson) is the brash hotshot and star of American television news. Henderson (Dillane), a British journalist, is quieter and more introspective. In the streets they see people die every day, and in its most innovative move, the film blends fact with fiction. Actual news film of the violence mingles with fictional recreations involving the characters. (Frank Cottrell Boyce's screenplay is based on Michael Nicholson's book *Natasha's Story,* itself a true story).

Behind the scenes, the tension between the two journalists and their entourages provides a counterpoint to the dangers they face. With international journalists thrown together, they compete with yet respect each other. Henderson has a simple decency, and for all his bravado Flynn shows unexpected courage when it's called for.

Uncharacteristically for Winterbottom, the film devolves into a soap opera about Henderson's efforts to save a tough young girl (Nusevic) orphaned by the war. But the movie also asks difficult questions, notably: Should journalists like Henderson leave their emotions and humanity at the border when they enter a war zone?

THE WELL

Pamela Rabe, Miranda Otto, Paul Chubb, Frank Wilson,
Steve Jacobs, Geneviève Lemon

Directed by Samantha Lang
1997. 101 minutes. No rating.

The first half of Lang's film sets up as an efficient study of two lonely women. Then, get set for the scariest exercise in cinematic sleight of hand since *The Blair Witch Project*.

Hester (Rabe) lives with her stern father on a desolate Australian sheep station, an invitation to repression and resentment if ever there was one. Hester's taste in music runs to German lieder. Her skirts are long, her shoes orthopedic; her hair is flat and colorless.

By contrast, her wayward young housekeeper, Katherine (Otto), prefers loud rock music and dances around the place in knee-high boots and short, gauzy skirts. Given the choice of loving or hating her, Hester buys her expensive gifts and learns how to laugh.

In fact, the flinty Hester starts thowing money around as if there were no tomorrow. When her father dies, she sells the station, and she and Katherine settle down in a cozy cottage with two cookie tins full of cash and begin fantasizing about a trip to Europe.

Just when the film seems to be headed nowhere interesting, Katherine accidentally runs over an unidentified man in Hester's new silver Toyota pickup. Faced with body disposal, they toss him down a deep dry well.

But will he stay put? Katherine begins to insist that he is alive and that he has fallen in love with her. Is she crazy? Or maybe Hester, who either believes Katherine or doesn't, has come unhinged. Or have you come unhinged? Strange things start to happen, or don't, as Lang pursues her puzzle with mathematical discipline and painterly emotion.

WHALE RIDER

*Keisha Castle-Hughes, Rawiri Paratene, Vicky Haughton,
Cliff Curtis*

Directed by Niki Caro
2002. 101 minutes. PG-13.

The Maori chief Koro (Paratene) doesn't hide his disappointment over the fact that the only family member who could succeed him is a girl, his 12-year-old granddaughter, Pai (Castle-Hughes). Pai lives in her grandfather's house on the New Zealand coast but without his recognition. The two are pals when it comes to her hitching rides on Koro's bike, but the chief stiffens with contempt at the suggestion that the girl stands in the direct line of leadership.

Pai is named for Paikea, the tribal ancestor who according to legend arrived on the back of a whale. Intelligent and a student of Maori ways, she takes to leadership naturally, or would if given a chance. Instead, Koro rounds up a half-dozen boys and tries to train them for the position. Their lack of aptitude, not to mention lack of interest, only adds to his frustration, which, not surprisingly, he takes out on Pai by banishing her from his household.

Then the whales take a hand. At this point, and at several earlier points, Caro's film could have lapsed into bathos, but it holds the line nicely.

WHAT ABOUT BOB?

*Bill Murray, Richard Dreyfuss, Julie Hagerty, Charlie
Korsmo, Kathryn Erbe*

Directed by Frank Oz
1991. 99 minutes. PG.

Some critics thought little of the idea, but Oz's comedy is on the right path when it sends the supremely neurotic Bob Wiley (Murray) off to leafy New Hampshire to find his psychiatrist, Dr. Leo Marvin (Dreyfuss).

It's August in New York, and with everybody's shrink out of town, things are a little crazy and completely out of hand for Bob, who has a particularly acute dependency problem. Bob can't last without Dr. Marvin. "Is this a bad time?" he bellows outside Marvin's vacation retreat.

Marvin, now busy in a distracted kind of way with his wife (Hagerty) and two children, named Sigmund and Anna (Korsmo and Erbe) after the Freuds, deems Bob's behavior "completely inappropriate."

A happy family in a remote setting suddenly stalked by a deranged man has possibilities along the lines of, say, *Cape Fear*. Instead, the psychiatrist's brood takes a liking to Bob and lets him fill in for Marvin, who can't seem to grasp the art of relaxation. ("It's as important for me to see you dive as it is for me to appear on *Good Morning America*," he tells Siggy.)

The tightly wound Dreyfuss and the unspooled Murray are automatically funny together, and Korsmo lends humor and dignity to Siggy's every move.

WHAT TIME IS IT THERE?

Lee Kang-Sheng, Miao Tien, Chen Shiang-Chyi

Directed by Tsai Ming-liang
2001. 116 minutes. Mandarin, Taiwanese and French with English subtitles. No rating.

They may not have been reaching for it, but Tsai and his co-screenwriter, Yang Pi-Ying, manage a Nouvelle Vague version of a Strindberg sitcom.

After his father's death in a cloud of cigarette smoke, Hsaio Kang (Lee Kang-Sheng) is stuck in the house with his distraught mother, who keeps expecting her husband's resurrection. To make a living, Hsaio sells watches on the streets of Taipei, and though he derides his mother's hope for a revival, he holds on to a dual-time watch that may have some tie to his departed father.

A customer who is moving to Paris and wants to see the time in both places finally badgers him into selling the watch, and from then on his world is never the same. Every clock he sees he resets to Paris time, or tries.

In an absurdist melodrama the camera never blinks at the dottiness, and the laughs, which are frequent, never are at the expense of the deeply moving scenario. The film never presses. Tsai Ming-liang not only gives us a chance to breathe but lets us bask in the mood of dead-pan melancholy.

WHO FRAMED ROGER RABBIT

Bob Hoskins, Christopher Lloyd, Joanna Cassidy, Charles Fleischer, Stubby Kaye, Joel Silver

Directed by Robert Zemeckis
1988. 103 minutes. PG.

Movies combining live characters with cartoon figures go way back, but until Zemeckis's film, Aljean Harmetz wrote in *The New York Times*, "no one has ever risked creating a movie which is breathtakingly complicated technically but can succeed artistically only if an animated character and a live man form a human bond."

This meant that the cartoon Roger, a big-time 1940's movie star, had to get along with the live Eddie Valiant (Hoskins), a private eye hired to check into allegations of hanky-panky on the part of Roger's stunning wife, a cartoon human named Jessica.

Valiant has to plunge back into Toontown, a place he dislikes because the endlessly adaptable toons can accomplish all kinds of things humans can't, like reinflating after being flattened by a steamroller or jumping up after being hit by a piano thrown off a high place, which was more than Valiant's brother could do when it happened to him.

Roger finds himself accused of knocking off the head of Maroon Studios, a live character, who has supposedly been having an affair with Jessica, a singer at the Ink and Print club. Valiant, a noirish figure in a snap-brim fedora, bonds with the bunny, finally becoming cartoonlike himself in a classic that remains a wonder even in the age of Pixar.

THE WIDOW OF ST. PIERRE

Juliette Binoche, Daniel Auteuil, Emir Kusturica, Philippe Magnan, Michel Duchaussoy

Directed by Patrice Leconte
2000. 112 minutes. French with English subtitles. No rating.

Leconte marries his considerable filmmaking gifts to a tale with the bold, earnest emotion of a classic 1940's Hollywood melodrama, and his three stars play their close-ups with the ardor and stoicism of the great movie stars of old.

In 1849, the fishing island of St. Pierre in the Maritimes is ruled by a garrison commanded by a dashing captain (Auteuil) whose surname is never mentioned. His aristocratic wife (Binoche) is known only as Mme. La.

A senseless murder by a couple of drunken fishermen has led to the impending execution of one of them, a rough-hewn fellow named Neel (Kusturica, the Yugoslav filmmaker). The prospect of his date with the guillotine, a secondhand contraption rented from authorities in Martinique, gives the film's spare, melodramatic plot the force and focus of tragedy.

From the first moment she sees him shackled and shuffling to his cell, Neel triggers intense emotion in Mme. La, who adopts him as a protégé to help her with chores and charitable missions to Dog Island, where most of the poorest fishing families live. Nothing indiscreet or improper transpires, but when she suggests that his escape would lead to her husband's execution, various translations of the remark present themselves.

Binoche is very strong as a liberal humanist opposed to the death penalty. One of the chief satisfactions of the film—one of the things that make it, perhaps paradoxically, so deeply entertaining—is its air of moral gravity.

WILDE

Stephen Fry, Jude Law, Vanessa Redgrave, Jennifer Ehle, Gemma Jones, Tom Wilkinson

Directed by Brian Gilbert
1997. 118 minutes. R.

Fry's may be the definitive portrait of Oscar Wilde, capturing both the razor-edged wit and the immense warmth of the writer and dandy, whom he plays with a mixture of superciliousness and vulnerability.

Marriage to Constance (Ehle) is obviously a mistake, but Oscar remains her good friend and a loving father to their two sons. After the successes of his plays, the middle-aged Wilde displays his true sexuality by falling passionately in love with the beautiful, young Lord Alfred Douglas (Law in an early role). Douglas, called Bosie, has the mocking petulance of a rock star, and he pays back his austere father by flaunting his scandalous relationship with the famous playwright.

Wilde remains tolerant even as Bosie turns flagrantly faithless. His trial for gross indecency and his imprisonment are handled almost as an epilogue here, but that doesn't mar the film, which emphasizes Wilde's character. It shows that one of the greatest, most acerbic social observers also had a profound, uncompromising capacity for love and forgiveness.

WINGED MIGRATION

Jacques Perrin (narrator) and puffins, sandbill cranes, pelicans, Canada geese and anything else that flies south (or north if they're in the lower latitudes) for the winter

Directed by Jacques Perrin
2001. 89 minutes. G.

Of all the birds that migrate thousands of miles every year, arctic terns may fly the farthest: 12,500 miles from Arctic to Antarctic. The white stork flies 3,100 miles from central Africa to western Europe; the bar-headed goose, 1,500 miles from India to the central Asian steppes; the whooper swan, 1,800 miles from the Far East to the Siberian tundra; the bald eagle, 1,800 miles from the American West to Alaska. Later they do it all in reverse.

As they flap, a film crew of 450 people—including 17 pilots and 14 cinematographers—creates a documentary that is truly majestic in look and effect. Flying beside and among the birds on the wing are photographers in ultra-light aircraft, staying with them through fair weather and foul to heights of thousands of feet and as low as the wave tops. That they could virtually become part of these flocks is beyond astonishing.

Skies are enormous, winds eternal, views endless. Incredibly, we take it all in, wing tip to wing tip.

THE WINSLOW BOY

Nigel Hawthorne, Guy Edwards, Rebecca Pidgeon, Jeremy Northam, Gemma Jones, Matthew Pidgeon

Directed by David Mamet
1999. 104 minutes. G.

Mamet can usually be found in twisty constructions like *The Spanish Prisoner* (page 377), but here he beautifully captures tensions in the more muffled confines of a handsome, stately adaptation of Terence Rattigan's play, set in 1910 and based on a true story, about a 13-year-old boy who was thrown out of Britain's Royal Naval Academy for stealing a five-shilling postal order. The case was a celebrated one in England.

Trouble lies ahead when the expelled Ronnie Winslow (Edwards) stands in a driving rain outside his house. His father, Arthur, played by Hawthorne with a stern but wonderfully warm sagaciousness, wants to know one thing: Did Ronnie steal the item? And don't lie, because if he does, Arthur will know it.

Flying in the face of authority and all the empire holds holy, Arthur mounts a defense of his son. A noted barrister (Northam), who prosecuted Oscar Wilde in a libel suit, agrees to defend Ronnie, but only after a tough grilling convinces him of the boy's innocence. Ronnie's edgy sister (Pidgeon), a cigarette-puffing suffragist, loses a proper fiancé and puts her old life on hold as she fights for her brother. Without all the money in the world, Arthur himself is threatened.

It's a sensational case, but a sedate film keeps the tabloids at bay. That makes it all the more exciting.

WINTER KILLS

Jeff Bridges, John Huston, Belinda Bauer, Anthony Perkins, Sterling Hayden, Dorothy Malone, Eli Wallach, Ralph Meeker

Directed by William Richert
1979. 97 minutes. R.

A greatly entertaining jet-black comedy, adapted from Richard Condon's novel, has its own take on the Kennedys. Papa Joe Kennedy in this case is Pa Kegan (Huston), an unscrupulous old womanizer who owns the world, including his own hospital, where he goes now and then to have his blood changed. Kegan's older son, president of the United States, was assassinated 19 years earlier. His younger son, Jeff (Bridges), runs Pa's oil rig in the North Sea, or he's supposed to.

The old man is flabbergasted when Jeff appears on the mainland bearing some cockeyed tale from a dying man who says he was the second shooter when Jeff's brother was killed. Jeff is determined to pick up the case, on the QT, of course; Pa humors his kid, but we get the feeling the old man will be more hindrance than help.

New theories take form: Pa's business rivals were at the bottom of the plot; Cuban gambling interests were involved; Hollywood was taking revenge for the suicide of a young starlet brushed off by President Kegan, a death that cost the studios $50 million.

Huston is the one to watch here in a picaresque film that stays big and bold in its eccentricities. Pa Kegan will figure in the scheme all right, leading to his famous plunge from a high building, tearing a giant American flag right down the middle.

WITHNAIL & I

Richard E. Grant, Paul McGann, Richard Griffiths

Directed by Bruce Robinson
1987. 107 minutes. No rating.

Robinson's comedy contemplates the bilious aftermath of that illusory era known as the 60's. Good-bye, Mary Quant, dropping out and turning on, *Oh! Calcutta!*, free love, public sex. The young would-be actors Marwood (McGann), the "I" of the title, and Withnail (Grant) wake up broke and crushingly hung over one morning to find only 90 days left in the decade. Something must be done.

So they decide to spend a soul-cleansing weekend in a primitive country cottage owned by Withnail's uncle, Monty (Griffiths), another actor. Withnail, tall, slim, vaguely Byronic, doesn't know what to make of the country, where they can't find aspirin. "It's not like H. E. Bates," he says. "I thought they'd be all out drinking cider and discussing butter."

To keep warm, they burn furniture in the fireplace. There's no food in the place, and about all they can order up is a live chicken. But how do they kill it? Uncle Monty appears, having been misled by his nephew into thinking he might make romantic inroads with Marwood.

Robinson has the good sense to focus not on the era but on specific characters and incidents. No social history, the film is about growing up, almost by accident.

WITHOUT LIMITS

Billy Crudup, Donald Sutherland

Directed by Robert Towne
1998. 117 minutes. PG-13.

A biography of Steve Prefontaine (Crudup), the charismatic miler who died in 1975 at age 24, becomes a broader parable with an especially evocative way of filtering a young man's headstrong nature through an older man's wiser point of view.

In Oregon, the renowned track coach Bill Bowerman (Sutherland), often tinkering with the rubber waffle he would turn into the Nike running shoe, has his hands full with the enigmatic Prefontaine, a maverick who usually ran (not always, but usually) as well as he talked about running.

There's a long, bravura re-creation of Prefontaine's performance in the 1972 Olympic Games in Munich, with Bowerman and the runner in conflict over strategy and ideas about running.

Not that the moody Prefontaine was a blowhard. Neither Bowerman nor anyone else ever got a handle on an elusive character who rarely revealed himself but never shied away from showing his stubbornness or expressing his confidence. "I can endure more pain than anyone you've ever met," he says. "That's why I can beat anyone you've ever met."

WONDER BOYS

Michael Douglas, Tobey Maguire, Frances McDormand, Robert Downey Jr., Katie Holmes, Rip Torn, Richard Knox, Jane Adams

Directed by Curtis Hanson
2000. 112 minutes. R.

Writers and writing are the focus in Hanson's edgy comedy, but one also is taken with the weather. It's always snowing or raining in Pittsburgh, and the dark wetness plays beautifully against the glistening red brick of old factory buildings in an industrial city that has seen better times.

At the university, the novelist and teacher Grady Tripp (Douglas) smokes pot and shepherds a class that has a couple of kids with some talent. Grady has one big novel to his credit, but that was years ago. Now he's in a funk. His wife—the latest wife, that is—has left him. His lover, Sara Gaskell (McDormand), dean of the college and wife of Grady's boss in the English department, tells Grady that she is pregnant. The piece of paper he cranks into his IBM Selectric is page 2,216 of a new novel he can never seem to end.

Grady just can't make choices, or so he's told by the sexy student (Holmes) who boards in his house and tempts him in short T-shirts. But at least there are some elements to hold on to. One is James Leer (Maguire), a promising but monumentally troubled student with a manuscript that could make him a star. Then there's Sara and the baby she and Grady could have together.

That is, if Grady has the guts to throw out his entire

previous life, including the 2,215 pages that fill several boxes. Perhaps Grady the mentor has something to learn from James the protégé.

WORKING GIRL

Melanie Griffith, Sigourney Weaver, Harrison Ford, Alec Baldwin, Joan Cusack, Philip Bosco, Nora Dunn

Directed by Mike Nichols
1988. 115 minutes. R.

In the 80's they called it big hair, but Tess McGill's locks are huge. And then there's the fact that she comes from the wrong island (Staten). Tess (Griffith) rides the ferry with her pal Cyn (Cusack) to the right island (Manhattan), where she labors as a secretary with thousands of others like her.

This is Mike Nichols in Cinderella mode. Tess's job as secretary to a conniving marketing executive (Weaver) leads to a big opportunity when the boss breaks her leg and is out of commission. Tess determines to step in, especially after she learns that the boss has stolen her good ideas and presented them as her own.

One total hair-and-sartorial makeover later, Tess is using her street smarts, business sense and sex appeal to hold her own in meetings and office suites. And how likely is this? Just relax and turn it over to Griffith, the ultimate baby-voiced bombshell.

WRITTEN ON THE WIND

*Rock Hudson, Lauren Bacall, Robert Stack, Dorothy
Malone, Robert Keith*

Directed by Douglas Sirk
1956. 99 minutes.

Sirk's big Texas melodrama, adapted from Robert Wilder's novel, overflows with lurid goings-on but still extends its storm-tossed characters and their tribulations a fair amount of sympathy and respect.

As is often the case in Sirk's films, a hidebound social environment is about to come apart at the seams. Stack gives a superb performance as the troubled, liquored-up Kyle Hadley, scion of the Texas oil Hadleys. Given Kyle's predilections, the Hadley patriarch, Jasper (Keith), looks to Mitch Wayne (Hudson), a young geologist he has hired for Hadley Oil and treats like a son. Also at home, when she's not sleeping around the oil town of Hadley and environs, is Kyle's sister, the nymphomaniacal Marlee Hadley (Malone, who won an Oscar as best supporting actress).

Trouble, or more of it than threatens already, arrives when Mitch meets an advertising executive named Lucy (Bacall). She immediately attracts Kyle but at first resists his advances, which include inducements like private-plane rides and hotel suites full of clothes.

Later they marry, but complications arise when he turns out to be sterile and she becomes pregnant. Kyle suspects Mitch, who is in love with Lucy. Meanwhile, Marlee has had matrimonial designs on Mitch, who decides he might be better off in Iran. Violence and tragedy ensue.

While Sirk was regarded as a master of space and color, critics tended to dismiss his work as "women's pictures." In reality, his films recorded the fears, frustrations and contradictions of America at the height of its postwar power and prestige. *Written on the Wind* is about the best example.

THE YARDS

James Caan, Mark Wahlberg, Charlize Theron, Joaquin Phoenix, Ellen Burstyn, Faye Dunaway

Directed by James Gray
2000. 115 minutes. R.

Wahlberg is a kinetic presence in this engrossing story of a small-time crime family, another neighborhood drama from James Gray. (See *Little Odessa*, page 226). Caan is all lethal charm as Frank Olchin, who makes a great deal of money in the business of repairing New York subway cars. He owes his success to a bribery-and-kickback scheme involving the Queens borough president.

Leo Handler (Wahlberg) is Frank's nephew, a young ex-convict who needs a job. A decent kid, Leo is the kind of guy who will wind up either dead or golden. We root for him, and so does his mother (Burstyn), Frank's sister-in-law.

Frank gives Leo a low-level position as a repairman, but Leo's best friend, Willie (Phoenix), also works for Frank, making a lot more money as a collector of payoffs. When Leo joins him on his rounds, there's a killing and Leo assaults a police officer. When all this threatens Frank's business, Leo is forced into hiding.

All the bad guys, including Frank, have extenuating circumstances and redeeming qualities, in a rare contemporary film that achieves moral complexity while creating a landscape of pure realistic detail.

THE YEAR OF LIVING DANGEROUSLY

Mel Gibson, Sigourney Weaver, Linda Hunt

Directed by Peter Weir
1982. 117 minutes. PG.

More than 20 years later (and after bigger Weir films like *Master and Commander*) this still holds up as a first-rate political thriller and an entertaining look at the young Gibson and Weaver on their way to becoming major stars. The exotic setting is Jakarta in 1965. President Sukarno, long Indonesia's nationalist hero, is placating the Communists, angering generals supported by the West. Corruption has stymied government, and people are starving.

Gibson is Guy Hamilton, an Australian journalist out to make a name for himself. Hamilton relies on contacts and insights provided by a very well-connected newsreel cameraman named Billy Kwan. As Billy, Hunt practically steals the film from its stars.

Billy would like to turn Hamilton into a journalist with a political conscience—an effort that seems futile. Kwan knows Jill Bryant (Weaver), an assistant in the British Embassy. He loves her, but that's an impossible situation so he presents her to Hamilton. The two begin an affair that seemingly ends disastrously when Hamilton betrays her as the source of a story that sends them both fleeing for their lives.

Weir is superb at big, riotous crowd scenes as well as the delicate drama of love and betrayal in this work of great imagination and atmospheric style.

YI YI (A ONE AND A TWO)

*Wu Nienjen, Jonathan Chang, Kelly Lee, Yupang
Chang, Chen Xisheng, Elaine Jin, Ke Suyun*

Directed by Edward Yang
2000. 173 minutes. Mandarin with English subtitles. No
rating.

Yang's charming, absorbing film serves up a bunch of
familiar middle-class pickles (well, some not so familiar), with the major difference being that this is Taipei and
not an American city.

At the center is N.J. (Wu Nienjen), the gentle, pensive
husband of the troubled Min-Min (Jin) and father of the
wise teenager Ting-Ting (Lee) and the precocious 8-year-
old Yang-Yang (Jonathan Chang). N.J. is having problems
at his software company. Min-Min is despondent over her
mother's stroke. Ting-Ting is caught in a romantic crisis,
torn between a safe friend and a slightly dangerous one, a
skinny boy named Fatty (Yupang Chang).

At school little Yang-Yang is badgered by bullies, and at
home he is a pint-size philosopher. "I can't see what you
see and you can't see what I see. So how can I know what
you see?" he asks his father.

N.J. encounters an old high school sweetheart who
leads him to believe he might have done things differently. Not the soul of satisfaction herself, Min-Min goes
off to join a cult. And there are a murder—outside the
family proper but scary nevertheless—and an attempted
suicide, which has a comical side.

But *Yi Yi* is not a soap opera. In a restrained mood, the
narrative meanders from story to story without ever becoming melodramatic. One of the nicest things about the
film is its universality. This is Taipei, but the story could be
taking place around the corner.

YOU CAN COUNT ON ME

Laura Linney, Mark Ruffalo, Matthew Broderick, Jon Tenney, Rory Culkin

Directed by Kenneth Lonergan
2000. 111 minutes. R.

A little gem of a movie proves that the everyday problems of ordinary people in a small town in upstate New York can be as compelling as the most bizarre personal circus in the tabloids, if portrayed with enough empathy and insight.

In the middle-to-working-class town of Scottville, a grown-up sister and brother, Samantha and Terry Prescott (Linney and Ruffalo), reunite after having not seen each other for a while. Sammy has an 8-year-old son, Rudy (Culkin), and a job as a loan officer at the local bank. Terry is a good-natured drifter who has done some jail time after a bar brawl and has a suicidally inclined girlfriend, whom he has impregnated.

As children, Sammy and Terry lost both parents in a car crash, an event the film wisely leaves largely to the imagination. As they quarrel and reminisce as adults, the trauma remains part of a sibling bond evoked with astounding depth and subtlety. As old wounds are torn open, Ruffalo's lost boy distinguishes a film that gets its characters and their world just right.

Y TU MAMÁ TAMBIÉN

Maribel Verdú, Gael García Bernal, Diego Luna

Directed by Alfonso Cuarón
2001. 105 minutes. Spanish with English subtitles. No rating.

Still waters run deep under Cuarón's film, which on the surface doubles very passably as a sex romp.

When her husband is unfaithful, the beautiful, sad-eyed Luisa (Verdú) accepts the invitation of two randy teenagers, Julio (García Bernal) and Tenoch (Luna), to accompany them to a Mexican beach they call Heaven's Mouth.

Used to sneaking quickies with their girlfriends in bedrooms of their parents' houses, the kids think they have landed a very hot lady in Luisa. They aren't wrong, but Luisa is a woman, not a kid, and while she is eventually willing to entertain their lust, the two pups find out that good sex is, or should be, a long and wondrous exercise.

Neither of them is up to it, but Luisa is a good sport about their adolescent ruttings. Besides, the boys are lively and fun to be with, and she could use the diversion. Something lonely and sad is happening with Luisa, and it goes beyond marital failure. Around them is the poverty of rural Mexico, unnoticed by two rich boys but very much in the fabric of a film that, for all the sex, has some profound things to say about people and society.

ZOOLANDER

Ben Stiller, Owen Wilson, Will Ferrell, Christine Taylor,
Milla Jovovich, Jerry Stiller, Jon Voight

Directed by Ben Stiller
2001. 89 minutes. PG-13.

A crazed clothier named Mugatu (Ferrell) needs a very dumb male model to assassinate the prime minister of Malaysia, who has pledged to shut down Mugatu's sweatshop operations in his country. Fabio is too smart for the job, but there is Derek Zoolander (Stiller), male model of the year for three years straight. Certain that he must have won a fourth time, Zoolander races to the podium even after another winner has been announced. Is that dumb enough?

Dumb, vacuous, empty—Zoolander is all these things, but still he longs to chuck modeling and take up a meaningful life teaching "kids who don't read good" at an institute financed by his efforts on the runway. Flouncing around his hall-of-the-mountain-king headquarters, Mugatu simply wants Zoolander programmed à la *The Manchurian Candidate* and put out to kill at a big show to be attended by the prime minister.

But Zoolander may be too addled to be programmed. After his defeat at the awards show, all he can think about is his rivalry with a younger model, Hansel (Wilson), and his newly flaming desire to return to his roots (leading to a brief stint in the coal mines).

During a runway walk-off to determine the better man, Hansel defeats Zoolander by removing his own underwear without taking his pants off. Later the two become friends. At the show, Mugatu tries to pass off the whole slave-labor thing as a kind of freedom movement. "Kids as young as 5 could work as they pleased," he tells the crowd. The prime minister looks contented, but will he survive?

GENRE LISTINGS

DRAMA

Adaptation

The Adventures of Sebastian Cole

The Age of Innocence

All About My Mother

All or Nothing

Almost Famous

American Beauty

American Splendor

Amores Perros

Angels in America

The Anniversary Party

Antonia's Line

Ararat

Atlantic City

Baran

Beau Travail

Beautiful People

Before Sunrise

Before the Rain

Better Luck Tomorrow

Billy Elliot

Black and White

Blind Shaft

Blow

Blue Sky

Blue Velvet

Boiler Room

Born on the Fourth of July

Bounce

The Boxer

Boycott

Boys Don't Cry

Boyz N the Hood

Bread and Roses

Brideshead Revisited

La Buche

The Business of Strangers

Butterfly

Carnage

Carrington

Casa de Los Babys

The Celebration

Chuck & Buck

The Cider House Rules

The Circle

City of God

The Claim

Close-Up

Contempt

The Cooler

Cop Land

The Crucible

The Crying Game

The Dancer Upstairs

Dangerous Liaisons

Days of Heaven

Dead Man Walking

Devil in a Blue Dress

The Devil's Backbone

Don Juan DeMarco

Donnie Darko

Door to Door

The Dreamers

Drugstore Cowboy

The Duellists

East-West

Elizabeth

Emma

Mifune

Mississippi Masala

Monsieur Ibrahim

Moonlight Mile

Morvern Callar

Mostly Martha

The Motorcycle Diaries

Mrs. Dalloway

Mumford

My Beautiful Launderette

My Dinner with Andre

My First Mister

My Life as a Dog

My Wife Is an Actress

Naked Lunch

Nelly and Monsieur Arnaud

Nobody's Fool

No Man's Land

Nora

Northfork

Nowhere in Africa

Of Mice and Men

Only Angels Have Wings

Osama

Our Lady of the Assassins

Our Song

Outskirts

Paid in Full

Panic

Personal Velocity

Persuasion

The Piano Teacher

Picnic at Hanging Rock

Pieces of April

Praise

Primary Colors

La Promesse

Queen Margot

The Quiet American

Quiz Show

Rabbit-Proof Fence

Rain

Rain Man

Rambling Rose

Read My Lips

Real Women Have Curves

Reckless

Restaurant

Return to Paradise

Reversal of Fortune

Richard III

Riding in Cars With Boys

Road to Perdition

Roger Dodger

The Rookie

The Safety of Objects

Salaam Bombay!

Salvador

Salvatore Giuliano

The Scarlet Empress

The Secret Lives of Dentists

Secrets and Lies

See the Sea

Sense and Sensibility

Shackleton

Shakespeare in Love

Shine

Shot Through the Heart

Silkwood

Sling Blade

The Spanish Prisoner

The Station Agent

Stealing Beauty

The Straight Story

Sunshine

Sunshine State

Sweet and Lowdown

The Sweet Hereafter

Ulee's Gold
Under the Sand
Unfaithful
Velvet Goldmine
The Verdict
The Virgin Suicides
Waking the Dead
Waking Life
Walkabout
A Walk on the Moon
Water Drops on Burning Rocks
Welcome to Sarajevo
Whale Rider
What Time Is It There?
The Widow of St. Pierre
Wilde
The Winslow Boy
Without Limits
Wonder Boys
Written on the Wind
Y Tu Mamá También
The Yards
The Year of Living
    Dangerously
Yi Yi (A One and a Two)
You Can Count on Me

COMEDY/SATIRE

About a Boy
Bad Santa
Bamboozled
The Barbarian Invasions
Bartleby
Barton Fink
Being Julia
Belle Epoque
Best in Show

Big Night
Bob Roberts
Bottle Rocket
Bring It On
Bulworth
Chasing Amy
Chicken Run
Children of the Revolution
Chris Rock: Bring the Pain
Citizen Ruth
Cold Comfort Farm
The Commitments
Confessions of a Dangerous
    Mind
Cookie's Fortune
The Dangerous Lives of Altar
    Boys
Dave
Day for Night
Dick
Dick Tracy
The Dinner Game
Dirty Rotten Scoundrels
Dr. T & the Women
Dogma
Down and Out in Beverly Hills
Eat Drink Man Woman
Eddie Izzard: Dress to Kill
Election
Flirting with Disaster
Freaky Friday
Freddy Got Fingered
The Freshman
Garden State
Get Shorty
Ghost World
Gosford Park
Grosse Pointe Blank
Groundhog Day

ACTION/THRILLER

American Psycho
Before the Rain
Behind Enemy Lines
Changing Lanes
Collateral
Dead Calm
The Deep End
Dirty Pretty Things
Diva
Don't Look Now
Enigma
Femme Fatale
The General
Get Shorty
Gosford Park
Grosse Pointe Blank
Heist
Hollywood Homicide
Identity
In the Line of Fire
Insomnia
Internal Affairs
The Italian Job
L.A. Confidential
The Limey
Manhunter
Memento
Merci Pour le Chocolat
Midnight in the Garden of Good and Evil
The Night of the Hunter
One False Move
Out of Time
Peeping Tom
A Perfect Murder
Ripley's Game
Ronin

Run Lola Run
Runaway Jury
Second Sight
Sexy Beast
Shallow Grave
Shot Through the Heart
A Simple Plan
Speed
Strange Days
Swimming Pool
The Tailor of Panama
The Talented Mr. Ripley
A Time to Kill
Tinker, Tailor, Soldier, Spy
Touching Evil
Traffik
The Trigger Effect
28 Days Later
Unfaithful
Vanilla Sky
The Vanishing
The Well

CRIME/FILM NOIR

Band of Outsiders
Baran
The Big Heat
Blind Shaft
Blood Simple
Collateral
The Cooler
Cop Land
Croupier
Devil in a Blue Dress
Donnie Brasco
The Good Thief
Gun Crazy
Hard Eight

I'll Sleep When I'm Dead
Internal Affairs
Kiss Me Deadly
L.A. Confidential
The Last Seduction
Little Odessa
Live Flesh
The Long Goodbye
M
Miami Blues
The Mighty Quinn
Mona Lisa
Mulholland Drive
The Naked Kiss
Nine Queens
One False Move
Out of the Past
Out of Time
Paid in Full
Panic
Pickup on South Street
Red Rock West
Road to Perdition
Runaway Jury
Stormy Monday
Touch of Evil
The Yards

Festival Express
The Gleaners and I
Grateful Dawg
Hoop Dreams
The Kid Stays in the Picture
Lost in La Mancha
My Architect
Only the Strong Survive
OT: Our Town
Pumping Iron
Spellbound
Stop Making Sense
To Be and To Have
Tom Dowd and the Language of Music
The Weather Underground
Winged Migration

ANIMATION

Chicken Run
Millennium Actress
Spirited Away
The Triplets of Belleville
Waking Life
Who Framed Roger Rabbit

DOCUMENTARY

The Battle Over Citizen Kane
The Blue Planet: Seas of Life
Brian Wilson: I Just Wasn't Made for These Times
Capturing the Friedmans
Concert for George
Crumb
Dogtown and Z-Boys
Fast, Cheap & Out of Control

MUSICAL

Dracula, Pages from a Virgin's Diary
Drumline
Hedwig and the Angry Inch
Moulin Rouge
South Park: Bigger, Longer & Uncut
Tango
Topsy-Turvy

481

Thirteen Days

The Widow of St. Pierre

ROMANCE

Before Sunrise

Bounce

Chasing Amy

East-West

Emma

Eternal Sunshine of the
    Spotless Mind

Great Expectations

High Fidelity

Il Postino

In the Mood for Love

My Wife Is an Actress

Persuasion

Punch-Drunk Love

Restaurant

Shakespeare in Love

The Shop Around the Corner

Triumph of Love

True Love

Truly Madly Deeply

A Walk on the Moon

COMING OF AGE

The Adventures of Sebastian
    Cole

Almost Famous

Belle Epoque

Better Luck Tomorrow

Billy Elliot

Boiler Room

Boyz N the Hood

The Dangerous Lives of Altar
    Boys

The Devil's Backbone

Drumline

Flirting

George Washington

The Good Girl

L'Auberge Espagnole

My First Mister

My Life as a Dog

The Night of the Hunter

Orange County

Our Song

Outside Providence

Rain

Raising Victor Vargas

Rambling Rose

Rushmore

Sweet Sixteen

Thirteen

Tumbleweeds

Whale Rider

Y Tu Mamá También

WAR

Beautiful People

Before the Rain

Behind Enemy Lines

Born on the Fourth of July

The Devil's Backbone

A Midnight Clear

Salvador

Shot Through the Heart

Three Kings

Underground

Welcome to Sarajevo

WESTERN

Ballad of Little Jo

My Darling Clementine

483

Once Upon a Time in the West
The Quick and the Dead
Ride with the Devil
Rio Bravo
Unforgiven

FOREIGN / SUBTITLED

All About My Mother
Amores Perros
Antonia's Line
Band of Outsiders
Baran
The Barbarian Invasions
Beau Travail
Before the Rain
Belle Epoque
Blind Shaft
La Buche
Butterfly
Carnage
The Celebration
The Circle
City of God
Close-Up
Contempt
Day for Night
The Devil's Backbone
Les Destinées
The Dinner Game
Diva
East-West
Eat Drink Man Woman
Europa Europa
The Fast Runner
The Gleaners and I
The Grandfather
Human Resources
Il Postino

In the Mood for Love
It All Starts Today
Kitchen Stories
Late Marriage
L'Auberge Espagnole
The Legend of Rita
L'Humanité
Like Water for Chocolate
Live Flesh
Maborosi
Man on the Train
The Man Without a Past
Maria Full of Grace
Me You Them
Merci Pour le Chocolat
Mifune
Millennium Actress
Mon Oncle
Monsieur Ibrahim
Mostly Martha
The Motorcycle Diaries
My Life as a Dog
My Wife Is an Actress
Nelly and Monsieur Arnaud
Nine Queens
No Man's Land
Nowhere in Africa
Osama
Our Lady of the Assassins
Outskirts
The Piano Teacher
La Promesse
Queen Margot
Read My Lips
Salaam Bombay!
Salvatore Guiliano
See the Sea
Talk to Her
Tango

Taste of Cherry

A Taxing Woman

The Three Colors Trilogy: Blue, White and Red

Time Out

To Be and To Have

Tokyo Story

Underground

Under the Sand

The Vanishing

Water Drops on Burning Rocks

What Time Is It There?

The Widow of St. Pierre

Yi Yi (A One and a Two)

Y Tu Mamá También

TELEVISION SERIES

The Office

Second Sight

Touching Evil

TELEVISION MINI-SERIES

Angels in America

The Blue Planet: Seas of Life

Brideshead Revisited

A History of Britain

Lillie

Reckless

Tinker, Tailor, Soldier, Spy

Traffik

CRITICS' TOP TEN

A. O. SCOTT

The Barbarian Invasions
The Fast Runner
George Washington
Man Without a Past
Punch-Drunk Love
Sexy Beast
Spellbound
The Triplets of Belleville
What Time Is It There?
Yi Yi
Primary Colors
Shallow Grave
South Park: Bigger, Longer & Uncut
Talk to Her
Waiting for Guffman

STEPHEN HOLDEN

All About My Mother
Amores Perros
Beau Travail
Best in Show
Dangerous Liaisons
Election
Happiness
L'Humanité
The Sweet Hereafter
Y Tu Mamá También

CARYN JAMES

The Age of Innocence
Brideshead Revisited
Eddie Izzard: Dress to Kill
The End of the Affair
Lolita

DAVE KEHR

The Big Heat
Contempt
Gun Crazy
M
The Night of the Hunter
Only Angels Have Wings
Peeping Tom
The Scarlet Empress
Touch of Evil
Trouble in Paradise

PETER M. NICHOLS

Before the Rain
The Deep End
Dirty Pretty Things
House of Sand and Fog
In the Bedroom
The Insider
Internal Affairs
Lone Star
Reversal of Fortune
The Triplets of Belleville

NOTES